A LABRADOR DOCTOR

THE AUTOBIOGRAPHY OF
WILFRED THOMASON GRENFELL

A LABRADOR DOCTOR

THE AUTOBIOGRAPHY OF
WILFRED THOMASON GRENFELL
M.D. (OXON.), C.M.G.

WITH ILLUSTRATIONS

BOSTON AND NEW YORK
HOUGHTON MIFFLIN COMPANY
The Riverside Press Cambridge

PREFACE

I HAVE long been resisting the strong pressure from friends that would force me to risk having to live alongside my own autobiography. It seems still an open question whether it is advisable, or even whether it is right — seeing that it calls for confessions. In the eyes of God the only alternative is a book of lies. Moreover, sitting down to write one's own life story has always loomed up before my imagination as an admission that one was passing the post which marks the last lap; and though it was a justly celebrated physician who told us that we might profitably crawl upon the shelf at half a century, that added no attraction for me to the effort, when I passed that goal.

Thirty-two years spent in work for deep-sea fishermen, twenty-seven of which years have been passed in Labrador and northern Newfoundland, have necessarily given me some experiences which may be helpful to others. I feel that this alone justifies the writing of this story.

To the many helpers who have coöperated with me at one time or another throughout these years, I owe a debt of gratitude which will never be forgotten, though it has been impossible to mention each one by name. Without them this work could never have been.

To my wife, who was willing to leave all the best the civilized world can offer to share my life on this lonely coast, I want to dedicate this book. Truth forces me to own that it would never have come into being without her, and her greater share in the work of its production declares her courage to face the consequences.

CONTENTS

ILLUSTRATIONS

A LABRADOR DOCTOR

CHAPTER I

EARLY DAYS

To be born on the 28th of February is not altogether
without its compensations. It affords a subject of conversation when you are asked to put your name in birthday books. It is evident that many people suppose it to
be almost an intrusion to appear on that day. However,
it was perfectly satisfactory to me so long as it was not
the 29th. As a boy, that was all for which I cared. Still,
I used at times to be oppressed by the danger, so nar-
rowly missed, of growing up with undue deliberation.

The event occurred in 1865 in Parkgate, near Chester,
England, whither my parents had moved to enable my
father to take over the school of his uncle. I was always
told that what might be called boisterous weather sig-
nalled my arrival. Experience has since shown me that
that need not be considered a particularly ominous
portent in the winter season on the Sands of Dee.

It is fortunate that the selection of our birthplace is
not left to ourselves. It would most certainly be one of
those small decisions which would later add to the things
over which we worry. I can see how it would have acted
in my own case. For my paternal forbears are really of
Cornish extraction — a corner of our little Island to
which attaches all the romantic aroma of the men, who,
in defence of England, "swept the Spanish Main," and
so long successfully singed the King of Spain's beard,
men whose exploits never fail to stir the best blood of
Englishmen, and among whom my direct ancestors had

the privilege of playing no undistinguished part. On the other hand, my visits thither have — romance aside — convinced me that the restricted foreshore and the precipitous cliffs are a handicap to the development of youth, compared with the broad expanses of tempting sands, which are after all associated with another kinsman, whose songs have helped to make them famous, Charles Kingsley.

My mother was born in India, her father being a colonel of many campaigns, and her brother an engineer officer in charge during the siege of Lucknow till relieved by Sir Henry Havelock. At the first Delhi Durbar no less than forty-eight of my cousins met, all being officers either of the Indian military or civil service.

To the modern progressive mind the wide sands are a stumbling-block. Silting up with the years, they have closed the river to navigation, and converted our once famous Roman city of Chester into a sleepy, second-rate market-town. The great flood of commerce from the New World sweeps contemptuously past our estuary, and finds its clearing-house under the eternal, assertive smoke clouds which camouflage the miles of throbbing docks and slums called Liverpool — little more than a dozen miles distant. But the heather-clad hills of Heswall, and the old red sandstone ridge, which form the ancient borough of the "Hundred of Wirral," afford an efficient shelter from the insistent taint of out-of-the-worldness.

Every inch of the Sands of Dee were dear to me. I learned to know their every bank and gutter. Away beyond them there was a mystery in the blue hills of the Welsh shore, only cut off from us children in reality by the narrow, rapid water of the channel we called the Deep. Yet they seemed so high and so far away. The people there spoke a different language from ours, and

VIEW FROM MOSTYN HOUSE, THE AUTHOR'S BIRTHPLACE, PARKGATE, CHESHIRE

all their instincts seemed diverse. Our humble neighbours lived by the seafaring genius which we ourselves loved so much. They made their living from the fisheries of the river mouth; and scores of times we children would slip away, and spend the day and night with them in their boats.

While I was still quite a small boy, a terrible blizzard struck the estuary while the boats were out, and for twenty-four hours one of the fishing craft was missing. Only a lad of sixteen was in charge of her — a boy whom we knew, and with whom we had often sailed. All my family were away from home at the time except myself; and I can still remember the thrill I experienced when, as representative of the " Big House," I was taken to see the poor lad, who had been brought home at last, frozen to death.

The men of the opposite shores were shopkeepers and miners. Somehow we knew that they could n't help it. The nursery rhyme about "Taffy was a Welshman; Taffy was a thief," because familiar, had not led us to hold any unduly inflated estimate of the Welsh character. One of my old nurses did much to redeem it, however. She had undertaken the burden of my brother and myself during a long vacation, and carried us off bodily to her home in Wales. Her clean little cottage stood by the side of a road leading to the village school of the State Mining District of Festiniog. We soon learned that the local boys resented the intrusion of the two English lads, and they so frequently chased us off the village green, which was the only playground offered us, that we at last decided to give battle. We had stored up a pile of slates behind our garden wall, and luring the enemy to the gates by the simple method of retiring before their advance, we saluted them with artillery fire from a comparatively safe entrenchment. To my horror, one of the first missiles struck a medium-sized boy right over the eye, and I saw the blood flow instantly. The awful comparison of David and Goliath flashed across my terror-stricken mind, and I fled incontinently to my nurse's protection. Subsequently by her adroit diplomacy, we were not only delivered from justice, but gained the freedom of the green as well.

Far away up the river came the great salt-water marshes which seemed so endless to our tiny selves. There was also the Great Cop, an embankment miles long, intended to reach "from England to Wales," but which was never finished because the quicksand swallowed up all that the workmen could pour into it. Many a time I have stood on the broken end, where the discouraged labourers had left their very shovels and picks and trucks and had apparently fled in dismay, as if convicted of the impiousness of trying to fill the Bottomless Pit. To my childish imagination the upturned wheelbarrows and wasted trucks and rails always suggested the banks of the Red Sea after the awful disaster had swept over Pharoah and his host. How the returning tide used to sweep through that to us fathomless gulch! It made the old river seem ever so much more wonderful, and ever so much more filled with adventure.

Many a time, just to dare it, I would dive into the very cauldron, and let the swirling current carry me to the grassy sward beyond — along which I would run till the narrowing channel permitted my crossing to the Great Cop again. I would be drying myself in the sunshine as I went, and all ready for my scanty garments when I reached my clothing once more.

Then came the great days when the heavy nor'westers howled over the Sands — our sea-front was exposed to

all the power of the sea right away to the Point of Ayr —
the days when they came in with big spring tides, when
we saw the fishermen doubling their anchors, and carefully overhauling the holding gear of their boats, before
the flooding tide drove them ashore, powerless to do
more than watch them battling at their moorings like
living things — the possessions upon which their very
bread depended. And then this one would sink, and another would part her cable and come hurtling before
the gale, until she crashed right into the great upright
blocks of sandstone which, riveted with iron bands to
their copings, were relied upon to hold the main road
from destruction. Sometimes in fragments, and sometimes almost entire, the craft would be slung clean over
the torturing battlements, and be left stranded high and
dry on our one village street, a menace to traffic, but a
huge joy to us children.

The fascination of the Sands was greatly enhanced by
the numerous birds which at all times frequented them,
in search of the abundant food which lay buried along
the edges of the muddy gutters. There were thousands
of sandpipers in enormous flocks, mixed with king
plovers, dunlins, and turnstones, which followed the ebb
tides, and returned again in whirling clouds before the
oncoming floods. Black-and-white oyster-catchers were
always to be found chattering over the great mussel
patches at low water. With their reddish bills, what a
trophy a bunch of them made as we bore them proudly
home over our shoulders! Then there were the big long-
billed curlews. What a triumph when one outwitted
them! One of my clearest recollections is discovering a
place to which they were flighting at night by the water's
edge; how, having no dog, I swam out for bird after bird
as they fell to my gun — shooting some before I had

even time to put on my shirt again; and my consequent blue-black shoulder, which had to be carefully hidden next day. There were wild ducks, too, to be surprised in the pools of the big salt marshes.

From daylight to dark I would wander, quite alone, over endless miles, entirely satisfied to come back with a single bird, and not in the least disheartened if I got none. All sense of time used to be lost, and often enough the sandwich and biscuit for lunch forgotten, so that I would be forced occasionally to resort to a solitary public house near a colliery on our side of the water, for "tea-biscuits," all that they offered, except endless beer for the miners. I can even remember, when very hard driven, crossing to the Welsh side for bread and cheese.

These expeditions were made barefoot as long as the cold was not too great. A diary that I assayed to keep in my eighth year reminds me that on my birthday, five miles from home in the marshes, I fell head over heels into a deep hole, while wading out, gun in hand, after some oyster-catchers which I had shot. The snow was still deep on the countryside, and the long trot home has never been quite forgotten. My grief, however, was all for the gun. There was always the joy of venture in those dear old Sands. The channels cut in them by the flowing tides ran deep, and often intersected. Moreover, they changed with the varying storms. The rapidly rising tide, which sent a bore up the main channel as far as Chester, twelve miles above us, filled first of all these treacherous waterways, quite silently, and often unobserved. To us, taught to be as much at home in the water as on the land, they only added spice to our wanderings. They were nowhere very wide, so by keeping one's head, and being able to swim, only our clothes suffered by it, and they, being built for that purpose, did not complain.

One day, however, I remember great excitement. The tide had risen rapidly in the channel along the parade front, and the shrimp fishermen, who used push-nets in the channels at low tide, had returned without noticing that one of their number was missing. Word got about just too late, and already there was half a mile of water, beyond which, through our telescopes, we could see the poor fellow making frantic signals to the shore. There was no boat out there, and a big bank intervening, there seemed no way to get to him. Watching through our glasses, we saw him drive the long handle of his net deep into the sand, and cling to it, while the tide rose speedily around him. Meanwhile a whole bevy of his mates had rowed out to the bank, and were literally carrying over its treacherous surface one of their clumsy and heavy fishing punts. It was a veritable race for life; and never have I watched one with keener excitement. We actually saw his post give way, and wash downstream with him clinging to it, just before his friends got near. Fortunately, drifting with the spar, he again found bottom, and was eventually rescued, half full of salt water. I remember how he fell in my estimation as a seaman — though I was only a boy at the time.

There were four of us boys in all, of whom I was the second. My next brother Maurice died when he was only seven, and the fourth, Cecil, being five years younger than I, left my brother Algernon and myself as the only real companions for each other. Moreover, an untoward accident, of which I was the unwitting cause, left my younger brother unable to share our play for many years. Having no sisters, and scarcely any boy friends, in the holidays, when all the boys in the school went home, it might be supposed that my elder brother and I were much thrown together. But as a matter of fact such was not the case, for our temperaments being entirely different, and neither of us having any idea of giving way to the other, we seldom or ever found our pleasures together. And yet most of the worst scrapes into which we fell were coöperative affairs. Though I am only anxious to shoulder my share of the responsibility in the escapades, as well as in every other line of life, my brother Algernon possessed any genius to which the family could lay claim, in that as in every other line. He was my father over again, while I was a second edition of my mother. Father was waiting to get into the sixth form at Rugby when he was only thirteen years old. He was a brilliant scholar at Balliol, but had been compelled to give up study and leave the University temporarily owing to brain trouble. He never published anything, but would reel off brilliant short poems or essays for friends at a moment's notice. I used always to remark that in whatever company he was, he was always deferred to as an authority in anything approaching classics. He could read and quote Greek and Latin like English, spoke German and French fluently, while he was an excellent geologist, and Fellow of the Geographical Society. Here is quite a pretty little effusion of his written at eight years of age:

O, Glorious Sun, in thy palace of light,
To behold thee methinks is a beautiful sight.
O, Glorious Sun, come out of thy cloud,
No longer thy brightness in darkness shroud.
Let thy glorious beams like a golden Flood
Pour over the hills and the valleys and wood.
See! Mountains of light around him rise,
While he in a golden ocean lies:
O, Glorious Sun, in thy Palace of Light
To behold thee methinks is a beautiful sight.

Algernon Sydney Grenfell
Aged eight years

Some of my brother's poems and hymns have been published in the school magazine, or printed privately; but he, too, has only published a Spanish grammar, a Greek lexicon, and a few articles in the papers. While at Oxford he ran daily, with some friends, during one "eights week" a cynical comic paper called "The Rattle," to boost some theories he held, and which he wished to enforce, and also to "score" a few of the dons to whom he objected. This would have resulted in his being asked to retire for a season from the seat of learning at the request of his enemies, had not our beloved provost routed the special cause of the whole trouble, who was himself contributing to a London society paper, by replying that it was not to be wondered at if the scurrilous rags of London found an echo in Oxford. Moreover, a set of "The Rattle" was ordered to be bound and placed in the college archives, where it may still be seen.

My father having a very great deal of responsibility and worry during the long school terms, as he was not only head master, but owned the school as well, which he had purchased from his great-uncle, used to leave almost the day the holidays began and travel abroad with my mother. This partly accounts for the very unusual latitude allowed to us boys in coming and going from the house — no one being anxious if now and again we did not return at night. The school matron was left in charge of the vast empty barracks, and we had the run of play-field, gymnasium, and everything else we wanted. To outwit the matron was always considered fair play by us boys, and on many occasions we were more than successful.

One time, when we had been acquiring some new lines of thought from some trashy boys' books of the period, we became fired with the desire to enjoy the ruling pas-

sion of the professional burglar. Though never kept
short of anything, we decided that one night we would
raid the large school storeroom while the matron slept.
As always, the planning was entrusted to my brother.
It was, of course, a perfectly easy affair, but we played
the whole game "according to Cavendish." We let ourselves out of the window at midnight, glued brown paper
to the window panes, cut out the putty, forced the catch,
and stole sugar, currants, biscuits, and I am ashamed
to say port wine — which we mulled in a tin can over
the renovated fire in the matron's own sanctum. In the
morning the remainder was turned over to fishermen
friends who were passing along shore on their way to
catch the early tide.

I had no share in two other of my brother's famous
escapades, though at the time it was a source of keen
regret, for we were sent to different public schools, as
being, I suppose, incompatible. But we heard with pride
how he had extracted phosphorus from the chemical
laboratory and while drawing luminous ghosts on the
wall for the benefit of the timorous, had set fire to the
large dormitory and the boys' underclothing neatly laid
out on the beds, besides burning himself badly. Later he
pleaded guilty to beeswaxing the seat of the boys in front
of him in chapel, much to the detriment of their trousers
and the destruction of the dignity of Sunday worship.

During the time that my parents were away we never
found a moment in which to be lonely, but on one occasion it occurred to us that the company of some friends
would add to our enjoyment. Why we waited till my
father and mother departed I do not know, but I recall that immediately they had gone we spent a much-
valued sixpence in telegraphing to a cousin in London
to come down to us for the holidays. Our message read:

"Dear Sid. Come down and stay the holidays. Father has gone to Aix." We were somewhat chagrined to receive the following day an answer, also by wire: "Not gone yet. Father." It appeared that my father and mother had stayed the night in London in the very house to which we had wired, and Sid. having to ask his father's permission in order to get his railway fare, our uncle had accepted the invitation to my father. It was characteristic of my parents that Sid. came duly along, but they could not keep from sharing the joke with my uncle.

During term-time some of our grown-up relatives would occasionally visit us. But alas, it was only their idiosyncrasies which used to make any impression upon us. One, a great-uncle, and a very distinguished person, being Professor of Political Economy at Oxford, and a great friend of the famous Dr. Jowett, the chancellor, was the only man we knew who ever, at any time, stood up long to my father in argument. It was only on rare occasions that we ever witnessed such a contest, but I shall never forget one which took place in the evening in our drawing-room. My great-uncle was a small man, rather stout and pink, and almost bald-headed. He got so absorbed in his arguments, which he always delivered walking up and down, that on this occasion, coming to an old-fashioned sofa, he stepped right up onto the seat, climbed over the back, and went on all the time with his remarks, as if only punctuating them thereby.

Whether some of our pranks were suggested by those of which we heard, I do not remember. One of my father's yarns, however, always stuck in my memory. For once, being in a very good humour, he told us how when some distinguished old lady had come to call on his father — a house master with Arnold at Rugby — he had been especially warned not to interrupt this important person,

who had come to see about her son's entering my grand-
father's "House." It so happened that quite unconsciously the lady in question had seated herself on an old
cane-bottomed armchair in which father had been playing, thus depriving him temporarily of a toy with which
he desired to amuse himself. He never, even in later life,
was noted for undue patience, and after endeavouring
in vain to await her departure, he somehow secured a
long pin. With this he crawled from behind under the
seat, and by discreetly probing upwards, succeeded suddenly in dislodging his enemy.

Our devotions on Sunday were carried out in the parish
church of the village of Neston, there being no place of
worhip of the Established Church in our little village.
In term-time we were obliged to go morning and evening
to the long services, which never made any concessions
to youthful capacities. So in holiday-time, though it was
essential that we should go in the morning to represent
the house, we were permitted to stay home in the evening. But even the mornings were a time of great weari-
ness, and oft-recurrent sermons on the terrible fate which
awaited those who never went to church, and the still
more untoward end which was in store for frequenters
of dissenting meeting-houses, failed to awaken in us the
respect due to the occasion.

On the way to church we had generally to pass by
those who dared even the awful fate of the latter. It was
our idea that to tantalize us they wore especially gorgeous apparel while we had to wear black Etons and a
top hat — which, by the way, greatly annoyed us. One
waistcoat especially excited our animosity, and from it
we conceived the title "specklebelly," by which we ever
afterwards designated the whole "genus nonconformist."
The entrance to the chapel (ours was the Church!) was

through a door in a high wall, over which we could not
see; and my youthful brain used to conjure up unright-
eous and strange orgies which we felt must take place in
those precincts which we were never permitted to enter.
Our Sunday Scripture lessons had grounded us very
familiarly with the perverse habits of that section of the
Chosen People who *would* serve Baal and Moloch, when
it obviously paid so much better not to do so. But although we counted the numbers which we saw going in,
and sometimes met them comimg out, they seemed never
to lessen perceptibly. On this account our minds, with
the merciless logic of childhood, gradually discounted
the threatened calamities.

This must have accounted for the lapse in our own
conduct, and a sort of comfortable satisfaction that the
Almighty contented Himself in merely counting noses
in the pews. For even though it was my brother who got
into trouble, I shall never forget the harangue on im-
piety that awaited us when a most unchristian sexton
reported to our father that the pew in front of ours had
been found chalked on the back, so as to make its occupants the object of undisguised attention from the
rest of the congregation. As circumstantial evidence also
against us, he offered some tell-tale squares of silver
paper, on which we had been cooking chocolates on the
steam pipes during the sermon.

In all my childhood I can only remember one single
punishment, among not a few which I received, which I
resented — and for years I never quite forgot it. Some
one had robbed a very favourite apple tree in our orchard
— an escapade of which I was perfectly capable, but in
this instance had not had the satisfaction of sharing.
Some evidence had been lodged against me, of which I
was not informed, and I therefore had no opportunity

to challenge it. I was asked before a whole class of my schoolmates if I had committed the act, and at once denied it. Without any hearing I was adjudged guilty, and promptly subjected to the punishment of the day — a good birching. On every occasion on which we were offered the alternative of detention, we invariably "plumped" for the rod, and got it over quickly, and, as we considered, creditably — taking it smiling as long as we could. But that one act of injustice, the disgrace which it carried of making me a liar before my friends, seared my very soul. I vowed I would get even whatever it cost, and I regret to say that I had n't long to wait the opportunity. For I scored both the apples and the lie against the punishment before many months. Nor was I satisfied then. It rankled in my mind both by day and by night; and it taught me an invaluable lesson — never to suspect or condemn rashly. It was one of Dr. Arnold's boys at Rugby, I believe, who summed up his master's character by saying, "The head was a beast, but he was always a just beast."

At fourteen years of age my brother was sent to Repton, to the house of an uncle by marriage — an arrangement which has persuaded me never to send boys to their relatives for training. My brother's pranks were undoubtedly many, but they were all boyish and legitimate ones. After a time, however, he was removed at his own request, and sent to Clifton, where he was head of the school, and the school house also, under Dr. Percival, the late Bishop of Hereford. From there he took an open scholarship for Oxford.

It was most wisely decided to send us to separate schools, and therefore at fourteen I found myself at Marlborough — a school of nearly six hundred resident boys, on entering which I had won a scholarship.

CHAPTER II

SCHOOL LIFE

MARLBOROUGH "COLLEGE," as we say in England for a large University preparatory school, is situated in Wiltshire, in a perfectly beautiful country, close to the Savernake Forest — one of the finest in all England. As everything and everybody was strange to me on my arrival, had I been brought up to be less self-reliant the events of my first day or two would probably have impressed themselves more deeply on my memory than is the case. Some Good Samaritan, hearing that I was bound for a certain house, allowed me to follow him from the station to the inn — for a veritable old inn it was. It was one of those lovely old wayside hostels along the main road to the west, which, with the decline of coaching days, found its way into the market, and had fallen to the hammer for the education of youth. Exactly how the adaptation had been accomplished I never quite understood. The building formed the end of a long avenue of trees and was approached through high gates from the main road. It was flanked on the east side by other houses, which fitted in somewhat inharmoniously, but served as school-rooms, dining-hall, chapel, racquets and fives courts, studies, and other dwelling-houses. The whole was entirely enclosed so that no one could pass in or out, after the gates were shut, without ringing up the porter from his lodge, and having one's name taken as being out after hours. At least it was supposed that no one could, though we boys soon found that there were more ways than one leading to Rome.

The separate dwelling-houses were named A, B, and C.

I was detailed to C House, the old inn itself. Each house was again divided into three, with its own house master, and its own special colour and badges. Our three were at the time "Sharps," "Upcutts," and "Bakers." Our particular one occupied the second floor, and was reached by great oak staircases, which, if you were smart, you could ascend at about six steps at a time. This was often a singular desideratum, because until you reached the fifth form, according to law you ascended by the less direct back stairway.

Our colours were white and maroon, and our sign a bishop's mitre — which effigy I still find scribbled all over the few book relics which I have retained, and which emblem, when borne subsequently on my velvet football cap, proved to be the nearest I ever was to approach to that dignified insignia.

My benefactor, on the night of my arrival, having done more for me than a new boy could expect of an old one, was whirled off in the stream of his returning chums long before I had found my resting-place for the night. The dormitory to which I at last found myself assigned contained no less than twenty-five beds, and seemed to me a veritable wilderness. If the coaches which used to stop here could have ascended the stairs, it might have accommodated several. What useful purpose it could have served in those far-off days I never succeeded in deciding. The room most nearly like it which I can recall is the old dining-hall of a great manor, into which the knights in armour rode on horseback to meals, that being far less trouble than removing one's armour, and quite as picturesque. More or less amicably I obtained possession of a bed in a good location, under a big window which looked out over the beautiful gardens below. I cannot remember that I experienced any of those heart-

searchings or forebodings which sentiment deplores as
the inevitable lot of the unprotected innocent.

One informal battle during the first week with a
boy possessed of the sanctity of having come up from
the lower school, and therefore being an "old boy,"
achieved for me more privileges than the actual decision
perhaps entitled one to enjoy, namely, being left alone.
I subsequently became known as the "Beast," owing to
my belligerent nature and the undue copiousness of my
hair.

The fact that I was placed in the upper fourth form
condemned me to do my "prep" in the intolerable bar-
rack called "Big School" — a veritable bear-garden to
which about three hundred small boys were relegated to
study. Order was kept by a master and a few monitors,
who wandered to and fro from end to end of the building,
while we were supposed to work. For my part, I never
tried it, partly because the work came very easy to me,
while the "repetition" was more readily learned from
a loose page at odd times like dinner and chapel, and
partly because, winning a scholarship during the term,
I was transferred to a building reserved for twenty-
eight such privileged individuals until they gained the
further distinction of a place in the house class-room,
by getting their transfer into the fifth form.

Besides those who lived in the big quad there were
several houses outside the gates, known as "Out-
Houses." The boys there fared a good deal better than
we who lived in college, and I presume paid more highly
for it. Our meals were served in "Big Hall," where the
whole four hundred of us were fed. The meals were exceptionally poor; so much so that we boys at the beginning of term formed what we called brewing companies — which provided as far as possible breakfasts

and suppers for ourselves all term. As a protection against early bankruptcy, it was our custom to deposit our money with a rotund but popular school official, known always by a corruption of his name as "the Slug." Every Saturday night he would dole out to you your deposit made on return from the holidays, divided into equal portions by the number of weeks in the term. Once one was in the fifth form, brewing became easy, for one had a right to a place on the class-room fire for one's kettle or saucepan. Till then the space over gas stoves in Big School being strictly limited, the right was only acquired "vi et armis." Moreover, most of the fourth form boys and the "Shells," a class between them and the fifth, if they had to work after evening chapel, had to sit behind desks around the house class-room facing the centre, in which as a rule the fifth form boys were lazily cooking and devouring their suppers. Certain parts of those repasts, like sausages, we would import ready cooked from the "Tuck Shop," and hence they only needed warming up. Breakfast in Big School was no comfort to one, and personally I seldom attended it. But at dinner and tea one had to appear, and remain till the doors were opened again. It was a kind of roll-call; and the penalty for being late was fifty lines to be written out. As my own habits were never as regular as they should have been, whenever I was able to keep ahead, I possessed pages of such lines, neatly written out during school hours and ready for emergencies. On other occasions I somewhat shamefacedly recall that I employed other boys, who devoted less time to athletics than was my wont, to help me out — their only remuneration being the "joy of service."

The great desire of every boy who could hope to do so was to excel in athletics. This fact has much to commend it in such an educational system, for it undoubtedly kept its devotees from innumerable worse troubles and dangers. All athletics were compulsory, unless one had obtained permanent exemption from the medical officer. If one was not chosen to play on any team during the afternoon, each boy had to go to gymnasium for drill and exercises, or to "flannel" and run round the Aylesbury Arms, an old public house three quarters of a mile distant. Any breach of this law was severely punished by the boys themselves. It involved a "fives batting," that is, a "birching" carried out with a hardwood fives bat, after chapel in the presence of the house. As a breach of patriotism, it carried great disgrace with it, and was very, very seldom necessary.

Experience would make me a firm believer in self-government — determination is the popular term now, I believe. No punishments ever touched the boys one tenth part as much as those administered by themselves. On one occasion two of the Big School monitors, who were themselves notorious far more for their constant breaches of school law than for their observance of it, decided to make capital at the expense of the sixth form. One day, just as the dinner-bell rang, they locked the sixth form door, while a conclave was being held inside. Though everyone was intended to know to whom the credit belonged, it was understood that no one would dream of giving evidence against them. But it so happened that their voices had been recognized from within by one of the sixth form boys — and "bullies" and unpopular though the culprits were, they would n't deny their guilt. Their condign punishment was to be "fives-batted" publicly in Big School — in which, however, they regained very considerable popularity by the way they took a "spanking" without turning a hair, though it cost no less than a dozen bats before it was over.

The publicity of Big School was the only redemption of such a bear-garden, but that was a good feature. It served to make us toe the line. After ten, it was the custom to have what we called "Upper School Boxing." A big ring was formed, boxing-gloves provided, and any differences which one might have to settle could be arranged there. There was more energy than science about the few occasions on which I appeared personally in the ring, but it was an excellent safety-valve and quite an evolutionary experience.

The exigency of having to play our games immediately after noon dinner had naturally taught the boys at the head of athletic affairs that it was not wise to eat too much. Dinner was the one solid meal which the college provided, and most of us wanted it badly enough when it came along, especially the suet puddings which went by the name of "bollies" and were particularly satisfying. But whenever any game of importance was scheduled, a remorseless card used to be passed round the table just after the meat stage, bearing the ominous legend "No bolly to-day." To make sure that there were no truants, all hands were forced to "Hooverize." Oddly enough, beer in large blue china jugs was freely served at every dinner. We called it "surpes," and boys, however small, helped themselves to as much as they liked. Moreover, as soon as the game was over, all who had their house colours might come in and get "surpes" served to them freely through the buttery window. Both practices, I believe, have long since fortunately fallen into desuetude.

To encourage the budding athlete there was an excellent custom of classifying not only the players who attained the first team; but beyond them there were "the

Forty" who wore velvet caps with tassels, "the Sixty" who wore velvet caps with silver braid, "the Eighty," and even "the Hundred" — all of whom were posted from time to time, and so stimulated their members to try for the next grade.

Like every other school there were bounds beyond which one might not go, and therefore beyond which one always wanted to go. Compulsory games limited the temptation in that direction very considerably; and my own breaches were practically always to get an extra swim. We had an excellent open-air swimming pool, made out of a branch of the river Kenneth, and were allowed one bathe a day, besides the dip before morning chapel, which only the few took, and which did not count as a bathe. The punishment for breaking the rule was severe, involving a week off for a first offence. But one was not easily caught, for even a sixth-former found hundreds of naked boys very much alike in the water, and the fact of any one having transgressed the limit was very hard to detect. Nor were we bound to incriminate ourselves by replying to leading questions.

"Late for Gates" was a more serious crime, involving detention from beloved games — and many were the expedients to which we resorted to avoid such an untoward contingency. I remember well waiting for an hour outside the porter's view, hoping for some delivery wagon to give me a chance to get inside. For it was far too light to venture to climb the lofty railings before "prep" time. Good fortune ordained, however, that a four-wheel cab should come along in time, containing the parents of a "hopeful" in the sick-room. It seemed a desperate venture, for to "run" the gate was a worse offence than being late and owning up. But we succeeded by standing on the off step, unquestioned by the person inside, who guessed at once what the trouble was, and who proved to be sport enough to engage the porter while we got clear. Later on a scapegrace who had more reason to require some by-way than myself, revealed to me a way which involved a long détour and a climb over the laundry roof. Of this, on another occasion, I was sincerely glad to avail myself. One of the older boys, I remember, made a much bolder venture. He waited till dusk, and then boldly walked in through the masters' garden. As luck would have it, he met our form master, whom we will call Jones, walking the other way. It so happened he possessed a voice which he knew was much like that of another master, so simply sprinting a little he called out, "Night, night, Jones," and got by without discovery.

Our chapel in those days was not a thing of beauty; but since then it has been rebuilt (out of our stomachs, the boys used to say) and is a model work of art. Attendance at chapel was compulsory, and no "cuts" were allowed. Moreover, once late, you were given lines, besides losing your chapel half-holiday. So the extraordinary zeal exhibited to be marked off as present should not be attributed to religious fervour. The chapel was entered from quad by two iron gates, with the same lofty railings which guarded the entrance on each side. The bell tolled for five minutes, then was silent one minute, and then a single toll was given, called "stroke." At that instant the two masters who stood by the pillars guarding each gate, jumped across, closing the gates if they could, and every one outside was late. Those inside the open walk — the length of the chapel that led to the doors at the far end — then continued to march in.

During prayers each form master sat opposite his form, all of which faced the central aisle, and marked off those present. Almost every morning half-dressed boys, with shirts open and collars unbuttoned, boots unlaced, and jumping into coats and waistcoats as they dashed along, could be seen rushing towards the gate during the ominous minute of silence. There was always time to get straight before the mass of boys inside had emptied into chapel; and I never remember a gate master stopping a boy before "stroke" for insufficiency of coverings. Many were the subterfuges employed to get excused, and naturally some form masters were themselves less regular than others, though you never could absolutely count on any particular one being absent. Twice in my time gates were rushed — that is, when "stroke" went such crowds of flying boys were just at the gate that the masters were unable to stop the onslaught, and were themselves brushed aside or knocked down under the seething mass of panic-stricken would-be worshippers. On one of these occasions we were forgiven — "stroke" was ten seconds early; on the other a half-holiday was stopped, as one of the masters had been injured. To trip one's self up, and get a bloody nose, and possibly a face scratched on the gravel, and then a "sick cut" from the kindly old school doctor, was one of the more common ways boys discovered of saving their chapel half — when it was a very close call.

The school surgery was presided over in my day by a much-beloved old physician of the old school, named Fergus, which the boys had so long ago corrupted into "Fungi" that many a lad was caught mistakenly addressing the old gentleman as Dr. Fungi — an error I always fancied to be rather appreciated.

By going to surgery you could very frequently escape evening chapel — a very desirable event if you had a "big brew" coming off in class-room, for you could get things cooked and have plenty of room on the fire before the others were out. But one always had to pay for the advantage, the old doctor being very much addicted to potions. I never shall forget the horrible tap in the corner, out of which "cough mixture" flowed as "a healing for the nations," but which, nasty as it was, was the cheapest price at which one could purchase the cut. Some boys, anxious to cut lessons, found that by putting a little soap in one's eye, that organ would become red and watery. This they practised so successfully that sometimes for weeks they would be forbidden to do lessons on account of "eye-strain." They had to use lotions, eye-shades, and every spectacle possible was tried, but all to no avail. Sometimes they used so much soap that I was sure the doctor would suspect the bubbles.

I had two periods in sick-room with a worrying cough, where the time was always made so pleasant that one was not tempted to hasten recovery. Diagnosis, moreover, was not so accurate in those days as it might have been, and the dear old doctor took no risks. So at the age of sixteen I was sent off for a winter to the South of France, with the diagnosis of congestion of the lungs.

One of my aunts, a Miss Hutchinson, living at Hyères in the South of France, was delighted to receive me. With a widowed friend and two charming and athletic daughters, she had a very pretty villa on the hills overlooking the sea. My orders — to live out of doors — were very literally obeyed. In light flannel costumes we roamed the hills after moths and butterflies, early and late. We kept the frogs in miniature ponds in boxes covered with netting, providing them with bamboo ladders to climb, and so tell us when it was going to be wet weather. We had also enclosures in which we kept banks of trap-door spiders, which used to afford us intense interest with their clever artifices. To these we added the breeding of the more beautiful butterflies and moths, and so, without knowing that we were learning, we were taught many and valuable truths of life. There were horses to ride also, and a beautiful "plage" to bathe upon. It was always sunny and warm, and I invariably look back on that winter as spent in paradise. I was permitted to go over with a young friend to the Carnival at Nice, where, disguised as a clown, and then as a priest, with the *abandon* of boys, we enjoyed every moment of the time — the world was so big and wonderful. The French that I had very quickly learned, as we always spoke it at our villa, stood me on this occasion in good stead. But better still, I happened, when climbing into one of the flower-bedecked carriages parading in the "bataille de fleurs" — which, being in costume, was quite the right thing to do — to find that the owner was an old friend of my family, one Sir William Hut. He at once carried me to his home for the rest of the Carnival, and, of course, made it doubly enjoyable.

A beautiful expedition, made later in that region, which lives in my memory, was to the gardens at La Mortola, over the Italian line, made famous by the frequent visits of Queen Victoria to them. They were owned by Sir Thomas Hanbury, whose wife was my aunt's great friend.

The quaintness of the memories which persist longest in one's mind often amuse me. We used, as good Episcopalians, to go every Sunday to the little English Church on the rue des Palmiers. Alas, I can remember only one thing about those services. The clergyman had a peculiar impediment in his speech which made him say his *h*'s and *s*'s, both as *sh*. Thus he always said *sh*uman for *h*uman, and invariably prayed that God might be pleased to "shave the Queen." He nearly got me into trouble once or twice through it.

About the middle of the winter I realized that I had made a mistake. In writing home I had so enthusiastically assured my father that the place was suiting my health, that he wrote back that he thought in that case I might stand a little tutoring, and forthwith I was despatched every morning to a Mr. B., an Englishman, whose house, called the "Hermitage," was in a thick wood. I soon discovered that Mr. B. was obliged to live abroad for his health, and that the coaching of small boys was only a means to that end. He was a good instructor in mathematics, a study which I always loved, but he insisted on my taking Latin and French literature, for neither of which I had the slightest taste. I consequently made no effort whatever to improve my mind, a fact which did not in the least disturb his equanimity. The great interest of those journeys to the Hermitage were the fables of La Fontaine — which I learned as repetition and enjoyed — and the enormous number of lizards on the walls, which could disappear with lightning rapidity when seen, though they would stay almost motionless, waiting for a fly to come near, which they then swallowed alive. They were so like the stones one could almost rub one's nose against them without seeing them. Each time I started, I used to cut a little switch for myself and try to switch them off their ledges before they vanished. The attraction to the act lay in that it was almost impossible to accomplish. But if you did they scored a bull's-eye by incontinently discarding their tails, which made them much harder to catch next time, and seemed in no way to incommode them, though it served to excuse my conscience of cruelty. At the same time I have no wish to pose as a protector of flies.

Returning to Marlborough School the following summer, I found that my father, who knew perfectly the thorough groundwork I had received in Greek and Latin, had insisted on my being given a remove into the lower fifth form "in absentia." Both he and I were aware that I could do the work easily; but the form master resented it, and had already protested in vain. I believe he was a very good man in his way, and much liked by those whom he liked. But alas, I was not one of them; and never once, during the whole time I was in his form, did I get one single word of encouragement out of him. My mathematical master, and "stinks," or chemical master, I was very fond of, and in both those departments I made good progress.

The task of keeping order in a chemistry class of boys is never easy. The necessary experiments divert the master's eye from the class, and always give opportunity for fooling. Added to this was the fact that our "stinks" master, like many scientific teachers, was far too good-natured, and half-enjoyed himself the diversion which his experiments gave. When obliged to punish a boy caught "flagrante delicto," he invariably looked out for some way to make it up to him later. It was the odd way he did it which endeared him to us, as if apologizing for the kindness. Thus, on one occasion, suddenly in most righteous anger, just as if a parenthesis to the remark he was making, he interposed, "Come and be caned, boy. My study, twelve o'clock." When the boy was leaving, very unrepentant after keeping the appointment, in the same parenthetical way the master remarked, "Go away, boy. Cake and wine, my room, five o'clock" — which proved eventually the most effective part of the correction.

To children there always appears a gap between them

and "grown-ups" as impassable as that which Abraham is made to describe as so great that they who would pass to and fro cannot. As we grow older, we cease to see it, but it exists all the same. As I write, five children are romping through this old wood on broom-handle horses. One has just fallen. A girl of twelve at once retorts, "Do get up, Willy, your horse is always throwing you off." The joys of life lie in us, not in things; and in childhood imagination is so big, its joys so entirely uncloyed. Sometimes grown-ups are apt to grudge the time and trouble put into apparently transient pleasures. A trivial strawberry feast, given to children on our dear old lawn under the jasmine and rose-bushes, something after the order of a New England clam-bake, still looms as a happy memory of my parents' love for children, punctuated by the fact that though by continuing a game in spite of warning I broke a window early in the afternoon, and was banished to the nursery "as advised," my father forgave me an hour later, and himself fetched me down again to the party.

To teach us independence, my father put us on an allowance at a very early age, with a small bank account, to which every birthday he added five pounds on our behalf. We had no pony at that time, indeed had not yet learned to ride, so our deposits always went by the name of "pony money." This was an excellent plan, for we didn't yet value money for itself, and were better able to appreciate the joy of giving because it seemed to postpone the advent of our pony. However, when we were thought to have learned to value so sentient a companion and to be likely to treat him properly, a Good Samaritan was permitted to present us with one of our most cherished friends. To us, she was an unparalleled beauty. How many times we fell over her head, and over her tail, no one can record. She always waited for you to remount, so it did n't much matter; and we were taught that great lesson in life, not to be afraid of falling, but to learn how to take a fall. My own bent, however, was never for the things of the land, and though gallops on the Dee Sands, and races with our cousins, who owned a broncho and generally beat us, had their fascination, boats were the things which appealed most to me.

Having funds at our disposal, we were allowed to purchase material, and under the supervision of a local carpenter, to build a boat ourselves. To this purpose our old back nursery was forthwith allocated. The craft which we desired was a canoe that would enable us to paddle or drift along the deep channels of the river, and allow us to steal upon the flocks of birds feeding at the edges. Often in memory I enjoy those days again — the planning, the modelling, the fitting, the setting-up, and at last, the visit of inspection of our parents. Alas, stiff-necked in our generation, we had insisted on straight lines and a square stern. Never shall I forget the indignation aroused in me by a cousin's remark, "It looks awful like a coffin." The resemblance had not previously struck either of us, and father had felt that the joke was too dangerous a one to make, and had said nothing. But the pathos of it was that we now saw it all too clearly. My brother explained that the barque was intended to be not "seen." Ugliness was almost desirable. It might help us if we called it the "Reptile," and painted it red — all of which suggestions were followed. But still I remember feeling a little crestfallen, when after launching it through the window, it lay offensively resplendent against the vivid green of the grass. It served, however, for a time, ending its days honourably by capsizing a friend and me, guns and all, into the half-frozen water of the lower estuary while we were stalking some curlew. I had to run home dripping. My friend's gun, moreover, having been surreptitiously borrowed from my cousin's father, was recovered the following day, to our unutterable relief. Out of the balance of the money spent on the boat, we purchased a pin-fire, breech-loading gun, the pride of my life for many days. I was being kept back from school at the time on account of a cold, but I was not surprised to find myself next day sitting in a train, bound for Marlborough, and "referred once more to my studies."

A little later my father, not being satisfied, took me away to read with a tutor for the London matriculation, in which without any trouble, I received a first class.

A large boarding-school in England is like a miniature world. One makes many acquaintances, who change as one gets pushed into new classes, so at that stage one makes few lasting friends. Those who remain till they attain the sixth form, and make the school teams, probably form more permanent friendships. I at least think of that period as one when one's bristles were generally up, and though many happy memories linger, and I have found that to be an old Marlburian is a bond of friendship all the world over, it is the little oddities which one remembers best.

A new scholarship boy had one day been assigned to the closed corporation of our particular class-room. To me he had many attractions, for he was a genius both in mathematics and chemistry. We used to love talking over the problems that were set us as voluntary tasks for our spare time; and our united excursions in those directions were so successful that we earned our class more than one "hour off," as rewards for the required number of stars given for good pieces of work. My friend

had, however, no use whatever for athletics. He had
never been from home before, had no brothers, and five
sisters, was the pet of his parents, and naturally somewhat of a square plug in a round hole in our school life.
He hated all conventions, and was always in trouble
with the boys, for he entirely neglected his personal appearance, while his fingers were always discoloured with
chemicals, and he would not even feign an interest in the
things for which they cared. I can remember him sitting
on the foot of my bed, talking me to sleep more than
once with some new plan he had devised for a self-steer-
ing torpedo or an absolutely reliable flying machine. He
had received the sobriquet of "Mad G.," and there was
some justice in it from the opposition point of view. I
had not realized, however, that he was being bullied —
on such a subject he would never say a syllable — till
one day as he left class-room I saw a large lump of coal
hit him square on the head, and a rush of blood follow it
that made me hustle him off to surgery. Scalp wounds
are not so dangerous as they are bloody to heads as thick
as ours. His explanation that he had fallen down was too
obvious a distortion of truth to deceive even our kindly
old doctor. But he asked no further question, seeing that
it was a point of honour. The matter, however, forced an
estrangement between myself and some of my fellows
that I realized afterwards was excellent for me. Forthwith
we moved my friend's desk into my corner of the room
which was always safe when I was around, though later
some practices of the others to which I took exception
led to a combination which I thought of then as that
made by the Jews to catch Paul, and which I foiled in a
similar way, watchfully eluding them when they were in
numbers together, but always ready to meet one or two
at a time. The fact that I had just taken up "racquets"

impressed it on my memory, for considering the class-room temporarily unsafe for "prep" work, I used that building as a convenient refuge for necessary study. It would have been far better to have fought it out and taken, if unavoidable, whatever came to me — had it been anywhere else I should probably have done so. But the class-room was a close corporation for Foundation scholars, and not one of my chums had access to it to see fair play.

My friendship for "Mad G." was largely tempered by my own love for anything athletic, and eccentricities paid a very heavy price among all boys. Thus, though I was glad to lend my protection to my friend, we never went about together — as such boys as he always lived the life of hermits in the midst of the crowd. I well remember one other boy, made eccentric by his peculiar face and an unfortunate impediment of speech. No such boy should have been sent to an English public school as it was in my day. His stutter was no ordinary one, for it consisted, not in repeating the first letter or syllable, but in blowing out both cheeks like a balloon, and making noises which resembled a back-firing motor engine. It was the custom of our form master to make us say our repetition by each boy taking one line, the last round being always "expressed" — that is, unless you started instantly the boy above you finished, the next boy began, and took your place. I can still see and hear the unfortunate J. getting up steam for his line four or five boys ahead of time, so that he might explode at the right moment, which desirable end, however, he but very rarely accomplished, and never catching up, he used, like the man in the parable, always to "begin with shame to take the lowest place." Sometimes the master in a merciful mood allowed us to write the line; but that was risky, for it was considered no disgrace to circumvent him, and under those circumstances it was very easy for the next boy to write his own and then yours, and pass it along if he saw you were in trouble.

There was, and I think with some reason, a pride among the boys on their appearance on certain occasions. It went by the name of "good form." Thus on Sundays at morning chapel, we always wore a button-hole flower if we could. My dear mother used to post me along a little box of flowers every week — nor was it by any means wasted energy, for not only did the love for flowers become a hobby and a custom with many of us through life, and a help to steer clear of sloppiness in appearance, but it was a habit quite likely to spread to the soul. But beyond that, the picture of my dear mother, with the thousand worries of a large school of small boys on her hands, finding time to gather, pack, address, and post each week with her own hands so fleeting and inessential a token of her love, has a thousand times arisen to my memory, and led me to consider some apparently quite unnecessary little labour of love as being well worth the time and trouble. It is these deeds of love — not words, however touching — that never fade from the soul, and to the last make their appeal to the wandering boy to "arise" and do things.

Like everything else this fastidiousness can be overdone, and I remember once a boy's legal guardian showing me a bill for a hundred pounds sterling that his ward had incurred in a single term for cut flowers. Yet "form" is a part of the life of all English schools, and the boys think much more of it than sin. At Harrow you may not walk in the middle of the road as a freshman; and in American schools and universities, such regulations as the "Fence" laws at Yale show that they have emulated and even surpassed us in these. It was, however, a very potent influence, and we were always ridiculously sensitive about breaches of it. Thus, on a certain prize day my friend "Mad G.," having singularly distinguished himself in his studies, his parents came all the way from their home, at great expense to themselves, to see their beloved and only son honoured. I presume that, though wild horses would not drag anything out of the boy at school, he had communicated to them the details of some little service rendered. For to my horror I was stopped by his mother, whom I subsequently learned to love and honour above most people, and actually kissed while walking in the open quad — strutting like a peacock, I suppose, for I remember feeling as if the bottom had suddenly fallen out of the earth. The sequel, however, was an invitation to visit their home in North Wales for the Christmas holidays, where there was rough shooting, — the only kind I really cared for, — boating, rock-climbing, bathing, and the companionship of as lively a family as it was possible to meet anywhere. Many a holiday afterwards we shared together, and the kindness showered upon me I shall never be able to forget, or, alas, return; for my dear friend "Mad G." has long ago gone to his rest, and so have both his parents, whom I loved almost as my own.

Another thing for which I have much to thank my parents is the interest which they encouraged me to take in the collecting and study of natural objects. We were taught that the only excuse that made the taking of animal life honourable was for some useful purpose, like food or study or self-preservation. Several cases of birds stuffed and set up when we were fourteen and sixteen years of age still adorn the old house. Every bit had to be done by ourselves, my brother making the cases, and

I the rock work and taxidermy. The hammering-up of sandstone and granite; to cover the glue-soaked brown paper that we moulded into rocks, satisfied my keenest instinct for making messes, and only the patience of the old-time domestics would have "stood for it." My brother specialized in birds' eggs, and I in butterflies and moths. Later we added seaweeds, shells, and flowers. Some of our collections have been dissipated; and though we have not a really scientific acquaintance with either of these kingdoms, we acquired a "hail-fellow-well-met" familiarity with all of them, which has enlivened many a day in many parts of the world as we have journeyed through life. Moreover, though purchased pictures have other values, the old cases set on the walls of one's den bring back memories that are the joy and solace of many idle moments later in life — each rarer egg, each extra butterfly picturing some day or place of keen triumph, otherwise long since forgotten. Here, for instance, is a convolvulus hawk father found killed on a mountain in Switzerland; there an Apollo I caught in the Pyrenees; here a "red burret" with "five eyes" captured as we raced through the bracken on Clifton Downs; and there are "purple emperors" wired down to "meat" baits on the Surrey Downs.

Many a night at school have I stolen into the great forest, my butterfly net under my coat, to try and add a new specimen to my hoard. We were always supplied with good "key-books," so that we should be able to identify our specimens, and also to search for others more intelligently. One value of my own specialty was that for the moths it demanded going out in the night, and the thrills of out of doors in the beautiful summer evenings, when others were "fugging" in the house or had gone to bed, used actually to make me dance around on the grass. The dark lantern, the sugaring of the tree stems with intoxicating potions, and the subsequent excitement of searching for specimens, fascinated me utterly. Our breeding from the egg, through the caterpillar stage, taught us many things without our knowing that we were learning.

One of our holidays was memorable, because as soon as our parents left we invited my friend and two sisters as well to come and stay with us. They came, fully expecting that mother had asked them, but were good enough sports to stay when they found it was only us two boys. They greatly added to the enjoyment of the days, and if they had not been such inveterate home letter-writers — a habit of which we were very contemptuous — it would have saved us boys much good-humoured teasing afterwards, for the matron would have been mum and no one the wiser.

CHAPTER III

EARLY WORK IN LONDON

In 1883 my father became anxious to give up teaching boys and to confine himself more exclusively to the work of a clergyman. With this in view he contemplated moving to London where he had been offered the chaplaincy of the huge London Hospital. I remember his talking it over with me, and then asking if I had any idea what I wanted to do in life. It came to me as a new conundrum. It had never occurred to me to look forward to a profession; except that I knew that the heads of tigers, deer, and all sorts of trophies of the chase which adorned our house came from soldier uncles and others who hunted them in India, and I had always thought that their occupation would suit my taste admirably. It never dawned on me that I would have to earn my bread and butter — that had always come along. Moreover, I had never seen real poverty in others, for all the fisherfolk in our village seemed to have enough. I hated dress and frills, and envied no one. At school, and on the Riviera, and even in Wales, I had never noticed any want. It is true that a number of dear old ladies from the village came in the winter months to our house once or twice a week to get soup. They used to sit in the back hall, each with a round tin can with a bucket handle. These were filled with hot broth, and the old ladies were given a repast as well before leaving. As a matter of fact I very seldom actually saw them, for that part of the house was cut off entirely by large double green-baize covered doors. But I often knew that they must have been there, because our Skye terrier, though fed to overflowing, usually attended these séances, and I presume, while the old ladies were occupied with lunch, sampled the cans of soup that stood in rows along the floor. He used to come along with dripping whiskers which betrayed his excursion, and the look of a connoisseur in his large round eyes — as if he were certifying that justice had been done once more in the kitchen.

While I was in France the mother of my best chum in school had been passing through Marseilles on her way home from India, and had most kindly taken me on a jolly trip to Arles, Avignon, and other historical places. She was the wife of a famous missionary in India. She spoke eight languages fluently, including Arabic, and was a perfect "vade mecum" of interesting information which she well knew how to impart. She had known my mother's family all her life, they being Anglo-Indians in the army service.

About the time of my father's question, my friend's mother was staying in Chester with her brother-in-law, the Lieutenant-Governor of Denbighshire. It was decided that as she was a citizeness of the world, no one could suggest better for what profession my peculiar talents fitted me. The interview I have long ago forgotten, but I recall coming home with a confused idea that tiger hunting would not support me, and that she thought I ought to become a clergyman, though it had no attraction for me, and I decided against it.

None of our family on either side, so far as I can find out, had ever practised medicine. My own experience of doctors had been rather a chequered one, but at my father's suggestion I gladly went up and discussed the matter with our country family doctor. He was a fine man, and we boys were very fond of him and his family, his daughter being our best girl friend near by. He had an enormous practice, in which he was eminently successful. The number of horses he kept, and the miles he covered with them, were phenomenal in my mind. He had always a kind word for every one, and never gave us boys away, though he must have known many of our pranks played in our parents' absence. The only remaining memory of that visit was that the old doctor brought down from one of his shelves a large jar, out of which he produced a pickled human brain. I was thrilled with entirely new emotions. I had never thought of man's body as a machine. That this weird, white, puckered-up mass could be the producer or transmitter of all that made man, that it controlled our physical strength and growth, and our responses to life, that it made one into "Mad G." and another into me — why, it was absolutely marvellous. It attracted me as did the gramophone, the camera, the automobile.

My father saw at once on my return that I had found my real interest, and put before me two alternative plans, one to go to Oxford, where my brother had just entered, or to join him in London and take up work in the London Hospital and University, preparatory to going in for medicine. I chose the latter at once — a decision I have never regretted. I ought to say that business as a career was not suggested. In England, especially in those days, these things were more or less hereditary. My forbears were all fighters or educators, except for an occasional statesman or banker. Probably there is some advantage in this plan.

The school had been leased for a period of seven years to a very delightful successor, it being rightly supposed that after that time my brother would wish to assume the responsibility.

Some of the subjects for the London matriculation

were quite new to me, especially "English." But with the fresh incentive and new vision of responsibility I set to work with a will, and soon had mastered the ten required subjects sufficiently to pass the examination with credit. But I must say here that Professor Huxley's criticisms of English public school teaching of that period were none too stringent. I wish with all my heart that others had spoken out as bravely, for in those days that wonderful man was held up to our scorn as an atheist and iconoclast. He was, however, perfectly right. We spent years of life and heaps of money on our education, and came out knowing nothing to fit us for life, except that which we picked up incidentally.

I now followed my father to London, and found every subject except my chemistry entirely new. I was not familiar with one word of botany, zoölogy, physics, physiology, or comparative anatomy. About the universe which I inhabited I knew as little as I did about cuneiform writings. Except for my mathematics and a mere modicum of chemistry I had nothing on which to base my new work; and students coming from Government free schools, or almost anywhere, had a great advantage over men of my previous education; I did not even know how to study wisely. Again, as Huxley showed, medical education in London was so divided, there being no teaching university, that the curriculum was ridiculously inadequate. There were still being foisted upon the world far too many medical men of the type of Bob Sawyer.

There were fourteen hospitals in London to which medical schools were attached. Our hospital was the largest in the British Isles, and in the midst of the poorest population in England, being located in the famous Whitechapel Road, and surrounded by all the purlieus of the East End of the great city. Patients came from

Tilbury Docks to Billingsgate Market, and all the river haunts between; from Shadwell, Deptford, Wapping, Poplar, from Petticoat Lane and Radcliffe Highway, made famous by crime and by Charles Dickens. They came from Bethnal Green, where once queens had their courts, now the squalid and crowded home of poverty; from Stratford and Bow, and a hundred other slums.

The hospital had some nine hundred beds, which were always so full that the last surgeon admitting to his wards constantly found himself with extra beds poked in between the regulation number through sheer necessity. It afforded an unrivalled field for clinical experience and practical teaching. In my day, however, owing to its position in London, and the fact that its school was only just emerging from primeval chaos, it attracted very few indeed of the medical students from Oxford and Cambridge, who are obliged to come to London for their last two or three years' hospital work — the scope in those small university towns being decidedly limited.

Looking back I am grateful to my alma mater, and have that real affection for her that every loyal son should have. But even that does not conceal from me how poor a teaching establishment it was. Those who had natural genius, and the advantages of previous scientific training, who were sons of medical men, or had served apprenticeships to them, need not have suffered so much through its utter inefficiency. But men in my position suffered quite unconsciously a terrible handicap, and it was only the influences for which I had nothing whatever to thank the hospital that saved me from the catastrophes which overtook so many who started with me.

To begin with, there was no supervision of our lives whatever. We were flung into a coarse and evil environment, among men who too often took pride in their shame, just to sink or swim. Not one soul cared which you did. I can still remember numerous cases where it simply meant that men paid quite large sums for the privilege of sending the sons they loved direct to the devil. I recall one lad whom I had known at school. His father lavished money upon him, and sincerely believed that his son was doing him credit and would soon return to share his large practice, and bring to it all the many new advances he had learned. The reports of examinations successfully passed he fully accepted; and the non-return of his son at vacation times he put down to professional zeal. It was not till the time came for the boy to get his degree and return that the father discovered that he had lived exactly the life of the prodigal in the parable, and had neither attended college nor attempted a single examination of any kind whatever. It broke the father's heart and he died.

Examinations for degrees were held by the London University, or the Royal College of Physicians and Surgeons, never by the hospital schools. These were practically race committees; they did no teaching, but when you had done certain things, they allowed you to come up and be examined, and if you got through a written and "viva voce" examination you were inflicted on an unsuspecting public "qualified to kill" — often only too literally so.

It is obvious on the face of it that this could be no proper criterion for so important a decision as to qualifications; special crammers studied the examiners, their questions, and their teachings, and luck had a great deal to do with success. While some men never did themselves justice in examinations, others were exactly the reverse. Thus I can remember one resident accoucheur being "ploughed," as we called it, in his special subject, obstetrics — and men to whom you would n't trust your cat getting through with flying colours.

Of the things to be done: First you had to be signed up for attending courses of lectures on certain subjects. This was simply a matter of tipping the beadle, who marked you off. I personally attended only two botany lectures during the whole course. At the first some practical joker had spilled a solution of carbon bisulphide all over the professor's platform, and the smell was so intolerable that the lecture was prorogued. At the second, some wag let loose a couple of pigeons, whereupon every one started either to capture them or stir them up with pea-shooters. The professor said, "Gentlemen, if you do not wish to learn, you are at liberty to leave." The entire class walked out. The insignificant sum of two and six-pence secured me my sign-up for the remainder of the course.

Materia medica was almost identical; and while we had better fortune with physiology, no experience and no apparatus for verifying its teachings were ever shown us.

Our chemistry professor was a very clever man, but extremely eccentric, and his class was pandemonium. I have seen him so frequently pelted with peas, when his head was turned, as to force him to leave the amphitheatre in despair. I well remember also an unpopular student being pushed down from the top row almost on to the experiment table.

There was practically no histology taught, and little or no pathology. Almost every bit of the microscope which I did was learned on my own instrument at home. Anatomy, however, we were well taught in the dissecting-room, where we could easily obtain all the work we needed. But not till Sir Frederick Treves became our lecturer in anatomy and surgery was it worth while doing more than pay the necessary sum to get signed up.

In the second place we had to attend in the dispensary, actually to handle drugs and learn about them — an admirable rule. Personally I went once, fooled around making egg-nogg, and arranged with a considerate druggist to do the rest that was necessary. Yet I satisfied the examiners at the College of Physicians and Surgeons, those of the London University at the examinations for Bachelor of Medicine — the only ones which they gave which carried questions in any of these subjects.

In the athletic life of the University, however, I took great interest, and was secretary in succession of the cricket, football, and rowing clubs. I helped remove the latter from the old river Lea to the Thames, to raise the inter-hospital rowing championship and start the united hospitals' rowing club. I found time to row in the inter-hospital race for two years and to play on the football team in the two years of which we won the inter-hospital football cup. A few times I played with the united hospitals' team; but I found that their ways were not mine, as I had been taught to despise alcohol as a beverage and to respect all kinds of womanhood. For three years I played regularly for Richmond — the best of the London clubs at the time — and subsequently for Oxford, being put on the team the only term I was in residence. I also threw the hammer for the hospital in the united hospitals' sports, winning second place for two years. Indeed, athletics in some form occupied every moment of my spare time.

It was in my second year, 1885, that returning from an out-patient case one night, I turned into a large tent erected in a purlieu of Shadwell, the district to which I happened to have been called. It proved to be an evangel-

OXFORD UNIVERSITY RUGBY UNION FOOTBALL TEAM

W. T. Grenfell at left of bottom row

istic meeting of the then famous Moody and Sankey. It
was so new to me that when a tedious prayer-bore began
with a long oration, I started to leave. Suddenly the
leader, whom I learned afterwards was D. L. Moody,
called out to the audience, "Let us sing a hymn while
our brother finishes his prayer." His practicality interested me, and I stayed the service out. When eventually
I left, it was with a determination either to make religion a real effort to do as I thought Christ would do in
my place as a doctor, or frankly abandon it. That could
only have one issue while I still lived with a mother like
mine. For she had always been my ideal of unselfish love.
So I decided to make the attempt, and later went down
to hear the brothers J. E. and C. T. Studd speak at some
subsidiary meeting of the Moody campaign. They were
natural athletes, and I felt that I could listen to them.
I could not have listened to a sensuous-looking man, a
man who was not a master of his own body, any more
than I could to a precentor, who coming to sing the
prayers at college chapel dedication, I saw get drunk on
sherry which he abstracted from the banquet table just
before the service. Never shall I forget, at the meeting
of the Studd brothers, the audience being asked to stand
up if they intended to try and follow Christ. It appeared
a very sensible question to me, but I was amazed how
hard I found it to stand up. At last one boy, out of
a hundred or more in sailor rig, from an industrial or
reformatory ship on the Thames, suddenly rose. It
seemed to me such a wonderfully courageous act — for
I knew perfectly what it would mean to him — that I
immediately found myself on my feet, and went out
feeling that I had crossed the Rubicon, and must do
something to prove it.

We were Church of England people, and I always attended service with my mother at an Episcopal church of the evangelical type. At her suggestion I asked the minister if I could in any way help. He offered me a class of small boys in his Sunday School, which I accepted with much hesitation. The boys, derived from houses in the neighbourhood, were as smart as any I have known. With every faculty sharpened by the competition of the street, they so tried my patience with their pranks that I often wondered what strange attraction induced them to come at all. The school and church were the property of a society known by the uninviting title of the "Episcopal Society for the promotion of Christianity among the Jews." It owned a large court, shut off from the road by high gates, around which stood about a dozen houses — with the church facing the gates at one end of a pretty avenue of trees. It was an oasis in the desert of that dismal region. It possessed also an industrial institution for helping its converts to make a living, when driven out of their own homes; and its main work was carried on for the most part by superannuated missionaries. One was from Bagdad, I remember, and one from Palestine, both themselves Jews by extraction. These missionaries were paid such miserable salaries that in their old age they were always left very poor.

One instance of a baptism I have never forgotten. I was then living in the court, having hired a nice separate house under the trees after my father had died and my mother had moved to Hampstead. In such a district the house was a Godsend. One Sunday I was strolling in the court when the clergyman came rushing out of the church and called to me in great excitement, "The church is full of Jews. They are going to carry off Abraham. Can't you go in and help while I fetch the police?" My friend and I therefore rushed in as directed to a narrow alleyway between high box pews which led into the vestry, into which "Abraham" had been spirited. The door being shut and our backs put to it, it was a very easy matter to hold back the crowd, who probably supposed at first that we were leading the abduction party. There being only room for two to come on at once, "those behind cried forward, and those in front back," till after very little blood spilt, we heard the police in the church, and the crowd at once took to flight. I regret to say that we expedited the rear-guard by football rather than strictly Christian methods. His friends then charged Abraham with theft, expecting to get him out of his place of refuge and then trap him, as we were told they had a previous convert. We therefore accompanied him personally through the mean streets, both to and fro, spoiling for more fun. But they displayed more discretion than valour, and to the best of my belief he escaped their machinations.

My Sunday-School efforts did not satisfy me. The boys were few, and I failed to see any progress. But I had resolved that I would do no work on Sundays except for others, so I joined a young Australian of my class in hospital in holding services on Sunday nights in half a dozen of the underground lodging-houses along the Radcliffe Highway. He was a good musician, so he purchased a fine little portable harmonium, and whatever else the lodgers thought of us, they always liked the music. We used to meet for evening tea at a place in the famous Highway known as "The Stranger's Rest," outside of which an open-air service was always held for the sailors wandering up and down the docks. At these a number of ladies would sing; and after the meetings a certain number of the sailors were asked to come in and have refreshments. There were always some who had spent their money on drink, or been robbed, or were out of ships, and many of them were very fine men. Some were foreigners — so much so that a bit farther down the road a Norwegian lady carried on another similar work, especially for Scandinavians.

A single story will illustrate the good points which some of these men displayed. My hospital chief, Sir Frederick Treves, had operated on a great big Norwegian, and the man had left the hospital cured. As a rule such patients do not even know the name of their surgeon. Some three weeks later, however, this man called at Sir Frederick Treves's house late one dark night. Having asked if he were the surgeon who had operated on him and getting a reply in the affirmative, he said he had come to return thanks, that since he left hospital he had been wandering about without a penny to his name, waiting for a ship, but had secured a place on that day. He proceeded to cut out from the upper edge of his trousers a gold Norwegian five-kronen piece which his wife had sewed in there to be his stand-by in case of absolute need. He had been so hungry that he had been tempted to use it, but now had come to present it as a token of gratitude — upon which he bowed and disappeared. Sir Frederick said that he was so utterly taken aback that he found himself standing in the hall, holding the coin, and bowing his visitor out. He said he could no more return it than you could offer your teacher a "tip," and he has preserved it as a much-prized possession.

The underground lodging-house work did me lots of good. It brought me into touch with real poverty — a very graveyard of life I had never surmised. The denizens of those miserable haunts were men from almost every rank of life. They were shipwrecks from the ocean of humanity, drifted up on the last beach. There were

large open fireplaces in the dens, over which those who
had any food cooked it. Often while the other doctor or
I was holding services, one of us would have to sit down
on some drunken man to keep him from making the
proceedings impossible; but there was always a modicum
who gathered around and really enjoyed the singing.

We soon found that there were no depths of contemptible treachery which some among these new acquaintances would not attempt. We became gradually
hardened to the piteous tales of ill luck, of malignant persecution, and of purely temporary embarrassments, and
learned soon to leave behind us purses, and watches,
and anything else of value, and to keep some specially
worn clothing for this service.

There was always a narrow passage from the front
door to the staircase which led down into those huge
underground basements. The guardians had a room
inside the door, with a ticket window, where they took
five or possibly eight cents from the boarders for their
night's lodging. At about eleven o'clock a "chucker out"
would go down and clear out all the gentlemen who had
not paid in advance for the night. This was always a
very melancholy period of the evening, and in spite of
our hardened hearts, we always had a score against us
there. That, however, had to be given in person, for there
were plenty among our audiences who had taken special
courses in imitative calligraphy. I.O.U.'s on odd bits of
paper were a menace to our banking accounts till we
sorrowfully abandoned that convenient way of helping
often a really deserving case.

In those houses, somewhat to my astonishment, we
never once received any physical opposition. We knew
that some considered us harmless and gullible imbeciles;
but the great majority were still able to see that it was

an attempt, however poor, to help them. Drink, of course, was the chief cause of the downfall of most; but as I have already said, there were cases of genuine, undeserved poverty — like our sailor friend, overtaken with sickness in a foreign port. We induced some to sign the pledge and to keep it, if only temporarily, but I think that we ourselves got most out of the work, both in pleasure and uplift. I recall one clergyman, one doctor, and many men from the business world and clerk's life in the flotsam and jetsam.

One poor creature, in the last stage of poverty and dirt, proved to be an honours man in Oxford. We looked up his record in the University. He assured us that he intended to begin again a new life, and we agreed to help start him. We took him to a respectable, temperance lodging-house, paid for a bed, a bath, and a supper, and purchased a good second-hand outfit of clothing for him. We were wise enough only to give this to him after we had taken away his own while he was having a bath in the tub. We did not give him a penny of money, fearing his lack of control. Next morning, however, when we went for him, he was gone — no one knew where. We had the neighbouring saloons searched, and soon got track of him. Some "friend" in the temperance house had given him sixpence. The barman offered him the whiskey; his hands trembled so that he could not lift the glass to his mouth, and the barman kindly poured it down his throat. We never saw him again.

. In this lodging-house work a friend, now a well-known artist and successful business man, often joined us two doctors.

My growing experience had shown me that there was a better way to the hearts of my Sunday-School boys than merely talking to them. Like myself, they worshipped the athlete, whether he were a prize-fighter or a big football player. There were no Y.M.C.A.'s or other places for them to get any physical culture, so we arranged to clear our dining-room every Saturday evening, and give boxing lessons and parallel-bar work: the ceiling was too low for the horizontal. The transformation of the room was easily accomplished. The furniture was very primitive, largely our own construction, and we could throw out through the window every scrap of it except the table, which was soon "adapted." We also put up a quoit pitch in our garden.

This is no place to discuss the spiritual influences of the "noble art of boxing." Personally I have always believed in its value; and my Sunday-School class soon learned the graces of fair play, how to take defeat and to be generous in victory. They began at once bringing "pals" whom my exegesis on Scripture would never have lured within my reach. We ourselves began to look forward to Saturday night and Sunday afternoon with an entirely new joy. We all learned to respect and so to love one another more — indeed, lifelong friendships were developed and that irrespective of our hereditary credal affiliations. The well-meaning clergyman, however, could not see the situation in that light, and declining all invitations to come and sample an evening's fun instead of condemning it unheard, or I should say, unseen, he delivered an ultimatum which I accepted — and resigned from his school.

My Australian friend was at that time wrestling with a real ragged school on the Highway on Sunday afternoons. The poor children there were street waifs and as wild as untamed animals. So, being temporarily out of a Sunday job, I consented to join him.

Our school-room this time owed no allegiance to any

one but ourselves, and the work certainly proved a real labour of love. If the boys were allowed in a minute before there was a force to cope with them, the room would be wrecked. Everything movable was stolen immediately opportunity arose. Boys turned out or locked out during session would climb to the windows, and triumphantly wave stolen articles. On one occasion when I had "chucked out" a specially obstreperous youth, I was met with a shower of mud and stones as I passed through a narrow alley on my return home. The police were always at war with the boys, who annoyed them in similar and many other ways. I remember two scholars whose eyes were blacked and badly beaten by a "cop" who happened to catch them in our doorway, as they declared, "only waiting for Sunday School to open." Old scores were paid off by both parties whenever possible. My own boys did not stay in the old school long after I left, but came and asked me to keep a class on Sunday in our dining-room — an arrangement in which I gladly acquiesced, though it involved my eventually abandoning the ragged school, which was at least two miles distant.

With the night work at the lodging-houses, we used to combine a very aggressive total abstinence campaign. The saloon-keepers as a rule looked upon us as harmless cranks, and I have no doubt were grateful for the leaflets we used to distribute to their customers. These served admirably for kindling purposes. At times, however, they got ugly, and once my friend, who was in a saloon talking to a customer, was trapped and whiskey poured into his mouth. On another occasion I noticed that the outer doors were shut and a couple of men backed up against them while I was talking to the bartender over the counter, and that a few other customers were closing in to repeat the same experiment on me. However, they greatly overrated their own stock of fitness and equally underrated my good training, for the scrimmage went all my own way in a very short time.

If ever I told my football chums (for in those days I was playing hard) of these adventures in a nether world, they always wanted to come and coöperate; but I have always felt that reliance on physical strength alone is only a menace when the odds are so universally in favour of our friend the enemy. At this time also at St. Andrew's Church, just across the Whitechapel Road from the hospital, the clergyman was a fine athlete and good boxer. He was a brother of Lord Wenlocks, and was one night returning from a mission service in the Highway when he was set upon by footpads and robbed of everything, including the boots off his feet. Meantime "Jack the Ripper" was also giving our residential section a most unsavoury reputation.

My long vacations at this time were always taken on the sea. My brother and I used to hire an old fishing smack called the "Oyster," which we rechristened the "Roysterer." This we fitted out, provisioned, and put to sea in with an entirely untrained crew, and without even the convention of caring where we were found so long as the winds bore us cheerily along. My brother was always cook — and never was there a better. We believed that he would have made a mark in the world as a chef, from his ability to satisfy our appetites and cater to our desires out of so ill-supplied a galley. We always took our departure from the north coast of Anglesea — a beautiful spot, and to us especially attractive as being so entirely out of the run of traffic that we could do exactly as we pleased. We invariably took our fishing gear with us, and thus never wanted for fresh food. We could replenish our bread, milk, butter, and egg supply at the numerous small ports at which we called. The first year the crew consisted of my brother and me — skipper, mate, and cook between us — and an Oxford boating friend as second mate. For a deckhand we had a young East London parson, whom we always knew as "the Puffin," because he so closely resembled that particular bird when he had his vestments on. We sailed first for Ireland, but the wind coming ahead we ran instead for the Isle of Man. The first night at sea the very tall undergraduate as second mate had the 12 P.M. to 4 A.M. night watch. The tiller handle was very low, and when I gave him his course at midnight before turning in myself, he asked me if it would be a breach of nautical etiquette to sit down to steer, as that was the only alternative to directing the ship's course with his ankles. No land was in sight, and the wind had died out when I came on deck for my 4 A.M. to 8 A.M. watch. I found the second mate sitting up rubbing his eyes as I emerged from the companion hatch.

"Well, where are we now? How is her head? What's my course?"

"Don't worry about such commonplace details," he replied. "I have made an original discovery about these parts that I have never seen mentioned before."

"What's that?" I asked innocently.

"Well," he replied, "when I sat down to steer the course you gave brought a bright star right over the topmast head and that's what I started to steer by. It's a perfect marvel what a game these heavenly bodies play. We must be in some place like Alice in Wonderland. I just shut my eyes for a second and when next I opened them the sun was exactly where I had left that star — " and he fled for shelter.

It is a wonder that we ever got anywhere, for we had

not so much as a chronometer watch, and so in spite of a decrepit sextant even our latitude was often an uncertain quantity. However, we made the port of Douglas, whence we visited quite a part of the historic island. As our parson was called home from there, we wired for and secured another chum to share our labours. Our generally unconventional attire in fashionable summer resorts was at times quite embarrassing. Barelegged, bareheaded, and "tanned to a chip," I was carrying my friend's bag along the fashionable pier to see him off on his homeward journey, when a lady stopped me and asked me if I were an Eskimo, offering me a job if I needed one. I have wondered sometimes if it were a seat in a sideshow which she had designed for me.

We spent that holiday cruising around the island. It included getting ashore off the north point of land and nearly losing the craft; and also in Ryde Harbour a fracas with the harbour authorities. We had run that night on top of the full spring tide. Not knowing the harbour, we had tied up to the first bollard, and gone incontinently to sleep. We were awakened by the sound of water thundering on top of us, and rushing up found to our dismay that we were lying in the mud, and a large sewer was discharging right on to our decks. Before we had time to get away or clean up, the harbour master, coming alongside, called on us to pay harbour duties. We stoutly protested that as a pleasure yacht we were not liable and intended to resist to the death any such insult being put upon us. He was really able to see at once that we were just young fellows out for a holiday, but he had the last word before a crowd of sight-seers who had gathered on the quay above us.

"Pleasure yacht, pleasure yacht, indeed!" he shouted as he rode away. "I can prove to any man with half an eye that you are nothing but one of them old coal or mud barges."

The following year the wind suited better the other way. We were practically all young doctors this time, the cook being a very athletic chum in whose rooms were collected as trophies, in almost every branch of athletics, over seventy of what we called silver "pots." As a cook he proved a failure except in zeal. It did n't really interest him, especially when the weather was lively. On one occasion I reported to the galley, though I was the skipper that year, in search of the rice-pudding for dinner — Dennis, our cook, being temporarily indisposed. Such a sight as met my view! Had I been superstitious I should have fled. A great black column the circumference of the boiler had risen not less than a foot above the top rim, and was wearing the iron cover jauntily on one side as a helmet. It proved to be rice. He had filled the saucepan with dry rice, crowded in a little water, forced the lid on very tight and left it to its own devices!

Nor, in his subsequent capacity as deckhand, did he redeem in our eyes the high qualities of seamanship which we had anticipated from him.

Our tour took us this time through the Menai Straits, *via* Carnarvon and the Welsh coast, down the Irish Channel to Milford Haven. In the region of very heavy tides and dangerous rocks near the south Welsh coast, we doubled our watch at night. One night the wind fell very light, and we had stood close inshore in order to pass inside the Bishop Rocks. The wind died out at that very moment, and the heavy current driving us down on the rocky islands threatened prematurely to terminate our cruise. The cook was asleep, as usual when called, and at last aroused to the nature of the alarm, was found leaning forward over the ship's bows with a lighted candle. When asked what he was doing, he explained, "Why, looking for those bishops, of course."

No holiday anywhere could be better sport than those cruises. There was responsibility, yet rest, mutual dependence, and a charming, unconventional way of getting acquainted with one's own country. We visited Carnarvon, Harlech, and other castles, lost our boat in a breeze of wind off Dynllyn, climbed Snowden from Pwllheli Harbour, and visited a dozen little out-of-the-world harbours that one would otherwise never see. Fishing and shooting for the pot, bathing and rowing, and every kind of healthy out-of-doors pleasure was indulged in along the road of travel. Moreover, it was all made to cost just as much or as little as you liked.

Another amusing memory which still remains with me was at one little seaport where a very small man not over five feet high had married a woman considerably over six. He was an idle, drunken little rascal, and I met her one day striding down the street with her intoxicated little spouse wrapped up in her apron and feebly protesting.

One result of these holidays was that I told my London boys about them, using one's experiences as illustrations; till suddenly it struck me that this was shabby Christianity. Why should n't these town cage-lings share our holidays? Thirteen accompanied me the following summer. We had three tents, an old deserted factory, and an uninhabited gorge by the sea, all to ourselves on the Anglesea coast, among people who spoke only Welsh. Thus we had all the joys of foreign travel at very little cost.

Among the many tricks the boys "got away with" was one at the big railway junction at Bangor, where we had an hour to wait. They apparently got into the baggage-room and stole a varied assortment of labels, which they industriously pasted over those on a large pile of luggage stacked on the platform. The subsequent tangle of destinations can better be imagined than described.

Camp rules were simple — no clothing allowed except short blue knickers and gray flannel shirts, no shoes, stockings, or caps except on Sundays. The uniform was provided and was as a rule the amateur production of numerous friends, for our finances were strictly limited. The knickers were not particularly successful, the legs frequently being carried so high up that there was no space into which the body could be inserted. Every one had to bathe in the sea before he got any breakfast. I can still see ravenous boys staving off the evil hour till as near midday as possible. No one was allowed in the boats who could n't swim, an art which they all quickly acquired. There was, of course, a regular fatigue party each day for the household duties. We had no beds — sleeping on long, burlap bags stuffed with hay. A very favourite pastime was afforded by our big lifeboat, an old one hired from the National Lifeboat Society. The tides flowed very strongly alongshore, east on the flood tide and west on the ebb. Food, fishing lines, and a skipper for the day being provided, the old boat would go off with the tide in the morning, the boys had a picnic somewhere during the slack-water interim, and came back with the return tide.

When our numbers grew, as they did to thirty the second year, and nearly a hundred in subsequent seasons, thirty or more boys would be packed off daily in that way — and yet we never lost one of them. If they had not had as many lives as cats it would have been quite another story. The boat had sufficient sails to give the appearance to their unfamiliar eyes of being a sailing vessel, but the real work was done with twelve huge oars, two boys to an oar being the rule. At nights they used to come drifting homeward on the returning tides singing their dirges, like some historic barge of old. There was one familiar hymn called "Bringing in the Sheaves," which like everything else these rascals adapted for the use of the moment; and many a time the returning barge would be announced to us cooking supper in the old factory or in the silent gorge, by the ringing echoes of many voices beating with their oars as they came on to the words:

> "Pulling at the sweeps,
> Pulling at the sweeps;
> Here we come rejoicing,
> Pulling at the sweeps."

As soon as the old boat's keel slid up upon the beach, there would be a rush of as appreciative a supper party as ever a cook had the pleasure of catering for.

An annual expedition was to the top of Mount Snowdon, the highest in England or Wales. It was attempted by land and water. Half of us tramped overland in forced marches to the beautiful Menai Straits, crossed the suspension bridge, and were given splendid hospitality and good beds on the straw of the large stables at the beautiful country seat of a friend at Treborth. Here the boat section who came around the island were to meet us, anchoring their craft on the south side of the Straits. Our second year the naval division did not turn up, and some had qualms of conscience that evil might have overtaken them. Nor did they arrive until we by land had conquered the summit, travelling by Bethesda and the famous slate quarries, and returning for the second evening at Treborth. We then found that they had been stranded on the sands in Red Wharf Bay, so far from shore that they could neither go forward nor back; had thus spent their first night in a somewhat chilly manner in old bathing machines by the land wash, and supped off the superfluous hard biscuit which they had been reserving for the return voyage. They were none the worse, however, our genial host making it up to them in an extra generous provision and a special evening entertainment. One of my smartest boys (a Jew by nationality, for we made no distinctions in election to our class), in recounting his adventures to me next day, said: "My! Doctor, I did have some fun kidding that waiter in the white choker. He took a liking to me so I let him pal up. I told him my name was Lord Shaftesbury when I was home, but I asked him not to let it out, and the old bloke promised he would n't." The "old bloke" happened to be our host, who was always in dress-clothes in the evening, the only time we were at his house.

These holidays were the best lessons of love I could show my boys. It drew us very closely together; and to make the boys feel it less a charitable affair, every one was encouraged to save up his railway fare and as much more as possible. By special arrangement with the railway and other friends, and by very simple living, the per caput charges were so much reduced that many of the boys not only paid their own expenses, but even helped their friends. The start was always attended by a crowd of relatives, all helping with the baggage. The father of one of my boys was a costermonger, and had a horse that he had obtained very cheap because it had a disease of the legs. He always kept it in the downstairs portion of his house, which it entered by the front door. It was a great pleasure to him to come and cart our things free to the station. The boys used to load his cart at our house, and I remember one time that they made him haul unconsciously all the way to the big London terminal at Euston half our furniture, including our coal boxes. His son, a most charming boy, made good in life in Australia and bought a nice house in one of the suburbs for his father and mother. I had the pleasure one night of meeting them all there. The father was terribly uneasy, for he said he just could not get accustomed to it. All his old "pals" were gone, and his neighbours' tastes and interests were a great gulf between them. I heard later that as soon as his son left England again the old man sold the house, and returned to the more congenial associations of a costermonger's life, where I believe he died in harness.

The last two years of my stay in London being occupied with resident work at hospital, I could not find time for such far-off holidays, and at the suggestion of my chief, Sir Frederick Treves, himself a Dorsetshire man, we camped by permission of our friends, the owners, in the grounds of Lulworth Castle, close by the sea. The class had now developed into a semi-military organization. We had acquired real rifles — old-timers from the Tower of London — and our athletic clubs were portions of the Anglesey Boys' Brigade, which antedated the Boys' Brigade of Glasgow, forerunner of the Church Lads' Brigade, and the Boy Scouts.

One of the great attractions of the new camping-ground was the exquisite country and the splendid coast, with chalk cliffs over which almost any one could fall with impunity. Lulworth Cove, one of the most picturesque in England, was the summer resort of my chief, and he being an expert mariner and swimmer used not only very often to join us at camp, but always gave the boys a fine regatta and picnic at his cottage. Our water

polo games were also a great feature here, the water
being warm and enabling us easily to play out the games.
There are also numerous beautiful castles and country
houses all the way between Swanage and Weymouth,
and we had such kindness extended to us wherever we
went that every day was a dream of joy to the lads.
Without any question they acquired new visions and
ideals through these experiences.

We always struck camp at the end of a fortnight, having sometimes arranged with other friends with classes
of their own to step into our shoes. The present head
master of Shrewsbury and many other distinguished
persons shared with us some of the educative joys of
those days. Among the many other more selfish portions
of the holidays none stand out more clearly in my memory than the August days when partridge and grouse
shooting used to open. Most of my shooting was done
over the delightful highlands around Bishop's Castle in
Shropshire, on the outskirts of the Welsh hills, in Clun
Forest, and on the heather-covered Longmynds. How I
loved those days, and the friends who made them possible — the sound of the beaters, the intelligent setters
and retrievers, the keepers in velveteens, the lunches
under the shade of the great hedges or in lovely cottages,
where the ladies used to meet us at midday, and every
one used to jolly you about not shooting straight, and
you had to take refuge in a thousand "ifs."

As one looks back on it all from Labrador, it breathes
the aroma of an old civilization and ancient customs.
Much of the shooting was over the old lands of the
Walcotts of Walcott Hall, a family estate that had been
bought up by Earl Clive on his return from India, and
was now in the hands of his descendant, an old bachelor who shot very little, riding from one good stand

to another on a steady old pony. There were many such estates, another close by being that of the Oakovers of Oakover, a family that has since sold their heritage.

A thousand time-honoured old customs, only made acceptable by their hoary age, added, and still continue to add in the pleasures of memory, to the joys of those days, with which golf and tennis and all the wonderful luxury of the modern summer hotel seem never able to compete. It is right, however, that such eras should pass.

The beautiful forest of Savernake, that in my school days I had loved so well, and which meant so much to us boys, spoke only too loudly of the evil heirloom of the laws of entail. Spendthrift and dissolute heirs had made it impossible for the land to be utilized for the benefit of the people, and yet kept it in the hands of utterly undeserving persons. Being of royal descent they still bore a royal name even in my day; but it was told of them that the last, who had been asked to withdraw from the school, on one occasion when, half drunk, he was defending himself from the gibes and jeers of grooms and 'ostlers whom he had made his companions, rose with ill-assumed dignity and with an oath declared that he was their king by divine right if only he had his dues. Looking back it seems to me that the germs of democratic tendencies were sown in me by just those very incidents.

CHAPTER IV

AT THE LONDON HOSPITAL

I HAVE never ceased to regret that there was not more corporate life in our medical school, but I believe that conditions have been greatly improved since my day. Here and there two or three classmates would "dig" together, but otherwise, except at lectures or in hospitals, we seldom met unless it was on the athletic teams. We had no playground of our own, and so, unable to get other hospitals to combine, when a now famous St. Thomas man and myself hired part of the justly celebrated London Rowing Club Headquarters at Putney for a united hospitals' headquarters, we used to take our blazers and more cherished possessions home with us at night for fear of distraint of rent.

They were great days. Rowing on the Thames about Putney is not like that at Oxford on a mill-pond, or as at Cambridge on what we nicknamed a drain that should be roofed over. Its turgid waters were often rough enough to sink a rowing shell, and its busy traffic was a thing with which to reckon. But it offered associations with all kinds of interesting places, historical and otherwise, from the Star and Garter at Richmond and the famous Park away to Boulter's Lock and Cleveden Woods, to the bathing pools about Taplow Court, the seat of the senior branch of our family, and to Marlow and Goring where our annual club outings were held. Twice I rowed in the inter-hospital race from Putney to Mortlake, once as bow and again as stroke. During those early days the "London" frequently had the best boat on the river.

Having now finished my second year at hospital and

taken my preliminary examinations, including the scientific preliminary, and my first bachelor of medicine for the University of London degree, I had advanced to the dignity of "walking the hospitals," carried a large shining stethoscope, and spent much time following the famous physicians and surgeons around the wards.

Our first appointment was clerking in the medical wards. We had each so many beds allotted to us, and it was our business to know everything about the patients who occupied them, to keep accurate "histories" of all developments, and to be ready to be quizzed and queried by our resident house physician, or our visiting consultant on the afternoon when he made his rounds, followed by larger or smaller crowds of students according to the value which was placed upon his teaching. I was lucky enough to work under the famous Sir Andrew Clark, Mr. Gladstone's great physician. He was a Scotchman greatly beloved, and always with a huge following to whom he imparted far more valuable truths than even the medical science of thirty years ago afforded. His constant message, repeated and repeated at the risk of wearying, was: "Gentlemen, you must observe for yourselves. It is your observation and not your memory which counts. It is the patient and not the disease whom you are treating."

Compared with the methods of diagnosis to-day those then were very limited, but Sir Andrew's message was the more important, showing the greatness of the man, who, though at the very top of the tree, never for a moment tried to convey to his followers that his knowledge was final, but that any moment he stood ready to abandon his position for a better one. On one occasion, to illustrate this point, while he was in one of the largest of our wards (one with four divisions and twenty beds each) he was examining a lung case, while a huge class of fifty young doctors stood around.

"What about the sputum, Mr. Jones?" he asked. "What have you observed coming from these lungs?"

"There is not much quantity, sir. It is greenish in colour."

"But what about the microscope, Mr. Jones? What does that show?"

"No examination has been made, sir."

"Gentlemen," he said, "I will now go to the other ward, and you shall choose a specimen of the sputum of some of these cases. When I return we will examine it and see what we can learn."

When he returned, four specimens awaited him, the history and diagnoses of the cases being known only to the class. The class never forgot how by dissolving and boiling, and with the microscope, he told us almost more from his examination of each case than we knew from all our other information. His was real teaching, and reminds one of the Glasgow professor who, in order to emphasize the same point of the value of observation, prepared a little cupful of kerosene, mustard, and castor oil, and calling the attention of his class to it, dipped a finger into the atrocious compound and then sucked his finger. He then passed the mixture around to the students who all did the same with most dire results. When the cup returned and he observed the faces of his students, he remarked: "Gentlemen, I am afraid you did not use your powers of obsairvation. The finger that I put into the cup was no the same one that I stuck in my mouth afterwards."

Sir Stephen Mackenzie, who operated on the Emperor Frederick, was another excellent teacher under whom we had the good fortune to study. Indeed, whatever could be said against the teaching of our college, in this much more important field of learning, the London Hospital was most signally fortunate, and, moreover, was famed not only in London, but all the world over. Our "walking class" used to number men from the United States to Australia, insomuch that the crowds became so large that the teachers could not get room to pass along. It was this fact which led to the practice, now almost universal, of carrying the patient in his bed with a nurse in attendance into the theatre for observation as more comfortable and profitable for all concerned.

On changing over to the surgical side in the hospital, we were employed in a very similar manner, only we were called "dressers," and under the house surgeon had all the care of a number of surgical patients. My good fortune now brought me under the chieftaincy of Sir Frederick Treves, the doyen of teachers. His great message was self-reliance. He taught dogmatically as one having authority, and always insisted that we should make up our minds, have a clear idea of what we were doing, and then do it. His ritual was always thought out, no detail being omitted, and each person had exactly his share of work and his share of responsibility. It used greatly to impress patients, and he never underestimated the psychical value of having their complete confidence. Thus, on one occasion asking a dresser for his diagnosis, the student replied:

"It might be a fracture, sir, or it might be only sprained."

"The patient is not interested to know that it might be measles, or it might be toothache. The patient wants to know what is the matter, and it is your business to tell it to him or he will go to a quack who will inform him at once."

All his teachings were, like Mark Twain's, enhanced
by such over-emphasis or exaggeration. He could make
an article in the "British Medical Journal" on Cholecys-
tenterostomy amusing to a general reader, and make an
ordinary remark as cutting as an amputation knife. He
never permitted laxity of any kind in personal appearance or dress, or any imposing on the patients. His habit
of saying openly exactly what he meant made many
people fear, as much as they respected, him. However,
he was always, in spite of it, the most popular of all the
chiefs because he was so worth while.

One incident recurs to my mind which I must recount
as an example when psychology failed. A Whitechapel
"lady," suffering with a very violent form of delirium
tremens, was lying screeching in a strait-jacket on the
cushioned floor of the padded room. With the usual huge
queue of students following, he had gone in to see her,
as I had been unable to get the results desired with a
reasonable quantity of sedatives and soporifics. It was a
very rare occasion, for cases which did not involve active
surgery he left strictly alone. After giving a talk on psychical influence he had the jacket removed as "a relic
of barbarism," and in a very impressive way looking into
her glaring eyes and shaking his forefinger at her, he
said: "Now, you are comfortable, my good woman, and
will sleep. You will make no more disturbance whatever."
There was an unusual silence. The woman remained
absolutely passive, and we all turned to follow the chief
out. Suddenly the "lady" called out, "Hi, hi," — and
some perverse spirit induced Sir Frederick to return.
Looking back with defiant eyes she screamed out, "You!
You with a faice! You do think yerself —— —— clever,
don't yer?" The strange situation was only relieved by
his bursting into a genuine fit of laughter.

Among other celebrated men who were admired and revered was Mr. Harry Fenwick on the surgical side, for whom I had the honour of illustrating in colours his prize Jacksonian essay. Any talent for sketching, especially in colours, is of great value to the student of medicine. Once you have sketched a case from nature, with the object of showing the peculiarity of the abnormality, it remains permanently in your mind. Besides this, it forces you to note small differences; in other words, it teaches you to "obsairve." Thus, in the skin department I was sent to reproduce a case of anthrax of the neck, a rare disease in England, though all men handling raw hides are liable to contract it. The area had to be immediately excised; yet one never could forget the picture on one's mind. On another occasion a case of genuine leprosy was brought in, with all the dreadful signs of the disease. The macula rash was entirely unique so far as I knew, but a sketch greatly helped to fix it on one's memory. The poor patient proved to be one of the men who was handling the meat in London's greatest market at Smithfield. A tremendous hue and cry spread over London when somehow the news got into the paper, and vegetarianism received a temporary boost which in my opinion it still badly needs for the benefit of the popular welfare.

Among the prophets of that day certainly should be numbered another of our teachers, Dr. Sutton, an author, and very much of a personality. For while being one of the consulting physicians of the largest of London hospitals, he was naturally scientific and strictly professional. He was very far, however, from being the conventionalist of those days, and the younger students used to look greatly askance at him. His message always was: "Drugs are very little use whatever. Nature is the source of healing. Give her a chance." Thus, a careful history would be read over to him; all the certain signs of typhoid would be noted — and his comment almost always was: "This case won't benefit by drugs. We will have the bed wheeled out into the sunshine." The next case would be acute lobar pneumonia and the same treatment would be adopted. "This patient needs air, gentlemen. We must wheel him out into the sunshine" — and so on. How near we are coming to his teaching in these days is already impressing itself upon our minds. Unfortunately the fact that the doctors realize that medicines are not so potent as our forbears thought has not left the public with the increased confidence in the profession which the infinitely more rational treatment of to-day justifies, and valuable time is wasted and fatal delays incurred, by a return of the more impressionable public to quacks with high-sounding titles, or to cults where faith is almost credulity.

Truly one has lived through wonderful days in the history of the healing art. The first operations which I saw performed at our hospitals were before Lord Lister's teaching was practised; though even in my boyhood I remember getting leave to run up from Marlborough to London to see my brother, on whom Sir Joseph Lister had operated for osteomyelitis of the leg. Our most famous surgeon in 1880 was Sir Walter Rivington; and to-day there rises in memory the picture of him removing a leg at the thigh, clad in a blood-stained, black velvet coat, and without any attempt at or idea of asepsis. The main thing was speed, although the patient was under ether, and in quickly turning round the tip of the sword-like amputation knife, he made a gash in the patient's other leg. The whole thing seemed horrible enough to us students, but the surgeon smiled, saying, "Fortunately it is of no importance, gentlemen. The man will not live."

The day came when every one worked under clouds of carbolic steam which fizzed and spouted from large brass boilers over everything; and then the time when every one was criticizing the new, young surgeon, Treves, who was daring to discard it, and getting as good results by scrupulous cleanliness. His aphorism was, "Gentlemen, the secret of surgery is the nailbrush." Now with blood examinations, germ cultures, sera tests, X-rays, and a hundred added improvements, one can say to a fisherman in far-off Labrador arriving on a mail steamer, and to whom every hour lost in the fishing season spells calamity, "Yes, brother, you can be operated on and the wound will be healed and you will be ready to go back by the next steamer, unless some utterly unforeseen circumstance arises."

The fallibility of diagnosis was at this very impressionable time fixed upon my mind — a fact that has since served me in good stead. For what can be more reactionary in human life than the man who thinks he knows it all, whether it be in science, philosophy, or religion?

During my Christmas vacation I was asked to go north and visit my father's brother, a well-known captain in Her Majesty's Navy, who was also an inventor in gun machinery and sighting apparatus, and who had been appointed the naval head of Lord Armstrong's great works at Yarrow-on-the-Tyne. All that I was told was that he had been taken with such severe pains in the back that he needed some one with him, and my new-fledged dignity of "walking the hospitals" was supposed to qualify me especially for the post. Already my uncle had seen many doctors in London and had been ordered to the Continent for rest. After some months, not a bit improved, he had again returned to London.

This time the doctor told his wife that it was a mental trouble, and that he should be sent to an asylum. This she most indignantly denied, and yet desired my company as the only medical Grenfell, who at such a crisis could stay in the house without being looked upon as a warder or keeper. Meantime they had consulted Sir C. P., who had told my uncle that he had an aneurism of his aorta, and that he must be prepared to have it break and kill him any minute. His preparations were accordingly all made, and personally I fully anticipated that he would fall dead before I left. He put up a wonderful fight against excruciating pain, of which I was frequently a witness. But the days went by and nothing happened, so I returned to town and another young doctor took my place. He also got tired of waiting and suggested it might be some spinal trouble. He induced them once more to visit London and see Sir Victor Horsley, whose work on the brains of animals and men had marked an epoch in our knowledge of the central nervous system. Some new symptoms had now supervened, and the famous neurologist at once diagnosed a tumour in the spinal canal. Such a case had never previously been operated on successfully, but there was no alternative. The operation was brilliantly performed and a wonderful success obtained. The case was quoted in the next edition of our surgical textbooks.

A little later my father's health began to fail in London, the worries and troubles of a clergyman's work among the poor creatures who were constantly passing under his care utterly overwhelming him. We had agreed that a long change of thought was necessary and he and I started for a fishing and sight-seeing tour in Norway. Our steamer was to sail from the Tyne, and we went up to Newcastle to catch it. There some evil fiend persuaded my father to go and consult a doctor about his illness, for Newcastle has produced some well-known names in medicine. Thus, while I waited at the hotel to start, my father became persuaded that he had some occult disease of the liver, and must remain in Newcastle for treatment. I, however, happened to be treasurer of the voyage, and for the first time asserting my professional powers, insisted that I was family physician for the time, and turned up in the evening with all our round-trip tickets and reservations taken and paid for. In the morning I had the trunks packed and conveyed aboard, and we sailed together for one of the most enjoyable holidays I ever spent. We travelled much afoot and in the little native carriages called "stolkjærre," just jogging along, staying anywhere, fishing in streams, and living an open-air life which the increasing flood of tourists in after years have made much less possible. We both came back fitter in body and soul for our winter's work.

My father's death a year later made a great difference to me, my mother removing to live with my grandmother at Hampstead, it being too lonely and not safe for her to live alone in East London. Twice our house had been broken into by burglars, though both times fruitlessly. The second occasion was in open daylight during the hour of evening service on a Sunday. Only a couple of maids would have been in the house had I not been suffering from two black eyes contracted during the Saturday's football game. Though I had accompanied the others out, decidedly my appearance might have led to misinterpretations in church, and I had returned unnoticed. The men escaped by some method which they had discovered of scaling a high fence, but I was close behind following them through the window by which they had entered. Shortly afterward I happened to be giving evidence at the Old Bailey on one of the many cases of assault and even murder where the victims were brought into hospital as patients. London was ringing with the tale of a barefaced murder at Murray Hill in North London, where an exceedingly clever piece of detective work, an old lantern discovered in a pawnbroker's shop in Whitechapel — miles away from the scene of the crime — was the means of bringing to trial four of the most rascally looking villains I ever saw. The trial preceded ours and we had to witness it. One of the gang had turned "Queen's evidence" to save his own neck. So great was the hatred of the others for him and the desire for revenge that even in the court they were handcuffed and in separate stands. Fresh from my own little fracas I learned what a fool I had been, for in this case also the deed was done in open daylight, and the lawn had tight wires stretched across it. The young son, giving chase as I did, had been tripped up and shot through his abdomen for his pains. He had, however, crawled back, made his will, and was subsequently only saved by a big operation. He looked in terrible shape when giving evidence at the trial.

The giving of expert evidence on such occasions was the only opportunity which the young sawbones had of earning money. True we only got a guinea a day and expenses, but there were no other movie shows in those days, and we learned a lot about medical jurisprudence, a subject which always greatly interested me. It was no uncommon sight either at the "London" or the "Poplar," at both of which I did interne work, to see a policeman always sitting behind the screen at the foot of the patient's bed. One man, quite a nice fellow when not occupied in crime, had when furiously drunk killed his wife and cut his own throat. By the curious custom of society all the skill and money that the hospital could offer to save a most valuable life was as usual devoted to restoring this man to health. He was weaned slowly back from the grave by special nurses and treatment, till it began to dawn upon him that he might have to stand his trial. He would ask me if I thought he would have to undergo a long term, for he had not been conscious of what he was doing. As he grew better, and the policeman arrived to watch him, he decided that it would probably be quite a long time. He had a little place of his own somewhere, and he used to have chickens and other presents sent up to fellow patients, and would have done so to the nurses, only they could not receive them. I was not personally present at his trial, but I felt really sorry to hear that they hanged him.

Many of these poor fellows were only prevented from ending their own lives by our using extreme care. The case of one wretched man, driven to desperation, I still remember. "Patient male; age forty-five; domestic trouble — fired revolver into his mouth. Finding no phenomena of interest develop, fired a second chamber into his right ear. Still no symptoms worthy of notice. Patient threw away pistol and walked to hospital." Both bullets had lodged in the thick parts of his skull, and doing no damage were left there. A subsequent note read: "Patient to-day tried to cut his throat with a dinner-knife which he had hidden in his bed. Patient met with no success." Another of my cases which interested me considerably was that of a professional burglar who had been operated upon in almost every part of the kingdom, and was inclined to be communicative, as the job which had brought him to hospital had cost him a broken spine. Very little hope was held out to him that he would ever walk again. He was clear of murder, for he said it was never his practice to carry firearms, being a nervous man and apt to use them if he had them and got alarmed when busy burglaring. He relied chiefly on his extraordinary agility and steady head to escape. His only yarn, however, was his last. He and a friend had been detailed by the gang to the job of plundering one of a row of houses. The plans of the house and of the enterprise were all in order, but some unexpected alarm was given and he fled upstairs, climbed through a sky-light onto the roof, and ran along the gables of the tiles, not far ahead of the police, who were armed and firing at him. He could easily have gotten away, as he could run along the coping of the brick parapet without turn-ing a hair, but he was brought up by a narrow side street on which he had not counted, not having anticipated, like cats, a battle on the tiles. It was only some twelve or fifteen feet across the gap, and the landing on the other side was a flat roof. Taking it all at a rush he cleared the street successfully, but the flat roof, black with ages of soot, proved to be a glass skylight, and he entered a house in a way new even to him. His falling on a stone floor many feet below accounted for his "unfortunate accident"! After many months in bed, the man took an unexpected turn, his back mended, and with only a slight leg paralysis he was able to return to the outside world. His long suffering and incarceration in hospital were accepted by the law as his punishment, and he assured me by all that he held sacred that he intended to retire into private life. Oddly enough, however, while on another case, I saw him again in the prisoner's dock and at once went over and spoke to him.

"Drink this time, Doctor," he said. "I was down on my luck and the barkeeper went out and left his till open. I climbed over and got the cash, but there was so little space between the bar and the wall that with my stiff back I could n't for the life of me get back. I was jammed like a stopper in a bottle."

Among many interesting experiences, one especially I shall never forget. Like the others, it occurred during my service for Sir Frederick Treves as house-surgeon, and I believe he told the story. A very badly burned woman had been brought into hospital. Her dress had somehow got soaked in paraffin and had then taken fire. Her terribly extensive burns left no hope whatever of her recovery, and only the conventions of society kept us from giving the poor creature the relief of euthanasia, or some cup of laudanum negus. But the law was interested. A magistrate was brought to the bedside and the husband sent for. The nature of the evidence, the meaning of an oath, the importance of the poor creature acknowledging that her words were spoken "in hopeless fear of immediate death," were all duly impressed upon what remained of her mind. The police then brought in the savage, degraded-looking husband, and made him stand between two policemen at the foot of the bed, facing his mangled wife. The magistrate, after preliminary questions, asked her to make her dying statement as to how she came by her death. There was a terrible moment of silence. It seemed as if her spirit were no longer able to respond to the stimuli of life on earth. Then a sudden rebound appeared to take place, her eyes lit up with a flash of light, and even endeavouring to raise her piteous body, she said, "It was an accident, Judge. I upset the lamp myself, so help me God"; and just for one moment her eyes met those of her miserable husband. It was the last time she spoke.

Tragedy and comedy ran hand in hand even in this work. St. Patrick's Day always made the hospital busy, just as Christmas was the season for burned children. Beer in an East London "pub" was generally served in pewter pots, as they were not easily broken. A common head injury was a circular scalp cut made by the heavy bottom rim, a wound which bled horribly. A woman was brought in on one St. Patrick's Day, her scalp turned forward over her face and her long hair a mass of clotted blood from such a stroke, made while she was on the ground. When the necessary readjustments had been made and she was leaving hospital cured, we asked her what had been the cause of the trouble. "'T was just an accidint, yer know. Sure, me an' another loidy was just havin' a few words."

On another occasion late at night, we were called out of bed by a cantankerous, half-drunken fellow whom the night porter could not pacify. "I'm a regular subscriber to this hospital, and I have never had my dues yet," he kept protesting. A new drug to produce immediate vomiting had just been put on the market, and as it was exactly the treatment he required, we gave him an injection. To our dismay, though the medicine is in common use to-day, either the poison which he had been drinking or the drug itself caused a collapse followed by head symptoms. He was admitted, his head shaved and icebags applied, with the result that next day he was quite well again. But when he left he had, instead of a superabundance of curly, auburn hair, a polished white knob oiled and shining like a State House at night. We debated whether his subscription would be as regular in future, though he professed to be profoundly grateful.

I have digressed, but the intimacy which grew up between some of my patients and myself seemed worth while recounting, for they showed me what I never in any other way could have understood about the seamy

side of life in great cities, of its terrible tragedies and
pathos, of how much good there is in the worst, and how
much need of courage, and what vast opportunities lie
before those who accept the service of man as their service to God. It proved to me how infinitely more needed
are unselfish deeds than orthodox words, and how much
the churches must learn from the Labour Party, the
Socialist Party, the Trades-Union, before tens of thousands of our fellow beings, with all their hopes and fears,
loves and aspirations, have a fair chance to make good.
I learned also to hate the liquor traffic with a loathing of
my soul. I met peers of the realm honoured with titles
because they had grown rich on the degradation of my
friends. I saw lives damned, cruelties of every kind per-
petrated, jails and hospitals filled, misery, want, starvation, murder, all caused by men who fattened off the
profits and posed as gentlemen and great people. I have
seen men's mouths closed whose business in life it was
to speak out against this accursed trade. I have seen
men driven from the profession of priests of God, making the Church a stench in the nostrils of men who knew
values just as well as those trained in the universities do,
all through alcohol, alcohol, alcohol. This awful war has
been dragging its weary course for over four years now,
and yet England has not tackled this curse which is
throttling her. We sing "God save the King," and pre-
tend to believe in the prayer, and yet we will not face
this glaring demon in our midst. Words may clothe ideas,
but it takes deeds to realize them.

My parents having gone, it became necessary for me
to find lodgings — which I did, "unfurnished," in the
house of a Portuguese widow. Her husband, who had a
good family name, had gone down in the world, and had

disappeared with another "lady." The eldest son, a mathematical genius, had been able to pay his way through Cambridge University by the scholarships and prizes which he had won. One beautiful little dark-eyed daughter of seven was playing in a West End Theatre as the dormouse in "Alice in Wonderland." She was second fiddle to Alice herself, also, and could sing all her songs. Her pay was some five pounds a week, poor enough for the attraction she proved, but more than all the rest of the family put together earned. At that time I never went to theatres. Acquaintances had persuaded me that so many of the girls were ruined on the stage that for a man taking any interest in Christian work whatever, it was wrong to attend. Moreover, among my acquaintances there were not a few theatre fans, and I had nothing in common with them. The "dormouse," however, used to come up and say her parts for my benefit, and that of occasional friends, and was so modest and winsome, and her earnings so invaluable to the family, that I entirely altered my opinion. Then and there I came to the conclusion that the drama was an essential part of art, and that those who were trying to elevate and cleanse it, like Sir Henry Irving, whose son I had met at Marlborough, must have the support of a public who demanded clean plays and good conditions both in front and behind the screen. When I came to London my father had asked me not to go to anything but Shakespearian or equally well-recognized plays until I was twenty-one. Only once did I enter a music hall and I had plenty to satisfy me in a very few minutes. Vaudevilles are better than in those days. The censor does good work, but it is still the demand which creates the supply, and whatever improvement has occurred has been largely due to the taste of the patrons. Medical students need all the open air they can get in order to keep body and soul fit, and our contempt for the theatre fan was justifiable.

My new lodgings being close to Victoria Park afforded the opportunity for training if one were unconventional. To practise throwing the sixteen-pound hammer requires rough ground and plenty of space, and as I was scheduled for that at the inter-hospital sports, it was necessary to work when not too many disinterested parties were around. Even an East-Ender's skull is not hammer proof, as I had seen when a poor woman was brought into hospital with five circular holes in her head, the result of blows inflicted by her husband with a hammer. The only excuse which the ruffian offered for the murder was that she had forgotten to wake him, he had been late, and lost his job.

A number of the boys in my class were learning to swim. There was only one bathing lake and once the waters were troubled we drew the line at going in to give lessons. So we used to meet at the gate at the hour of opening in the morning, and thus be going back before most folks were moving. Nor did we always wait for the park keeper, but often scaled the gates and so obtained an even more exclusive dip. Many an evening we would also "flannel," and train round and round the park, or Hackney Common, to improve one's wind before some big event. For diet at that time I used oatmeal, milk, and eggs, and very little or no meat. It was cheaper and seemed to give me more endurance; and the real value of money was dawning on me.

Victoria Park is one of those open forums where every man with a sore spot goes out to air his grievance. On Sundays there were little groups around the trees where orators debated on everything from a patent medicine to the nature of God. Charles Bradlaugh and Mrs. Annie

Besant were associated together in iconoclastic efforts against orthodox religion, and there was so much truth in some of their contentions that they were making no little disturbance. Hanging on their skirts were a whole crowd of ignorant, dogmatic atheists, who published a paper called "The Freethinker," which, while it was a villainous and contemptible rag, appealed to the passions and prejudices of the partially educated. To answer the specious arguments of their propaganda an association known as the Christian Evidence Society used to send out lecturers. One of them became quite famous for his clever arguments and answers, his ready wit, and really extensive reading. He was an Antiguan, a black man named Edwards, and had been a sailor before the mast. I met him at the parish house of an Episcopal clergyman of a near-by church, who, under the caption of Christian socialism, ran all kinds of social agencies that really found their way to the hearts of the people. His messages were so much more in deeds than in words that he greatly appealed to me, and I transferred my allegiance to his church, which was always well filled. I particularly remember among his efforts the weekly parish dance. My religious acquaintances were apt to class all such simple amusements in a sort of general category as "works of the Devil," and turn deaf ears to every invitation to point out any evil results, being satisfied with their own statement that it was the "thin edge of the wedge." This good man, however, was very obviously driving a wedge into the hearts of many of his poor neighbours who in those days found no opportunity for relief in innocent pleasures from the sordid round of life in the drab purlieus of Bethnal Green. This clergyman was a forerunner of his neighbour, the famous Samuel Barnett of Mile End, who thought out, started, and for many years pre-

sided over Toynbee House, the first big university settlement in East London. His workers preached their gospel
through phrases and creeds which they accepted with
mental reservations, but just exactly in such ways as
they believed in absolutely. At first it used to send a
shiver down my spine to find a church worker who did n't
believe in the Creed, and stumbled over all our funda-
mentals. At first it amazed me that such men would pay
their own expenses to live in a place like Whitechapel,
only to work on drain committees, as delinquent land-
lord mentors, or just to give special educational chances
to promising minds, or physical training to unfit bodies.
Yet one saw in their efforts undeniable messages of real
love. Personally I could only occasionally run up there
to meet friends in residence or attend an art exhibition,
but they taught me many lessons.

Exactly opposite the hospital was Oxford House, only
two minutes distant, which combined definite doctrinal
religion with social work. Being an Oxford effort it had
great attractions for me. Moreover, right alongside it in
the middle of a disused sugar refinery I had hired the
yard, converted it into a couple of lawn-tennis courts,
and ran a small club. There I first met the famous Dr.
Hensley Henson, now Bishop of Hereford, and also the
present Bishop of London, Dr. Winnington-Ingram —
a good all-round athlete. He used to visit in our wards,
and as we had a couple of fives courts, a game which
takes little time and gives much exercise, we used to
have an afternoon off together, once a week, when he
came over to hospital. Neither of these splendid men
were dignitaries in those days, or I am afraid they would
have found us medicals much more stand-offish. I may
as well admit that we had not then learned to have any
respect for bishops or church magnates generally. We

liked both of these men because they were unconventional and good sports, and especially in that they were not afraid to tackle the atheist's propaganda in the open. I have seen Dr. Henson in Whitechapel debating alone against a hall full of opponents and with a fairness and infinite restraint, convincing those open to reason that they were mistaken. Moreover, I have seen Dr. Ingram doing just the same thing standing on a stone in the open park. It may all sound very silly when one knows that by human minds, or to the human mind, the Infinite can never be demonstrated as a mathematical proposition. But the point was that these clergy were proving that they were real men — men who had courage as well as faith, who believed in themselves and their message, who deserved the living which they were supposed to make out of orthodoxy. This the audience knew was more than could be said of many of the opponents. Christ himself showed his superb manhood in just such speaking out.

Indelibly impressed on my mind still is an occasion when one of the most blatant and vicious of these opponents of religion fell ill. A Salvation Army lass found him deserted and in poverty, nursed and looked after him and eventually made a new man of him.

Far and away the most popular of the Park speakers was the Antiguan. His arguments were so clever it was obvious that he was well and widely read. His absolute understanding of the crowd and his witty repartee used frequently to cause his opponents to lose their tempers, and that was always their undoing. The crowd as a rule was very fair and could easily distinguish arguments from abuse. Thus, on one Sunday the debate was as to whether nature was God. The atheist representative was a very loud-voiced demagogue, who when angry betrayed his Hibernian origin very markedly. Having been completely worsted and the laugh turned against him by a clever correction of some one's, he used the few minutes given him to reply in violent abuse, ending up that "ladies and gentlemen did not come out on holidays to spend their time being taught English by a damned nigger."

"Sir," Edwards answered from the crowd, "I am a British subject, born on the island of Antigua, and as much an Englishman as any Irishman in the country."

Edwards possessed an inexhaustible stock of good-humour and his laugh could be heard halfway across the Park. As soon as his turn came to mount the stone, he got the crowd so good-natured that they became angry at the interruptions of the enemy, and when some one suggested that if nature were that man's God, the near-by duckpond was the natural place for him, there was a rush for him, and for several subsequent Sundays he was not in evidence. Edwards was a poor man, his small salary and incessant generosity left him nothing for holidays, and he was killing himself with overwork. So we asked him to join us in the new house which we were fitting up in Palestine Place. He most gladly did so and added enormously to our fun. Unfortunately tuberculosis long ago got its grip upon him, and removed a valuable life from East London.

It was a queer little beehive in which we lived in those days, and a more cosmopolitan crowd could hardly have been found: one young doctor who has since made his name and fortune in Australia; another in whose rooms were nearly a hundred cups for prowess in nearly every form of athletics, and who also has "made good" in professional life, besides several others who for shorter or longer periods were allotted rooms in our house.

Among the more unusual was the "C. M.," a Brahmin from India, a priest in his youth, who had been brought back to England by some society to be educated in medical missionary work, but whom for some reason they had dropped. For a short time a clever young Russian of Hebrew extraction who was studying for the Church helped to render our common-room social engagements almost international affairs.

As I write this I am at Charleston, South Carolina, and I see how hard it will be for an American to understand the possibility of such a motley assembly being reasonable or even proper. It seems to me down here that there must have been odd feelings sometimes in those days. I can only say, however, that I never personally even thought of it. East London is so democratic that one's standards are simply those of the value of the man's soul as we saw it. If he had been yellow with pink stripes it honestly would not have mattered one iota to most of us.

It so happened that there was at that time in hospital under my care a patient known as "the elephant man." He had been starring under that title in a cheap vaudeville, had been seen by some of the students, and invited over to be shown to and studied by our best physicians. The poor fellow was really exceedingly sensitive about his most extraordinary appearance. The disease was called "leontiasis," and consisted of an enormous over-development of bone and skin on one side. His head and face were so deformed as really to resemble a big animal's head with a trunk. My arms would not reach around his hat. A special room in a yard was allotted to him, and several famous people came to see him — among them Queen Alexandra, then the Princess of Wales, who afterward sent him an autographed photograph of herself.

He kept it in his room, which was known as the "elephant house," and it always suggested beauty and the beast. Only at night could the man venture out of doors, and it was no unusual thing in the dusk of nightfall to meet him walking up and down in the little courtyard. He used to talk freely of how he would look in a huge bottle of alcohol — an end to which in his imagination he was fated to come. He was of a very cheerful disposition and pathetically proud of his left side which was normal. Very suddenly one day he died — the reason assigned being that his head fell forward and choked him, being too heavy for him to lift up.

In 1886 I passed my examinations and duly became a member of the College of Physicians and of the Royal College of Surgeons of England; and sought some field for change and rest, where also I could use my newly acquired license to my own, if to no one else's, benefit. Among the patients who came to the London Hospital, there were now and again fishermen from the large fishing fleets of the North Sea. They lived out, as it were, on floating villages, sending their fish to market every day by fast cutters. Every two or three months, as their turn came round, a vessel would leave for the home port on the east coast, being permitted, or supposed to be permitted, a day at home for each full week at sea. As the fleets kept the sea summer and winter and the boats were small, not averaging over sixty tons, it was a hazardous calling. The North Sea is nowhere deeper than thirty fathoms, much of it being under twenty, and in some places only five. Indeed, it is a recently sunken and still sinking portion of Europe, so much so that the coasts on both sides are constantly receding, and when Heligoland was handed over by the English to the Kaiser, it was said that he would have to keep jacking it up or soon there would be none left. Shallow waters exposed to the fierce gales which sweep the German Ocean make deep and dangerous seas, which readily break and wash the decks of craft with low freeboard, such as the North Sea vessels are obliged to have in order to get boats in and out to ferry their fish to the cutter.

There being no skilled aid at hand, the quickest way to get help used to be to send an injured man to market with the fish. Often it was a long journey of many days, simple fractures became compound, and limbs and faculties were often thus lost. It so happened that Sir Frederick Treves had himself a love for navigating in small sailing craft. He had made it a practice to cross the English Channel to Calais in a sailing lugger every Boxing Day — that is, the day after Christmas. He was especially interested in those "that go down to the sea in ships" and had recently made a trip among the fishing fleets. He told me that a small body of men, interested in the religious and social welfare of the deep-sea fishermen, had chartered a small fishing smack, sent her out among the fishermen to hold religious services of a simple, unconventional type, in order to afford the men an alternative to the grog vessels when fishing was slack, and to carry first aid, the skipper of the vessel being taught ambulance work. They wanted, however, very much to get a young doctor to go out, who cared also for the spiritual side of the work, to see if they could use the additional attraction of proper medical aid to gain the men's sympathies. His advice to me was to go and have a look at it. "If you go in January you will see some fine seascapes, anyhow. Don't go in summer when all of the old ladies go for a rest."

I therefore applied to go out the following January, and that fall, while working near the Great London docks, I used often to look at the tall East Indiamen, thinking that I soon should be aboard just such a vessel in the North Sea. It was dark and raining when my train ran into Yarmouth, and a dripping, stout fisherman in a blue uniform met me at that then unattractive and ill-lighted terminus. He had brought a forlorn "growler" or four-wheeled cab. Climbing in we drove a mile or more along a deserted road, and drew up at last apparently at the back of beyond.

"Where is the ship?" I asked.

"Why, those are her topmasts," replied my guide, pointing to two posts projecting from the sand. "The tide is low and she is hidden by the quay."

"Heavens!" I thought; "she's no tea clipper, any-how."

I climbed up the bank and peered down in the darkness at the hull of a small craft, a little larger than our old Roysterer. She was just discernible by the dim rays of the anchor light. I was hesitating as to whether I should n't drive back to Yarmouth and return to London when a cheery voice on deck called out a hearty welcome. What big things hang on a smile and a cheery word no man can ever say. But it broke the spell this time and I had my cabby unload my bags on the bank and bade him good-night. As his wheels rumbled away into the rain and dark, I felt that my cables were cut beyond recall. Too late to save me, the cheery voice shouted, "Mind the rigging, it's just tarred and greased." I was already sliding down and sticking to it as I went. Small as the vessel was she was absolutely spotless. Her steward, who cooked for all hands, was smart and in a snow-white suit. The contrast between-decks and that above was very comforting, though my quarters were small. The crew were all stocky, good-humoured, and independent.

Democratic as East London had made me, they impressed me very favourably, and I began to look forward to the venture with real pleasure.

Drink was the worst enemy of these men. The quaysides of the fisherman's quarters teemed with low saloons. Wages were even paid off in them or their annexes, and grog vessels, luring the men aboard with cheap tobacco and low literature, plied their nefarious calling with the fleets, and were the death, body and soul, of many of these fine specimens of manhood.

There was never any question as to the real object of the Mission to Deep-Sea Fishermen. The words "Heal the sick" carved in large letters adorned the starboard bow. "Preach the Word" was on the port, and around the brass rim of the wheel ran the legend, "Jesus said, Follow me and I will make you fishers of men." Thirty years ago we were more conventional than to-day, and I was much surprised to learn from our skipper that we were bound to Ostend to ship four tons of tobacco, sent over from England for us in bond, as he might not take it out consigned to the high seas. In Belgium, however, no duty was paid. The only trouble was that our vessel, to help pay its expenses, carried fishing gear, and as a fishing vessel could not get a clearance in Belgium. Our nets and beams, therefore, had to go out to the fishing grounds in a friendly trawler while we passed as a mercantile marine during the time we took on our cargo.

So bitter was the cold that in the harbour we got frozen in and were able to skate up the canals. We had eventually to get a steamer to go around us and smash our ice bonds when we were again ready for sea. During the next two months we saw no land except Heligoland and Terschelling — or Skilling, as the fishermen called it —

far away in the offing. Nor was our deck once clear of ice and snow during all the time.

Our duty was to visit as many fleets as we could, and arrange with some reliable vessel to take a stock of tobacco for the use of their special fleet. The ship was to carry about six feet of blue bunting on her foretopmast stay, a couple of fathoms above her bowsprit end, so that all the fleet might know her. She was to sell the tobacco at a fixed price that just covered the cost, and undersold the "coper" by fifty per cent. She was to hoist her flag for business every morning, while the small boats were out boarding fish on the carrier, and was to lie as far to leeward of the coper as possible so that the men could not go to both. Nineteen such floating depots were eventually arranged for, with the precaution that if any one of them had to return to port, he should bring no tobacco home, but hand over his stock and accounts to a reliable friend.

These deep-sea fisheries were a revelation to me, and every hour of the long trip I enjoyed. It was amazing to me to find over twenty thousand men and boys afloat — the merriest, cheerfullest lot which I had ever met. They were hail-fellow-well-met with every one, and never thought of deprivation or danger. Clothing, food, customs, were all subordinated to utility. They were the nearest possible thing to a community of big boys, only needing a leader. In efficiency and for their daring resourcefulness in physical difficulties and dangers, they were absolutely in a class by themselves, embodying all the traits of character which make men love to read the stories of the buccaneers and other seamen of the sixteenth-century period.

Each fleet had its admiral and vice-admiral, appointed partly by the owner, and partly by the skippers of the vessels. The devil-may-care spirit was always a great factor with the men. The admiral directed operations by flags in the daytime and by rockets at night, thus indicating what the fleet was to do and where they were to fish. Generally he had the fastest boat, and the cutters, hunting for the fleet always lay just astern of the admiral, the morning after their arrival. Hundreds of men would come for letters, packages, to load fish, to get the news of what their last assignment fetched in market. Moreover, a kind of Parliament was held aboard to consider policies and hear complaints.

At first it was a great surprise to me how these men knew where they were, for we never saw anything but sky and sea, and not even the admirals carried a chronometer or could work out a longitude; and only a small percentage of the skippers could read or write. They all, however, carried a sextant and could by rule of thumb find a latitude roughly. But that was only done at a pinch. The armed lead was the fisherman's friend. It was a heavy lead with a cup on the bottom filled fresh each time with sticky grease. When used, the depth was always called out by the watch, and the kind of sand, mud, or rock which stuck to the grease shown to the skipper. "Fifteen fathoms and coffee grounds — must be on the tail end of the Dogger. Put her a bit more to the westward, boy," he would remark, and think no more about it, though he might have been three or four days looking for his fleet, and not spoken to a soul since he left land. I remember one skipper used to have the lead brought down below, and he could tell by the grit between his teeth after a couple of soundings which way to steer. It sounds strange even now, but it was so universal, being just second-nature to the men, who from boyhood had lived on the sea, that we soon ceased to marvel at it.

Skippers were only just being obliged to have certificates. These they obtained by *viva voce* examinations. You would sometimes hear an aspiring student, a great black-bearded pirate over forty-seven inches around the chest, and possibly the father of eight or ten children, as he stamped about in his watch keeping warm, repeating the courses — "East end of the Dogger to Horn S.E. by E. $\frac{1}{2}$ and W. point of the island [Heligoland] to Barkum S. $\frac{1}{2}$ W. Ower Light to Hazebrough N.N.W." — and so on. Their memories were not burdened by a vast range of facts, but in these things they were the nearest imaginable to Blind Tom, the famous slave musician.

Our long round only occupied us about a month, and after that we settled down with the fleet known as the Great Northerners. Others were the Short Blues, the Rashers (because they were streaked like a piece of bacon), the Columbia, the Red Cross, and so on. Sometimes during the night while we were fishing into the west, a hundred sail or more of vessels, we would pass through another big fleet coming the other way, and some of our long trawls and warps would tangle with theirs. Beyond the beautiful spectacle of the myriads of lights bobbing up and down often enough on mighty rough seas — for it needed good breezes to haul our trawls — would be the rockets and flares of the entangled boats, and often enough also rockets and flares from friends, and from cutters. One soon became so friendly with the men that one would not return at night to the ship, but visit around and rejoin the Mission ship boarding fish next day, to see patients coming for aid. Though it was strictly against sea rules for skippers to be off their vessels all night, that was a rule, like all others on the North Sea, as often marked in the breach as in the observance. A goodly company would get to-

gether yarning and often singing and playing games until
it was time to haul the trawl and light enough to find
their own vessel and signal for the boat.

The relation of my new friends to religion was a very
characteristic one. Whatever they did, they did hard.
Thus one of the admirals, being a thirsty soul, and the
grog vessels having been adrift for a longer while than
he fancied, conceived the fine idea of holding up the
Heligoland saloons. So one bright morning he "hove his
fleet to" under the lee of the island and a number of
boats went ashore, presumably to sell fish. Altogether
they landed some five hundred men, who held up the few
saloons for two or three days. As a result subsequently
only one crew selling fish to the island was allowed
ashore at one time. The very gamble of their occupation
made them do things hard. Thus it was a dangerous task
to throw out a small boat in half a gale of wind, fill her
up with heavy boxes of fish, and send her to put these
over the rail of a steamer wallowing in the trough of a
mountainous sea.

But it was on these very days when less fish was sent
to market that the best prices were realized, and so there
were always a number of dare-devils, who did not care if
lives were lost so long as good prices were obtained and
their record stood high on the weekly list of sales which
was forwarded to both owners and men. I have known
as many as fourteen men upset in one morning out of
these boats; and the annual loss of some three hundred
and fifty men was mostly from this cause. Conditions
were subsequently improved by the Board of Trade, who
made it manslaughter against the skipper if any man
was drowned boarding fish, unless the admiral had shown
his flags to give the fleet permission to do so. In those
days, however, I often saw twenty to thirty boats all

tied up alongside the cutter at one time, the heavy seas every now and again rolling the cutter's sail right under water, and when she righted again it might come up under the keels of some of the boats and tip them upside down. Thus any one in them was caught like a mouse under a trap or knocked to pieces trying to swim among the rushing, tossing boats.

As a rule we hauled at midnight, and it was always a fresh source of wonder, for the trawl was catholic in its embrace and brought up anything that came in its way. To emphasize how comparatively recently the Channel had been dry land, many teeth and tusks of mammoths who used to roam its now buried forests were given up to the trawls by the ever-shifting sands. Old wreckage of every description, ancient crockery, and even a water-logged, old square-rigger that must have sunk years before were brought one day as far as the surface by the stout wire warp. After the loss of a large steamer called the Elbe many of the passengers who had been drowned were hauled up in this way; and on one occasion great excitement was caused in Hull by a fisher lad from that port being picked up with his hands tied behind his back and a heavy weight on his feet. The defence was that the boy had died, and was thus buried to save breaking the voyage — supported by the fact that another vessel had also picked up the boy and thrown him overboard again for the same reason. But those who were a bit superstitious thought otherwise, and more especially as cruelty to these boys was not unknown.

These lads were apprenticed to the fishery masters largely from industrial or reformatory schools, had no relations to look after them, and often no doubt gave the limit of trouble and irritation. On the whole, however, the system worked well, and a most excellent class of capable seamen was developed. At times, however, they were badly exploited. During their apprenticeship years they were not entitled to pay, only to pocket money, and yet sometimes the whole crew including the skipper were apprentices and under twenty-one years of age. Even after that they were fitted for no other calling but to follow the sea, and had to accept the master's terms. There were no fishermen's unions, and the men being very largely illiterate were often left victims of a peonage system in spite of the Truck Acts. The master of a vessel has to keep discipline, especially in a fleet, and the best of boys have faults and need punishing while on land. These skippers themselves were brought up in a rough school, and those who fell vicitms to drink and made the acquaintance of the remedial measures of our penal system of that day were only further brutalized by it. Religion scarcely touched the majority; for their brief periods of leave ashore were not unnaturally spent in having a good time. To those poisoned by the villainous beverages sold on the sordid grog vessels no excess was too great. Owners were in sympathy with the Mission in trying to oust the coper, because their property, in the form of fish, nets, stores, and even sails, were sometimes bartered on the high seas for liquor. On one occasion during a drunken quarrel in the coper's cabin one skipper threw the kerosene lamp over another lying intoxicated on the floor. His heavy wool jersey soaked in kerosene caught fire. He rushed for the deck, and then, a dancing mass of flames, leaped overboard and disappeared.

Occasionally skippers devised punishments with a view to remedying the defects of character. Thus one lad, who through carelessness had on more than one occasion cooked the "duff" for dinner badly, was made to take his cinders on deck when it was his time to turn in, and go forward to the fore-rigging. Then he had to take one cinder, go up to the cross-tree, and throw it over into the sea, come down the opposite rigging and repeat the act until he had emptied his scuttle. Another who had failed to clean the cabin properly had one night, instead of going to bed, to take a bucketful of sea water and empty it with a teaspoon into another, and so to and fro until morning. On one occasion a poor boy was put under the ballast deck, that is, the cabin floor, and forgotten. He was subsequently found dead, drowned in the bilge water. It was easy to hide the results of cruelty, for being washed overboard was by no means an uncommon way of disappearing from vessels with low freeboards in the shallow water of the North Sea.

A very practical outcome in the mission work was the organization of the Fisher Lads' Letter-Writing Association. The members accepted so many names of orphan lads at sea and pledged themselves to write regularly to them. Also, if possible, they were to look them up when they returned to land, and indeed do for them much as the War Camp Community League members are to-day trying to accomplish for our soldiers and sailors. As every practical exposition of love must, it met with a very real response, and brought, moreover, new interests and joys into many selfish lives.

I remember one lady whose whole care in life had been her own health. She had nursed it, and worried over it, and enjoyed ill health so long, that only the constant recourse to the most refined stimulants postponed the end which would have been a merciful relief — to others. The effort of letter-writing remade her. Doctors were forgotten, stimulants were tabooed, the insignia of invalidism banished, and to my intense surprise I ran across her at a fishing port surrounded by a bevy of blue-jerseyed lads, who were some of those whom she was being blessed by helping.

The best of efforts, however, sometimes "gang aft agley." One day I received a letter, evidently written in great consternation, from an elderly spinster of singularly aristocratic connections and an irreproachableness of life which was almost painful. The name sent to her by one of our skippers as a correspondent who needed help and encouragement was one of those which would be characterized as common — let us say John Jones. By some perverse fate the wrong ship was given as an address, and the skipper of it happened to have exactly the same name. It appeared that lack of experience in just such work had made her letter possibly more affectionate than she would have wished for under the circumstances which developed. For in writing to me she enclosed a ferocious letter from a lady of Billingsgate threatening, not death, but mutilation, if she continued making overtures to "her John."

CHAPTER V

NORTH SEA WORK

I HAVE dwelt at length upon the experiences of the North Sea, because trivial as they appear on the surface, they concern the biggest problem of human life — the belief that man is not of the earth, but only a temporary sojourner upon it. This belief, that he is destined to go on living elsewhere, makes a vast difference to one's estimate of values. Life becomes a school instead of a mere stage, the object of which is that our capacities for usefulness should develop through using them until we reach graduation. What life gives to us can only be of permanent importance as it develops our souls, thus enabling us to give more back to it, and leaves us better prepared for any opportunities than may lie beyond this world. The most valuable asset for this assumption is love for the people among whom one lives.

The best teachers in life are far from being those who know most, or who think themselves wisest. Show me a schoolmaster who does not love his boys and you show me one who is of no use. Our faith in our sonship of God is immensely strengthened by the puzzling fact that even God cannot force goodness into us, His sons, because we share His nature.

These convictions, anyhow, were the mental assets with which I had to begin work, and no others. A scientific training had impressed upon me that big and little are very relative terms; that one piece of work becomes unexpectedly permanent and big, while that which appears to be great, but is merely diffuse, will be temporary and ineffective. Experience has taught me that one human life has its limits of direct impetus, but that its most lasting value is its indirect influence. The greatest Life ever lived was no smaller for being in a carpenter's shop, and largely spent among a few ignorant fishermen. The Scarabee had a valid *apologia pro vita sua* in spite of Dr. Holmes. Tolstoy on his farm, Milton without his sight, Bunyan in his prison, Pasteur in his laboratory, all did great things for the world.

There is so much that is manly about the lives of those who follow the sea, so much less artificiality than in many other callings, and with our fishermen so many fewer of what we call loosely "chances in life," that to sympathize with them was easy — and sympathy is a long step toward love. Life at sea also gives time and opportunity for really knowing a man. It breaks down conventional barriers, and indeed almost compels fellowship and thus an intelligent understanding of the difficulties and tragedies of the soul of our neighbour. That rare faculty of imagination which is the inspiration of all great lovers of men is not alone indispensable. Hand in hand with this inevitably goes the vision of one's own opportunity to help and not to hinder others, even though it be through the unattractive medium of the collection box — for that gives satisfaction only in proportion to the sacrifice which we make.

In plain words the field of work offered me was attractive. It seemed to promise me the most remunerative returns for my abilities, or, to put it in another way, it aroused my ambitions sufficiently to make me believe that my special capacities and training could be used to make new men as well as new bodies. Any idea of sacrifice was balanced by the fact that I never cared very much for the frills of life so long as the necessities were forthcoming.

The attention that Harold Begbie's book "Twice-Born Men" received, was to me later in life a source of surprise. One forgets that the various religions and sects which aimed at the healing of men's souls have concerned themselves more with intellectual creeds than material, Christ-like ends. At first it was not so. Paul rejoiced that he was a new man. There can be no question but that the Gospels show us truly that the change in Christ's first followers was from men, the slaves of every ordinary human passion, into men who were self-mastered — that Christ taught by what he was and did rather than by insistence on creeds and words. It has been seeing these changes in men's lives, not only in their surroundings, though those improve immediately, that reconcile one to our environment, and has induced me to live a lifetime in the wilds.

Another movement that was just starting at this time also interested me considerably. A number of keen young men from Oxford and Cambridge, having experienced the dangers that beset boys from big English public schools who enter the universities without any definite help as to their attitude toward the spiritual relationships of life, got together to discuss the question. They recognized that the formation of the Boys' Brigade in our conservative social life only touched the youth of the poorer classes. Like our English Y.M.C.A., it was not then aristocratic enough for gentlemen. They saw, however, that athletic attainments carried great weight, and that all outdoor accomplishments had a strong attraction for boys from every class. Thus it happened that an organization called the Public School Camps came into being. Its ideal was the uplift of character, and the movement has grown with immense strides on both sides of the Atlantic.

An integral part of my summer holidays during these years was spent as medical officer at one of these camps. For many reasons it was wise in England to run them on military lines, for besides the added dignity, it insured the ability to maintain order and discipline. Some well-known commandant was chosen who was a soldier also in the good fight of faith. Special sites were selected, generally on the grounds of some big country seat which were loaned by the interested lord of the manor, and every kind of outdoor attraction was provided which could be secured. Besides organized competitive games, there was usually a yacht, good bathing, always a gymkhana, and numerous expeditions and "hikes." Not a moment was left unoccupied. All of the work of the camp was done by the boys, who served in turn on orderly duty. The officers were always, if possible, prominent athletes, to whom the boys could look up as being capable in physical as well as spiritual fields. There was a brief address each night before "taps" in the big marquee used for mess; and one night was always a straight talk on the problems of sex by the medical officers, whom the boys were advised to consult in their perplexities. These camps were among the happiest memories of my life, and many of the men to-day gratefully acknowledge that the camps were the turning-point of their whole lives. The secret was unconventionality and absolute naturalness with no "shibboleths." The boys were allowed to be boys absolutely in an atmosphere of sincere if not omniscient fervour. On one occasion when breaking up camp, a curly-headed young rascal in my tent, being late on the last morning — unknown to any one — went to the train in his pajamas, hidden only by his raincoat. At a small wayside station over a hundred miles from London, whither he was bound, leaving his coat in the carriage, he ventured into the refreshment stall of the waiting-room. Unfortunately, however, he came out only to find his train departed and himself in his night-clothes on the platform without a penny, a ticket, or a friend. Eluding the authorities he reached the huge Liverpool terminus by night to find a faithful friend waiting on the platform for him with the sorely needed overgarment.

No one was ever ashamed to be a Christian, or of what Christ was, or what he did and stood for. However, to ignore the fact that the mere word "missionary" aroused suspicion in the average English unconventional mind — such as those of these clean, natural-minded boys — would be a great mistake. Unquestionably, as in the case of Dickens, a missionary was unpractical if not hypocritical, and mildly incompetent if not secretly vicious. I found myself always fighting against the idea that I was termed a missionary. The men I loved and admired, especially such men as those on our athletic teams, felt really strongly about it. Henry Martyn — as a scholar — was a hero to those who read of him, though few did. Moreover, who does not love Charles Kingsley? Even as boys, we want to be "a man," though Kingsley was a "Parson Lot." It always seemed that a missionary was naturally discounted until he had proved his right to be received as an ordinary being. Once after being the guest of a bank president, he told me that my stay was followed by that of their bishop, who was a person of great importance. When the bishop had gone, he asked his two boys one day. "Well, which do you like best, the bishop or the doctor?" "Ach," was the reply, "the bishop can't stand on his head." On another occasion during a visit — while lecturing on behalf of the fishermen — and doing my usual evening physical drill in my bedroom, by a great mischance I missed a straight-arm-balance on a chair, fell over, and nearly brought the chandelier of the drawing-room down on the heads of some guests. That a so-called "missionary" should be so worldly as to wish to keep his body fit seemed so unusual that I heard of that trifle a hundred times.

The Church of Christ that is coming will be interested in the forces that make for peace and righteousness in this world rather than in academic theories as to how to get rewards in another. That will be a real stimulus to fitness and capacity all round instead of a dope for failures. It is that element in missions to-day, such as the up-to-date work of the Rockefeller Institute and other medical missions in China and India, which alone holds the respect of the mass of the people. The value of going out merely to make men of different races think as we think is being proportionately discounted with the increase of education.

Our North Sea work grew apace. Vessel after vessel was added to the fleet. Her Majesty, Queen Victoria, became interested, and besides subscribing personally toward the first hospital boat, permitted it to be named in her honour. According to custom the builders had a beautiful little model made which Her Majesty agreed to accept. It was decided that it should be presented to her in Buckingham Palace by the two senior mission captains.

The journey to them was a far more serious undertaking than a winter voyage on the Dogger Bank. However, arrayed in smart blue suits and new guernseys and polished to the last degree, they set out on the eventful expedition. On their return every one was as anxious to know "how the voyage had turned out" as if they had been exploring new fishing grounds around the North Cape in the White Sea. "Nothing to complain of, boys, till just as we had her in the wind's eye to shoot the gear," said the senior skipper. "A big swell in knee-breeches opened the door and called out our names, when I was brought up all standing, for I saw that the peak halliard was fast on the port side. The blame thing was too small for me to shift over, so I had to leave it. But, believe me, she never said a word about it. That's what I call something of a lady."

At this time we had begun two new ventures, an institute at Yarmouth for fishermen ashore and a dispensary vessel to be sent out each spring among the thousands of Scotch, Manx, Irish, and French fishermen, who carried on the herring and mackerel fishery off the south and west coast of Ireland.

The south Irish spring fishery is wonderfully interesting. Herring and mackerel are in huge shoals anywhere from five to forty miles off the land, and the vessels run in and out each day bringing back the catch of the night. Each vessel shoots out about two miles of net, while some French ones will shoot out five miles. Thus the aggregate of nets used would with ease stretch from Ireland to New York and back. Yet the undaunted herring return year after year to the disastrous rendezvous. The vessels come from all parts. Many are the large tan-sailed luggers from the Scottish coasts, their sails and hulls marked "B.F." for Banff, "M.E." for Montrose, "C.N." for Campbelltown, etc. With these come the plucky little Ulster boats from Belfast and Larne, Loch Swilling and Loch Foyle; and not a few of the hereditary seafaring men from Cornwall, Devon, and Dorset. Others also come from Falmouth, Penzance, and Exmouth. Besides these are the Irish boats — few

enough, alas, for Paddy is not a sailor. A good priest
had tried to induce his people to share this rich harvest
by starting a fishery school for boys at Baltimore, where
net-making and every other branch of the industry was
taught. It was to little purpose, for I have met men
hungry on the west coast, who were trying to live on
potato-raising on that bog land who were graduates of
Father D.'s school.

There was one year when we ourselves were trying out
the trawling in Clew Bay and Blackwood, and getting
marvellous catches; so much so that I remember one
small trawler from Grimsby on the east coast of England
making two thousand dollars in two days' work, while
the Countess of Z. fund was distributing charity to the
poverty-stricken men who lived around the bay itself.
The Government of Ireland also made serious efforts to
make its people take up the fishery business. About one
million dollars obtained out of the escheated funds of
the Church of England in Ireland, when that organization was disestablished by Mr. Gladstone, was used as a
loan fund which was available for fishermen, resident six
months, at two per cent interest. They were permitted
to purchase their own boat and gear for the fishery out
of the money thus provided.

While we lay in Durham Harbour at the entrance to
Waterford Harbour, we met many Cornishmen who were
temporarily resident there, having come over from Cornwall to qualify for borrowing the money to get boats and
outfit. During one week in which we were working from
that port, there were so many saints' days on which the
Irish crews would not go out fishing, but were having
good times on the land, that the skippers, who were
Cornishmen, had to form a crew out of their own numbers and take one of their boats to sea.

One day we had landed on the Arran Islands, and I was hunting ferns in the rock crevices, for owing to the warmth of the Gulf current the growth is luxuriant. On the top of the cliffs about three hundred feet high, I fell in with two Irishmen smoking their pipes and sprawling on the edge of the precipice. The water below was very deep and they were fishing. I had the fun of seeing dangling codfish hauled leisurely up all that long distance, and if one fell off on the passage, it was amusing to note the absolute insouciance of the fishermen, who assured me that there were plenty more in the sea.

It has always been a puzzle to me why so few tourists and yachtsmen visit the south and west coast of Ireland. Its marvellous wild, rock scenery, its exquisite bays, — no other words describe them, — its emerald verdure, and its interesting and hospitable people have given me, during the spring fishing seasons that I spent on that coast, some of the happiest memories of my life. On the contrary, most of the yachts hang around the Solent, and the piers of Ryde, Cowes, and Southampton, instead of the magnificent coast from Queenstown to Donegal Cliffs, and from there all along West Scotland to the Hebrides.

About this time our work established a dispensary and social centre at Crookhaven, just inside the Fastnet Lighthouse, and another in Tralee on the Kerry coast, north of Cape Clear. Gatherings for worship and singing were also held on Sundays on the boats, for on that day neither Scotch, Manx, nor English went fishing. The men loved the music, the singing of hymns, and the conversational addresses. Many would take some part in the service, and my memories of those gatherings are still very pleasant ones.

On this wild coast calls for help frequently came from

the poor settlers as well as from the seafarers. A summons coming in one day from the Fastnet Light, we rowed out in a small boat to that lovely rock in the Atlantic. A heavy sea, however, making landing impossible, we caught hold of a buoy, anchored off from the rock, and then rowing in almost to the surf, caught a line from the high overhanging crane. A few moments later one was picked out of the tumbling, tossing boat like a winkle out of a shell, by a noose at the end of a line from a crane a hundred and fifty feet above, swung perpendicularly up into the air, and then round and into a trap-door in the side of the lighthouse. On leaving one was swung out again in the same fashion, and dangled over the tumbling boat until caught and pulled in by the oarsmen.

Another day we rowed out nine miles in an Irish craft to visit the Skerry Islands, famous for the old Beehive Monastery, and the countless nests of gannets and other large sea-birds. The cliffs rise to a great height almost precipitously, and the ceaseless thunder of the Atlantic swell jealously guards any landing. There being no davit or crane, we had just to fling ourselves into the sea, and climb up as best we could, carrying a line to haul up our clothing from the boat and other apparatus after landing, while the oarsmen kept her outside the surf. To hold on to the slippery rock we needed but little clothing, anyhow, for it was a slow matter, and the clinging power of one's bare toes was essential. The innumerable gannets sitting on their nests gave the island the appearance of a snowdrift; and we soon had all the eggs that we needed lowered by a line. But some of the gulls, of whose eggs we wanted specimens also, built so cleverly onto the actual faces of the cliffs, that we had to adopt the old plan of hanging over the edge and raising the eggs on the back of one's foot, which is an exploit not devoid of excitement. The chief difficulty was, however, with one of our number, who literally stuck on the top, being unable to descend, at least in a way compatible with comfort or safety. The upshot was that he had to be blindfolded and helped.

One of our Council, being connected at this time with the Irish Poor-Relief Board and greatly interested in the Government efforts to relieve distress in Ireland, arranged that we should make a voyage around the entire island in one of our vessels, trying the trawling grounds everywhere, and also the local markets available for making our catch remunerative. There has been considerable activity in these waters of late years, but it was practically pioneer work in those days, the fishery being almost entirely composed of drift nets and long lines. It was supposed that the water was too deep and the bottom too uneven and rocky to make trawling possible. We had only a sailing vessel of about sixty tons, and the old heavy beam trawl, for the other trawl and steam fishing boats were then quite in their infancy. The quantity and variety of victims that came to our net were prodigious, and the cruise has remained as a dream in my memory, combined as it was with so many chances of helping out one of the most interesting and amiable — if not educated — peoples in the world. It happened to be a year of potato scarcity; as one friend pointed out, there was a surplus of Murphys in the kitchen and a scarcity of Murphys in the cellar — "Murphys" being another name for that vegetable which is so large a factor in Irish economic life. As mentioned before, a fund, called the Countess of Z.'s fund, had been established to relieve the consequent distress, and while we were fishing in Black Sod Bay, the natives around the shore were accepting all that they could secure. Yet one steam trawler cleared four hundred pounds within a week; and our own fine catches, taken in so short a while, made it seem a veritable fishermen's paradise for us, who were accustomed to toil over the long-combed-out and stormy banks of the North Sea. The variety of fish taken alone made the voyage of absorbing interest, numbering cod, haddock, ling, hake, turbot, soles, plaice, halibut, whiting, crayfish, shark, dog-fish, and many quaint monsters unmarketable then, but perfectly edible. Among those taken in was the big angler fish, which lives at the bottom with his enormous mouth open, dangling an attractive-looking bait formed by a long rod growing out from his nose, which lures small victims into the cavern, whence, as he possesses row upon row of spiky teeth which providentially point down his throat, there is seldom any returning.

Among the many memories of that coast which gave me a vision of the land question as it affected the people in those days, one in particular has always remained with me. We had made a big catch in a certain bay, a perfectly beautiful inlet. To see if the local fishermen could find a market within reach of these fishing grounds, with one of the crew, and the fish packed in boxes, we sailed up the inlet to the market town of Bell Mullet. Being Saturday, we found a market day in progress, and buyers, who, encouraged by one of the new Government light railways, were able to purchase our fish. That evening, however, when halfway home, a squall suddenly struck our own lightened boat, which was rigged with one large lugsail, and capsized her. By swimming and manœuvring the boat, we made land on the low, muddy flats. No house was in sight, and it was not until long after dark that we two shivering masses of mud reached an isolated cabin in the middle of a patch of the redeemed ground right in the centre of a large bog. A miserably clad woman greeted us with a warm Irish welcome. The house had only one room and accommodated the live-stock as well as the family. A fine cow stood in one corner; a donkey tied to the foot of the bed was patiently looking down into the face of the baby. Father was in England harvesting. A couple of pigs lay under the bed, and the floor space was still further encroached upon by a goodly number of chickens, which were encouraged by the warmth of the peat fire. They not only thought it their duty to emphasize our welcome, but — misled by the firelight — were saluting the still far-off dawn. The resultant emotions which we experienced during the night led us to suggest that we might assist toward the erection of a cattle pen. Before leaving, however, we were told, "Shure t' rint would be raised in the fall," if such signs of prosperity as farm buildings greeted the land agent's arrival.

The mouth of Loch Foyle, one of the most beautiful bays in Ireland, gave us a fine return in fish. Especially I remember the magnificent turbot which we took off the wild shore between the frowning basalt cliffs of the Giant's Causeway, and the rough headlands of Loch Swilly. We sold our fish in the historic town of Londonderry, where we saw the old gun Morris Meg, which once so successfully roared for King William, still in its place on the old battlements. By a packet steamer plying to Glasgow, we despatched some of the catch to that greedy market. At Loch Foyle there is a good expanse of sandy and mud bottom which nurses quite a harvest of the sea, though — oddly enough — close by off Rathlin Island is the only water over one hundred fathoms deep until the Atlantic Basin is reached. The Irish Sea like the North Sea is all shallow water. Crossing to the

Isle of Man, we delayed there only a short while, for those grounds are well known to the Fleetwood trawlers, who supply so much fish to the dense population of North Central England. We found little opportunity of trawling off the west of Scotland, the ocean's bottom being in no way suited to it. On reaching the Western Hebrides, however, we were once more among many old friends. From Stornaway on the Isle of Lewis alone some nine hundred drifters were pursuing the retreating armies of herring.

The German hordes have taught us to think of life in large numbers, but were the herring to elect a Kaiser, he would dominate in reality an absolutely indestructible host. For hundreds of years fishermen of all countries have without cessation been pursuing these friends of mankind. For centuries these inexhaustible hordes have followed their long pathways of the sea, swimming by some strange instinct always more or less over the same courses — ever with their tireless enemies, both in and out of the water, hot foot on their tracks. Sharks, dog-fish, wolf-fish, cod, and every fish large enough to swallow them, gulls, divers, auks, and almost every bird of the air, to say nothing of the nets set now from steam-propelled ships, might well threaten their speedy extermination. This is especially true when we remember that even their eggs are preyed upon in almost incalculable bulk as soon as they are deposited. But phœnix-like they continue to reappear in such vast quantities that they are still the cheapest food on the market. Such huge numbers are caught at one time that they have now and again to be used for fertilizer, or dumped overboard into the sea. The great bay of Stornaway Harbour was so deeply covered in oil from the fish while we lay there, that the sailing boats raced to and fro before fine breezes and yet the wind could not even ripple the surface of the sea, as if at last millennial conditions had materialized. Many times we saw nets which had caught such quantities of fish at once that they had sunk to the bottom. They were only rescued with great difficulty, and then the fish were so swollen by being drowned in the net that it took hours of hard work and delay to shake their now distended bodies out again.

The opportunities for both holding simple religious services and rendering medical help from our dispensary were numerous, and we thought sufficiently needed to call for some sort of permanent effort; so later the Society established a small mission room in the harbour.

Alcohol has always been a menace to Scotch life, though their fishermen were singularly free from rioting and drunkenness. Indeed, their home-born piety was continually a protest to the indulgence of the mixed crowd which at that time followed King Henry. Scores of times have I seen a humble crew of poor fishermen, who themselves owned their small craft, observing the Sunday as if they were in their homes, while the skippers of large vessels belonging to others fished all the week round at the beck of their absent owners, thinking they made more money in that way.

In 1891 the present Lord Southborough, then Mr. Francis Hopwood, and a member of the Mission Board, returned from a visit to Canada and Newfoundland. He brought before the Council the opportunities for service among the fishermen of the northwest Atlantic, and the suggestion was handed on to me in the form of a query. Would I consider crossing the Atlantic in one of our small sailing vessels, and make an inquiry into the problem?

Some of my older friends have thought that my de-

cision to go was made under strong religious excitement,
and in response to some deep-seated conviction that
material sacrifices or physical discomforts commended
one to God. I must, however, disclaim all such lofty
motives. I have always believed that the Good Samaritan
went across the road to the wounded man just because
he wanted to. I do not believe that he felt any sacrifice
or fear in the matter. If he did, I know very well that I
did not. On the contrary, there is everything about such
a venture to attract my type of mind, and making preparations for the long voyage was an unmitigated delight.

The boat which I selected was ketch-rigged — much
like a yawl, but more comfortable for lying-to in heavy
weather, the sail area being more evenly distributed.
Her freeboard being only three feet, we replaced her
wooden hatches, which were too large for handling
patients, by iron ones; and also sheathed her forward
along the water-line with greenheart to protect her
planking in ice. For running in high seas we put a large
square sail forward, tripping the yard along the fore-
mast, much like a spinnaker boom. Having a screw
steering gear which took two men to handle quickly
enough when she yawed and threatened to jibe in a big
swell, it proved very useful.

It was not until the spring of 1892 that we were ready
to start. We had secured a master with a certificate, for
though I was myself a master mariner, and my mate had
been in charge of our vessel in the North Sea for many
years, we had neither of us been across the Atlantic before. The skipper was a Cornishman, Trevize by name,
and a martinet on discipline — an entirely new experience to a crew of North Sea fishermen. He was so particular about everything being just so that quite a few
days were lost in starting, though well spent as far as

preparedness went. Nothing was wanting when at last, in the second week of June, the tugboat let us go, and crowds of friends waved us good-bye from the pier-head as we passed out with our bunting standing. We had not intended to touch land again until it should rise out of the western horizon, but off the south coast of Ireland we met with heavy seas and head winds, so we ran into Crookhaven to visit our colleagues who worked at that station. Our old patients in that lonely corner were almost as interested as ourselves in the new venture, and many were the good eggs and "meals of greens" which they brought down to the ship as parting tokens. Indeed, we shrewdly guessed that our "dry" principles alone robbed us of more than "one drop o' potheen" whose birth the light of the moon had witnessed.

As we were not fortunate in encountering fair winds, it was not until the twelfth day that we saw our first iceberg, almost running into it in a heavy fog. The fall in the temperature of the sea surface had warned us that we were in the cold current, and three or four days of dense fog emphasized the fact. As it was midsummer, we felt the change keenly, when suddenly on the seventeenth day the fog lifted, and a high evergreen-crowned coastline greeted our delighted eyes. A lofty lighthouse on a rocky headland enabled us almost immediately to discover our exact position. We were just a little north of St. John's Harbour, which, being my first landfall across the Atlantic, impressed me as a really marvellous feat; but what was our surprise as we approached the high cliffs which guard the entrance to see dense columns of smoke arising, and to feel the offshore wind grow hotter and hotter as the pilot tug towed us between the headlands. For the third time in its history the city of St. John's was in flames.

The heat was fierce when we at last anchored, and had the height of the blaze not passed, we should certainly have been glad to seek again the cool of our icy friends outside. Some ships had even been burned at their anchors. We could count thirteen fiercely raging fires in various parts of the city, which looked like one vast funeral pyre. Only the brick chimneys of the houses remained standing blackened and charred. Smoke and occasional flame would burst out here and there as the fickle eddies of wind, influenced, no doubt, by the heat, whirled around as if in sport over the scene of man's discomfitures. On the hillside stood a solitary house almost untouched, which, had there been any reason for its being held sacred, might well have served as a demonstration of Heaven's special intervention in its behalf. As it was, it seemed to mock the still smouldering wreck of the beautiful stone cathedral just beside it. Among the ruins in this valley of desolation little groups of men darted hither and thither, resembling from the harbour nothing so much as tiny black imps gloating over a congenial environment. I hope never again to see the sight that might well have suggested Gehenna to a less active imagination than Dante's.

Huts had been erected in open places to shelter the homeless; long queues of hungry human beings defiled before temporary booths which served out soup and other rations. Every nook and corner of house-room left was crowded to overflowing with derelict persons and their belongings. The roads to the country, like those now in the environs of the towns in northern France, were dotted with exiles and belated vehicles, hauling in every direction the remnants of household goods. The feeling as of a rudely disturbed antheap dominated one's mind, and yet, in spite of it all, the hospitality and wel-

come which we as strangers received was as wonderful
as if we had been a relief ship laden with supplies to replace the immense amount destroyed in the ships and
stores of the city. Moreover, the cheerfulness of the town
was amazing. Scarcely a "peep" or "squeal" did we
hear, and not a single diatribe against the authorities.
Every one had suffered together. Nor was it due to any
one's fault. True, the town water-supply had been temporarily out of commission, some stranger was said to
have been smoking in the hay loft, Providence had not
specially intervened to save property, and hence this
result. Thus to our relief it was a city of hope, not of
despair, and to our amazement they were able to show
most kindly interest in problems such as ours which
seemed so remote at the moment. None of us will ever
forget their kindness, from the Governor Sir Terence
O'Brien, and the Prime Minister, Sir William Whiteway,
to the humblest stevedore on the wharves.

I had expected to spend the greater part of our time
cruising among the fishing schooners out of sight of land
on the big Banks as we did in the North Sea; but I was
advised that owing to fog and isolation, each vessel
working separately and bringing its own catch to market,
it would be a much more profitable outlay of time, if
we were to follow the large fleet of over one hundred
schooners, with some thirty thousand fishermen, women,
and children which had just sailed North for summer
work along the coast of Labrador. To better aid us the
Government provided a pilot free of expense, and their
splendid Superintendent of Fisheries, Mr. Adolph Niel-
sen, also accepted the invitation to accompany us, to
make our experiment more exhaustive and valuable by
a special scientific inquiry into the habits and manner
of the fish as well as of the fishermen. Naturally a good

deal of delay had occurred owing to the unusual congestion of business which needed immediate attention and the unfortunate temporary lack of facilities; but we got under way at last, and sailing "down North" some four hundred miles and well outside the land, eventually ran in on a parallel and made the Labrador coast on the 4th of August.

The exhilarating memory of that day is one which will die only when we do. A glorious sun shone over an oily ocean of cerulean blue, over a hundred towering icebergs of every fantastic shape, and flashing all of the colours of the rainbow from their gleaming pinnacles as they rolled on the long and lazy swell. Birds familiar and strange left the dense shoals of rippling fish, over which great flocks were hovering and quarrelling in noisy enjoyment, to wave us welcome as they swept in joyous circles overhead.

CHAPTER VI

THE LURE OF THE LABRADOR

TWENTY years have passed away since that day, and a thousand more important affairs which have occurred in the meantime have faded from my memory; but still its events stand out clear and sharp. The large and lofty island, its top covered with green verdure, so wonderful a landmark from the sea, its peaks capped with the fleecy mist of early morning, rose in a setting of the purest azure blue. For the first time I saw the faces of its ruddy cliffs, their ledges picked out with the homes of myriad birds. Its feet were bathed in the dark, rich green of the Atlantic water, edged by the line of pure white breakers, where the gigantic swell lazily hurled immeasurable mountains of water against its titanic bastions, evoking peals of sound like thunder from its cavernous recesses — a very riot of magnificence. The great schools of whales, noisily slapping the calm surface of the sea with their huge tails as in an *abandon* of joy, dived and rose, and at times threw the whole of their mighty carcasses right out of water for a bath in the glorious morning sunshine. The shoals of fish everywhere breaching the water, and the silver streaks which flashed beneath our bows as we lazed along, suggested that the whole vast ocean was too small to hold its riches.

When we realized that practically no man had ever lived there, and few had even seen it, it seemed to overwhelm us, coming as we did from the crowded Island of our birth, where notices not to trespass haunted even the dreams of the average man.

A serried rank of range upon range of hills, reaching

north and south as far as the eye could see from the masthead, was rising above our horizon behind a very surfeit of islands, bewildering the minds of men accustomed to our English and North Sea coast-lines.

In a ship just the size of the famous Matthew, we had gone west, following almost the exact footsteps of the great John Cabot when just four hundred years before he had fared forth on his famous venture of discovery. We seemed now almost able to share the exhilaration which only such experiences can afford the human soul, and the vast potential resources for the blessing of humanity of this great land still practically untouched.

At last we came to anchor among many schooners in a wonderful natural harbour called Domino Run, so named because the Northern fleets all pass through it on their way North and South. Had we been painted scarlet, and flown the Black Jack instead of the Red Ensign, we could not have attracted more attention. Flags of greeting were run up to all mastheads, and boats from all sides were soon aboard inquiring into the strange phenomenon. Our object explained, we soon had calls for a doctor, and it has been the experience of almost every visitor to the coast from that day to this that he is expected to have a knowledge of medicine.

One impression made on my mind that day undoubtedly influenced all my subsequent actions. Late in the evening, when the rush of visitors was largely over, I noticed a miserable bunch of boards, serving as a boat, with only a dab of tar along its seams, lying motionless a little way from us. In it, sitting silent, was a half-clad, brown-haired, brown-faced figure. After long hesitation, during which time I had been watching him from the rail, he suddenly asked:

"Be you a real doctor?"

Cape Uivuk

The Tickle Anchorage

THE LABRADOR COAST

"That's what I call myself," I replied.

"Us has n't got no money," he fenced, "but there's a very sick man ashore, if so be you'd come and see him."

A little later he led me to a tiny sod-covered hovel, compared with which the Irish cabins were palaces. It had one window of odd fragments of glass. The floor was of pebbles from the beach; the earth walls were damp and chilly. There were half a dozen rude wooden bunks built in tiers around the single room, and a group of some six neglected children, frightened by our arrival, were huddled together in one corner. A very sick man was coughing his soul out in the darkness of a lower bunk, while a pitiably covered woman gave him cold water to sip out of a spoon. There was no furniture except a small stove with an iron pipe leading through a hole in the roof.

My heart sank as I thought of the little I could do for the sufferer in such surroundings. He had pneumonia, a high fever, and was probably tubercular. The thought of our attractive little hospital on board at once rose to my mind; but how could one sail away with this husband and father, probably never to bring him back. Advice, medicine, a few packages of food were only temporizing. The poor mother could never nurse him and tend the family. Furthermore, their earning season, "while the fish were in," was slipping away. To pray for the man, and with the family, was easy, but scarcely satisfying. A hospital and a trained nurse was the only chance for this bread-winner — and neither was available.

I called in a couple of months later as we came South before the approach of winter. Snow was already on the ground. The man was dead and buried; there was no provision whatever for the family, who were destitute, except for the hollow mockery of a widow's grant of twenty dollars a year. This, moreover, had to be taken up in goods at a truck store, less debts *if* she owed any.

Among the nine hundred patients that still show on the records of that long-ago voyage, some stand out more than others for their peculiar pathos and their utter helplessness. I shall never forget one poor Eskimo. In firing a cannon to salute the arrival of the Moravian Mission ship, the gun exploded prematurely, blowing off both the man's arms below the elbows. He had been lying on his back for a fortnight, the pathetic stumps covered only with far from sterile rags dipped in cold water. We remained some days, and did all we could for his benefit; but he too joined the great host that is forever "going west," for want of what the world fails to give them.

It is not given to every member of our profession to enjoy the knowledge that he alone stands between the helpless and suffering or death, for in civilization modern amenities have almost' annihilated space and time, and the sensations of the Yankee at the Court of King Arthur are destroyed by the realization of competitors, "just as good," even if it often does leave one conscious of limitations. The successful removal of a molar which has given torture for weeks in a dentistless country, gains one as much gratitude as the amputation of a limb. One mere boy came to me with necrosis of one side of his lower jaw due to nothing but neglected toothache. It had to be dug out from the new covering of bone which had grown up all around it. The whimsical expression of his lop-sided face still haunts me.

Deformities went untreated. The crippled and blind halted through life, victims of what "the blessed Lord saw best for them." The torture of an ingrowing toe-nail, which could be relieved in a few minutes, had incapacitated one poor father for years. Tuberculosis and rickets carried on their evil work unchecked. Preventable poverty was the efficient handmaid of these two latter diseases.

There was also much social work to be done in connection with the medical. Education in every one of its branches — especially public health — was almost non-existent — as were many simple social amenities which might have been so easily induced.

At one village a woman with five children asked us if we could marry her to her husband. They had never been together when a parson happened along, and they now lived in a lonely cove three miles away. This seemed a genuine case of distress; and as it happened a parson was taking a passage with us, we sent two of our crew over in a boat to round up the groom. Apparently he was not at all anxious, but being a very small man and she a large woman, he discreetly acquiesced. The wedding was held on board our ship, every one entering into the spirit of the unusual occasion. The main hold was crammed with guests, bells were rung and flags flown, guns fired, and at night distress rockets were sent up. We kept in touch with the happy couple for years, till once more they moved away to try their luck elsewhere.

Obviously the coast offered us work that would not be done unless we did it. Here was real need along any line on which one could labour, in a section of our own Empire, where the people embodied all our best sea traditions. They exhibited many of the attractive characteristics which, even when buried beneath habits and customs the outcome of their environment, always endear men of the sea to the genuine Anglo-Saxon. They were uncomplaining, optimistic, splendidly resourceful, cheerful and generous — and after all in one sense soap and water only makes the outside of the platter clean.

I confess that we had greatly enjoyed the adventure *qua* adventure. Mysterious fjords which wound out of sight into the fastnesses of unknown mountains, and which were entirely uncharted, fairly shouted an invitation to enter and discover what was round the next corner. Islands by the hundred, hitherto never placed on any map, challenged one's hydrographic skill. Families of strange birds, which came swinging seaward as the season advanced, suggested a virgin field for hunting. Berries and flowering plants, as excellent as they were unfamiliar, appealed for exploration. Great boulders perched on perilous peaks, torn and twisted strata, with here and there raised beaches, and great outcrops of black trap-rock piercing through red granite cliffs in giant vertical seams — all piqued one's curiosity to know the geology of this unknown land. Some stone arrowheads and knives, brought to me by a fisherman, together with the memories that the Norse Vikings and their competitors on the scroll of discovery made their first landfall on this the nearest section of the American coast to Europe, excited one's curiosity to know more of these shores. The dense growth of evergreen trees abounding in every river valley, and the exquisite streams with trout and salmon and seals attracted one whose familiarity with sport and forests was inseparably connected with notices to trespassers.

It only wanted an adventure such as we had one day while sailing up a fjord on a prosaic professional call, when we upset our cutter and had to camp for the night, to give spice to our other experiences, and made us wish to return another year, better equipped, and with a more competent staff.

I am far from being the only person from the outside world who has experienced what Wallace describes as "the Lure of the Labrador." It was a genuine surprise to me one morning to find ice on deck — a scale of sparkling crystals most beautifully picking out the water-line of our little craft. It was only then that I realized that October had come. The days, so full of incident, had passed away like ships in the night. Whither away was the question? We could not stay even though we felt the urgent call to remain. So "Heigho for the southward bar" and a visit to St. John's to try and arouse interest in the new-discovered problems, before we should once more let go our stern lines and be bowling homeward before the fall nor'westers to dear old England.

Home-going craft had generously carried our story before us to the city of St. John's. The Board of Trade commended our effort. The papers had written of the new phenomenon; the politicians had not refrained from commendation. His Excellency the Governor made our path plain by calling a meeting in Government House, where the following resolution was passed:

"That this meeting, representing the principal merchants and traders carrying on the fisheries, especially on the Labrador coast, and others interested in the welfare of this colony, desires to tender its warmest thanks to the directors of the Deep-Sea Mission for sending their hospital ship Albert to visit the settlement on the Labrador coast.

"Much of our fishing industry is carried on in regions beyond the ordinary reach of medical aid, or of charity, and it is with the deepest sense of gratitude that this meeting learns of the amount of medical and surgical work done. . . .

"This meeting also desires to express the hope that the directors may see their way to continue the work thus begun, and should they do so, they may be assured of the earnest coöperation of all classes of this community."

When at last we said good-bye on our homeward voyage, our cabins were loaded with generous souvenirs for the journey, and no king on his throne was happier than every man of the crew of the good ship Albert.

Our report to the Council in London, followed by the resolution sent by the Newfoundland Committee, induced the Society to repeat the experiment on a larger scale the following spring. Thus, with two young doctors, Elliott Curwen of Cambridge and Arthur Bobardt from Australia, and two nurses, Miss Cawardine and Miss Williams, we again set out the following June.

The voyage was uneventful except that I was nearly left behind in mid-Atlantic. While playing cricket on deck our last ball went over the side, and I after it, shouting to the helmsman to tack back. This he did, but I failed to cut him off the first time, as he got a bit rattled. However, we rescued the ball.

We had chosen two islands two hundred miles apart for cottage hospitals, one at Battle Harbour, on the north side of the entrance of the St. Lawrence (Straits of Belle Isle), and the other at Indian Harbour, out in the Atlantic at the mouth of the great Hamilton Inlet. Both places were the centres of large fisheries, and were the "bring-ups" for numberless schooners of the Labrador fleet on their way North and South. The first, a building already half finished, was donated by a local fishery firm by the name of Baine, Johnston and Company. This was quickly made habitable, and patients were admitted under Dr. Bobardt's care. The second building, assembled at St. John's, was shipped by the donors, who were the owners of the Indian Harbour fishery, Job Brothers and Company. Owing to difficulties in landing, this building was not completed and ready for use until the following year, so Dr. Curwen took charge of the hospital ship Albert, and I cruised as far north as Okkak (lat. 57°) in the Princess May, a midget steam launch, eight feet wide, with a cook and an engineer. As there was no coal obtainable in the North, we used wood, and her fire-box being small the amount of cutting entailed left a permanent impression on our biceps.

A friend from Ireland had presented this little boat, which I found lying up on the Chester Race-Course, near our home on the Sands of Dee. We had repaired her and steamed her through the canal into the Mersey, where, somewhat to our humiliation, she had been slung up onto the deck of an Allan liner for her trans-Atlantic passage, as if she were nothing but an extra hand satchel. Nor was our pride restored when on her arrival it was found that her funnel was missing among the general baggage in the hold. We had to wait in St. John's for a new one before starting on our trip North. The close of the voyage proved a fitting corollary. In crossing the Straits of Belle Isle, the last boat to leave the Labrador, we ran short of fuel, and had to burn our cabin-top to make the French shore, having also lost our compass overboard. Here we delayed repairing and refitting so long that the authorities in St. John's became alarmed and despatched their mail steamer in search of us. I still remember my astonishment, when, on boarding the steamer, the lively skipper, a very tender-hearted father of a family, threw both arms around me with a mighty hug and exclaimed, "Thank God, we all thought you were gone. A schooner picked up your flagpole at sea." Poor fellow, he was a fine Christian seaman, but only a year or two later he perished with his large steamer while I still rove this rugged coast.

That summer we visited the stations of the Moravian Brethren, who were kindness personified to us. Their stations, five in number, dated back over a hundred and thirty [years, yet they had never had a doctor among them. It would scarcely be modest for me to protest that they were the worse off for that circumstance. Each station was well armed with homœopathic pills, and at least those do no harm; while one old German house-father had really performed with complete success craniotomy and delivery of a child *en morcellement,* in the case of a colleague's wife. During our stay they gave us plenty of work among their Eskimos, and were good enough to report most favourably of our work to their home Committee.

As there was no chart of any use for the coast north of Hopedale, few if any corrections having been made in the topographic efforts of the long late Captain Cook, of around-the-world reputation, one of the Brethren, Mr. Christopher Schmidt, joined the Princess May to help me find their northern stations among the plethora of islands which fringe the coast in that vicinity. Never in my life had I expected any journey half so wonderful. We travelled through endless calm fjords, runs, tickles, bays, and straits without ever seeing the open sea, and with hardly a ripple on the surface. We passed high mountains and lofty cliffs, crossed the mouths of large rivers, left groves of spruce and fir and larches on both sides of us, and saw endless birds, among them the Canada goose, eider duck, surf scoters, and many commoner sea-fowl. As it was both impossible and dangerous to proceed after dark, when no longer able to run we would go ashore and gather specimens of the abundant and beautiful sub-arctic flora, and occasionally capture a bird or a dish of trout to help out our diminutive larder.

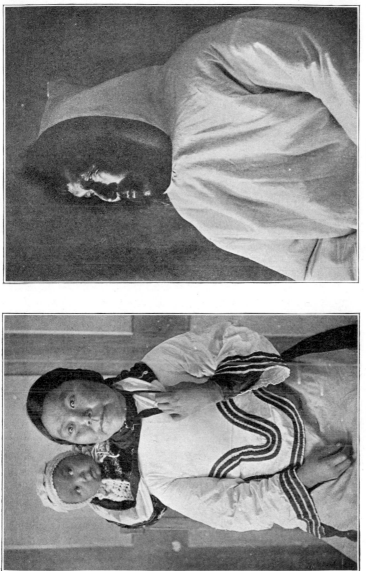

ESKIMO MAN

ESKIMO WOMAN AND BABY

Among the Eskimos I found a great deal of tuberculosis and much eye trouble. Around the Moravian Mission stations wooden houses had largely replaced the former "tubiks," or skin tents, which were moved as occasion required and so provided for sanitation. These wooden huts were undrained, dark and dirty to a remarkable degree. No water supply was provided, and the spaces between the houses were simply indescribable garbage heaps, presided over by innumerable dogs. The average life was very short and infant mortality high. The best for which we could hope in the way of morals among these people was that a natural unmorality was some offset to the existing conditions. The features of the native life which appealed most to us were the universal optimism, the laughing good-nature and contentment, and the Sunday cleanliness of the entire congregation which swarmed into the chapel service, a welcome respite from the perennial dirt of the week days. Moreover, nearly all had been taught to read and write in Eskimo, though there is no literature in that language to read, except such books as have been translated by the Moravian Brethren. At that time a strict policy of teaching no English had been adopted. Words lacking in the language, like "God," "love," etc., were substituted by German words. Nearly every Eskimo counted "ein, zwei, drei." In one of my lectures, on returning to England, I mentioned that as the Eskimos had never seen a lamb or a sheep either alive or in a picture, the Moravians, in order to offer them an intelligible and appealing simile, had most wisely substituted the kotik, or white seal, for the phrase "the Lamb of God." One old lady in my audience must have felt that the good Brethren were tampering unjustifiably with Holy Writ, for the following summer, from the barrels of clothing sent out to the

Labrador, was extracted a dirty, distorted, and much-mangled and wholly sorry-looking woolly toy lamb. Its *raison d'être* was a mystery until we read the legend carefully pinned to one dislocated leg, "Sent in order that the heathen may know better."

Their love for music and ability to do part-playing and singing also greatly impressed us, and we spent many evenings enjoying their brass bands and their Easter and Christmas carols. We made some records of these on our Edison phonograph, and they were overpowered with joy when they heard their own voices coming back to them from the machine. The magic lantern also proved exceedingly popular, and several tried to touch the pictures and see if they could not hold them. We were also able to show some hastily made lantern slides of themselves, and I shall never forget their joyful excitement. The following season, in giving them some lantern views, we chanced to show a slide of an old Eskimo woman who had died during the winter. The subsequent commotion caused among the "little people" was unintelligible to us until one of the Moravian Brethren explained that they thought her spirit had taken visible form and returned to her own haunts.

I happened to be in the gardens at Nain when a northerly air made it feel chilly and the thermometer stood only a little above freezing. A troop of Eskimo women came out to cover up the potatoes. Every row of potatoes is covered with arched sticks and long strips of canvas along them. A huge roll of sacking is kept near each row and the whole is drawn over and the potatoes are tucked in bed for the night. I could not resist the temptation to lift the bedclothes and shake hands and say good-night to one of the nearest plants, whereat the merry little people went off into convulsions of laughter.

At Hopedale there was a large Danish ship with over six hundred tons of cargo for the new Moravian buildings. The Brethren do not build as we are doing from coast material. In order to save time and also to have more substantial buildings, they are cut out and built in Germany, photographed, and each piece marked. Then they are taken to pieces, shipped, and sent out here for erection.

Some years ago in Germany, when the Socialists were wearing beards and mustaches, all respectable people used to shave. Therefore the missionaries being Germans insisted on the Eskimos shaving as they did. The result is that at one store at least a stock of ancient razors are left on hand, for now neither missionary nor Eskimo shaves in the inhospitable climate of this country. A small stock of these razors was, therefore, left on my account in some graves from which one or two Eskimos were good enough to go and get us a few ancient stone implements. It is a marvellous thing how superstition still clings around the very best of native Christian communities.

The Moravian Mission is a trading mission. This trading policy in some aspects is in its favour. It is unquestionably part of a message of real love to a brother to put within his reach at reasonable rates those adjuncts of civilized life that help to make less onerous his hard lot. Trade, however, is always a difficult form of charity, and the barter system, common to this coast, being in vogue at the Moravian Mission stations also, practically every Eskimo was in debt to them. In reality this caused a vicious circle, for it encouraged directly the outstanding fault of the Eskimo, his readiness to leave the morrow to care for itself so long as he does not starve to-day. Like a race of children, they need the stimulus of necessity to make them get out and do their best while the opportunity exists. In the past twenty-six years I have made many voyages to one and another of the stations of the Brethren, and have learned to love them all very sincerely as individuals, though their mission policies are their own and not mine.

I remember once in Nain the slob ice had already made ballicaters and the biting cold of winter so far north had set in with all its vigour. There was a heavy sea and a gale of wind. One of two boats which had been out all day had not come in. The sea was so rough and the wind so strong that the occupants of the first boat could not face it, and so had run in under the land and walked all the way round, towing their boat by a long line from the shore. Night came on and the second boat had not appeared. Next morning the Nain folk knew that some accident must have happened. Some men reported that the evening before they had seen through a glass the boat trying to beat against the storm, and then disappear. The Eskimos gathered together to see what could be done and then decided that it was kismet — and went their way. The following evening a tiny light was seen on the far shore of the bay — some one must be alive there. There was no food or shelter there, and it was obvious that help was needed. The gale was still blowing in fury and the sea was as rough as ever, and Eskimos and missionaries decided that in their unseaworthy boats they could do nothing. There was one dissentient voice — Brother Schmidt; and he went and rescued them. One was nearly spent. When their boat had capsized, one man, a woman, and a lad had been drowned, but two men had succeeded in getting into their kajaks and floated off when the disaster happened.

With October came the necessity for returning South,

ESKIMO GIRLS

and the long dark nights spent at the little fishing stations as we journeyed from place to place proved all too short. The gatherings for lantern meetings, for simple services, for spinning yarns, together with medicine and such surgery as we could accomplish under the circumstances, made every moment busy and enjoyable. One outstanding feature, however, everywhere impressed an Englishman — the absolute necessity for some standard medium of exchange. Till one has seen the truck system at work, its evil effects in enslaving and demoralizing the poor are impossible to realize.

All the length and breadth of the coast, the poorer people would show me their "settling up" as they called their account, though many never got as far as having any "settling up" given them — so they lived and died in debt to their merchant. They never knew the independence of a dollar in their pockets and the consequent incentive and value of thrift.

It was incredible to me that even large concerns like the Hudson Bay Company would not pay in cash for valuable furs, and that so many dealers in the necessities of life should be still able to hold free men in economic bondage. It seemed a veritable chapter from "Through the Looking Glass," to hear the "grocer" and "haberdasher" talking of "my people," meaning their patrons, and holding over them the whip of refusal to sell them necessities in their hour of need if at any time they dealt with outsiders, however much to their advantage such a course might be.

This fact was first impressed upon me in an odd way. Early in the summer an Eskimo had come aboard the hospital ship with a bear skin and a few other furs to sell. We had not only been delighted with the chance to buy them, but had spread them all around the cabin and taken a picture of him in the middle. Later in the season, while showing my photograph album to a trader, he had suddenly remarked, "Why, what's —— doing here?"

"Selling me some beautiful furs," I replied.

"Oh! was he?" said the man. "I'll make him sing for selling the furs for which I supplied him."

It was no salve to his fretfulness when I assured him that I had paid in good English gold, and that his "dealer" would be as honest with the money as the system had made him. But the trader knew that the truck system creates slippery, tricky men; and the fisherman openly declares war on the merchant, making the most of his few opportunities to outwit his opponent.

A few years later a man brought a silver fox skin aboard my ship, just such a one as I had been requested by an English lady to secure for her. As fulfilling such a request would involve me in hostilities (which, however, I do not think were useless), I asked the man, who was wretchedly poor, if he owed the skin to the trader.

"I am in debt," he replied, "but they will only allow me eight dollars off my account for this skin, and I want to buy some food."

"Very well," I answered. "If you will promise to go at once and pay eight dollars off your debt, I will give you eight gold sovereigns for this skin."

To this he agreed, and faithfully carried out the agreement — while the English lady scored a bargain, and I a very black mark in the books of my friend the trader.

On another occasion my little steamer had temporarily broken down, and to save time I had journeyed on in the jolly-boat, leaving the cook to steer the vessel after me. I wanted to visit a very poor family, one of whose eight children I had taken to hospital for bone tuberculosis the previous year, and to whom the Mission had made a liberal grant of warm clothing. As the steamer had not come along by night, I had to sleep in the tiny one-roomed shack which served as a home. True, since it stood on the edge of the forest, there was little excuse that it was no larger; but the father, a most excellent, honest, and faithful worker, was obviously discouraged. He had not nearly enough proper food for his family; clothing was even more at a discount; tools with which to work were almost as lacking as in a cave man's dwelling; the whole family was going to pieces from sheer discouragement. The previous winter on the opposite bank of the same river, called Big River, a neighbour had in desperation sent his wife and eldest boy out of the house, killed his young family, and then shot himself.

When night came five of the children huddled together for warmth in one bed, and the parents and balance of the family in the other. I slept on the floor near the door in my sleeping-bag, with my nose glued to the crack to get a breath of God's cold air, in spite of the need for warmth — for not a blanket did the house possess. When I asked, a little hurt, where were the blankets which we had sent last year, the mother somewhat indignantly pointed to various trousers and coats which betrayed their final resting-place, and remarked, "If you'se had five lads all trying to get under one covering to onct, Doctor, you'd soon know what would happen to that blanket."

Early in the morning I made a boiling of cocoa, and took the two elder boys out for a seal hunt while waiting for my steamer. I was just in time to see one boy carefully upset his mug of cocoa, when he thought I was not looking, and replace it with cold spring water. "I 'lows I'se not accustomed to no sweetness" was his simple explanation. It was raw and damp as we rowed into the estuary at sunrise in search of the seals. I was chilly even in a well-lined leather coat. But the two shock-headed boys, clad in ancient cotton shirts, and with what had once been only cotton overall jackets, were as jolly as crickets, and apparently almost unduly warm. The Labrador has taught me one truth, which as a physician I never forget, that is, coddling is the terrible menace of civilization, and "to endure hardness" is the best preparation for a "good soldier." On leaving, I promised to send to those boys, whose contentment and cheerfulness greatly endeared them to me, a dozen good fox traps in order to give them a chance for the coming winter. Such a gift as those old iron rat traps seemed in their eyes! When at last they arrived, and were really their own possessions, no prince could have been prouder than they. The next summer as I steamed North, we called in at D—— B——'s house. The same famine in the land seemed to prevail; the same lack of apparently everything which I should have wanted. But the old infective smile was still presented with an almost religious ceremonial, and my friend produced from his box a real silver fox skin. "I kept it for you'se, Doctor," he said, "though us had n't ne'er a bit in t' house. I know'd you'd do better 'n we with he."

I promised to try, and on my way called in at some northern islands where my friend, Captain Bartlett, father of the celebrated "Captain Bob" of North Pole fame, carried on a summer trade and fishery. He himself was a great seal and cod fisherman, and a man known for his generous sympathy for others.

"Do your best for me, Captain Will," I asked as I handed over the skin — and on coming South I found a complete winter diet laid out for me to take to D—— B——'s little house. It was a veritable full load for the small carrying capacity of my little craft.

When we arrived at the house on the promontory, however, it was locked up and the family gone. They were off fishing on the outer islands, so all we could do was to break in the door, pile up the things inside, bar it up again, affixing a notice warning off bears, dogs, and all poachers, and advising Dick that it was the price of his pelt. In the note we also told him to put all the fur he caught the following winter in a barrel and "sit on it" till we came along, if he wanted a chance to get ahead. This he did almost literally. We ourselves took his barrel to the nearest cash buyer, and ordered for him goods for cash in St. John's to the full amount realized. The fur brought more than his needs, and he was able to help out neighbours by reselling at cash prices. This he did till the day of his death, when he left me, as his executor, with a couple of hundred good dollars in cash to divide among his children.

It was experiments like this which led me in later years to start the small coöperative distributive stores, in spite of the knowledge of the opposition and criticism it would involve. How can one preach the gospel of love to a hungry people by sermons, or a gospel of healing to under-fed children by pills, while one feels that practical teaching in home economics is what one would most wish if in their position? The more broad-minded critics themselves privately acknowledged this to me. One day a Northern furrier, an excellent and more intelligent man than ordinary, came to me as a magistrate to insist that a trading company keep its bargain by paying him in cash for a valuable fox skin. They were trying to compel him to take flour and supplies from them at prices far in excess of those at which he could purchase the goods in St. John's, *via* the mail steamer.

When asked to act as a justice of the peace for the

Colony, I had thought it my duty to accept the responsibility. Already it had led me into a good deal of trouble. But that I should be forced to seize the large store of a company, and threaten an auction of goods for payment, without even a policeman to back me up, had never entered my mind. It was, however, exactly what I now felt called upon to do. To my intense surprise and satisfaction the trader immediately turned round and said: "You are quite right. The money shall be paid at once. The truck system is a mistaken policy, and loses us many customers." It was Saturday night. We had decided to have a service for the fishermen the next day, but had no place in which to gather. Therefore, after we had settled the business I took my pluck in my hands, and said:

"It's Sunday to-morrow. Would you lend us your big room for prayers in the morning?"

"Why, certainly," he replied; and he was present himself and sang as heartily as any man in the meeting. Nor did he lose a good customer on account of his open-mindedness.

CHAPTER VII

THE PEOPLE OF LABRADOR

SINCE the publication of the book "Labrador, the Country and the People," the means of transportation to the coast have been so improved that each year brings us an increasing number of visitors to enjoy the attractions of this sub-arctic land. So many misconceptions have arisen, however, as to the country and its inhabitants, and one is so often misrepresented as distorting conditions, that it seems wise at this point to try and answer a few questions which are so familiar to us who live on the coast as to appear almost negligible.

The east coast of Labrador belongs to Newfoundland, and is not part of the territory of Canada, although the ill-defined boundary between the two possessions has given rise to many misunderstandings. Newfoundland is an autonomous government, having its own Governor sent out from England, Prime Minister, and Houses of Parliament in the city of St. John's. Instead of being a province of Canada, as is often supposed, and an arrangement which some of us firmly believe would result in the ultimate good of the Newfoundlanders, it stands in the same relationship to England as does the great Dominion herself. Labrador is owned by Newfoundland, so that legally the Labradormen are Newfoundlanders, though they have no representation in the Newfoundland Government. At Blanc Sablon, on the north coast in the Straits of Belle Isle, the Canadian Labrador begins, so far as the coast-line is concerned. The hinterland of the Province of Ungava is also a Canadian possession.

The original natives of the Labrador were Eskimos

and bands of roving Indians. The ethnologist would find fruitful opportunities in the country. The Eskimos, one of the most interesting of primitive races, have still a firm foothold in the North — chiefly around the five stations of the Moravian Brethren, upon whose heroic work I need not now dilate. The Montaignais Indians roam the interior. They are a branch of the ancient Algonquin race who held North America as far west as the Rockies. They are the hereditary foes of the Eskimos, whole settlements of whom they have more than once exterminated. Gradually, with the influx of white settlers from Devon and Dorset, from Scotland and France, the "Innuits" were driven farther and farther north, until there are only some fifteen hundred of them remaining to-day. Among them the Moravians have been working for the past hundred and thirty-five years. A few bands of Indians still continue to rove the interior, occasionally coming out to the coast to dispose of their furs, and obtain such meagre supplies as their mode of life requires. The balance of the inhabitants of the country are white men of our own blood and religion — men of the sea and dear to the Anglo-Saxon heart.

During the past years it has been the experience of many of my colleagues, as well as myself, that as soon as one mentions the fact that part of our work is done on the north shore of Newfoundland, one's audience loses interest, and there arises the question: "But Newfoundland is a prosperous island. Why is it necessary to carry on a charitable enterprise there?"

There is a sharp demarcation between main or southern Newfoundland and the long finger of land jutting northward, which at Cape Bauld splits the polar current, so that the shores of the narrow peninsula are continuously bathed in icy waters. The country is swept by

BATTLE HARBOUR

biting winds, and often for weeks enveloped in a chilly
and dripping blanket of fog. The climate at the north end
of the northward-pointing finger is more severe than on
the Labrador side of the Straits. Indeed, my friend, Mr.
George Ford, for twenty-seven years factor of the Hudson
Bay Company at Nakvak, told me that even in the extreme north of Labrador he never really knew what cold
was until he underwent the penetrating experience of a
winter at St. Anthony. The Lapp reindeer herders whom
we brought over from Lapland, a country lying well
north of the Arctic Circle, after spending a winter near
St. Anthony, told me that they had never felt anything
like that kind of cold, and that they really could not put
up with it! The climate of the actual Labrador is clear,
cold, and still, with a greater proportion of sunshine than
the northern peninsula of Newfoundland. As a matter of
fact, our station at St. Anthony is farther north and
farther east than two of our hospitals on the Labrador
side of the Straits of Belle Isle. Along that north side the
gardens of the people are so good that their produce
affords a valuable addition to the diet — but not so here.

The dominant industry of the whole Colony is its fisheries — the ever-recurrent pursuit of the luckless cod,
salmon, herring, halibut, and lobster in summer, and the
seal fishery in the month of March. It is increasingly difficult to overestimate the importance, not merely to the
British Empire, but to the entire world, of the invaluable
food-supply procured by the hardy fishermen of these
northern waters. Only the other day the captain of a
patrol boat told me that he had just come over from
service on the North Sea, and in his opinion it would be
years before those waters could again be fished, owing to
the immense numbers of still active mines which would
render such an attempt disproportionately hazardous.

From this point of view, if from no other more disinterested angle, we owe a great and continuous debt to the splendid people of Britain's oldest colony. It was among these white fishermen that I came out to work primarily, the floating population which every summer, some twenty thousand strong, visits the coasts of Labrador; and later including the white resident settlers of the Labrador and North Newfoundland coasts as well.

The conditions prevailing among some of the people at the north end of Newfoundland and of Labrador itself should not be confused with those of their neighbours to the southward. Chronic poverty is, however, very far from being universally prevalent in the northern district. Some of the fishermen lead a comfortable, happy, and prosperous life; but my old diaries, as well as my present observations, furnish all too many instances in which families exist well within the danger-line of poverty, ignorance, and starvation.

The privations which the inhabitants of the French or Treaty shore and of Labrador have had to undergo, and their isolation from so many of the benefits of civilization, have had varying effects on the residents of the coast to-day. While a resourceful and kindly, hardy and hospitable people have been developed, yet one sometimes wonders exactly into what era an inhabitant of say the planet Mars would place our section of the North Country if he were to alight here some crisp morning in one of his unearthly machines. For we are a reactionary people in matters of religion and education; and our very "speech betrays us," belonging as so many of its expressions do to the days when the Pilgrims went up to Canterbury, or a certain Tinker wrote of another and more distant pilgrimage to the City of Zion.

The people are, naturally, Christians of a devout and

simple faith. The superstitions still found among them are attributable to the remoteness of the country from the current of the world's thought, the natural tendency of all seafaring people, and the fact that the days when the forbears of these fishermen left "Merrie England" to seek a living by the harvest of the sea, and finally settled on these rocky shores, were those when witches and hobgoblins and charms and amulets were accepted beliefs.

Nevertheless, to-day as a medical man one is startled to see a fox's or wolf's head suspended by a cord from the centre, and to learn that it will always twist the way from which the wind is going to blow. One man had a barometer of this kind hanging from his roof, and explained that the peculiar fact was due to the nature of the animals, which in life always went to windward of others; but if you had a seal's head similarly suspended, it would turn from the wind, owing to the timid character of that creature. Moreover, it surprises one to be assured, on the irrefutable and quite unquestioned authority of "old Aunt Anne Sweetapple," that aged cats always become playful before a gale of wind comes on.

"I never gets sea boils," one old chap told me the other day.

"How is that?" I asked.

"Oh! I always cuts my nails on a Monday, so I never has any."

There is a great belief in fairies on the coast. A man came to me once to cure what he was determined to believe was a balsam on his baby's nose. The birthmark to him resembled that tree. More than one had given currency if not credence to the belief that the reason why the bull's-eye was so hard to hit in one of our running deer rifle matches was that we had previously charmed it. If a woman sees a hare without cutting out and keeping a portion of the dress she is then wearing, her child will be born with a hare-lip.

When stripping a patient for examination, I noticed that he removed from his neck what appeared to be a very large scapular. I asked him what it could be. It was a haddock's fin-bone — a charm against rheumatism. The peculiarity of the fin consists in the fact that the fish must be taken from the water and the fin cut out before the animal touches anything whatever, especially the boat. Any one who has seen a trawl hauled knows how difficult a task this would be, with the jumping, squirming fish to cope with.

Protestant and Catholic alike often sew up bits of paper, with prayers written on them, in little sacks that are worn around the neck as an amulet; and green worsted tied around the wrist is reported to be a never-failing cure for hemorrhage.

Every summer some twenty thousand fishermen travel "down North" in schooners, as soon as ever the ice breaks sufficiently to allow them to get along. They are the "Labrador fishermen," and they come from South Newfoundland, from Nova Scotia, from Gloucester, and even Boston. Some Newfoundlanders take their families down and leave them in summer tilts on the land near the fishing grounds during the season. When fall comes they pick them up again and start for their winter homes "in the South," leaving only a few hundreds of scattered "Liveyeres" in possession of the Labrador.

We were much surprised one day to notice a family moving their house in the middle of the fishing season, especially when we learned that the reason was that a spirit had appropriated their dwelling.

Stephen Leacock would have obtained much valuable

data for his essay on "How to Become a Doctor" if he had ever chanced to sail along "the lonely Labrador." In a certain village one is confidently told of a cure for asthma, as simple as it is infallible. It consists merely of taking the tips of all one's finger-nails, carefully allowed to grow long, and cutting them off with sharp scissors. In another section a powder known as "Dragon's Blood" is very generally used as a plaster. It appears quite inert and harmless. A little farther south along the coast is a baby suffering from ophthalmia. The doctor has only been called in because blowing sugar in its eyes has failed to cure it.

A colleague of mine was visiting on his winter rounds in a delightful village some forty miles south of St. Anthony Hospital. The "swiles" (seals) had struck in, and all hands were out on the ice, eager to capture their share of these valuable animals. But snow-blindness had incontinently attacked the men, and had rendered them utterly unable to profit by their good fortune. The doctor's clinic was long and busy that night. The following morning he was, however, amazed to see many of his erstwhile patients wending their way seawards, each with one eye treated on his prescription, but the other (for safety's sake) doctored after the long-accepted methods of the talent of the village — tansy poultices and sugar being the acknowledged favourites. The consensus of opinion obviously was that the stakes were too high for a man to offer up both eyes on the altar of modern medicine.

In the course of many years' practice the methods for the treatment and extraction of offending molars which have come to my attention are numerous, but none can claim a more prompt result than the following: First you attach a stout, fine fish-line firmly to the tooth. Next you lash the other end to the latch of the door — we do not use knobs in this country. You then make the patient stand back till there is a nice tension on the line, when suddenly you make a feint as if to strike him in the eye. Forgetful of the line, he leaps back to avoid the blow. Result, painless extraction of the tooth, which should be found hanging to the latch.

Although there have been clergyman of the Church of England and Methodist denominations on the coast for many years past — devoted and self-sacrificing men who have done most unselfish work — still, their visits must be infrequent. One of them told me in North Newfoundland that once, when he happened to pass through a little village with his dog team on his way South, the man of one house ran out and asked him to come in. "Sorry I have no time," he replied. "Well, just come in at the front door and out at the back, so we can say that a minister has been in the house," the fisherman answered.

Even to-day, to the least fastidious, the conditions of travel leave much to be desired. The coastal steamers are packed far beyond their sleeping or sitting capacity. On the upper deck of the best of these boats I recall that there are two benches, each to accommodate four people. The steamer often carries three hundred in the crowded season of the fall of the year. One retires at night under the misapprehension that the following morning will find these seats still available. On ascending the companionway, however, one's gaze is met by a heterogeneous collection of impedimenta. The benches are buried as irretrievably as if they "had been carried into the midst of the sea." Almost anything may have been piled on them, from bales of hay — among which my wife once sat for two days — to the nucleus of a chicken farm, destined, let us say, for the Rogues' Roost Bight.

As the sturdy little steamer noses her way into some picturesque harbour and blows a lusty warning of her approach, small boats are seen putting off from the shore and rowing or sculling toward her with almost indecorous rapidity. Lean over the rail for a minute with me, and watch the freight being unloaded into one of these bobbing little craft. The hatch of the steamer is opened, a most unmusical winch commences operations — and a sewing machine emerges *de profundis*. This is swung giddily out over the sea by the crane and dropped on the thwarts of the waiting punt. One shudders to think of the probably fatal shock received by the vertebræ of that machine. One's sympathies, however, are almost immediately enlisted in the interest and fortunes of a young and voiceful pig, which, poised in the blue, unwillingly experiences for the moment the fate of the coffin of the Prophet. Great shouting ensues as a baby is carried down the ship's ladder and deposited in the rocking boat. A bag of beans, of the variety known as "haricot," is the next candidate. A small hole has been torn in a corner of the burlap sack, out of which trickles a white and ominous stream. The last article to join the galaxy is a tub of butter. By a slight mischance the tub has "burst abroad," and the butter, a golden and gleaming mass, — with unexpected consideration having escaped the ministrations of the winch, — is passed from one pair of fishy hands to another, till it finds a resting-place by the side of the now quiescent pig.

We pass out into the open again, bound for the next port of call. If the weather chances to be "dirty," the sufferers from *mal-de-mer* lie about on every available spot, be it floor or bench, and over these prostrate forms must one jump as one descends to the dining-saloon for lunch. It may be merely due to the special keenness of

my professional sense, but the apparent proportion of
the halt, lame, and blind who frequent these steamers
appears out of all relation to the total population of the
coast. Across the table is a man with an enormous white
rag swathing his thumb. The woman next him looks out
on a blue and altered world from behind a bandaged eye.
Beside one sits a young fisherman, tenderly nursing his
left lower jaw, his enjoyment of the fact that his appetite
is unimpaired by the vagaries of the North Atlantic
tempered by an unremitting toothache.

But the cheerful kindliness and capability of the captain, the crew, and the passengers, on whatever boat you
may chance to travel, pervades the whole ship like an
atmosphere, and makes one forget any slight discomfort
in a justifiable pride that as an Anglo-Saxon one can
claim kinship to these "Vikings of to-day."

Life is hard in White Bay. An outsider visiting there in
the spring of the year would come to the conclusion that
if nothing further can be done for these people to make
a more generous living, they should be encouraged to go
elsewhere. The number of cases of tubercle, anæmia, and
dyspepsia, of beri-beri and scurvy, all largely attributable to poverty of diet, is very great; and the relative
poverty, even compared with that of the countries
which I have been privileged to visit, is piteous. The solution of such a problem does not, however, lie in removing a people from their environment, but in trying
to make the environment more fit for human habitation.

The hospitality of the people is unstinted and beautiful. They will turn out of their beds at any time to make
a stranger comfortable, and offer him their last crust into
the bargain, without ever expecting or asking a penny of
recompense. But here, as all the world over, the sublime
and the ridiculous go hand in hand. On one of my dog

trips the first winter which I spent at St. Anthony, the bench on which I slept was the top of the box used for hens. This would have made little difference to me, but unfortunately it contained a youthful and vigorous rooster, which, mistaking the arrival of so many visitors for some strange herald of morning, proceeded every half-hour to salute it with premature and misdirected zeal, utterly incompatible with unbroken repose just above his head. It was possible, without moving one's limbs much, to reach through the bars and suggest better things to him; but owing to the inequality which exists in most things, one invariably captured a drowsy hen, while the more active offender eluded one with ease. Lighting matches to differentiate species under such exceptional circumstances in the pursuit of knowledge was quite out of the question.

A visit to one house on the French shore I shall not easily forget. The poor lad of sixteen years had hip disease, and lay dying. The indescribable dirt I cannot here picture. The bed, the house, and everything in it were full of vermin, and the poor boy had not been washed since he took to bed three or four months before. With the help of a clergyman who was travelling with me at the time, the lad was chloroformed and washed. We then ordered the bedding to be burned, provided him with fresh garments, and put him into a clean bed. The people's explanation was that he was in too much pain to be touched, and so they could do nothing. We cleansed and drained his wounds and left what we could for him. Had he not been so far gone, we should have taken him to the hospital, but I feared that he would not survive the journey.

Although at the time it often seemed an unnecessary expenditure of effort in an already overcrowded day,

one now values the records of the early days of one's
life on the coast. In my notebook for 1895 I find the
following: "The desolation of Labrador at this time
is easy to understand. No Newfoundlanders were left
north of us; not a vessel in sight anywhere. The
ground was all under snow, and everything caught over
with ice except the sea. I think that I must describe
one house, for it seems a marvel that any man could
live in it all winter, much less women and children.
It was ten feet by twenty, one storey high, made of mud
and boards, with half a partition to divide bedroom
from the sitting-room kitchen. If one adds a small
porch filled with dirty, half-starved dogs, and refuse
of every kind, an ancient and dilapidated stove in the
sitting part of the house, two wooden benches against
the walls, a fixed rude table, some shelves nailed to the
wall, and two boarded-up beds, one has a fairly accurate description of the furnishings. Inside were fourteen persons, sleeping there, at any rate for a night or
two. The ordinary regular family of a man and wife and
four girls was to be increased this winter by the man's
brother, his wife, and four boys from twelve months to
seven years of age. His brother had 'handy enough
flour,' but no tea or molasses. The owner was looking
after Newfoundland Rooms, for which he got flour, tea,
molasses, and firewood for the winter. The people assure me that one man, who was aboard us last fall just
as we were going South, starved to death, and many
more were just able to hold out till spring. The man,
they tell me, ate his only dog as his last resource."

I sent one day a barrel of flour and some molasses
to a poor widow with seven children at Stag Islands.
She was starving even in summer. She was just eating
fish, which she and her eldest girl caught, and drinking

water — no flour, no tea, nothing. Two winters before she and her eldest girl sawed up three thousand feet of planking to keep the wolf from the little ones. The girl managed the boat and fished in summer, drove the dogs and komatik and did the shooting for which they could afford powder in winter.

A man, having failed to catch a single salmon beyond what he was forced to eat, left in his little boat to row down to the Inlet to try for codfish. To get a meal — breakfast — and a little flour to sustain life on the way, he had to sell his anchor before he left.

The life of the sea, with all its attractions, is at best a hazardous calling, and it speaks loud in the praise of the capacity and simple faith of our people that in the midst of a trying and often perilous environment, they retain so quiet and kindly a temper of mind. During my voyage to the seal fishery I recall that one day at three o'clock the men were all called in. Four were missing. We did not find them till we had been steaming for an hour and a half. They were caught on pans some mile or so apart in couples, and were in prison. We were a little anxious about them, but the only remark which I heard, when at last they came aboard, was, "Leave the key of your box the next time, Ned."

To those who claim that Labrador is a land of plenty I would offer the following incident in refutation. At Holton on a certain Sunday morning the leader of the church services came aboard the hospital steamer and asked me for a Bible. Some sacrilegious pigs which had been brought down to fatten on the fish, driven to the verge of starvation by the scarcity of that article, had broken into the church illicitly one night, and not only destroyed the cloth, but had actually torn up

and eaten the Bible. In reply to inquiry I gave it as
my opinion that it would be no sin to eat the pork of
the erring quadrupeds.

Once when I was cruising on the North Labrador
coast I anchored one day between two desolate islands
some distance out in the Atlantic, a locality which
in those days was frequented by many fishing craft.
My anchors were scarcely down when a boat from a
small Welsh brigantine came aboard, and asked me to
go at once and see a dying girl. She proved to be the
only woman among a host of men, and was servant
in one of the tiny summer fishing huts, cooking and
mending for the men, and helping with the fish when required. I found her in a rude bunk in a dark corner
of the shack. She was almost eighteen, and even by
the dim light of my lantern and in contrast with the
sordid surroundings, I could see that she was very
pretty. A brief examination convinced me that she was
dying. The tender-hearted old captain, whose aid had
been called in as the only man with a doctor's box and
therefore felt to be better qualified to use it than
others, was heart-broken. He had pronounced the case
to be typhoid, to be dangerous and contagious, and had
wisely ordered the fishermen, who were handling food
for human consumption, to leave him to deal with the
case alone. He told me at once that he had limited
his attentions to feeding her, and that though helpless for over a fortnight, and at times unconscious, the
patient had not once been washed or the bed changed.
The result, even with my experience, appalled me.
But while there is life in a young patient there is always hope, and we at once set to work on our Augean
task. By the strangest coincidence it was an inky dark
night outside, with a low fog hanging over the water,

and the big trap boat, with a crew of some six men, among them the skipper's sons, had been missing since morning. The skipper had stayed home out of sympathy for his servant girl, and his mind was torn asunder by the anxiety for the girl and his fear for his boys.

When night fell, the old captain and I were through with the hardest part of our work. We had new bedding on the bed and the patient clean and sleeping quietly. Still the boat and its precious complement did not come. Every few minutes the skipper would go out and listen, and stare into the darkness. The girl's heart suddenly failed, and about midnight her spirit left this world. The captain and I decided that the best thing to do was to burn everything — and in order to avoid publicity to do it at once. So having laboriously carried it all out onto the edge of the cliff, we set a light to the pile and were rewarded with a bonfire which would have made many a Guy Fawkes celebration. Quite unintentionally we were sending out great streams of light into the darkness over the waters away down below us, and actually giving the longed-for signal to the missing boat. Her crew worked their way in the fog to life and safety by means of the blazing and poor discarded "properties" of the soul preceding us to our last port.

Although our work has lain almost entirely among the white population of the Labrador and North Newfoundland coasts, still it has been our privilege occasionally to come in contact with the native races, and to render them such services, medical or otherwise, as lay within our power. Our doctor at Harrington on the Canadian Labrador is appointed by the Canadian Government as Indian Agent.

Once, when my own boat was anchored in Davis Inlet, a band of roving Indians had come to the post for barter and supplies. Our steamer was a source of great interest to them. Our steam whistle they would gladly have purchased, after they had mastered their first fears. At night we showed them some distress rockets and some red and blue port flares. The way those Indians fled from the port flares was really amusing, and no one enjoyed it more than they did, for the shouting and laughter, after they had picked themselves out of the scuppers where they had been rolling on top of one another, wakened the very hills with their echoes. Next morning one lonely-looking brave came on board, and explained to me by signs and grunts that during the entertainment a white counter, or Hudson Bay dollar, had rolled out of the lining of his hat into our woodpile. An elaborate search failed to reveal its whereabouts, but as there was no reason to doubt him, I decided to make up the loss to him out of our clothesbag. Fortunately a gorgeous purple rowing blazer came readily to hand, and with this and a helmet, both of which he put on at once, the poor fellow was more than satisfied. Indeed, on the wharf he was the envy of the whole band.

At night they slept in the bunkhouse, and they presented a sight which one is not likely to forget — especially one lying on his back on the table, with his arms extended and his head hanging listlessly over the edge. One felt sorely tempted to put a pin into him to see if he really were alive, but we decided to abstain for prudential reasons.

We had among the garments on board three not exactly suited to the white settlers, so I told the agent to let the Indians have a rifle shooting match for them.

They were a fox huntsman's red broadcloth tail-coat,
with all the glory of gilt buttons, a rather dilapidated
red golf blazer, and a white, cavalryman's Eton coat,
with silver buttons, and the coat-of-arms on. Words fail
me to paint the elation of the winner of the fox hunting
coat; while the wearer of the cavalry mess jacket was
not the least bit daunted by the fact that when he got
it on he could hardly breathe. I must say that he wore
it over a deerskin kossak, which is not the custom of
cavalrymen, I am led to believe.

The coast-line from Ramah to Cape Chidley is just
under one hundred miles, and on it live a few scattered
Eskimo hunters. Mr. Ford knew every one of them
personally, having lived there twenty-seven years. It
appears that a larger race of Eskimos called "Tunits,"
to whom the present race were slaves, used to be on
this section of the coast. At Nakvak there are remains of them. In Hebron, the same year that we
met the Indians at Davis Inlet, we saw Pomiuk's
mother. Her name is Regina, and she is now married
to Valentine, the king of the Eskimos there. I have
an excellent photograph of a royal dinner party, a thing
which I never possessed before. The king and queen
and a solitary courtier are seated on the rocks, gnawing
contentedly raw walrus bones — "ivik" they call it.

. The Eskimos one year suffered very heavily from an
epidemic of influenza — the germ doubtless imported
by some schooner from the South. Like all primitive
peoples, they had no immunity to the disease, and the
suffering and mortality were very high. It was a pathetic sight as the lighter received its load of rude coffins
from the wharf, with all the kindly little people gathered
to tow them to their last resting-place in the shallow
sand at the end of the inlet. The ten coffins in one

grave seemed more the sequence of a battle than of a summer sickness in Labrador. Certainly the hospital move on the part of the Moravians deserved every commendation; though I understand that at their little hospital in Okkak they have not always been able to have a qualified medical man in residence.

One old man, a patient on whose hip I had operated, came and insisted that I should examine the scars. Oddly enough during the operation the Eskimo, who was the only available person whom I had been able to find to hold the light, had fainted, and left me in darkness. I had previously had no idea that their sensibilities were so akin to ours.

At Napatuliarasok Island are some lovely specimens of blue and green and golden Labradorite, a striated feldspar with a glorious sheen. Nothing has ever really been done with this from a commercial point of view; moreover, the samples of gold-bearing quartz, of which such good hopes have been entertained, have so far been found wanting also. In my opinion this is merely due to lack of persevering investigation — for one cannot believe that this vast area of land can be utterly unremunerative.

On one of the old maps of Labrador this terse description is written by the cartographer: "Labrador was discovered by the English. There is nothing in it of any value"; and another historian enlarges on the theme in this fashion: "God made the world in five days, made Labrador on the sixth, and spent the seventh throwing stones at it." It is so near and yet so far, so large a section of the British Empire and yet so little known, and so romantic for its wild grandeur, and many fastnesses still untrodden by the foot of man! The polar current steals from the unknown

A LABRADOR BURIAL

North its ice treasures, and lends them with no niggard hand to this seaboard. There is a never-wearying charm in these countless icebergs, so stately in size and so fantastic in shape and colouring.

The fauna and flora of the country are so varied and exquisite that one wonders why the world of science has so largely passed us by. Perhaps with the advent of hydroplanes, Labrador will come to its own among the countries of the world. Not only the ethnologist and botanist, but the archæologist as well reaps a rich harvest for his labours here. Many relics of a recent stone age still exist. I have had brought to me stone saucepans, lamps, knives, arrow-heads, etc., taken from old graves. It is the Eskimo custom to entomb with the dead man all and every possession which he might want hereafter, the idea being that the spirit of the implement accompanies the man's spirit. Relics of ancient whaling establishments, possibly early Basque, are found in plenty at one village, while even to-day the trapper there needing a runner for his komatik can always hook up a whale's jaw or rib from the mud of the harbour. Relics of rovers of the sea, who sought shelter on this uncharted coast with its million islands, are still to be found. A friend of mine was one day looking from his boat into the deep, narrow channel in front of his house, when he perceived some strange object in the mud. With help he raised it, and found a long brass "Long Tom" cannon, which now stands on the rocks at that place. Remains of the ancient French occupation should also be procurable near the seat of their deserted capital near Bradore.

My friend, Professor Reginald Daly, head of the Department of Geology at Harvard University, after having spent a summer with me on the coast, wrote as follows:

"We crossed the Straits of Belle Isle once more, homeward bound. Old Jacques Cartier, searching for an Eldorado, found Labrador, and in disgust called it the 'Land of Cain.' A century and a half afterward Lieutenant Roger Curtis wrote of it as a ' country formed of frightful mountains, and unfruitful valleys, a prodigious heap of barren rock'; and George Cartwright, in his gossipy journal, summed up his impressions after five and twenty years on the coast. He said, 'God created this country last of all, and threw together there the refuse of his materials as of no use to mankind.'

"We have learned at last the vital fact that Nature has set apart her own picture galleries where men may resort if for a time they would forget human contrivances. Such a wilderness is Labrador, a kind of mental and moral sanitarium. The beautiful is but the visible splendor of the true. The enjoyment of a visit to the coast may consist not alone in the impressions of the scenery; there may be added the deeper pleasure of reading out the history of noble landscapes, the sculptured monuments of elemental strife and revolutions of distant ages."

CHAPTER VIII

LECTURING AND CRUISING

WE had now been coming for some two years to the coast, and the problem was assuming larger proportions than I felt the Society at home ought to be called on to finance. It seemed advisable, therefore, to try and raise money in southern Newfoundland and Canada. So under the wing of the most famous seal and fish killer, Captain Samuel Blandford, I next visited and lectured in St. John's, Harbour Grace, and Carbonear.

The towns in Newfoundland are not large. Its sectarian schools and the strong denominational feeling between the churches so greatly divide the people that united efforts for the Kingdom of God were extremely rare before the war. Even now there is no Y.M.C.A. or Y.W.C.A. in the Colony. The Boys' Brigade, which we initiated our first year, divided as it grew in importance, into the Church Lads Brigade, the Catholic Cadet Corps, and the Methodist Guards.

Dr. Bobardt, my young Australian colleague, and I now decided to cross over to Halifax. We had only a certain amount of money for the venture; it was our first visit to Canada, and we knew no one. We carried credentials, however, from the Marquis of Ripon and other reputable persons. If we had had experience as commercial travellers, this would have been child's play. But our education had been in an English school and university; and when finally we sat at breakfast at the Halifax hotel we felt like fish out of water. Such success as we obtained subsequently I attribute entirely to what then seemed to me my colleague's colonial "cheek." He insisted that we should call on the most prominent persons at once, the Prime Minister, the General in charge of the garrison, the Presidents of the Board of Trade and University, the Governor of the Province, and all the leading clergymen. There have been times when I have hesitated about getting my anchors for sea, when the barometer was falling, the wind in, and a fog-bank on the horizon — but now, years after, I still recall my reluctance to face that ordeal. But like most things, the obstacles were largely in one's own mind, and the kindness which we received left me entirely overwhelmed. Friends formed a regular committee to keep a couple of cots going in our hospital, to collect supplies, and sent us to Montreal with introductions and endorsements. Some of these people have since been lifelong helpers of the Labrador Mission.

By the time we reached Montreal, our funds were getting low, but Dr. Bobardt insisted that we must engage the best accommodations, even if it prevented our travelling farther west. The result was that reporters insisted on interviewing him as to the purpose of an Australian coming to Montreal; and I was startled to see a long account which he had jokingly given them published in the morning papers, stating that his purpose was to materialize the All Red Line and arrange closer relations between Australia and Canada. According to his report my object was to inspect my ranch in Alberta. Life to him, whether on the Labrador Coast, in an English school, or in his Australian home, was one perpetual picnic.

Naturally, our most important interview was with Lord Strathcona. He was President of the Hudson Bay Company, the Canadian Pacific Railroad, and the

Bank of Montreal. As a poor Scotch lad named Donald Smith he had lived for thirteen years of his early life in Labrador. There he had found a wife and there his daughter was born. From the very first he was thoroughly interested in our work, and all through the years until his death in 1914 his support was maintained, so that at the very time he died we were actually due to visit him the following month at Knelsworth.

We hired the best hall and advertised Sir Donald as our chairman. To save expense Dr. Bobardt acted in the ticket-box. When Sir Donald came along, not having seen him previously, he insisted on collecting fifty cents from him as from the rest. When Sir Donald strongly protested that he was our chairman, the shrewd young doctor merely replied that several others before him had made the same remark. Every one in the city knew Sir Donald; and when the matter was explained to him in the greenroom, he was thoroughly pleased with the business-like attitude of the Mission. As we had never seen Canada he insisted that we must take a holiday and visit as far west as British Columbia. All of this he not only arranged freely for us, but even saw to such details as that we should ride on the engine through the Rocky Mountains, and be entertained at his home called "Silver Heights" while in Winnipeg. It was during this trip that I visited "Grenfell Town," a queer little place called after Pascoe Grenfell, of the Bank of England. The marvel of the place to me was the thousands and thousands of acres of splendid farm-land on which no one lived. I promised that I would send the hotel-keeper the Grenfell crest.

Lord Strathcona later presented the Mission with a fine little steamer, the Sir Donald, purchased and equipped at his expense through the Committee in Montreal.

We went back to England very well satisfied with our work. Dr. Bobardt left me and entered the Navy, while I returned the following year and steamed the new boat from Montreal down the St. Lawrence River and the Straits to Battle Harbour. There the Albert, which had sailed again from England with doctors, nurses, and supplies, was to meet me. We had made a fine voyage, visiting all along the coast as we journeyed, and had turned in from sea through the last "run," or passage between islands. We had polished our brass-work, cleaned up our decks, hoisted our flags, all that we might make a triumphant entry on our arrival a few minutes later — when sudddenly, *Buff — Bur–r — Buff*, we rose, staggered, and fell over on a horrible submerged shoal. Our side was gored, our propeller and shaft gone, our keel badly splintered, and the ship left high and dry. When we realized our mistake and the dreadful position into which we had put ourselves, we rowed ashore to the nearest island, walked three or four miles over hill and bog, and from there got a fisherman with a boat to put us over to Battle Harbour Island. The good ship Albert lay at anchor in the harbour. Our new colleagues and old friends were all impatiently waiting to see our fine new steamer speed in with all her flags up — when, instead, two bedraggled-looking tramps, crestfallen almost to weeping, literally crept aboard.

Sympathy took the form of deeds and a crowd at once went round in boats with a museum of implements. Soon they had her off, and our plucky schooner took her in tow all the three hundred miles to the nearest dry-dock at St. John's.

Meanwhile Sir Thomas Roddick, of Montreal, an old Newfoundlander, had presented us with a splendid twenty-foot jolly-boat, rigged with lug-sail and centre-boom. In this I cruised north to Eskimo Bay, harbouring at nights if possible, getting a local pilot when I could, and once being taken bodily on board, craft and all, by a big friendly fishing schooner. It proved a most profitable summer. I was so dependent on the settlers and fishermen for food and hospitality that I learned to know them as would otherwise have been impossible. Far the best road to a seaman's heart is to let him do something for you. Our impressions of a landscape, like our estimates of character, all depend on our viewpoint. Fresh from the more momentous problems of great cities, the interests and misunderstandings of small isolated places bias the mind and make one censorious and resentful. But from the position of a tight corner, that of needing help and hospitality from entire strangers, one learns how large are the hearts and homes of those who live next to Nature. If I knew the Labrador people before (and among such I include the Hudson Bay traders and the Newfoundland fishermen), that summer made me love them. I could not help feeling how much more they gladly and freely did for me than I should have dreamed of doing for them had they come along to my house in London. I have sailed the seas in ocean greyhounds and in floating palaces and in steam yachts, but better than any other I love to dwell on the memories of that summer, cruising the Labrador in a twenty-footer.

That year I was late returning South. Progress is slow in the fall of the year along the Labrador in a boat of that capacity. I was weather-bound, with the snow already on the ground in Square Island Harbour. The fishery of the settlers had been very poor. The traders coming South had passed them by. There were eight

months of winter ahead, and practically no supplies
for the dozen families of the little village. I shall never
forget the confidence of the patriarch of the settlement,
Uncle Jim, whose guest I was. The fact that we were
without butter, and that "sweetness" (molasses) was
low, was scarcely even noticed. I remember as if it
were yesterday the stimulating tang of the frosty air
and the racy problem of the open sea yet to be covered.
The bag of birds which we had captured when we had
driven in for shelter from the storm made our dry-diet
supper sweeter than any Delmonico ten-course dinner,
because we had wrested it ourselves from the reluc-
tant environment. Then last of all came the general
meeting in Uncle Jim's house at night to ask the Lord
to open the windows of heaven for the benefit of the
pathetic little group on the island. Next morning the
first thing on which our eyes lighted was the belated
trader, actually driven north again by the storm, anchored right in the harbour. Of course Uncle Jim
knew that it would be there. Personally, I did not
expect her, so can claim no credit for the telepathy;
but if faith ever did work wonders it was on that occasion. There were laughing faces and happy hearts as
we said good-bye, when my dainty little lady spread her
wings to a fair breeze a day or so later.

The gallant little Sir Donald did herself every credit
the following year, and we not only visited the coast
as far north as Cape Chidley, but explored the narrow
channel which runs through the land into Ungava Bay,
and places Cape Chidley itself on a detached island.

There were a great many fishing schooners far north
that season, and the keen pleasures of exploring a truly
marvellous coast, practically uncharted and unknown,
were redeemed from the reproach of selfishness by the

THE LABRADOR DOCTOR IN SUMMER

numerous opportunities for service to one's fellow men.

Once that summer we were eleven days stuck in the ice, and while there the huge mail steamer broke her propeller, and a boat was sent up to us through the ice to ask for our help. The truck on my mastheads was just up to her deck. The ice was a lot of trouble, but we got her into safety. On board were the superintendent of the Moravian Missions and his wife. They were awfully grateful. The great tub rolled about so in the Atlantic swell that the big ice-pans nearly came on deck. My dainty little lady took no notice of anything and picked her way among the pans like Agag "treading delicately." We had five hours' good push, however, to get into Battle Harbour. It was calm in the ice-field, only the heavy tide made it run and the little "alive" steamer with human skill beat the massive mountains of ice into a cocked hat.

At Indian Tickle there is a nice little church which was built by subscription and free labour the second year we came on the coast. There is one especially charming feature about this building. It stands in such a position that you can see it as you come from the north miles away from the harbour entrance, and it is so situated that it leads directly into the safe anchorage. There are no lights to guide sailors on this coast at all, and yet during September, October, and November, three of the most dangerous months in the year, hundreds of schooners and thousands of men, women, and children are coming into or passing through this harbour on their way to the southward. By a nice arrangement the little east window points to the north — if that is not Irish — and two large bracket lamps can be turned on a pivot, so that the lamps and their reflectors throw a light out to sea. The good planter, at his own expense, often maintains a light here on stormy or dark nights, and "steering straight for it" brings one to safety.

While cruising near Cape Chidley, a schooner signalling with flag at half-mast attracted our attention. On going aboard we found a young man with the globe of one eye ruptured by a gun accident, in great pain, and in danger of losing the other eye sympathetically. Having excised the globe, we allowed him to go back to his vessel, intensely grateful, but full of apprehension as to how his girl would regard him on his return South. It so happened that we had had a gift of false eyes, and we therefore told him to call in at hospital on his way home and take his chance on getting a blue one. While walking over the hill near the hospital that fall I ran into a crowd of young fishermen, whose schooner was wind-bound in the harbour, and who had been into the country for an hour's trouting. One asked me to look at his eye, as something was wrong with it. Being in a hurry, I simply remarked, "Come to hospital, and I'll examine it for you"; whereupon he burst out into a merry laugh, "Why, Doctor, I'm the boy whose eye you removed. This is the glass one you promised. Do you think it will suit her?"

Another time I was called to a large schooner in the same region. There were two young girls on board doing the cooking and cleaning, as was the wont in Newfoundland vessels. One, alas, was seriously ill, having given birth to a premature child, and having lain absolutely helpless, with only a crew of kind but strange men anywhere near. Rolling her up in blankets, we transferred her to the Sir Donald, and steamed for the nearest Moravian station. Here the

necessary treatment was possible, and when we left
for the South a Moravian's good wife accompanied us
as nurse. The girl, however, had no wish to live. "I
want to die, Doctor; I can never go home again." Her
physical troubles had abated, but her mind was made
up to die, and this, in spite of all our care, she did a few
days later. The pathos of the scene as we rowed the
poor child's body ashore for interment on a rocky and
lonely headland, looking out over the great Atlantic,
wrapped simply in the flag of her country, will never be
forgotten by any of us — the silent but unanswerable
reproach on man's utter selfishness. Many such scenes
must rise to the memory of the general practitioner; at
times, thank God, affording those opportunities of doing
more for the patients than simply patching up their
bodies — opportunities which are the real reward for the
"art of healing." Some years later I revisited the grave
of this poor girl, marked by the simple wooden cross
which we had then put up, and bearing the simple inscription:

Suzanne
"Jesus said, Neither do I condemn thee."

The fall trip lasted till late into November, without
our even realizing the fact that snow was on the ground.
Indeed the ponds were all frozen and we enjoyed drives
with dog teams on the land before we had finished
our work and could think of leaving. We had scarcely
left Flowers Cove and were just burying our little
steamer — loaded to the utmost with wood, cut in return for winter clothing — in the dense fog which almost universally maintains in the Straits, and were
rounding the hidden ledges of rock which lie half a
mile offshore, when we discovered a huge trans-Atlantic

liner racing up in our wake. We instantly put down
our helm and scuttled out of the way to avoid the wash,
and almost held our breath as the great steamer dashed
by at twenty miles an hour, between us and the hidden
shoal. She altered her helm as she did so, no doubt
catching her first sight of the lighthouse as she emerged
from the fog-bank, but as it was, she must have passed
within an ace of the shoal. We expected every minute
to see her dash on the top of it, and then she passed out
of sight once more, her light-hearted passengers no
doubt completely unconscious that they had been in
any danger at all.

The last port of call was Henley, or Château, where
formerly the British had placed a fort to defend it against
the French. We had carried round with us a prospective bridegroom, and we were privileged to witness the
wedding, a simple but very picturesque proceeding.
A parson had been fetched from thirty miles away, and
every kind of hospitality provided for the festive event.
But in spite of the warmth of the occasion the weather
turned bitterly cold, the harbour "caught over," and
for a week we were prisoners. When at last the young
ice broke up again, we made an attempt to cross the
Straits, but sea and wind caught us halfway and forced
us to run back, this time in the thick fog. The Straits'
current had carried us a few miles in the meanwhile —
which way we did not know — and the land, hard to
make out as it was in the fog, was white with snow.
However, with the storm increasing and the long dark
night ahead, we took a sporting chance, and ran direct
in on the cliffs. How we escaped shipwreck I do not
know now. We suddenly saw a rock on our bow and
a sheer precipice ahead, twisted round on our heel,
shot between the two, and we knew where we were,

as that is the only rock on a coast-line of twenty miles of beach — but there really is no room between it and the cliff.

All along the coast that year we noticed a change of attitude toward professional medical aid. Confidence in the wise woman, in the seventh son and his "wonderful" power, in the use of charms like green worsted, haddock fins, or scrolls of prayer tied round the neck, had begun to waver. The world talks still of a blind man made to see nineteen hundred years ago; but the coast had recently been more thrilled by the tale of a blind man made to see by "these yere doctors." One was a man who for seventeen years had given up all hope; and two others, old men, parted for years, and whose first occasion of seeing again had revealed to them the fact that they were brothers.

Some lame had also been made to walk — persons who had abandoned hope quite as much as he who lay for forty years by the Pool of Siloam, or for a similar period at the Golden Gate.

One of my first operations had been rendered absolutely inescapable by the great pain caused by a tumour in the leg. The patient had insisted on having five men sit on her while the operation proceeded, as she did not believe it was right to be put to sleep, and, moreover, she secretly feared that she might not wake up again. But now the conversion of the coast had proceeded so far that many were pleading for a winter doctor. At first we did not think it feasible, but my colleague, Dr. Willway, finally volunteered to stay at Battle Harbour. We loaded him up with all our spare assets against the experiment, the hospital being but very ill-equipped for an Arctic winter. When the following summer we approached the coast, it was with real trepidation that I scanned the land for signs of my derelict friend. We felt that he would be gravely altered at least, possibly having grown hair all over his face. When an alert, tanned, athletic figure, neatly tonsured and barbered, at last leaped over our rail, all our sympathy vanished and gave way to jealousy.

One detail, however, had gone wrong. We had anchored our beautiful Sir Donald in his care in a harbour off the long bay on the shores of which he was wintering. He had seen her once or twice in her ice prison, but when he came to look for her in the spring, she had mysteriously disappeared. The ice was there still. There wasn't a vestige of wreckage. She must have sunk, and the hole frozen up. Yet an extended period of "creeping" the bottom with drags and grapples had revealed nothing, and, anyhow, the water not being deep, her masts should have been easily visible. It was not till some time later that we heard from the South that our trusty craft had been picked up some three hundred miles to the southward and westward, well out in a heavy ice-pack, and right in amongst a big patch of seals, away off on the Atlantic. The whole of the bay ice had evidently gone out together, taking the ship with it, and the bay had then neatly frozen over again. The seal hunters laughingly assured me that they found a patch of old "swiles" having tea in the cabin. As the hull of the Sir Donald was old, and the size of the boat made good medical work aboard impossible, we decided to sell her and try and raise the funds for a more seaworthy and capable craft.

Years of experience have subsequently emphasized the fact that if you are reasonably resistant, and want to get tough and young again, you can do far worse than come and winter on "the lonely Labrador."

CHAPTER IX

THE SEAL FISHERY

RETURNING South in the fall of 1895, business necessitated my remaining for some time in St. John's, where as previously the Governor, Sir Terence O'Brien, very kindly entertained me. It proved to be a most exciting time. There were only two banks in the Colony, called respectively the Union and the Commercial. These issued all the notes used in the country and except for the savings bank had all the deposits of the fishermen and people. Suddenly one day I was told, though with extreme secrecy, that the two banks were unsound and would not again open after Monday morning. This was early on Saturday. Business went on as usual, but among the leaders of the country consternation was beginning to spread. The banks closed at their usual hour — three o'clock on Saturday, and so far as I knew no one profited by the secret knowledge, though later accusations were made against some people. The serious nature of the impending disaster never really dawned on me, not being either personally concerned in either bank or having any experience of finance. When the collection came around at the cathedral on Sunday my friend whispered to me, "That silver will be valuable to-morrow." It so happened that on Sunday I was dining with the Prime Minister, who had befriended all our efforts, and his tremendously serious view of the position of the Colony sent me to bed full of alarms for my new friends. We were to have sailed for England next day and I went down after breakfast to buy my ticket. The agent sold it, but remarked, "I am not sure if Newfoundland money is good any longer. It is a speculation selling you this ticket." Before we sailed the vessel was held up by the Government, as only a few of the ships were taking notes at face value. Those of the Commercial Bank were only fetching twenty cents. Besides the banks quite a number of commercial firms also closed. The directors of the banks were all local merchants, and many were heavily indebted to them for supplies given out to their "planters," as they call the fishermen whom they supply with goods in advance to catch fish for them. It was a sorry mix-up, and business was very difficult to carry on because we had no medium of exchange. Even the Governor to pay his gardener had to give I.O.U. orders on shops — there simply being no currency available.

Matters have long since adjusted themselves, though neither bank ever reopened. Larger banks of good standing came in from Canada, and no one can find anything of which to complain in the financial affairs of the "oldest Colony," even in these days of war.

Newfoundland has a large seal as well as cod fishery. The great sealing captains are all aristocrats of the fishermen and certainly are an unusually fine set of men. The work calls for peculiar training in the hardest of schools, for great self-reliance and resource, besides skill in handling men and ships. In those days the doyen of the fleet was Captain Samuel Blandford. He fired me with tales of the hardships to be encountered and the opportunities and needs for a doctor among three hundred men hundreds of miles from anywhere. The result was a decision to return early from my lecture tour and go out with the seal hunters of the good ship Neptune.

I look back on this as one of the great treats of my life; though I believe it to be an industry seriously detrimental to the welfare of the people of the Colony and the outside world. For no mammal bringing forth but one young a year can stand, when their young are just born and are entirely helpless, being attacked by huge steel-protected steamers carrying hundreds of men with modern rifles or even clubs. Advantage is also taken of the maternal instinct to get the mothers as well as the young "fat," if the latter is not obtainable in sufficient quantities. Meanwhile the poor scattered people of the northern shores of Newfoundland are being absolutely ruined and driven out. They need the seals for clothing, boots, fresh food, and fats. They use every portion of the few animals which each catches, while the big steamers lose thousands which they have killed, by not carrying them at once to the ship and leaving them in piles to be picked up later. Moreover, in the latter case all the good proteid food of their carcasses is left to the sharks and gulls.

At twelve o'clock of March 10, 1896, the good ship Neptune hauled out into the stream at St. John's Harbour, Newfoundland, preparatory to weighing anchor for the seal fishery. The law allows no vessels to sail before 2 p.m. on that day, under a penalty of four thousand dollars fine — nor may any seals be killed from the steamers until March 14, and at no time on Sundays. The whole city of St. John's seemed to be engrossed in the one absorbing topic of the seal fishery. It meant if successful some fifty thousand pounds sterling at least to the Colony — it meant bread for thousands of people — it meant for days and even weeks past that men from far-away outports had been slowly collecting at the capital, till the main street was peopled all day with anxious-looking crowds, and all the wharves where there was any chance of a "berth" to the ice were fairly in a state of siege.

Now let us go down to the dock and visit the ship before she starts. She is a large barque-rigged vessel, with auxiliary steam, or rather one should say a steamer with auxiliary sails. The first point that strikes one is her massive build, her veritable bulldog look as she sits on the water. Her sides are some eighteen inches thick, and sheathed and resheathed with "greenheart" to help her in battering the ice. Inside she is ceiled with English oak and beech, so that her portholes look like the arrow slits of the windows of an old feudal castle. Her bow is double-stemmed — shot with a broad band of iron, and the space of some seventeen feet between the two stems solid with the choicest hardwoods. Below decks every corner is adapted to some use. There are bags of flour, hard bread, and food for the crew of three hundred and twenty men; five hundred tons of coal for the hungry engine in her battle with the ice-floe. The vessel carries only about eighteen hundred gallons of water and the men use five hundred in a day. This, however, is of little consequence, for a party each day brings back plenty of ice, which is excellent drinking after being boiled. This ice is of very different qualities. Now it is "slob" mixed with snow born on the Newfoundland coast. This is called "dirty ice" by the sealers. Even it at times packs very thick and is hard to get through. Then there is the clearer, heavy Arctic ice with here and there huge icebergs frozen in; and again the smoother, whiter variety known as "whelping ice" — that is, the Arctic shore ice, born probably in Labrador, on which the seals give birth to their pups.

The masters of watches are also called "scunners" — they go up night and day in the forebarrel to "scun" the ship — that is, to find the way or leads through the ice. This word comes from "con" of the conning tower on a man-of-war.

When the morning of the 10th arrives, all is excitement. Fortunately this year a southwest wind had blown the ice a mile or so offshore. Now all the men are on board. The vessels are in the stream. The flags are up; the whistles are blowing. The hour of two approaches at last, and a loud cheering, renewed again and again, intimates that the first vessel is off, and the S.S. Aurora comes up the harbour. Cheers from the ships, the wharves, and the town answer her whistle, and closely followed by the S.S. Neptune and S.S. Windsor, she gallantly goes out, the leader of the sealing fleet for the year.

There have been two or three great disasters at the seal fishery, where numbers of men astray from their vessels in heavy snow blizzards on the ice have perished miserably. Sixteen fishermen were once out hunting for seals on the frozen ice of Trinity Bay when the wind changed and drove the ice offshore. When night came on they realized their terrible position and that, with a gale of wind blowing, they could not hope to reach land in their small boats. Nothing but an awful death stared them in the face, for in order to hunt over the ice men must be lightly clad, so as to run and jump from piece to piece. Without fire, without food, without sufficient clothing, exposed to the pitiless storm on the frozen sea, they endured thirty-six hours without losing a life. Finally, they dragged their boats ten miles over the ice to the land, where they arrived at last more dead than alive.

It is the physical excitement of travelling over broken loose ice on the bosom of the mighty ocean, and the skill and athletic qualities which the work demands, that makes one love the voyage. Jumping from the side of the

ship as she goes along, skurrying and leaping from ice-pan
to ice-pan, and then having killed, "sculped," and
"pelted" the seal, the exciting return to the vessel! But
it has its tragic side, for it takes its regular tribute of
fine human life.

A Mr. Thomas Green, of Greenspond, while a boy,
with his father and another man and a 'prentice lad, was
tending his seal nets when a "dwey" or snowstorm came
on, and the boat became unmanageable and drifted off
to sea. They struck a small island, but drifted off again.
That night the father and the 'prentice lad died, and
next morning the other man also. The son dressed himself in all the clothes of the other three, whose bodies he
kept in the boat. He ate the flesh of an old harp seal they
had caught in their net. On the third day by wonderful
luck he gaffed an old seal in the slob ice. This he hauled
in and drank the warm blood. On the fifth day he killed
a white-coat, and thinking that he saw a ship he walked
five miles over the floe, leaving his boat behind. The
phantom ship proved to be an island of ice, and in the
night he had to tramp back to his open punt. On the
seventh day he was really beginning to give up hope
when a vessel, the Flora, suddenly hove in sight. He
shouted loudly as it was dark, whereupon she immediately tacked as if to leave him. Again he shouted, "For
God's sake, don't leave me with my dead father here!"
The words were plainly heard on board, and the vessel
hove to. The watch had thought that his previous shouting was of supernatural origin. He and his boat with its
pitiful load were picked up and sent back home by a
passing vessel.

On this particular voyage we were lucky enough to
come early into the seals. From the conner's barrel, in
which I spent a great deal of time, we saw one morning

black dots spread away in thousands all over the ice-floes through which we were butting, ramming, and fighting our way. All hands were over the side at once, and very soon patients began needing a doctor. Here a cut, there a wrench or sprain, and later came thirty or forty at a time with snow-blindness or conjunctivitis — very painful and disabling, though not fatal to sight.

One morning we had been kept late relieving these various slight ailments, and the men being mostly out on the ice made me think that they were among the seals; so I started out alone as soon as I could slip over the side to join them. This, however, I failed to do till late in the afternoon, when the strong wind, which had kept the loose ice packed together, dropped, and in less than no time it was all "running abroad." The result naturally is that one cannot get along except by floating on one piece to another, and that is a slow process without oars. It came on dark and a dozen of us who had got together decided to make for a large pan not far distant; but were obliged to give it up, and wait for the ship which had long gone out of sight. To keep warm we played "leap-frog," "caps," and "hop, skip, and jump" — at which some were very proficient. We ate our sugar and oatmeal, mixed with some nice clear snow; and then, shaving our wooden seal bat handles, and dipping them into the fat of the animals which we had killed, we made a big blaze periodically to attract the attention of the ship.

It was well into the night before we were picked up; and no sooner had we climbed over the rail than the skipper came and gave us the best or worst "blowing-up" I ever received since my father spanked me. He told me afterwards that his good heart was really so relieved by our safe return that he was scarcely conscious of what he said. Indeed, any words which might have been considered as unparliamentary he asked me to construe as gratitude to God.

Our captain was a passenger on and prospective captain of the S.S. Tigris when she picked up those members of the ill-fated Polaris expedition who had been five months on the ice-pans. He had gone below from his watch and daylight was just breaking when the next watch came and reported a boat and some people on a large pan, with the American flag flying. A kayak came off and Hans, an Eskimo, came alongside and said, "Ship lost. Captain gone." Boats were immediately lowered and nineteen persons, including two women and one baby, born on the ice-pan, came aboard amidst cheers renewed again and again. They had to be washed and fed, cleaned and clothed. The two officers were invited to live aft and the remainder of the rescued party being pestered to death by the sealing crew in the forecastle, it was decided to abandon the sealing trip, and the brave explorers were carried to St. John's, the American people eventually indemnifying the owners of the Tigris.

In hunting my patients I started round with a book and pencil accompanied by the steward carrying a candle and matches. The invalids were distributed in the four holds — the after, the main, forecastle, and foretop-gallant-forecastle. I never went round without a bottle of cocaine solution in my pocket for the snow-blind men, who suffered the most excruciating pain, often rolling about and moaning as if in a kind of frenzy, and to whom the cocaine gave wonderful relief. Very often I found that I must miss one or even both holds on my first rounds, for the ladders were gone and seals and coals were exchanging places in them during the first part of the day. Once down, however, one shouts out, "Is there any one here?" No answer. Louder still, "Is there any one here?" Perhaps a distant cough answers from some dark recess, and the steward and I begin a search. Then we go round systematically, climbing over on the barrels, searching under sacks, and poking into recesses, and after all occasionally missing one or two in our search. It seems a peculiarity about the men, that though they will lie up, they will not always say anything about it. The holds were very damp and dirty, but the men seemed to improve in health and fattened like the young seals. It must have been the pork, doughs, and excellent fresh meat of the seal. We had boiled or fried seal quite often with onions, and I must say that it was excellent eating — far more palatable than the dried codfish, which, when one has any ice work, creates an intolerable thirst.

The rats were making a huge noise one night and a barrel man gave it as his opinion that we should have a gale before long; but a glorious sunshine came streaming down upon us next morning, and we decided perforce the rats were evidently a little previous.

On Sunday I had a good chance to watch the seals. They came up, simply stared at the ship; now from sheer fat rolling on their backs, and lying for a few seconds tail and flippers beating the air helpless. These baby seals resemble on the ice nothing so much as the South Sea parrot fish — that is, a complete round head, with somewhere in the sphere two huge black dots for eyes and a similar one for a nose. These three form the corners of a small triangle, and except for the tail one could not easily tell which was the back and which the belly of a young white-coat — especially in stormy weather. For it is a well-ascertained fact that Nature makes the marvellous provision that in storm and snow they grow fattest and fastest. I have marvelled greatly how it is possible for any hot-blooded creature to enjoy so immensely this terribly cold water as do these old seals. They paddle about, throw themselves on their backs, float and puff out their breasts, flapping their flippers like paws over their chests.

Sunday morning we were lying off Fogo Island when some men came aboard and reported the wreck of the S.S. Wolf in the ice. She got round the island, a wind off-shore having cleared the ice from the land. Three other vessels were behind her. Hardly, however, had she got round when the northerly wind brought the ice back. The doomed ship now lay between the main or fixed frozen shore ice and the immense floe which was impelled by the north wind acting on its whole irregular surface. The force was irresistible. The Wolf backed and butted and got twenty yards into a nook in the main ice, and lay there helpless as an infant. On then swept the floe, crashed into the fixed ice, shattered its edge, rose up out of water over it, which is called "rafting," forced itself on the unfortunate ship, rose over her bulwarks, crushed in her sides, and only by nipping her tightly avoided sinking her immediately. Seeing that all was lost, Captain Kean got the men and boats onto the pans, took all they could save of food and clothes, but before he had saved his own clothing, the ice parted enough to let her through and she sank like a stone, her masts catching and breaking in pieces as she went. A sorrowful march for the shore now began over the ice, as the three hundred men started for home, carrying as much as they could on their backs. Many would have to face empty cupboards and hard times; all would have days of walking and rowing and camping before they could get home. One hundred miles would be the least, two and even three hundred for some, before they could reach their own villages. Some of these poor fellows had walked nearly two hundred miles to get a chance of going on the lost ship, impelled by hunger and necessity. Alas, we felt very sad for them and for Captain Kean, who had to face almost absolute ruin on account of this great loss.

The heaving of the great pans, like battering-rams against the sides of the Neptune, made a woesome noise below decks. I was often glad of her thirty-six inches of hardwood covering. Every now and then she steamed ahead a little and pressed into the ice to prevent this. I tried to climb on one of the many icebergs, but the heavy swell made it dangerous. At every swell it rolled over and back some eight feet, and as I watched it I understood how an iceberg goes to wind. For it acted exactly like a steam plough, crashing down onto one large pan as it rolled, and then, as it rolled back, lifting up another and smashing it from beneath. A regular battle seemed to be going on, with weird sounds of blows and groanings of the large masses of ice. Sometimes as pieces fell off the water would rush up high on the side of the berg. For some reason or other the berg had red-and-white streaks, and looked much like an ornamental pudding.

At latitude 50.18, about Funk Island, is one of the last refuges of the great auk. A few years ago, the earth, such as there is on these lonely rocks, was sifted for the bones of that extinct bird, and I think three perfect skeletons, worth a hundred pounds sterling each, were put together from the remnants discovered. One day the captain told me that he held on there in a furious gale for some time. Masses of ice, weighing thirty or forty tons, were hurled high up and lodged on the top of the island. Some men went out to "pan" seals on a large pan. Seven hundred of the animals had been placed on one of them, and the men had just left it, when a furious breaking sea took hold of the pan and threw it completely upside down.

I am never likely to forget the last lovely Sunday. We had nearly "got our voyage"; at least no one was anxious now for the credit of the ship. The sunshine was blazing hot as it came from above and below at the same time, and the blue sky over the apparently boundless field of heaving "floe" on which we lay made a contrast which must be seen to be appreciated. I had brought along a number of pocket hymn-books and in the afternoon we lay out on the high fore-deck and sang and talked, unworried by callers and the thousand interruptions of the land. Then we had evening prayers together, Catholic and Protestant alike; and for my part I felt the nearness of God's presence as really as I have felt it in the mysterious environment of the most magnificent cathedral. Eternal life seemed so close, as if it lay just over that horizon of ice, in the eternal blue beyond.

CHAPTER X

THREE YEARS' WORK IN THE BRITISH ISLES

In the spring of 1897 I was asked by the Council to sail to Iceland with a view to opening work there, in response to a petition sent in to the Board by the Hearn long-liners and trawlers, who were just beginning their vast fishery in those waters from Hull and Grimsby.

Having chosen a smaller vessel, so as to leave the hospital ship free for work among the fleets, we set sail for Iceland in June. The fight with the liquor traffic which the Mission had been waging had now been successful in driving the sale of intoxicants from the North Sea by international agreement; but the proverbial whiskey still continued its filibustering work in the Scotch seaports. As our men at times had to frequent these ports we were anxious to make it easier for them to walk straight while they were ashore.

We therefore called at Aberdeen on the way and anchored off the first dock. The beautiful Seaman's Home there was on the wrong side of the harbour for the vessels, and was not offering exactly what was needed. So we obtained leave to put a hull in the basin, with a first-aid equipment, refreshments, lounge and writing-rooms, and with simple services on Sunday. This boat commenced then and there, and was run for some years under Captain Skiff; till she made way for the present homely little Fishermen's Institute exactly across the road from the docks before you came to the saloons.

I shall not soon forget our first view of the cliffs of the southern coast of Iceland. We had called at Thorshaven in the Faroë group to see what we could learn of the boats fishing near Rockall; but none were there at the time. As we had no chronometers on our own boat we were quite unable to tell our longitude — a very much-needed bit of information, for we had had fog for some days, and anyhow none of us knew anything about the coast.

We brought up under the shadow of the mighty cliffs and were debating our whereabouts, when we saw an English sailing trawler about our own size, with his nets out close in under the land. So we threw out our boat and boarded him for information. He proved to be a Grimsby skipper, and we received the usual warm reception which these Yorkshire people know so well how to give. But to my amazement he was unable to afford us the one thing which we really desired. "I've been coming this way, man and boy, for forty years," he assured me. "But I can't read the chart, and I knows no more of the lay of the land than you does yourself. I don't use no chart beyond what's in my head."

With this we were naturally not content, so we sent back to the boat for our own sheet chart to try and get more satisfactory information. But when it lay on the table in this old shellback's cabin all he did was to put down on it a huge and horny thumb that was nearly large enough to cover the whole historic island, and "guess we were somewhere just about here."

Our cruise carried us all round the island — the larger part of our time being spent off the Vestmann Islands and the mouth of Brede Bugt, the large bay in which Reikyavik lies. It was off these islands that Eric the Red threw his flaming sticks into the sea. The first brand which alighted on the land directed him where to locate his new headquarters. Reikyavik means "smoking village," so called from the vapours of the hot streams which come out of the ground near by.

There is no night on the coast in summer; and even though we were a Mission ship we found it a real difficulty to keep tab of Sundays. The first afternoon that I went visiting aboard a large trawler, the extraordinary number of fish and the specimens of unfamiliar varieties kept me so interested that I lost all count of time, and when at last hunger prompted me to look at my watch I found that it was exactly 1.30 A.M.

At that time so many plaice and flatfish were caught at every haul, and they were so much more valuable than cod and haddock, that it was customary not to burden the vessel on her long five days' journey to market with round fish at all. These were, however, hauled up so rapidly to the surface from great depths that they had no time to accommodate the tension in their swimming bladders to the diminished pressure, with the result that when thrown overboard they were all left swimming upside down. A pathetic wake of white-bellied fish would stretch away for half a mile behind the vessel, over which countless screaming gulls and other birds were fighting. A sympathy for their horribly unprotected helplessness always left an uneasy sinking feeling at the pit of my own stomach. The waste has, however, righted itself in the course of years by the simple process of an increasing scarcity of the species, making it pay to save all haddock, cod, hake, ling, and other fish good for food, formerly so ruthlessly cast away.

One had many interesting experiences in this voyage, some of which have been of no small value subsequently. But the best lesson was the optimism and contentment of one's fellows, who had apparently so few of the things that only tyrannize the lives of those who live for them.

They were a simple, kindly, helpful people, living in a country barren and frigid beyond all others, with no trees except in one extreme corner of the island. The cows were literally fed on salt codfish and the tails of whales, and the goats grazed on the roofs of the houses, where existed the only available grass. There were dry, hard, and almost larval deposits over the whole surface of the land which is not occupied by perpetual snow and ice. The hot springs which abound in some regions only suggest a forlorn effort on the part of Nature at the last moment to save the situation. The one asset of the country is its fisheries, and of these the whale and seal fisheries were practically handed over to Norwegians; while large French and English boats fell like wolves on the fish, which the poor natives had no adequate means of securing for themselves.

We were fishing one day in Seyde Fjord on the east coast, when suddenly with much speed and excitement the great net was hauled, and we started with several other trawlers to dash pell-mell for the open sea. The alarm of masts and smoke together on the horizon had been given — the sign manual of the one poor Danish gunboat which was supposed to control the whole swarm of far smarter little pirates, which lived like mosquitoes by sucking their sustenance from others. The water was as a general rule too deep outside the three-mile limit for legitimate fishing.

The mention of Iceland brings to every one's mind the name of Pierre Loti. We saw many of the "pêcheurs d'islande" whom he so effectively portrays; and often felt sorry enough for them, fishing as they still were from old square-rigged wind-jammers. On some of these which had been months on the voyage, enough green weed had grown "to feed a cow" — as the mate put it.

On our return home we reported the need of a Mission vessel on the coast, but the difficulty of her being where she was wanted at the right time, over such an extended fishery ground, was very considerable. We decided that only a steam hospital trawler would be of any real value — unless a small cottage hospital could be started in Seyde Fjord, to which the sick and injured could be taken.

It was now thought wise that I should take a holiday, and thus through the kindness of my former chief, Sir Frederick Treves, then surgeon to the King, whose life he had been the means of saving, I found myself for a time his guest on the Scilly Islands. There we could divert our minds from our different occupations, conjuring up visions of heroes like Sir Cloudesley Shovel, who lost his life here, and of the scenes of daring and of death that these beautiful isles out in the Atlantic have witnessed. Nor did we need Charles Kingsley to paint for us again the visit of Angus Lee and Salvation Yeo, for Sir Frederick, as his book, "The Cradle of the Deep," shows, is a past-master in buccaneer lore. Besides that we had with us his nephew, the famous novel writer, A. E. W. Mason.

Treves, with his usual insatiable energy, had organized a grand regatta to be held at St. Mary's, at which the Governor of the island, the Duke of Wellington, and a host of visiting big-wigs were to be present. One event advertised as a special attraction was a life-saving exhibition to be given by local experts from the judges' stage opposite the grand stand on the pier. This, Mason and I, being little more than ornaments in the other events, decided to try and improve upon. Dressed as a somewhat antiquated lady, just at the psychological moment Mason fell off the pier head with a loud scream

— when, disguised as an aged clergyman, wildly gesticulating, and cramming my large beaver hat hard down on my head, I dived in to rescue him. A real scene ensued. We were dragged out with such energy that the lady lost her skirt, and on reaching the pier fled for the boat-house clad only in a bonnet and bodice over a bathing-suit. Although the local press wrote up the affair as genuine, the secret somehow leaked out, and we had to make our bow at the prize distribution the following evening.

Only parts of the winter seasons could be devoted to raising money. The general Mission budget had to be taken care of as well as the special funds; besides which one had to superintend the North Sea work. Thus the summer of 1897 was spent in Iceland as above described, and some of the winter in the North Sea. The spring, summer, and part of the fall of 1898 were occupied by the long Irish trip, which established work among the spring herring and mackerel men from Crookhaven.

On leaving England for one of these North Sea trips I was delayed and missed the hospital ship, so that later I was obliged to transfer to her on the high seas from the little cutter which had kindly carried me out to the fishing grounds. Friends had been good enough to give me several little delicacies on my departure, and I had, moreover, some especially cherished personal possessions which I desired to have with me on the voyage. These choice treasures consisted of some eggs, a kayak, a kodak, a chronometer, and a leg of mutton! After I was safely aboard the Mission hospital ship I found to my chagrin that in my anxiety to transfer the eggs, the kayak, the kodak, the chronometer, and especially the leg of mutton to the Albert, I had forgotten my personal clothing. I appreciated the fact that a soaking meant a serious matter, as I had to stay in bed till my things, which were drenched during my passage in the small boat, were dry again.

It was on this same voyage that a man, badly damaged, sent off for a doctor. It was a dirty dark morning, "thick o' rain," and a nasty sea was running, but we were really glad of a chance of doing anything to relieve the monotony. So we booted and oil-skinned, sou'-westered and life-jacketed, till we looked like Tweedledum and Tweedledee, and felt much as I expect a German student does when he is bandaged and padded till he can hardly move, preparatory to his first duel. The boat was launched and eagerly announcing the fact by banging loudly and persistently on the Albert's side. Our two lads, Topsy and Sam, were soon in the boat, adopting the usual North Sea recipe for transit: (1) Lie on the rail full length so as not to get your legs and hands jammed. (2) Wait till the boat bounces in somewhere below you. (3) Let go! It is not such a painful process as one might imagine, especially when one is be-padded as we were. The stretcher was now handed in, and a bag of splints and bandages. "All gone!" shouted simultaneously the mate and crew, who had risked a shower bath on deck to see us off; and after a vicious little crack from the Albert's quarter as we dropped astern, we found ourselves rushing away before the rolling waters, experiencing about the same sensation one can imagine a young sea-gull feels when he begins to fly.

While the skipper was at work in the tobacco locker one morning he heard a fisherman say that he had taken poison.

"Where did you get it?"

"I got it from the Albert."

"Who gave it to you?"

"Skipper ——" mentioning the skipper's name.

At this the skipper came out trembling, wondering what he had done wrong now.

"Well, you see it was this way. Our skipper had a bad leg, so as I was going aboard for some corf mixture, he just arst me to get him a drop of something to rub in. Well, the skipper here gives me a bottle of red liniment for our skipper's leg, and a big bottle of corf mixture for me, but by mistake I drinks the liniment and gave the corf mixture to our skipper to rub in his leg. I only found out that there yesterday, so I knew I were poisoned, and I've been lying up ever since."

"How long ago did you get the medicine?"

"About a fortnight."

This man had got it into his head that he was poisoned, and nothing on earth would persuade him to the contrary, so he was put to bed in the hospital. For three meals he had nothing but water and a dose of castor oil. By the next time dinner came round the patient really began to think he was on the mend, and remarked that "he began to feel real hungry like." It was just marvellous how much better he was before tea. He went home to his old smack, cured, and greatly impressed with the capacity of the medical profession.

The first piece of news that reached us in the spring was that the Sir Donald had been found frozen in the floe ice far out on the Atlantic. No one was on board her, and there was little of any kind in her, but even the hardy crew of Newfoundland sealers who found her, as they wandered over the floating ice-fields in search of seals, did not fail to appreciate the weird and romantic suggestions of a derelict Mission steamer, keeping her lonely watch on that awful, deathlike waste. She had been left at Assizes Harbour, usually an absolutely safe haven of rest. But she was not destined to end her chequered career so peacefully, for the Arctic ice came surging in and froze fast to her devoted sides, then bore her bodily into the open sea, as if to give her a fitting burial. The sealing ship Ranger passed her a friendly rope, and she at length felt the joyful life of the rolling ocean beneath her once more, and soon lay safely ensconced in the harbour at St. John's. Here she was sold by auction, and part of the proceeds divided as her ransom to her plucky salvors.

The money which could be especially devoted to the new steamer for Labrador, over and above the general expenses, was not forthcoming until 1899, when the contract for building the ship was given to a firm at Dartmouth in Devon. The chief donor of the new boat was again Lord Strathcona, after whom she was subsequently named.

On June 27, 1899, the Strathcona was launched, and christened by Lady Curzon-Howe. When the word was given to let go, without the slightest hitch or roll the ship slid steadily down the ways into the water. The band played "Eternal Father," "God save the Queen," and "Life on the Ocean Wave." Lord Curzon-Howe was formerly commodore upon the station embracing the Newfoundland and Labrador coast. Lord Strathcona regretted his enforced absence and sent "Godspeed" to the new steamer.

She arrived at Gorleston July 18, proving an excellent sea-boat, with light coal consumption. She is larger than the vessel in which Drake sailed round the world, or Dampier raided the Spanish Main, or than the Speedy, which Earl Dundonald made the terror of the French and Spanish.

In the fall of 1899 the hull of the Strathcona was completely finished, and I brought her round, an empty shell, to fit her up at our Yarmouth wharf; after which, in company with a young Oxford friend, Alfred Beattie, we left for the Labrador, crossing to Tilt Cove, Newfoundland, direct from Swansea in an empty copper ore tanker, the Kilmorack. On this I was rated as purser at twenty-five cents for the trip. Most tramps can roll, but an empty tanker going west against prevailing winds in the "roaring forties" can certainly give points to the others. Her slippery iron decks and the involuntary sideways excursions into the scuppers still spring into my mind when a certain Psalm comes round in the Church calendar, with its "that thy footsteps slip not." We were a little delayed by what is known as wind-jamming, and we used to kill time by playing tennis in the huge empty hold. This occupation, under the circumstances, supplied every kind of diversion.

The mine at Tilt Cove is situated in a hole in the huge headland which juts out far into the Atlantic, in the northern end of Newfoundland. Communication in these days was very meagre. No vessel would be available for us to get North for a fortnight. It so happened, however, that the Company's doctor had long been waiting a chance to get married, but his contract never allowed him to leave the mine without a medical man while it was working. I therefore found myself welcomed with open arms, and incidentally practising in his place the very next day — he having skipped in a boat after his bride. The exchange had been ratified by the captain of the mine on the assurance that I would not leave before he returned. It was absolutely essential that I should not let the next north-bound steamer go by. The season was already far advanced; and yet when the day on

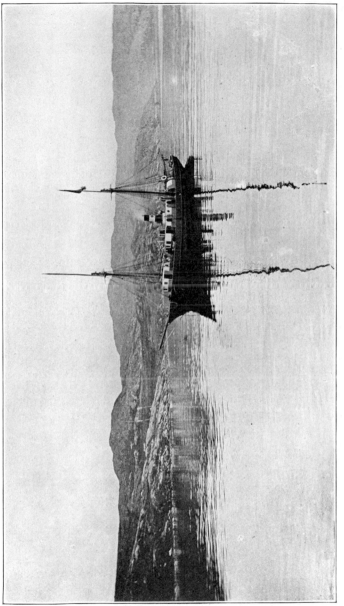

THE STRATHCONA

which she was due arrived, there was no sign of the doctor
and his wife. It was a kind of Damon and Pythias experience — only Pythias got back late by a few hours
in spite of all his efforts, and Damon would have had to
pay the piper if the captain of the mine had not permitted me to proceed.

The narrow road around the cavernous basin in the
cliffs leaves only just room for the line of houses between
the lake in the middle and the precipice behind. Only a
few years later an avalanche overwhelmed the house of
Captain Williams, and he and his family perished in it.
During the days I was at the mine the news travelled by
grapevine telegraph that the Mission doctor from England had come to the village, and every one took
advantage of it. The plan there was to pay so much
per month, well or ill, for the doctor. The work was
easy at first, but by the time I left every living being
seemed to me to have contracted some disease. For each
succeeding day my surgery got fuller, until on the last
morning even the yard and road contained waiting patients. Whose fault it was has always been a problem
to me; but it added a fresh reason for wishing to leave
punctually, so that one might not risk outliving one's
reputation.

In October, 1899, I wrote to my mother: "We have
just steamed into Battle Harbour and guns and flags
gave us a welcome after our three years' absence. The
hospital was full and looked splendid. What a change
from the day, now seven years ago, that we first landed
and had only a partially finished house! What an oasis
for patients from the bleak rocks outside! I never thought
to remain so long in this country."

Here we boarded the little Mission steamer, but no
human agency is perfect, and even the Julia Sheriden

had her faults. Her gait on this fall voyage was suggestive of inebriety, and at times gave rise to the anxious
sensations one experiences when one sees a poor victim
of the saloon returning home along a pavement near
much traffic.

While in England we had received letters from the
north coast of Newfoundland, begging us to again include their shores in our visits, and especially to establish
a definite winter station at St. Anthony. The people
claimed, and rightly, to be very poor. One man with a
large family, whom I knew well, as he had acted guide
for me on hunting expeditions, wrote: "Come and start
a station here if you can. My family and I are starving."
Dr. Aspland wrote that every one was strongly in favour
of our taking up a Mission hospital in North Newfoundland. We felt that we should certainly reach a very large
number of people whom we now failed to touch, and
that careful inquiries should be made.

Life on the French shore has been a struggle with too
many families to keep off actual starvation. For instance, one winter at St. Anthony a man with a large
family, and a fine, capable, self-respecting fellow, was
nine days without tasting any flour or bread, or anything
besides roast seal meat. Others were even worse off, for
this man was a keen hunter, and with his rickety old
single-barrel, boy's muzzle-loading gun used to wander
alone far out over the frozen sea, with an empty stomach
as well, trying to get a seal or a bird for his family. At
last he shot a square flipper seal and dragged it home.
The rumour of his having killed it preceded his arrival,
and even while skinning it a crowd of hungry men were
waiting for their share of the fat. Not that any was due
to them, but here there is a delightful semi-community
of goods.

Fish was then only fetching two or three dollars a hundredweight, salted and dried. The price of necessities depended on the conscience of the individual supplier and the ignorance of the people. The truck system was universal; thrift at a discount — and the sin of Ananias an all too common one; that is, taking supplies from one man and returning to him only part of the catch. The people in the north end of Newfoundland and Labrador were very largely illiterate; the sectarian schools split up the grants for teachers — as they still most unfortunately do — and miserable salaries, permitting teachers only for a few months at a time, were the rule.

I had once spent a fortnight at St. Anthony, having taken refuge there in the Princess May when I was supposed to be lost by those who were cut off from communication with us. I had also looked in there each summer to see a few patients. My original idea was to get a winter place established for our Indian Harbour staff, and I proposed opening up there each October when Indian Harbour closed, and closing in June when navigation was reopened, Battle Harbour again accessible, and when the man-of-war doctors are more on this section of the coast.

The snow was deep on the ground long before our voyage ended. There is always a romantic charm about cruising in the fall of the year on the Labrador. The long nights and the heavy gales add to the interest of the day's work. The shelter of the islands becomes a positive joy; the sense of safety in the harbours and fjords is as real a pleasure as the artificial attractions of civilization. The tang of the air, the young ice that makes every night, the fantastic midnight dances of the November auroras in the winter sky, all make one forget the petty worries of the daily round.

As Beattie agreed to stay with me it was with real

keenness to sample a sub-arctic winter that in November we disembarked from the Julia Sheriden. We made only the simplest preparations, renting a couple of rooms in the chief trader's house and hiring my former guide as dog-driver.

CHAPTER XI

FIRST WINTER AT ST. ANTHONY

Not one of the many who have wintered with us in the North has failed to love our frozen season. To me it was one long delight. The dog-driving, the intimate relationships with the people on whom one was so often absolutely dependent, the opportunity to use to the real help of good people in distress the thousand and one small things which we had learned — all these made the knowledge that we were shut off from the outside world rather a pleasure than a cause for regret.

Calls for the doctor were constant. I spent but three Sundays at home the whole time, and my records showed fifteen hundred miles covered with dogs.

The Eskimo dog is so strong and enduring that he is the doyen of traction power in the North, when long distances and staying qualities are required. But for short, sharp dashes of twenty to thirty miles the lighter built and more vivacious Straits dog is the speedier and certainly the less wolfish. We have attempted crossbreeding our somewhat squat-legged Eskimo dogs with Kentucky wolf hounds, to combine speed with endurance. The mail-carrier from Fullerton to Winnipeg found that combination very desirable. With us, however, it did not succeed. The pups were lank and weedy and not nearly so capable as the ordinary Straits breed.

The real Labrador dog is a very slightly modified wolf. A good specimen stands two feet six inches, or even two feet eight inches high at the shoulder, measures over six feet six inches from the tip of the nose to the tip of the tail, and will scale a hundred pounds. The hair is thick and straight; the ears are pointed and stand directly up. The large, bushy tail curves completely over on to the back, and is always carried erect. The colour is generally tawny, like that of a gray wolf, with no distinctive markings. The general resemblance to wolves is so great that at Davis Inlet, where wolves come out frequently in winter, the factor has seen his team mixed with a pack of wolves on the beach in front of the door, and yet could not shoot, being unable to distinguish one from the other. The Eskimo dog never barks, but howls exactly like a wolf, in sitting posture with the head upturned. The Labrador wolf has never been known to kill a man, but during the years I have spent in that country I have known the dogs to kill two children and one man, and to eat the body of another. Our dogs have little or no fear, and unlike the wolves, will unhesitatingly attack even the largest polar bear.

No amount of dry cold seems to affect the dogs. At 50° F. below zero, a dog will lie out on the ice and sleep without danger of frost-bite. He may climb out of the sea with ice forming all over his fur, but he seems not to mind one iota. I have seen his breath freeze so over his face that he had to rub the coating off his eyes with his paws to enable him to see the track.

The dogs have a wonderful instinct for finding their way under almost insurmountable difficulties, and they have oftentimes been the means of saving the lives of their masters. Once I was driving a distance of seventy miles across country. The path was untravelled for the winter, and was only a direction, not being cut or blazed. The leading dog had been once across the previous year with the doctor. The "going" had then been very bad; with snow and fog the journey had taken three days. A large part of the way lay across

THREE OF THE DOCTOR'S DOGS

wide frozen lakes, and then through woods. As I had never been that way before I had to leave it to the dog. Without a single fault, as far as we knew, he took us across, and we accomplished the whole journey in twelve hours, including one and a half hours for rest and lunch.

The distance travelled and the average speed attained depends largely on other factors than the dog power. We have covered seventy-five miles in a day with comfort; we have done five with difficulty. Ordinary speed would be six miles an hour, but I once did twenty-one miles in two hours and a quarter over level ice. Sails can sometimes be used with advantage on the komatik as an adjunct. The whole charm of dog-team driving lies in its infinite variety of experiences, the personal study of each dog, and the need for one's strength, courage, and resourcefulness.

South and north of the little village of St. Anthony where we had settled were other similar villages; and we decided that we could make a round tour every second month at least. We soon found, however, a great difficulty in getting started, because we always had some patients in houses near about, whom we felt that we could not leave. So we selected a motherly woman, whom we had learned that we could trust to obey orders and not act on her own initiative and judgment, and trained her as best we could to deal with some of these sick people. Then, having borrowed and outfitted a couple of rooms in a friend's house, we left our serious cases under her care, and started for a month's travel with all the optimism of youth.

Weight on your komatik is a vital question, and not knowing for what you may be called upon, makes the outfitting an art. I give the experience of years. The sledge should be eleven feet long. Its runners should be constructed of black spruce grown in the Far North where wood grows slowly and is very tough, and yet quite light. The runners should be an inch thick, eleven inches high, and about twenty-six inches apart, the bottoms rising at the back half an inch, as well as at the front toward the horns. The laths are fastened on with alternate diagonal lashings, are two inches wide, and close together. Such a komatik will "work" like a snake, adapting itself to the inequalities of the ground, and will not spread or "buckle." Long nails are driven up right through the runners, and clinched on the top to prevent splitting. The runners should be shod with spring steel, one inch wide; and a second runner, two and a half inches wide, may be put between the lower one and the wood, to hold up the sledge when the snow is soft. Thus one has on both a skate and a snowshoe at once. The dogs' traces should be of skin and fastened with toggles or buttons to the bowline. Dog food must be distributed along the komatik trail in summer — though the people will make great sacrifices to feed "the Doctor's team."

Clothing must be light; to perspire in cold weather is unpardonable, for it will freeze inside your clothes at night. Fortunately warmth depends only on keeping heat in; and we find an impervious, light, dressed canvas best. The kossak should be made with, so to speak, no neck through which the heat which one produces can leak out. The headpiece must be attached to the tunic, which also clips tight round the wrists and round the waist to retain the heat. The edges may be bound with fur, especially about the hood, so as to be soft and tight about the face, and to keep the air out. The Eskimo cuts his own hair so as to fill that function. Light sealskin boots are best for all weathers, but in very cold, dry seasons, deerskin dressed very soft is warmer. The skin boot should be sewn with sinew which swells in water and thus keeps the stitches water-tight. These skin boots are made by the Eskimo women who chew the edges of the skin to make them soft before sewing them with deer sinew. The little Eskimo girls on the North Labrador coast are proficient in the art of chewing, as they are brought up from childhood to help their mothers in this way, the women having invariably lost their teeth at a very early age.

A light rifle should always be lashed on the komatik, as a rabbit, a partridge, or a deer gives often a light to the eyes with the fresh proteids they afford, like Jonathan's wild honey. In these temperatures, with the muscular exercise required, my strictest of vegetarian friends should permit us to bow in the House of Rimmon. One day while crossing a bay I noticed some seals popping up their heads out of the water beyond the ice edge. I had a fine leading dog bearing the unromantic name of Podge, and pure white in colour. But he was an excellent water dog, trained not only to go for birds, but to dive under water for sunken seals. Owing to their increasing fat in winter, seals as a rule float, though they invariably sink in summer. On this particular occasion, having hitched up the team we crept out to the ice edge, Podge following at my heels. Lying still on the ice, and just occasionally lifting and waggling one's leg when the seal put up his head, he mistook one for a basking brother, and being a very curious animal, he again dived, and came up a few feet away. We shot two, both of which Podge dived after and retrieved, to the unbounded joy both of ourselves and his four-footed chums, who more than gladly shared the carcasses with him later.

A friend, returning from an island, was jogging quietly along on the bay ice, when his team suddenly went wild. A bear had crossed close ahead, and before he could unlash his rifle the komatik had dashed right onto the animal, who, instead of running, stood up and showed fight. The team were all around him, rapidly snarling themselves up in their own traces. He had just time to draw his hunting knife across the traces and so save the dogs, caring much more for them than he did for the prey. Whilst his dogs held the attention of the bear, he was able, though only a few feet away, to unlash his rifle at his leisure, and very soon ended the conflict.

A gun, however, is a temptation, even to a doctor, and nearly cost one of my colleagues his life. He was crossing a big divide, or neck of land, between bays, and was twenty miles from anywhere, when his dogs took the trail of some deer, which were evidently not far off. Being short of fresh food, he hitched up his team, and also his pilot's team, leaving only his boy driver in charge, while the men pursued the caribou. He enjoined the boy very strictly not to move on any account. By an odd freak a sudden snowstorm swept out of a clear sky just after they left. They missed their way, and two days later, starving and tired out, they found their first refuge, a small house many miles from the spot where they had left the sledges. When, however, they sent a relief team to find the komatiks, they discovered the boy still "standing by" his charge.

When crossing wide stretches of country we are often obliged to camp if it comes on dark. It is quite impossible to navigate rough country when one cannot see stumps, windfalls, or snags; and I have more than once, while caught in a forest looking for our tilt, been obliged to

A Hilly Trail   Crossing a Brook

A KOMATIK JOURNEY

walk ahead with a light, and even to search the snow
for tracks with the help of matches, when one's torch
has carelessly been left at home. On one occasion, having stopped our team in deep snow at nightfall, we left
it in the woods to walk out to a village, only five or six
miles distant, on our snowshoes. We entirely lost our
way, and ended up at the foot of some steep cliffs which
we had climbed down, thinking that our destination
lay at their feet. The storm of the day had broken the
sea ice from the land, and we could not get round the
base of the cliffs, though we could see the village lights
twinkling away, only a mile or two across the bay.
Climbing steep hills through dense woods in deep snow
in the dark calls for some endurance, especially as a
white snow-bank looks like an open space through the
dark trees. I have actually stuck my face into a per-
pendicular bluff, thinking that I was just coming out
into the open. Oddly enough, when after much struggling
we had mounted the hill, we heard voices, and suddenly
met two men, who had also been astray all day, but
now knew the way home. They were "all in" for want
of food, and preferred camping for the night. A good
fire and some chunks of sweet cake so greatly restored
them, however, that we got under way again in a couple
of hours, further stimulated to do so by the bitter cold,
against which, in the dark, we could not make adequate shelter. Moreover, we had perspired with the
violent exercise and our clothes were freezing from the
inside out.

You must always carry an axe, not only for firewood,
but for getting water — unless you wish to boil snow,
which is a slow process, and apt to burn your kettle.
Also when you have either lost the trail or there is none,
you must have an axe to clear a track as you march

ahead of your dogs. Then there is, of course, the unfortunate question of food. Buns baked with chopped pork in them give one fine energy-producing material, and do not freeze. A sweet hard biscuit is made on the coast which is excellent in one's pocket. Cocoa, cooked pork fat, stick chocolate, are all good to have. Our sealers carry dry oatmeal and sugar in their "nonny bags," which, mixed with snow, assuage their thirst and hunger as well. Pork and beans in tins are good, but they freeze badly. I have boiled a tin in our kettle for fifteen minutes, and then found a lump of ice in the middle of the substance when it was turned out into the dish.

Winter travelling on this coast oftentimes involves considerable hardships, as when once our doctor lost the track and he and his men had to spend several nights in the woods. They were so reduced by hunger that they were obliged to chew pieces of green sealskin which they cut from their boots and to broil their skin gloves over a fire which they had kindled.

One great joy which comes with the work is the sympathy one gets with the really poor, whether in intelligence, physical make-up, or worldly assets. One learns how simple needs and simple lives preserve simple virtues that get lost in the crush of advancing civilization. Many and many a time have the poor people by the wayside refused a penny for their trouble. On one occasion I came in the middle of the night to a poor man's house. He was in bed and the lights out, and it was bitter cold. He got out of bed in a trice and went down to his stage carrying an old hurricane lantern to feed my dogs, while his wife, after he had lit a fire in the freezing cold room, busied herself making me some cocoa. Milk and sugar were provided, and not till long afterwards did I know that it was a special little hoard kept for visitors. Later

I was sent to bed — quite unaware that the good folk had spent the first part of the night in it, and were now themselves on the neighbouring floor. Nor would a sou's return be asked. "It's the way of t' coast," the good fellow assured me.

Another time my host for the night had gone when I rose for breakfast. I found that he had taken the road which I was intending to travel to the next village, some fourteen miles distant, just to break and mark a trail for us as we did not know the way; and secondly to carry some milk and sugar to "save the face" of my prospective host for the next day, who had "made a bad voyage" that year. Still another time no less than forty men from Conche marched ahead on a twenty-mile track to make it possible for our team to travel quickly to a neighbouring settlement.

Often I have thought how many of these things would I do for my poorer friends. We who speak glibly of the need of love for our neighbours as being before that for ourselves, would we share a bed, a room, or give hospitality to strangers even in our kitchens, after they had awakened us in the middle of the night by slinging snowballs at our bedroom windows?

One day that winter a father of eight children sent in from a neighbouring island for immediate help. His gun had gone off while his hand was on the muzzle, and practically blown it to pieces. To treat him ten miles away on that island was impossible, so we brought him in for operation. To stop the bleeding he had plunged his hand into a flour barrel and then tied it up in a bag, and as a result the wounded arm was poisoned way up above the elbow. He preferred death to losing his right arm. Day and night for weeks our nurse tended him, as he hovered between life and death with general blood poisoning. Slowly his fine constitution brought him through, and at last a secondary operation for repair became possible. We took chances on bone-grafting to form a hand; and he was left with a flipper like a seal's, able, however, to oppose one long index finger and "nip a line" when he fished. But there was no skin for it. So Dr. Beattie and I shared the honours of supplying some. Pat — for that was his name — has been a veritable apostle of the hospital ever since, and has undoubtedly been the means of enabling others to risk the danger of our suspected proselytizing. For though he had English Episcopal skin on the palm of his hand and Scotch Presbyterian skin on the back, the rest of him still remained a devout Roman Catholic.

Another somewhat parallel case occurred the following year, when a dear old Catholic lady was hauled fifty miles over the snow by her two stalwart sons, to have her leg removed for tubercular disease of the ankle. She did exceedingly well, and the only puzzle which we could not solve was where to raise the necessary hundred dollars for a new leg — for her disposition, even more than her necessity, compelled her to move about. While lecturing that winter in America, I asked friends to donate to me any of their old legs which they no longer needed, and soon I found myself the happy possessor of two good wooden limbs, one of which exactly suited my requirements. A departed Methodist had left it, and the wife's clergyman, a Congregationalist, had handed it to me, an Episcopalian, and I had the joy of seeing it a real blessing to as good a Roman Catholic as I know. As the priest says, there is now at least one Protestant leg established in his parish.

We once reached a house at midnight, found a boy with a broken thigh, and had to begin work by thawing out frozen board in order to plane it for splints, then pad and fix it, and finally give chloroform on the kitchen table. On another occasion we had to knock down a partition in a tiny cottage, make a full-length wooden bath, pitching the seams to make it water-tight, in order to treat a severe cellulitis. Now it would be a maternity case, now a dental one, now a gunshot wound or an axe cut with severed tendons to adjust, now pneumonia, when often in solitary and unlearned homes, we would ourselves do the nursing and especially the cooking, as that art for the sick is entirely uncultivated on the coast.

The following winter I lectured in England and then crossed in the early spring to the United States and lectured both there and in Canada, receiving great kindness and much help for the work.

As I have stated in the previous chapter we had raised, largely through the generosity of Lord Strathcona, the money for a suitable little hospital steamer, and she had been built to our design in England. I had steamed her round to our fitting yard at Great Yarmouth, and had her fitted for our work before sailing. While I was in America, my old Newfoundland crew went across and fetched her over, so that June found us once more cruising the Labrador coast.

While working with the large fleet of schooners, which at that time fished in August and September from Cape Mugford to Hudson Bay Straits, I visited as usual the five stations of the Moravian Brethren. They were looking for a new place to put a station, and at their request I took their representative to Cape Chidley in the Strathcona.

This northern end of Labrador is extremely interesting to cruise. The great Appalachian Mountain Range runs out here right to the water edge, and forms a marvellous sea-front of embattled cliffs from two thousand to three thousand feet in height. The narrow passages which here and there run far into the mountains, and represent old valleys scooped out by ice action, are dominated all along by frowning peaks, whose pointed summits betray the fact that they overtopped the ice stream in the glacial age. The sharp precipices and weather-worn sides are picked out by coloured lichens, and tiny cold-proof Arctic plants, and these, with the deep blue water and unknown vistas that keep constantly opening up as one steams along the almost fathomless fjords, afford a fascination beyond measure.

Once before in the Sir Donald we had tried to navigate the narrow run that cuts off the island on which Cape Chidley stands from the mainland of Labrador, but had missed the way among the many openings, and only noted from a hilltop the course we should have taken, by the boiling current which we saw below, whose vicious whirlpools like miniature maelstroms poured like a dashing torrent from Ungava Bay into the Atlantic.

It was, however, with our hearts somewhere near our mouths that we made an attempt to get through this year, for we knew nothing of the depth, except that the Eskimos had told us that large icebergs drove through at times. We could steam nine knots, and we essayed to cover the tide, which we found against us, as we neared the narrowest part, which is scarcely one hundred yards wide. The current carried us bodily astern, however, and glad enough we were to drive stern foremost into a cove on one side and find thirteen fathoms of water to hold on in till the tide should turn. When at last it did turn, and got under way, it fairly took us in its teeth, and we shot through, an impotent plaything on the heaving bosom of the resistless waters. We returned safely, with a site selected and a fair chart of the "Tickle" (Grenfell Tickle).

When winter closed in, I arranged for an old friend, a clerk of the Hudson Bay Company, to stay with me at St. Anthony, and once more we settled down in rooms hired in a cottage. We had a driver, a team of dogs, and an arrangement with a paternal Government to help out by making an allowance of twenty-five cents for medicine for such patients as could not themselves pay that amount, and in those days the number was quite large.

When early spring came the hospital question revived. An expedition into the woods was arranged, and with a hundred men and thrice as many dogs, we camped in the trees, and at the end of the fortnight came home hauling behind us the material for a thirty-six by thirty-six hospital. Being entirely new to us it proved a very happy experience. We were quartermasters and general providers. Our kitchen was dug down in thick woods through six feet of snow, and our main reliance was on boiled "doughboys" — the "sinkers" among which, with a slice of fat pork or a basin of bird soup, were as popular as lobster à la Newburg at Delmonico's or Sherry's.

The next summer we had trouble with a form of selfishness which I have always heartily hated — the liquor traffic. Suppose we do allow that a man has a right to degrade his body with swallowing alcohol, he certainly has no more right to lure others to their destruction for money than a filibuster has a right to spend his money in gunpowder and shoot his fellow countrymen. To our great chagrin we found that an important neighbour near one of our hospitals was selling intoxicants to the people — girls and men. One girl found drunk on the hillside brought home to me the cost of this man's right to "do as he liked." We promptly declared war, and I thanked God who had made "my hands to war, and my fingers to fight" — when that is the only way to resist the Devil successfully and to hasten the kingdom of peace.

This man and I had had several disagreements, and I had been warned not to land on the premises on pain of being "chucked into the sea." But when I tested the matter out by landing quite alone from a rowboat, after a "few wor-r-r-ds" his coast-born hospitality overcame him, and as his bell sounded the dinner call, he promptly invited me to dine with him. I knew that he would not poison the food, and soon we were glowering at one another over his own table — where his painful efforts to convince me that he was right absolutely demonstrated the exact opposite.

My chance came that summer. We were steaming to our Northern hospital from the deep bay which runs in a hundred and fifty miles. About twenty miles from the mouth a boat hailed us out of the darkness, and we stopped and took aboard a wrecked crew of three men. They had struck our friend's well-insured old steam launch on a shoal and she had sunk under them. We took them aboard, boat and all, wrote down carefully their tale of woe, and then put the steamer about, pushed as near the wreck as we dared and anchored. Her skipper came forward and asked me what I intended doing, and I told him I was going to survey the wreck. A little later he again came to ask permission to go aboard the wreck to look for something he had forgotten. I told him certainly not. Just before sunrise the watch called me and said that the wrecked crew had launched their boat, and were rowing toward the steamer. "Launch ours at once, and drive them back" was an order which our boys obeyed with alacrity and zest. It was a very uneasy three men who faced me when they returned. They were full of bluff at what they would do for having their liberties thus interfered with, but obviously uneasy at heart.

With some labour we discovered that the water only entered the wreck at low tide and forward; so by buoying her with casks, tearing up her ballast deck, and using our own pumps as well as buckets — at which all hands of my crew worked with a good will, we at last found the hole. It was round. There were no splinters on the inside. We made a huge bung from a stick of wood, plugged the opening, finished pumping her out, and before dark had her floating alongside us. Late that night we were once more anchored — this time opposite the dwelling-house of my friend the owner. We immediately went ashore and woke him up. There is a great deal in doing things at the psychological moment; and by midnight I had a deed duly drawn up, signed and sealed, selling me the steamer for fifty cents. I still see the look in his eyes as he gave me fifty cents change from a dollar. He was a self-made man, had acquired considerable money, and was keen as a ferret at business. The deed was to me a confession that he was in the plot for barratry, to murder the boat for her insurance.

On our trip South we picked up the small steamer, and towing her to a Hudson Bay Company's Post we put her "on the hard," photographed the hole, with all the splintering on the outside, and had a proper survey of the hull made by the Company's shipwright. The unanimous verdict was "wilful murder." In the fall as her own best witness, we tried to tow her to St. John's, but in a heavy breeze of wind and thick snow we lost her at sea — and with her our own case as well. The law decided that there was no evidence, and my friend, making out that he had lost the boat and the insurance, threatened to sue me for the value.

The sequel of the story may as well be told here. A year or so later I had just returned from Labrador. It used to be said always that our boat "brought up the keel of the Labrador"; but this year our friend had remained until every one else had gone. Just as we were about to leave for England, the papers in St. John's published the news of the loss of a large foreign-going vessel, laden with fish for the Mediterranean, near the very spot where our friend lived. On a visit a little later to the shipping office I found the event described in the graphic words of the skipper and mate. Our friend the consignee had himself been on board at the time the "accident" occurred. After prodigies of valour they had been forced to leave the ship, condemn her, and put her up for sale. Our friend, the only buyer at such a time on the coast, had bought her in for eighty dollars.

It was the end of November, and already a great deal of ice had made. The place was six hundred miles north. The expense of trying to save the ship would be great. But was she really lost? The heroics sounded too good to be true. All life is a venture. Why not take one in the cause of righteousness? That night in a chartered steam trawler, with a trusty diver, we steamed out of the harbour, steering north. Our skipper was the sea rival of the famous Captain Blandford; and the way he drove his little craft, with the ice inches thick from the driving spray all over the bridge and blocking the chart-room windows, made one glad to know that the good sea genius of the English was still so well preserved.

When our distance was run down we hauled in for the land, but had to lay "hove to" (with the ship sugared like a Christmas cake), as we were unable to recognize our position in the drifting snow. At length we located the islands, and never shall I forget as we drew near hearing the watch call out, "A ship's top-masts over the land." It was the wreck we were looking for.

It took some hours to cut through the ice in which she lay, before ever we could get aboard; and even the old skipper showed excitement when at last we stood on her deck. Needless to say, she was not upside down, nor was she damaged in any way, though she was completely stripped of all running gear. The diver reported no damage to her bottom, while the mate reported the fish in her hold dry, and the hatches still tightly clewed, never having been stirred.

With much hearty good-will our crew jettisoned fish enough into our own vessel to float the craft. Fearing that so late in the year we might fail to tow her safely so far, and remembering the outcome of our losing the launch, we opened the stores on the island, and finding both block and sails, neatly labelled and stowed away, we soon had our prize not only refitted for sea, but also stocked with food, water, chart, and compass and all essentials for a voyage across the Atlantic, if she were to break loose and we to lose her. The last orders were to the mate, who was put on board her with a crew, "If not St. John's then Liverpool."

No such expedient, however, proved necessary. Though we had sixty fathoms of anchor chain on each of our wire cables to the ship, we broke one in a seaway and had to haul under the lee of some cliffs and repair damages. Often for hours together the vessel by day and her lights by night would disappear, and our hearts would jump into our mouths for fear we might yet fail. But at last, with all our bunting up, and both ships dressed as if for a holiday, we proudly entered the Narrows of St. John's, the cynosure of all eyes. The skipper and our friend had gone to England, so the Government had them extradited. The captain, who was ill with a fatal disease, made a full confession, and both men were sent to prison.

That was how we "went dry" in our section of Labrador.

CHAPTER XII

THE COÖPERATIVE MOVEMENT

BEING a professional and not a business man, and having no acquaintance with the ways of trade, the importance of a new economic system as one of the most permanent messages of helpfulness to the coast was not at first obvious to me. But the ubiquitous barter system, which always left the poor men the worst end of the bargain, is as subtle a danger as can face a community — subtle because it impoverishes and enslaves the victims, and then makes them love their chains.

As a magistrate I once heard a case where a poor man paid one hundred dollars in cash to his trader in the fall to get him a new net. The trader could not procure the twine, and when spring arrived the man came to get on credit his usual advance of "tings." From the bill for these the trader deducted the hundred dollars cash, upon which the man actually came to me as a justice of the peace to have him punished!

Lord Strathcona told me that in his day on this coast, when a man had made so good a hunt that he had purchased all he could think of, he would go round to the store again asking how much money was still due him. He would then take up purchases to exceed it by a moderate margin, saying that he liked to keep his name on the Company's books. In those days the people felt that they had the best part of the bargain if they were always a little in debt. The tendency to thrift was thus annihilated. The fishermen simply turned in all their catch to the merchant, and took what was coming to them as a matter of course. Many even were afraid to ask for certain supplies. This fact often became evident when we were trying to order special diets — the patient would reply, "Our trader won't give out that." Naturally the whole system horrified us, as being the nearest possible approach to English slavery, for the poor man was in constant fear that the merchant "will turn me off." On the other hand, the traders took precautions that their "dealers" should not be able to leave them, such as not selling them traps outright for furring, or nets for fishing, but only loaning them, and having them periodically returned. This method insured their securing all the fur caught, because legally a share of the catch belonged to them in return for the loan of the trap. They thus completely minimized the chance for competition, which is "the life of trade."

Soon after my arrival on the coast I saw the old Hudson Bay Company's plan of paying in bone counters of various colours; and a large lumber company paying its wages in tin money, stamped "Only valuable at our store." If, to counteract this handicap, the men sold fish or fur for cash to outsiders, and their suppliers found it out, they would punish them severely.

On another occasion, sitting by me on a gunning point where we were shooting ducks as they flew by on their fall migration, was a friend who had given me much help in building one of our hospitals. I suddenly noticed that he did not fire at a wonderful flock of eiders which went right over our heads. "What's the matter, Jim?" I asked. "I settled with the merchant to-day," he replied, "and he won't give me nothing for powder. A duck or two won't matter. 'T is the children I'm minding." The fishery had been poor, and not having enough to meet his advances, he had sold a few quintals of fish for cash, so as to get things like milk which he would not be allowed on winter credit, and had been caught doing so. He was a grown man and the father of four children. We went to his trader to find out how much he was in debt. The man's account on the books was shown us, and it read over three thousand dollars against our friend. It had been carried on for many years. A year or two later when the merchant himself went bankrupt with a debt of $686,000 to the bank of which he was a director, the people of that village, some four hundred and eleven souls in all, owed his firm $64,000, an asset returned as value nil. The whole thing seemed a nightmare to any one who cared about these people.

In Labrador no cereals are grown and the summer frosts make potato and turnip crops precarious, so that the tops of the latter are practically all the green food to which we can aspire — except for the few families who remain at the heads of the long bays all summer, far removed from the polar current. Furthermore, until some one invents a way to extract the fishy taste from our fish oils, we must import our edible fats; for the Labrador dogs will not permit cows or even goats to live near them. I have heard only this week that a process has just been discovered in California for making a pleasant tasting butter out of fish oil. Our "sweetness" must all be imported, for none of our native berries are naturally sweet, and we can grow no cultivated fruits. The same fact applies to cotton and wool. Thus nearly all our necessities of life have to be brought to us. Firewood, lumber, fish and game, boots or clothing of skins, are all that we can provide for ourselves. On the other hand, we must export our codfish, salmon, trout, whales, oil, fur, and in fact practically all our products. An exchange medium is therefore imperative; and we must have some gauge like cash by which to measure, or else we shall lose on all transactions; for all the prices of both exports and imports fluctuate very rapidly, and besides this, we had then practically no way to find out what prices were maintaining in our markets.

Government relief had failed to stop the evils of the barter system. In the opinion of thinking men it only made matters worse. We were therefore from every point of view encouraged to start the coöperative plan which had proved so successful in England. I still believe that the people are honest, and that the laziness of indolence, from the stigma of which it is often impossible to clear them, is due to despair and inability to work properly owing to imperfect nourishment.

Things went from bad to worse as the years went by. The fact of the sealing steamers killing the young seals before they could swim greatly impoverished the Labrador inshore seal fishery. The prices of fish were so low that a man could scarcely catch enough to pay for his summer expenses out of it.

With us the matter came to a head in a little fishing village called Red Bay, on the north side of the Straits of Belle Isle. When we ran in there on our last visit one fall, we found some of our good friends packed up and waiting on their stages to see if we would remove them from the coast. A meeting was called that night to consider the problem, and it was decided that the people must try to be their own merchants, accepting the risks and sharing the profits. The fisherman's and trapper's life is a gamble, and naturally, therefore, they like credit advances, for it makes the other man carry the risks. We then and there decided, however, to venture a coöperative store, hiring a schooner to bring our freight and carry our produce straight to market; and if necessary eat grass for a year or so. Alas,

THE FIRST COÖPERATIVE STORE

after a year's saving the seventeen families could raise
only eighty-five dollars among them for capital, and we
had to loan them sufficient to obtain the first cargo. A
young fisherman was chosen as secretary, and the store
worked well from the beginning. That was in 1905. He
is still secretary, and to-day in 1918 the five-dollar
shares are worth one hundred and four dollars each, by
the simple process of accumulation of profits. The loan
has been repaid years ago. Not a barrow load of fish
leaves the harbour except through the coöperative store.
Due to it, the people have been able to tide over a series
of bad fisheries; and every family is free of debt.

At the time of the formation one most significant
fact was that every shareholder insisted that his name
must not be registered, for fear some one might find
out that he owned cash. They were even opposed to a
label on the building to signify that it was a store. However, I chalked all over its face "Red Bay Coöperative
Store."

The whole effort met with very severe criticism, not
to say hostility, at the hands of the smaller traders,
but the larger merchants were most generous in their
attitude, and though doubtful of the possibility of
realizing a cash basis, were without exception favourable
to the attempt. This store has been an unqualified success, only limited in its blessings by its lack of larger
capital. It has enabled its members to live independently,
free of debt and without want; while similar villages,
both south and east and west, have been gradually de-
leted by the people being forced to leave through inability to meet their needs.

During my first winter at St. Anthony, the young
minister of the little church on more than one occasion
happened to be visiting on his rounds in the very house

where we were staying on ours, and the subject of co-operation was frequently discussed over the evening pipe with the friends in the place. He had himself been trading, and had so disliked the methods that he had retired. He would certainly help us to organize a store on the Newfoundland side of the Straits.

At last the day arrived for the initial meeting. We gave notice everywhere. The chosen rendezvous was in a village fourteen miles north. The evening before, however, the minister sent word that he could not be present, as he had to go to a place twenty miles to the northwest to hold service. Knowing for how much his opinion counted in the minds of some of the people, this was a heavy blow, especially as the traders had notified me that they would all be on hand. Fortunately an ingenious suggestion was made — "He does n't know the way. Persuade his driver, after starting out, to gradually work round and end up at the coöperative meeting." This was actually done, and our friend was present willy-nilly. He proved a broken reed, however, for in the face of the traders he went back on coöperation.

As fortune would have it, our own komatik fell through the ice in taking a short cut across a bay, and we arrived late, having had to borrow some dry clothing from a fisherman on the way. Our trader friends had already appeared on the scene, and were joking the parson for being tricked, saying that evidently we had made a mistake and were really at Cape Norman, the place to which he had intended to go.

It was a dark evening, crisp and cold, and hundreds of dogs that had hauled people from all over the countryside to the meeting made night dismal outside. We began our meeting with prayer for guidance, wisdom, and good temper, for we knew that we should need them all

— and then we came down to statistics, prices, debts, possibilities, and the story of coöperation elsewhere.

The little house was crammed to overflowing. But the fear of the old régime was heavy on the meeting. The traders occupied the whole time for speaking. Only one old fisherman spoke at all. He had been an overseas sailor in his early days, and he surprised himself by turning orator. His effort elicited great applause. "Doctor — I means Mr. Chairman — if this here copper store buys a bar'l of flour in St. John's for five dollars, be it going to sell it to we fer ten? That's what us wants to know."

Outside, after the meeting, Babel was let loose. The general opinion was that there must be something to it or the traders would not have so much to say against the project. The upshot of the matter was that for a long time no one could be found who would take the managership; but at length the best-beloved fisherman on the shore stepped into the breach. He was not a scholar — in fact could scarcely read, write, and figure — but his pluck, optimism, and unselfishness carried him through.

That little store has been preaching its vital truths ever since. It is a still small text, but it has had vast influences for good. There has proved to be one difficulty. It is the custom on the coast to give all meals to travellers free, both men and dogs, and lodging to boot. Customers came from so far away that they had to stay overnight at least, and of course it was always Harry's house to which they went. The profit on a twenty-five cent purchase was slender under these circumstances, and as cash was scarce in those days, a twenty-five-cent purchase was not so rare as might be supposed. We therefore printed, mounted, framed, and sent to our friend the legend, "No more free meals. Each meal will cost ten cents." Later we received a most grateful reply from him in his merry way, saying that he had hung up the card in his parlour, but begging us not to defer visits if we had not the requisite amount, as he was permitted to give credit to that extent. But when next we suddenly "blew in" to Harry's house, the legend was hanging with its face to the wall.

Our third store was seventy-five miles to the westward at a place called Flowers Cove. Here the parson came in with a will. Being a Church of England man, he was a more permanent resident, and, as he said,"he was a poor man, but he would sell his extra pair of boots to be able to put one more share in the store." What was infinitely more important he put in his brains. Every one in that vicinity who had felt the slavery of the old system joined the venture. One poor Irishman walked several miles around the coast to catch me on my next visit, and secretly give me five dollars. "'T is all I has in the world, Doctor, saving a bunch of children, but if it was ten times as large, you should have every cent of it for the store." "Thanks, Paddy, that's the talking that tells." For some years afterwards, every time that he knew I was making a visit to that part of the coast, he would come around seeking a private interview, and inquire after the health of "the copper store"; till he triumphantly brought another five dollars for a second share "out of my profits, Doctor."

That store is now a limited liability company with a capital of ten thousand dollars owned entirely by the fishermen, it has paid consistently a ten per cent dividend every year, and is located in fine premises which it bought and owns outright.

A fourth store followed near the lumber mill which we started to give winter labour at logging; but owing to bad management and lack of ability to say "no" to men seeking credit, it fell into debt and we closed it up. Number five almost shared the same fate. Unable to get local talent to manage it, we hired a Canadian whose pretensions proved unequal to his responsibility. He was, however, found out in time to reorganize the store; but the loss which he had caused was heavy, and it was his notice of leaving for Canada which alone betrayed the truth to us. The most serious aspect of the matter was that many of the local fishermen lost confidence in the ability of the store to succeed, and returning to the credit system, they found it modified enough to appear to them a lamb instead of a wolf. However, number five is growing all the time again and will yet be a factor in the people's deliverance.

Numbers six and seven were in poor and remote parts of Labrador, very small, and with insufficient capital and brains. One has closed permanently. They were simply small stores under the care of one settler, who guaranteed to charge the people only a fixed percentage over St. John's prices for goods, as the return for his responsibility. Number eight was the result of a night spent in a miserable shack on a lonely promontory called Adlavik.

God forbid that I should judge traders or doctors or lawyers or priests by their profession or their intellectual attitude. There are noble men in all walks of life. Alas, some are more liable than others to yield to temptation, and the temptations to which they are exposed are more insistent.

Number nine was on the extreme northern edge of the white settlers at Ford's Harbour. The story of it is too long to relate, but the trade there, in spite of many difficulties, still continues to preach a gospel and spell much blessing to poor people. To help out, we have sent north to this station three of our boys from the orphanage, as they grew old enough to go out into the world for themselves.

One disaster, in the form of a shipwreck, overtook the fine fellow in charge of this most northerly venture. For the first time in his life he came south, to seek a wife, his former wife having succumbed to tuberculosis. He brought with him his year's products of fur and skin boots. The mail steamer on which he was travelling struck a rock off Battle Harbour, and most of his goods were lost uninsured, he himself gladly enough escaping with his life.

It remained for our tenth venture to bring the hardest battle, and in a sense the greatest measure of success. Spurred by the benefits of the Red Bay store, the people of a little village about forty miles away determined to combine also. The result was a fine store near our hospital at Battle Harbour — which during the first year did sixty thousand dollars' worth of business. This served to put a match to the explosive wrath of those whose opposition hitherto had been that of rats behind a wainscot. They secured from their friends a Government commission appointed to inquire into the work of the Mission as "a menace to honest trade." The leading petitioner had been the best of helpers to the first venture. When the traders affected by it had first boycotted the fish, he had sent his steamer and purchased it from the company. Now the boot was on the other leg. The Commission and even the lawyers have all told me that they were prejudiced against the whole Mission by hearsay and misinterpretations, before they even began their exhaustive inquiry. Their findings, however, were a complete refutation of all charges, and the best advertisement possible.

It would not be the time to say that the whole coöperative venture has been an unqualified success; but the causes of failure in each case have been perfectly obvious, and no fault of the system. Lack of business ability has been the main trouble, and the lack of courage and unity which everywhere characterizes mankind, but is perhaps more emphasized on a coast where failure means starvation, and where the coöperative spirit has been rendered very difficult to arouse owing to mistrust born of religious sectarianism and denominational schools. These all militate very strongly against that unity which alone can enable labour to come to its own without productive ability.

There is one aspect for which we are particularly grateful. Politics, at any rate, has not been permitted to intrude, and the stress laid on the need of brotherliness, forbearance, and self-development — if ever these producers are to reap the rewards of being their own traders — has been very marked. Only thus can they share in the balance of profit which makes the difference between plenty and poverty on this isolated coast.

CHAPTER XIII

THE MILL AND THE FOX FARM

THE argument for coöperation had been that life on the coast was not worth living under the credit system. A short feast and a long famine was the local epigram. If our profits could be maintained on the coast, and spent on the coast, then the next-to-nature life had enough to offer in character as well as in maintenance to attract a permanent population, especially with the furring in winter. For the actual figures showed that good hunters made from a thousand to fifteen hundred dollars in a season, besides the salmon and cod fishery. There was, moreover, game for food, free firewood, water, homes, and no taxation except indirect in duties on their goods.

These same conditions prevailed on the long, narrow slice of land known as the "French shore" in northern Newfoundland. There the people were more densely settled, the hinterland was small, and many therefore could not go furring. Moreover, the polar current, entering the mouth of the Straits of Belle Isle, makes this section of land more liable to summer frosts, with a far worse climate than the Labrador bays, and gardening is less remunerative. We puzzled our brains for some way to add to our earning capacities, some coöperative productive as well as distributive enterprise.

The poverty which I had witnessed in Canada Bay in North Newfoundland, some sixty miles south of St. Anthony Hospital, had left me very keen to do something for that district which might really offer a solution of the problem. I had been told that there was plenty of timber to justify running a mill in the bay; but that no

ST. ANTHONY

sawmills paid in Newfoundland. This was emphasized in St. John's by my friends who still own the only venture out of the eleven which have operated in that city that has been able to continue. They have succeeded by adopting modern methods and erecting a factory for making furniture, so as to supply finished articles direct to their customers. We knew that in our case labour would be cheaper than ordinarily, for our labour in winter had generally to go begging. It was mainly this fact which finally induced us to make the attempt.

Having talked the matter over with the people we secured from the Government a special grant, as the venture, if it succeeded, would relieve them of the necessity of having poor-relief bills. The whole expense of the enterprise fell upon myself, for the Mission Board considered it outside their sphere; and already we had built St. Anthony Hospital in spite of the fact that they thought that we were undertaking more than they would be able to handle, and had discouraged it from the first.

The people had no money to start a mill, and the circumstances prohibited my asking aid from outside, so it was with considerable anxiety that we ordered a mill, as if it were a pound of chocolates, and arranged with two young friends to come out from England as volunteers, except for their expenses, to help us through with the new effort. At the same time there was three hundred dollars to pay for the necessary survey and line cutting, and supplies of food for the loggers for the winter. Houses must also be erected and furnished.

Ignorance undoubtedly supplied us with the courage to begin. Personally I knew nothing whatever of mills, having never even seen one. Nor had I seen the grant of land, or selected a site for the building. This was left entirely to the people themselves; and as none of them had ever seen a mill either, we all felt a bit uneasy about our capacities. I had left orders with the captain of the Coöperator (our schooner) to fetch the mill and put it where the people told him; but when I heard that there was one piece which included the boiler which weighed three tons, it seemed to me that they could never handle it. We had no wharf ready to receive it and no boat capable of carrying it. I woke many times that summer wondering if it had not gone to the bottom while they were attempting the landing. There was no communication whatever with them as we were six hundred miles farther north on our summer cruise; and we had not the slightest control over the circumstances in which we might become involved.

It was late in the season and the snow was already deep on the ground when eventually we were piloted to the spot selected. It was nine miles up the bay on a well-wooded promontory of a side inlet. The water was deep to the shore and the harbour as safe as a house. The boys from England had arrived, and a small cottage had been erected, tucked away in the trees. It was very small, and very damp, the inside of the walls being white with frost in the morning until the fire had been under way for some time. But it was a merry crowd, emerging from various little hutlets around among the trees, which greeted the Strathcona.

The big boiler, the "bugaboo" of my dreams all summer, lay on the bank. "How did you get it there?" was my first query. "We warped the vessel close to the land, and then hove her close ashore and put skids from the rocks off to her. On these we slid the boiler, all hands hauling it up with our tackles."

Having left the few supplies which we had with us, for the Strathcona has no hold or carrying space, we returned to the hospital, mighty grateful for the successful opening of the venture. The survey had been completed and accepted by the Government, and though unfortunately it was but very poorly marked, and we have had lots of trouble since, — as we have never been able to say exactly where our boundaries lie, nor even to find marks enough to follow over the original survey again, — yet it enabled us to get to work, which was all that we wanted at the moment.

The fresh problems at the hospital, and the constant demands on our energies, made Christmas and New Year go by with our minds quite alienated from the cares of the new enterprise. But when after Christmas the dogs had safely carried us over many miles of snow-covered wastes, and our immediate patients gave us a chance to look farther afield, I began to wonder if we might not pay the mill a visit. By land it was only fifty miles distant to the southward, possibly sixty if we had to go round the bays. The only difficulty about the trip was that there were no trails, and most of the way led through virgin forest, where windfalls and stumps and dense undergrowth mixed with snow made the ordinary obstacle race a sprint in the open in comparison. We knew what it meant, because in our eagerness to begin our dog-driving when the first snow came, we had wandered over small trees crusted with snow, fallen through, and literally floundered about under the crust, unable to climb to the top again. It was the nearest thing to the sensations of a man who cannot swim struggling under the surface of the water. Moreover, on a tramp with the minister, he had gone through his snow racquets and actually lost the bows later, smashing them all up as he repeatedly fell through between logs and tree-trunks and "tuckamore." His summons for help and the idea that there were still eight miles to go still haunted me. On that occasion we had cut down some spruce boughs and improvised some huge webbed feet for ourselves, which had saved the situation; but whether they would have served for twenty or thirty miles, we could not tell. Not so long before a man named Casey, bringing his komatik down the steep hill at Conche, missed his footing and fell headlong by a bush into the snow. The heavy, loaded sledge ran over him and pressed him still farther into the bank. Struggling only made him sink the deeper, and an hour later the poor fellow was discovered smothered to death.

No one knew the way. We could not hear of a single man who had ever gone across in winter, though some said that an old fellow who had lived farther south had once carried the mails that way. At length we could stand it no longer, and arranging with four men and two extra teams, we started off. We hoped to reach the mill in two days, but at the end of that time we were still trying to push through the tangle of these close-grown forests. To steer by compass sounded easy, but the wretched instrument seemed persistently to point to precipitous cliffs or impenetrable thickets. There were no barren hilltops after the first twenty miles. Occasionally we would stop, climb a tree, and try to get a view. But climbing a conifer whose boughs are heavily laden with ice and snow is no joke, and gave very meagre returns. At last, however, we struck a high divide, and from an island in the centre of a lake, occupied only by two lone fir trees, we got a view both ways, showing the Cloudy Hills which towered over the south side of the bay in which the mill stood.

A very high, densely wooded hill lay, however, directly in our path; and which way to get round it best none of

us knew. We "tossed up" and went to the eastward —
the wrong side, of course. We soon struck a river, and at
once surmised that if we followed it, it must bring us to
the head of the bay, which meant only three miles of
salt water ice to cover. Alas, the stream proved very
torrential. It leaped here and there over so many rapid
falls that great canyons were left in the ice, and instead
of being able to dash along as when first we struck it, we
had painfully to pick our way between heavy ice-blocks,
which sorely tangled up our traces, and our dogs ran
great danger of being injured. Nor could we leave the
river, for the banks were precipitous and utterly impassable with undergrowth. At length when we came to
a gorge where the boiling torrent was not even frozen,
and as prospects of being washed under the ice became
only too vivid, we were forced to cut our way out on the
sloping sides. The task was great fun, but an exceedingly slow process.

It was altogether an exciting and delightful trip. Now
we have a good trail cut and blazed, which after some
years of experience we have gradually straightened out,
with two tilts by the roadside when the weather makes
camping imperative, or when delay is caused by having
helpless patients to haul, till now it is only a "joy-ride"
to go through that beautiful country "on dogs." There
is always a challenge, however, left in that trail — just
enough to lend tang to the toil of it. Once, having missed
the way in a blizzard, we had to camp on the snow with
the thermometer standing at twenty below zero. The
problem was all the more interesting as we struck only
"taunt" timberwoods with no undergrowth to halt the
wind. On another occasion we attempted to cross Hare
Bay, and one of the dogs fell through the ice. There was
a biting wind blowing, and it was ten degrees below zero.

When we were a mile off the land I got off the sledge to try the ice edge, when suddenly it gave way, and in I fell. It did not take me long to get out — the best advice being to "keep cool." I had as hard a mile's running as ever I experienced, for my clothing was fast becoming like the armour of an ancient knight; and though in my youth I had been accustomed to break the ice in the morning to bathe, I had never run in a coat of mail.

Never shall I forget dragging ourselves in among those big trees with our axes, and tumbling to sleep in a grave in the snow, in spite of the elements. In this hole in a sleeping-bag, protected by the light drift which blew in, one rested as comfortably as in a more conventional type of feather bed. Nor, when I think of De Quincey's idea of supreme happiness before the glowing logs, can I forget that gorgeous blaze which the watch kept up by felling trees full length into the fire, so that our Yule logs were twenty feet long, and the ruddy glow and crackling warmth went smashing through the hurtling snowdrift. True, it was cold taking off our dripping clothing, which as it froze on us made progress as difficult as if we were encased in armour. But dancing up and down before a huge fire in the crisp open air under God's blue sky gave as pleasing a reaction as doing the same thing in the dusty, germ-laden atmosphere of a ballroom in the small hours of the night, when one would better be in bed, if the joys of efficiency and accomplishment are the durable pleasure of life.

It was a real picnic which we had at the mill. Our visit was as welcome as it was unexpected, and we celebrated it by the whole day off, when all hands went "rabbiting." When at the end, hot and tired, we gathered round a huge log fire in the woods and discussed boiling cocoa and pork buns, we all agreed that it had been a day worth living for.

Logging had progressed favourably. Logs were close at hand; and the whole enterprise spelled cash coming in that the people had never earned before. The time had also arrived to prepare the machinery for cutting the timber boxes were being unpacked, and weird iron "parts" revealed to us, that had all the interest of a Chinese puzzle, with the added pleasure of knowing that they stood for much if we solved the problems rightly.

When next we saw the mill it was spring, and the puffing smoke and white heaps of lumber that graced the point and met our vision as we rounded Breakheart Point will not soon be forgotten. Only one trouble had proved insurmountable. The log-hauler would not deliver the goods to the rotary saw. Later, with the knowledge that the whole apparatus was upside down, it did not seem so surprising after all. One accident also marred the year's record. While a party of children had been crossing the ice in the harbour to school, a treacherous rapid had caused it to give way and leave a number of them in the water. One of my English volunteers, being a first-class athlete, had by swimming saved five lives, but two had been lost, and the young fellow himself so badly chilled that it had taken the hot body of one of the fathers of the rescued children, wrapped up in bed with him in lieu of a hot-water bottle, to restore his circulation.

The second fall was our hardest period. The bills for our lumber sold had not been paid in time for us to purchase the absolutely essential stock of food for the winter; and if we could not get a store of food, we knew that our men could not go logging. It was food, not cash, which they needed in the months when their own slender stock

of provisions gave out, and when all communication was
cut off by the frozen sea.

For a venture which seemed to us problematical in its
outcome, we did not dare to borrow money or to induce
friends to invest; and of course Mission funds were not
available. For the day has not yet arrived when all those
who seek by their gifts to hasten the coming of the Kingdom of God on earth recognize that to give the opportunity to men to provide decently for their families and
homes is as effective work for the Master, whose first
attribute was love, as patching up the unfortunate victims of semi-starvation. The inculcation of the particular intellectual conception which the donor may hold
of religion, or as to how, after death, the soul can get into
heaven, is, as the result of the Church teaching, still considered far the most important line of effort. The emphasis on hospitals is second, partly at least because, so
it has seemed to me as a doctor of medicine, the more
obvious personal benefit thereby conferred renders the
recipients more impressionable to the views considered
desirable to promulgate. Yet only to-day, as I came home
from our busy operating-room, I felt how little real gain
the additional time on earth often is either to the world
outside or even to the poor sufferers themselves. In order
to have one's early teachings on these matters profoundly
shaken, one has only to work as a surgeon in a country
where tuberculosis, beri-beri, and other preventable diseases, and especially the chronic malnutrition of poverty
fills your clinic with suffering children, who at least
are victims and not responsible spiritually for their
"punishment." Of course, the magnitude of service to
the world of every act of unselfishness, and much more
of whole lives of devotion, such as that of Miss Sullivan,
the teacher of Miss Helen Keller, can never be rightly

estimated by any purely material conception of human life.

Love is dangerously near to sentimentality when we actually prefer remedial to prophylactic charity — and I personally feel that it is false economy even from the point of view of mission funds. The industrial mission, the educational mission, and the orphanage work at least rank with and should go hand in hand with hospitals in any true interpretation of a gospel of love.

In subsequent years the nearest attempt to finance such commonly called "side issues of the work" has been with us through the medium of a discretionary fund. Into this are put sums of money specially given by personal friends, who are content to leave the allocation of their expenditure in the hands of the worker on the actual field. This fund is, of course, paid out in the same way as other mission funds, and is as strictly supervised by the auditors. While it leaves possibly more responsibility than some of us are worthy of, it enables individuality to play that part in mission business which every one recognizes to be all-important in the ordinary business of the world. No money, however, from this fund has ever gone into the mill or in assisting the coöperative stores.

Sorry as one feels to confess it, I have seen money wasted and lost through red tape in the mission business. And after all is not mission business part of the world's business, and must not the measure of success depend largely on the same factors in the one case as in the other? Has one man more than another the right to be called "missionary," for of what use is any man in the world if he has no mission in it? Christ's life is one long emphasis on the point that in the last analysis, when something has to be done, it is the individual who has to do it It is, we believe, a fact of paramount importance for efficiency and economy; and the loyalty of God in committing such trust to us, when He presumably knows exactly how unworthy we are of it, is the explanation of life's enigma.

When at last our food and freight were purchased for the loggers for the winter and landed by the mail steamer nine miles from the mill, the whole bay was frozen and five miles of ice already over six inches thick. The hull of the Strathcona was three eighths of an inch soft steel; but there was no other way to transport the goods but on her, excepting by sledges — a very painful and impracticable method.

It was decided that as we could not possibly butt through the ice, we must butt over it. The whole company of some thirty men helped us to move everything, including chains and anchors, to the after end of the ship, and to pile up the barrels of pork, flour, sugar, molasses, etc., together with boats and all heavy weights, so that her fore foot came above the water level and she looked as if she were sinking by the stern. We then proceeded to crash into the ice. Up onto it we ran, and then broke through, doing no damage whatever to her hull. The only trouble was that sometimes she would get caught fast in the trough, and it was exceedingly hard to back her astern for a second drive. To counteract this all hands stood on one rail, each carrying a weight, and then rushed over to the other side, backward and forward at the word of command, thus causing the steamer to roll. It was a very slow process, but we got there, though in true Biblical fashion, literally "reeling to and fro like drunken men."

While the mill was in its cradle, we in the Strathcona were cruising the northern Labrador waters. We witnessed that year, off the mighty Kaumajets, the most remarkable storm of lightning that I have ever seen in those parts. Inky masses hid the hoary heads of those tremendous cliffs. Away to the northwest, over the high land called Saeglek, a lurid light just marked the sharp outline of the mills. Ahead, where we were trying to make the entrance to Hebron Bay, an apparently impenetrable wall persisted. Seaward night had already obscured the horizon; but the moon, hidden behind the curtain of the storm, now and again fitfully illuminated some icebergs lazily heaving on the ocean swell. Almost every second a vivid flash, now on one side, now on the other, would show us a glimpse of the land looming darkly ahead. The powers of darkness seemed at play; while the sea, the ice, the craggy cliffs, and the flashing heavens were advertising man's puny power.

An amusing incident took place in one isolated harbour. A patient came on board for medicine, and after examining him I went below to make it up. When I came on deck again I gave the medicine to one I took to be my man, and then sent him ashore to get the twenty-five cent fee for the Mission which he had forgotten. No sooner had he gone than another man came and asked if his medicine was ready. I had to explain to him that the man just climbing over the rail had it. The odd thing was that the latter, having paid for it, positively refused to give it up. True, he had not said that he was ill, but the medicine looked good (Heaven save the mark!) and he "guessed that it would suit his complaint all right."

At the mill we found that quite a large part of the timberland was over limestone, while near our first dam there was some very white marble. We fully intended to erect a kiln, using our refuse for fuel, for the land is loaded with humic acid, and only plants like blueberries, conifers, and a very limited flora flourish on it. Some friends in England, however, hearing of marble in the bay, which it was later discovered formed an entire mountain, commenced a marble mine near the entrance. The material there is said to be excellent for statuary. Even this small discovery of natural resources encouraged us. For having neither road, telegraph, nor mail service to the mill, we hoped that the development of these things might help in our own enterprise.

For ten years the little mill has run, giving work to the locality, better houses, a new church and school, and indeed created a new village.

The only trouble with this North country's own peculiar winter work, fur-hunting, is that its very nature limits its supply. In my early days in the country, fur in Labrador was very cheap. Seldom did even a silver fox fetch a hundred dollars. Beaver, lynx, wolverine, wolves, bears, and other skins were priced proportionately. Still, some men lived very well out of furring. We came to the conclusion that the only way to improve conditions in this line was to breed some of the animals in captivity. We did not then know of any enterprise of that kind, but I remembered in the zoölogical gardens at Washington seeing a healthy batch of young fox pups born in captivity.

Life is short. Things have to be crowded into it. So we started that year an experimental fox farm at St. Anthony. A few uprights from the woods and some rolls of wire are a fox farm. We put it close by the hospital, thinking that it would be less trouble. The idea, we rejoice to know, was perfectly right; but we had neither time, study, nor experience to teach us how to manage the animals. Very soon we had a dozen couples, red, white, patch, and one silver pair. Some of the young fox pups were very tame, for I find an old record written by a professor of Harvard University, while he was on board the Strathcona on one trip when we were bringing some of the little creatures to St. Anthony. He describes the state of affairs as follows: "Dr. Grenfell at one time had fifteen little foxes aboard which he was carrying to St. Anthony to start a fox farm there. Some of these little animals had been brought aboard in blubber casks, and their coats were very sticky. After a few days they were very tame and played with the dogs; were all over the deck, fell down the companionway, were always having their tails and feet stepped on, and yelping for pain, when not yelling for food. The long-suffering seaman who took care of them said, 'I been cleaned out that fox box. It do be shockin'. I been in a courageous turmoil my time, but dis be the head smell ever I witnessed.'"

When the farm was erected, every schooner entering the harbour was interested in it, and a deep-cut pathway soon developed as the crews went up to see the animals. The reds and one patch were very tame, and always came out to greet us. One of the reds loved nothing better than to be caught and hugged, and squealed with delight like a child when you took notice of it. The whites, and still more the silvers, were always very shy; and though we never reared a single pup, there were some born and destroyed by the old ones.

As the years passed we decided to close up the little farm, particularly after a certain kind of sickness which resembled strychnine poisoning had attacked and destroyed three of the animals which were especial pets. We then converted the farm into a garden with a glass house for our seedling vegetables.

Meanwhile the industry had been developed by a Mr. Beetz in Quebec Labrador with very marked economic success; and in Prince Edward Island with such tremendous profit that it soon became the most important industry in the Province. Enormous prices were paid for stock. I remembered a schooner in the days of our farm (1907) bringing me in four live young silvers, and asking two hundred dollars for the lot. We had enough animals and refused to buy them. In 1914 one of our distant neighbours, who had caught a live slut in pup, sold her with her little brood for ten thousand dollars. We at once started an agitation to encourage the industry locally, and the Government passed regulations that only foxes bred in the Colony could be exported alive. The last wild one sold was for twenty-five dollars to a buyer, and resold for something like a thousand dollars by him. A large number of farms grew up and met with more or less success, one big one especially in Labrador, which is still running. We saw there this present year some delightful little broods, also some mink and marten (sables), the prettiest little animals to watch possible. For some reason the success of this farm so far has not been what was hoped for it. Indeed, even in Prince Edward Island the furor has somewhat died down owing to the war; though at the close of the war it is anticipated that the industry will go on steadily and profitably. Are not sheep, angora goats, oxen, and other animals just the result of similar efforts? If fox-farming some day should actually supersede the use of the present sharp-toothed leg trap, no small gain would have been effected. A fox now trapped in those horrible teeth remains imprisoned generally till he perishes of cold, exhaustion, or fear. Though the fur trapper as a rule is a most gentle creature, the "quality of mercy is not strained" in furring.

CHAPTER XIV

THE CHILDREN'S HOME

"What's that schooner bound South at this time of year for?" I asked the skipper of a fishing vessel who had come aboard for treatment the second summer I was on the coast.

"I guess, Doctor, that that's the Yankee what's been down North for a load of Huskeymaws. What do they want with them when they gets them?"

"They'll put them in a cage and show them at ten cents a head. They're taking them to the World's Fair in Chicago."

People of every sort crowded to see the popular Eskimo Encampment on the Midway. The most taking attraction among the groups displayed was a little boy, son of a Northern Chieftain, Kaiachououk by name; and many a nickel was thrown into the ring that little Prince Pomiuk might show his dexterity with the thirty-foot lash of his dog whip.

One man alone of all who came to stare at the little people from far-off Labrador took a real interest in the child. It was the Rev. C. C. Carpenter, who had spent many years of his life as a clergyman on the Labrador coast. But one day Mr. Carpenter missed his little friend. Pomiuk was found on a bed of sickness in his dark hut. An injury to his thigh had led to the onset of an insidious hip disease.

The Exhibition closed soon after, and the Eskimos went north. But Pomiuk was not forgotten, and Mr. Carpenter sent him letter after letter, though he never received an answer. The first year the band of Eskimos reached as far north as Ramah, but Pomiuk's increasing sufferings made it impossible for them to take him farther that season.

Meanwhile in June, 1895, we again steamed out through the Narrows of St. John's Harbour, determined to push as far north as the farthest white family. A dark foggy night in August found us at the entrance of that marvellous gorge called Nakvak. We pushed our way cautiously in some twenty miles from the entrance. Suddenly the watch sang out, "Light on the starboard bow!" and the sound of our steamer whistle echoed and reëchoed in endless cadences between those mighty cliffs. Three rifle shots answered us, soon a boat bumped our side, and a hearty Englishman sprang over the rail.

It was George Ford, factor of the Hudson Bay Company at that post. During the evening's talk he told me of a group of Eskimos still farther up the fjord having with them a dying boy. Next day I had my first glimpse of little Prince Pomiuk. We found him naked and haggard, lying on the rocks beside the tiny "tubik."

The Eskimos were only too glad to be rid of the responsibility of the sick lad, and, furthermore, he was "no good fishing." So the next day saw us steaming south again, carrying with us the boy and his one treasured possession — a letter from a clergyman at Andover, Massachusetts. It contained a photograph, and when I showed it to Pomiuk he said, "Me even love him."

A letter was sent to the address given, and some weeks later came back an answer. "Keep him," it said. "He must never know cold and loneliness again. I write for a certain magazine, and the children in 'The Corner' will become his guardians." Thus the "Corner Cot" was founded, and occupied by the little Eskimo Prince for the brief remainder of his life.

On my return the following summer the child's joyful laughter greeted me as he said, "Me Gabriel Pomiuk now." A good Moravian Brother had come along during the winter and christened the child by the name of the angel of comfort.

In a sheltered corner of a little graveyard on the La-brador coast rests the tiny body of this true prince. When he died the doctor in charge of the hospital wrote me that the building seemed desolate without his smiling, happy face and unselfish presence. The night that he was buried the mysterious aurora lit up the vault of heaven. The Innuits, children of the Northland, call it "the spirits of the dead at play." But it seemed to us a shining symbol of the joy in the City of the King that another young soldier had won his way home.

The Roman Catholic Church is undoubtedly correct in stating that the first seven years of his life makes the child. Missions have always emphasized the importance of the children from a purely propaganda point of view. But our Children's Home was not begun for any such reason. Like Topsy, "it just grow'd." I had been sum-moned to a lonely headland, fifty miles from our hos-pital at Indian Harbour, to see a very sick family. Among the spruce trees in a small hut lived a Scotch salmon fisher, his wife and five little children. When we anchored off the promontory we were surprised to re-ceive no signs of welcome. When we landed and entered the house we found the mother dead on the bed and the father lying on the floor dying. Next morning we improvised two coffins, contributed from the wardrobes of all hands enough black material for a "seemly" funeral, and later, steaming up the bay to a sandy stretch of land, buried the two parents with all the ceremonies of the Church — and found ourselves left with five little mortals in black sitting on the grave mound. We thought that we had done all that could be expected of a doctor, but we now found the difference. It looked as if God expected more. An uncle volunteered to assume one little boy and we sailed away with the remainder of the children. Having no place to keep them, we wrote to a friendly newspaper in New England and advertised for foster parents. One person responded. A young farmer's wife wrote: "I am just married to a farmer in the country, and miss the chance to teach children in Sunday-School, or even to get to church, it is so far away. I think that I can feed two children for the Lord's sake. If you will send them along, I will see that they do not want for anything." We shipped two, and began what developed into our Children's Home with the balance of the stock.

We had everything to learn in the rearing of children, having had only the hygienic side of their development to attend to previously. One of the two which we kept turned out very well, becoming a fully trained nurse. The other failed. Both of those who went to New England did well, the superior discipline of their foster mother being no doubt responsible. The following fall I made a special journey to see the latter. It was a small farm on which they lived, and a little baby had just arrived. Only high ideals could have persuaded the woman to accept the added responsibility. The children were as bright and jolly as possible.

Among the other functions which have fallen to my lot to perform is the ungrateful task of unpaid magistrate, or justice of the peace. In this capacity a little later I was called on to try a mother, who in a Labrador

village had become a widow and later married a man
with six children who refused to accept her three-year-
old little girl. When I happened along, the baby was
living alone in the mother's old shack, a mud-walled
hut, and she or the neighbours went in and tended it
as they could. None of the few neighbours wanted permanently to assume the added expense of the child, so
dared not accept it temporarily. It was sitting happily
on the floor playing with a broken saucer when I came
in. It showed no fear of a stranger; indeed, it made most
friendly overtures. I had no right to send the new husband to jail. I could not fine him, for he had no money.
There was no jail in Labrador, anyhow. My special con-
stable was a very stout fisherman, a family man, who
proposed to nurse the child till I could get it to some
place where it could be properly looked after. When we
steamed away, we had the baby lashed into a swing cot.
It became very rough, and the baby, of course, crawled
out and was found in the scuppers. It did everything
that it ought not to do, but which we knew that it would.
But we got it to the hospital at last and the nurse received it right to her heart.

In various ways my family grew at an alarming rate,
once the general principle was established. On my early
summer voyage to the east coast of Labrador I found
at Indian Harbour Hospital a little girl of four. In the
absence of her father, who was hunting, and while her
mother lay sick in bed, she had crawled out of the
house and when found in the snow had both legs badly
frozen. They became gangrenous halfway to the knee,
and her father had been obliged to chop them both off.
An operation gave her good stumps; but what use was
she in Labrador with no legs? So she joined our family,
and we gave her such good new limbs that when I brought

her into Government House at Halifax, where one of our nurses had taken her to school temporarily, and she ran into the room with two other little girls, the Governor could scarcely tell which was our little cripple Kirkina.

The following fall as we left for the South our good friend, the chief factor of the Hudson Bay Company, told me that on an island in the large inlet known to us as Eskimo Bay a native family, both hungry and naked, were living literally under the open sky. We promised to try and find them and help them with some warm clothing.

Having steamed round the island and seen no signs of life, we were on the point of leaving when a tiny smoke column betrayed the presence of human life — and with my family-man mate we landed as a search party. Against the face of a sheer rock a single sheet of light cotton duck covered the abode of a woman with a nursing baby. They were the only persons at home. The three boys and a father comprised the remainder of the family. We soon found the two small boys. They were practically stark naked, but fat as curlews, being full of wild berries with which their bodies were stained bright blues and reds. They were a jolly little couple, as unconcerned about their environment as Robinson Crusoe after five years on his island. Soon the father came home. I can see him still — the vacant brown face of a very feeble-minded half-breed, ragged and tattered and almost bootless. He was carrying an aged single-barrelled boy's gun in one hand and a belated sea-gull in the other, which bird was destined for the entire evening meal of the family. A half-wild-looking hobbledehoy boy of fifteen years also joined the group.

It was just beginning to snow, a wet sleet. Eight

months of winter lay ahead. Yet not one of the family
seemed to think a whit about that which was vivid
enough to the minds of the mate and myself. We sat
down for a regular pow-wow beside the fire sputtering
in the open room, from which thick smoke crept up the
face of the rock, and hung over us in a material but symbolic cloud. It was naturally cold. The man began with
a plea for some "clodin." We began with a plea for some
children. How many would he swap for a start in clothing
and "tings for his winter"? He picked out and gave us
Jimmie. The soft-hearted mate, on whose cheeks the
tears were literally standing, grabbed Jimmie — as the
latter did his share of the gull. But we were not satisfied.
We had to have Willie. It was only when a breaking of
diplomatic relations altogether was threatened that
Willie was sacrificed on the altar of "tings." I forget the
price, but I think that we threw in an axe, which was
one of the trifles which the father lacked — and in this
of all countries! The word was no sooner spoken than our
shellback again excelled himself. He pounced on Willie
like a hawk on its prey, and before the treaty was really
concluded he was off to our dory with a naked boy kicking violently in the vice of each of his powerful arms.
The grasping strength of our men, reared from childhood to haul heavy strains and ponderous anchors, is
phenomenal.

Whatever sins Labrador has been guilty of, Malthu-
sianism is not in the category. Nowhere are there larger
families. Those of Quebec Labrador, which is better
known, are of almost world-wide fame. God is, to Labrador thinking, the Giver of all children. Man's responsibility is merely to do the best he can to find food and
clothing for them. A man can accomplish only so much.
If these "gifts of God" suffer and are a burden to others

that is kismet. It is the animal philosophy and makes women's lives on this coast terribly hard. The opportunity for service along child-welfare lines is therefore not surprising from this angle also.

One day, passing a group of islands, we anchored in a bight known as Rogues' Roost. It so happened that a man who many years before had shot off his right arm, and had followed up his incapacity with a large family of dependants, had just died. Life cannot be expected to last long in Labrador under those conditions. There were four children, one being a big boy who could help out. The rest were offered as a contribution to the Mission. A splendid Newfoundland fisherman and his wife had a summer fishing station here, and with that generous open-heartedness which is characteristic of our seafarers, they were only too anxious to help. "Of course, she would make clothing while I was North" — out of such odd garments as a general collection produced. "She would n't think of letting them wear it till I came along South, not she." She would "put them in the tub as soon as she heard our whistle." When after the long summer's work we landed and went up to her little house, three shining, red, naked children were drying before a large stove, in which the last vestige of connection with their past was contributing its quota of calories toward the send-off. A few minutes later we were off to the ship with as sweet a batch of jolly, black-haired, dark-eyed kiddies as one could wish for. Our good friend could not keep back the tears as she kissed them good-bye on deck. The boy has already put in three years on the Western Front. The girls have both been educated, the elder having had two years finishing at the Pratt Institute in New York.

A grimy note saying, "Please call in to Bird Island as

you pass and see the sick," brought me our next donation. "There be something wrong with Mrs. B's twins,
Doctor," greeted me on landing. "Seems as if they was
like kittens, and couldn't see yet a wink." It was only
too true. The little twin girls were born blind in both
eyes. What could they do in Labrador? Two more for
our family without any question. After leaving our Orphanage, these two went through the beautiful school
for the blind at Halifax, and are now able to make their
own living in the world.

So the roll swelled. Some came because they were or-
phans; some because they were not. Thus, poor Sammy.
The home from which he came was past description.
From the outside it looked like a tumble-down shed.
Inside there appeared to be but one room, which measured six by twelve feet, and a small lean-to. The family
consisted of father and mother and three children. The
eldest boy was about twelve, then came Sam, and lastly
a wee girl of five, with pretty curly fair hair, but very
thin and delicate-looking. She seemed to be half-starved
and thoroughly neglected. The father was a ne'er-do-
well and the mother an imbecile who has since died of
tuberculosis. The filth inside was awful. The house was
built of logs, and the spaces in between them were partly
filled in with old rags and moss. The roof leaked. The
room seemed to be alive with vermin, as were also the
whole family. The two boys were simply clothed in a pair
of men's trousers apiece and a dilapidated pair of boots
between them. The trousers they found very hard to
keep on and had to give them frequent hoists up. They
were both practically destitute of underclothing. To hide
all deficiencies, they each wore a woman's long jacket
of the oldest style possible and green with age, which
reached down to their heels. Round their waists they

each wore a skin strap. They were stripped of their rags, and made to scrub themselves in the stream and then indoors before putting on their new clean clothes. Sammy and the little sister joined the family.

One of our boys is from Cape Chidley itself; others come from as far south and west as Bay of Islands in South Newfoundland. So many erroneous opinions seem to persist regarding the difference between Newfoundland and Labrador that I am constantly asked: "But why do you have a Children's Home in Newfoundland? Can't the Newfoundlanders look out for themselves and their dependent children?" As I have tried to make clear in a previous chapter North and South Newfoundland should be sharply differentiated as to wealth, education, climate, and opportunity. Though for purposes of efficiency and economy the actual building of the Home is situated in the north end of the northern peninsula of Newfoundland, the children who make up the family are drawn almost entirely from the Labrador side of the Straits; unless, as is often the case, the poverty and destitution of a so-called Newfoundland family on the south side of Belle Isle makes it impossible to leave children under such conditions.

It is obvious that something had to be built to accommodate the galaxy; and some one secured who understood the problem of running the Home. She — how often it is "she" — was found in England, a volunteer by the name of Miss Eleanor Storr. She was a true Christian lady and a trained worker as well. The building during the years grew with the family, so that it is really a wonder of odds and patches. The generosity of one of our volunteers, Mr. Francis Sayre, the son-in-law of President Wilson, doubled its capacity. But buildings that are made of green wood, and grow like Topsy, are

INSIDE THE ORPHANAGE

apt to end like Topsy — turvy. Now we are straining
every nerve to obtain a suitable accommodation for the
children. We sorely need a brick building, economically
laid out and easily kept warm, with separate wings for
girls and boys and a crêche for babies. Miss Storr was
obliged to leave us, and now for over six years a splendid
and unselfish English lady, Miss Katie Spalding, has
been helping to solve this most important of all problems — the preparation of the next generation to make
their land and the world a more fit place in which to live.
Miss Spalding's contribution to this country has lain
not only in her influence on the children and her un-
ceasing care of them, but she has given her counsel and
assistance in other problems of the Mission, where also
her judgment, experience, and wisdom have proven invaluable.

There is yet another side of the orphanage problem.
We have been obliged, due to the lack of any boarding-
school, to accept bright children from isolated homes
so as to give them a chance in life. It has been the truest
of love messages to several. The children always repay,
whether the parents pay anything or not; and as so
much of the care of them is volunteer, and friends have
assumed the expenses of a number of the children, the
budget has never been unduly heavy. They do all their
own work, and thanks to the inestimably valuable help
of the Needlework Guild of America through its Labrador branch, the clothing item has been made possible.
In summer we use neither boots nor stockings for the
children unless absolutely necessary. Our harbour people
still look on that practice askance; but ours are the
healthiest lot of children on the coast, and their brown
bare legs and tough, well-shaped feet are a great asset
to their resistance to tuberculosis, their arch-enemy, and

no small addition to the attraction of their merry faces and hatless heads.

Even though Gabriel, Prince Pomiuk, never lived within its walls, the real beginning of the idea of our Children's Home was due to him; and one feels sure that his spirit loves to visit the other little ones who claim this lonely coast as their homeland also.

The one test for surgery which we allow in these days is its "end results." Patients must not be advertised as cured till they have survived the treatment many years. Surely that is man's as well as God's test. Certainly it is the gauge of the outlay in child life. What is the good of it all? Does it pay? In the gift of increasing joy to us, in its obvious humanity and in its continuous inspiration, it certainly does make the work of life here in every branch the better.

The solution of the problem of inducing the peace of God and the Kingdom of God into our "parish" is most likely to be solved by wise and persevering work among the children. For in them lies the hope of the future of this country, and their true education and upbringing to fit them for wise citizenship have been cruelly neglected in this "outpost of Empire."

Another menace to the future welfare of the coast has been the lack of careful instruction and suitable opportunities for the development, physical, mental, and spiritual, of its girls. Without an educated and enlightened womanhood, no country, no matter how favored by material prosperity, can hope to take its place as a factor in the progress of the world. In our orphanage and educational work we have tried to keep these two ideas constantly before us, and to offer incentives to and opportunities for useful life-work in whatever branch, from the humblest to the highest, a child showed aptitude.

Through the vision, ability, and devotion of Miss Storr, Miss Spalding, and their helpers, in training the characters as well as the bodies of the children at the Home, and by the generous support of friends of children elsewhere, we have been able to turn out each year from its walls young men and women better fitted to cope with the difficult problems of this environment, and to offer to its service that best of all gifts — useful and consecrated personalities.

CHAPTER XV

PROBLEMS OF EDUCATION

Every child should be washed. Every child should be educated. The only question is how to get there. The "why's" of life interest chiefly the academic mind. The "how's" interest every one. It is a pleasure sometimes to be out in dirty weather on a lee shore; it permits you to devote all your energies to accomplishing something. When secretary for our hospital rowing club on the Thames, a fine cup was given for competition by Sir Frederick Treves on terms symbolic of his attitude to life. The race was to be in ordinary punts with a coxswain "in order that every ounce of energy should be devoted to the progress of the boat."

That is the whole trouble with the Newfoundland Labrador. All moneys granted for education are handed to the churches for sectarian schools. It is almost writing ourselves down as still living in the Middle Ages, when the Clergy had a monopoly of polite learning. In more densely populated countries this division of grants need not be so disastrous. Here it means that one often finds a Roman Catholic, a Church of England, a Methodist, and a Salvation Army school, all in one little village — and no school whatever in the adjoining place.

The denominational spirit, fostered by these sectarian schools and societies, is so emphasized that Catholic and Protestant have little in common. Some preferred to let their children or themselves suffer pain and inefficiency, rather than come for relief to a hospital where the doctors were Protestant. This has in some measure passed away, but it was painfully real at first —

so much so that once a rickety, crippled child, easily cured, though he actually came to the harbour, was forbidden to land and returned home to be a cripple for life.

The salaries available offer no attraction to enter the teaching profession in this island; and there is no compulsory education law to assist those who with lofty motives remain loyal to the profession when "better chances" come along. Gauged rightly, there is no such thing as a better chance for fulfilling life's purposes than an education; and modern conditions concede the right of a decent living wage to all who render service to the world in whatever line.

In the little village where are our headquarters there was already a Church of England and a Methodist school when we came there, and a Salvation Army one has since been added. Threats of still another "institution of learning" menaced us at one time — almost like a new Egyptian plague, with more permanency of results thrown in.

If the motor power of the school boat is dissipated in sectarian religious education, not to say focussed on it, the arrival of the cargo must be seriously handicapped. The statistical returns may show a majority of our fishermen as "able to read and write"; but as a matter of fact the illiteracy and ignorance of North Newfoundland and Labrador is the greatest handicap in the lives of the people.

My first scholar came from North Labrador, long before we aspired to a school of our own. He was a lad of Scotch extraction and name, and came aboard the hospital ship one night, as she lay at anchor among some northern islands, with the request that we would take him up with us to some place where he could get an hour's schooling a day. He offered to work all the rest of the time in return for his food and clothing. To-day he holds a Pratt certificate, is head of our machine shop, has a sheet-metal working factory of his own which fills a most valuable purpose on the shore, is general consultant for the coast in matters of engineering, as well as being the Government surveyor for his district. He is also chief musician for the church, having fitted himself for both those latter posts in his "spare time." The inspiration which his life has been is in itself an education to many of us — a reflex result which is the really highest value of all life.

As each transferred individual has come back North for service, desire has at once manifested itself for similar privileges in young people who had not previously shown even interest enough to attend our winter night schools. This is the best evidence that inroads are being made into that natural apathy which is content with mediocrity or even inferiority. This is everywhere the world's most subtle enemy. Even if selfishness or envy has been the motive, the fact remains that they have often kindled that discontent with the past which Charles Kingsley preached as necessary to all progress. Nowhere could the pathology of the matter be more easily traced than in these concrete examples carrying the infection which could come from no other quarter into our isolation. It has been in very humble life an example of the return of the "Yankee to the Court of King Arthur."

There was a time when Lord Haldane proposed that every English child, who in the Board schools had proved his ability to profit by it, should be given a college or university education at the expense of the State — as a remunerative outlay for the nation. This proposal was turned down as being too costly, though the expenditure for a single day's runnng of this war would have gone a long way to provide such a fund. We now know that it can be done and must be done as a sign manual of real freedom, which is not the leaving of parents or forbears, incompetent for any reason, free to damn their country with a stream of stunted intellects.

America has already honoured herself forever by being a pioneer in this movement for the higher education of the people. Religion surely need not fear mental enlightenment. The dangers of life lie in ignorance, and after all is not true religion a thing of the intellect as well as of the heart? Can that really be inculcated in "two periods of forty minutes each week devoted to sectarian teaching," which was one of the concessions demanded of us in our fight for a free public or common school at St. Anthony? My own mental picture of myself at the age of seven sitting on a bench for forty minutes twice every week learning to be "religious" made me sympathize with Scrooge when the Ghost of the Past was paying him a visit.

One thing was certain. The young lives entrusted to us were having as good medical care for their bodies as we could provide; and if we could compass it, we were going to have that paralleled for their minds. The parents of the village children could do as they liked with those committed to them — and they did it. There is nothing so thoroughly reactionary that I know of as religious prejudice well ground in. As regards the treatment of physical ailments the prejudices of what Dr. Holmes called "Homœopathy and Kindred Delusions" always are strong in proportion as they are impregnated with some religious bias.

Our efforts to combine the local schools having failed, we had to provide a building of our own. This we felt must be planned for the future. For some day the halcyon days of peace on earth shall be permitted in our community, and the true loyalty of efficient service to our brothers will, it is to be hoped, become actually the paramount object of our Christian religion. Perhaps this terrible war will have convinced the world that the loftiest aspirations of mankind are no more to save yourself hereafter than here. Is it not as true as ever that if we are not ourselves possessors of Christ's spirit, ourselves we cannot save?

The only schoolhouse available, anyhow, was not nearly so good a building as that which we have since provided for the accommodation of our pigs! Fat pork is considered an absolute essential "down North"; and it was cheaper and safer, according to Upton Sinclair, to raise pigs than buy the salted or tinned article. So we had instituted what we deemed a missionary enterprise in that line. (*Pace* our vegetarian friends.)

As soon as a sum of three thousand dollars had been raised, architect friends at the Pratt Institute sent down to us competitive designs, and one of our Labrador boys, who had studied there, erected the building. Having at the beginning no funds whatever for current expenses, we had to look for volunteer teachers. One denomination helped with part of its harbour grant, but the Government would not make any special donation toward the union school project. Even the caput grant, to which we had hoped that we were entitled for our own orphanage children, had by law to go to the denomination to which their parents had belonged. This was not always easy to decide correctly. On the occasion of taking the last census in Labrador, a well-dressed stranger suddenly visited one of our settlements on the east coast. It so happened that a very poor man with a large and growing family of eight children under ten years, who resided there, was not so loyal to his church as we are taught we ought to be. When the stranger entered his tilt a vision of material favours to be obtained was the dominant idea in the fisherman's mind. He was therefore on tenterhooks all the while that the questioning was going on lest some blunder of his might alienate the sympathy on which he was banking for "getting his share." At length it came to the momentous point of "What denomination do you belong to?" — a very vital matter when it comes to sympathy and sharing up. In some hesitation he gazed at the row of his eight unwashed and but half-clad offspring, whose treacly faces gaped open-mouthed at the visitor. Then with sudden inspiration he decided to play for safety, and replied, "Half of them is Church of England, and half is Methodist!"

Being an unrecognized school, and so far off, some years went by before the innovation of bringing up scholars from our northern district entered our heads. We realized at length, however, that we should close one channel of criticism to the enemy if we proved that we could justify our school by their standard of annual examinations. Our teachers, being mostly volunteers, had to come from outside the Colony. Having no funds to purchase books and other supplies, we made use of books also sent us from outside. The real value of the local examination becomes questionable as a standard of success when far more highly educated teachers, and at least as cleverly laid-out study books, prevented the children in our school from passing them.

Moreover, further to waken their faculties, we had included in our facilities a large upper hall of the school building and a library of some thousands of books collected from all quarters. The former afforded the stimulus which entertainments given by the children could carry, and also space for physical drill; the latter, that greatest incentive of all, access to books which lure people to wish to read them. In summer the parents and older children are busy with the fisheries day and night, and the little children run more or less wild, so this form of occupation was doubly desirable.

The generous help of summer volunteers, especially a trained kindergartner, Miss Olive Lesley, gave us a regular summer school. All the expensive outfit needed was also donated. Eye and hand were enlisted in the service of brain evolution; while a piano, which it is true had seen better days, pressed the ear and the imagination into the service as well.

One of the great gaps in child development in Labrador had been the almost entire lack of games. The very first year of our coming the absence of dolls had so impressed itself upon us that the second season we had brought out a trunkful. Even then we found later that the dolls were perched high up on the walls as ornaments, just out of reach of the children. In one little house I found a lad playing with some marbles. For lack of better these were three-quarter-inch bullets which "Dad had given him," while the alley was a full-inch round ball, which belonged to what my host was pleased to call "the little darlint" — a hoary blunderbuss over six feet in length. The skipper informed me that he had plenty of "fresh" for the winter, largely as a result of the successful efforts of the "darlint"; though it appeared to have exploded with the same fatal effect this year as the season previous. "I hear that you made a good shot the other day, Uncle Joe," I remarked. "Nothing to speak on," he answered. "I only got forty-three, though I think there was a few more if I could have found them on the ice."

The pathos of the lack of toys and games appealed especially to the Anglo-Saxon, who believes that if he has any advantage over competitors, it is not merely in racial attributes, but in the reaction of those attributes which develop in him the ineradicable love of athletics and sport. The fact that he dubs the classmate whom he admires most "a good sport," shows that he thinks so, anyway.

So organized play was carefully introduced on the coast. It caught like wildfire among the children, and it was delightful to see groups of them naïvely memorizing by the roadside school lessons in the form of "Ring-of-Roses," "Looby-Loo," "All on the Train for Boston." To our dismay in the minds of the local people the very success of this effort gave further evidence of our incompetence.

Our people have well-defined, though often singular, ideas as to what Almighty God does and does not allow; and among the pursuits which are irrevocably condemned by local oracles is dancing. The laxity of "foreigners" on this article of the Creed is proverbial. At the time there were two ministers in the place, and realizing that the people considered that our kindergarten was introducing the thin edge of the wedge, and that our whole effort might meet with disaster unless the rumours were checked, I went in search of them without delay. Three o'clock found us knocking at the kindergarten door. The teacher and source of the reputed scandal seemed in no way disconcerted by the visitation. The first game was irreproachable — every child was sitting on the floor. But next the children were choosing partners, and though the boys had chosen boys, and the girls girls, the suspicions of the vigilance committee were aroused. No danger, however, to the three R's transpired, and we were next successfully piloted clear of condemnation through a game entitled "Piggie-wig and Piggie-wee." Our circulation was just beginning to operate once more in its normal fashion when we were told that the whole company would now "join hands and move around in a circle" to music. The entire jury sensed that the crucial moment had come. We saw boys and girls alternating, hand held in hand — and all to the undeniably secular libretto of "Looby-Loo." It was, moreover, noted with inward pain that many of the little feet actually left the ground. We adjourned to an adjacent fish stage to discuss the matter. I need not dilate on the vicissitudes of the session. It was clear that all but "Looby-Loo" could obviously be excluded from the group of "questionables" — but the last game was of a different calibre and must be put to vote. My readers will be relieved to learn that the resultant ballot was unanimously in favour of non-interference, and that from the pulpit the following Sunday the clergy gave to the kindergarten the official sanction of the Church.

Other outsiders now began telling the people that we could not pass the Colony's examinations because we wasted our efforts on teaching "foolishness"; and the denomination which had hitherto lent us aid withdrew it, and tried again to run a midget sectarian school right alongside. The first occasion, however, on which this institution came seriously to my attention was when the minister and another young man came to call during the early weeks of our winter school session. The stranger was their special teacher. He was undoubtedly a smart lad; he had passed the preliminary examination. But he was only sixteen, and in temperament a very young sixteen at that. He was engaged at a more generous salary than usual, and was perfectly prepared to revolutionize our records. But, alas, not only was their little building practically unfit for habitation, but after a week's waiting not one single scholar had come to his school. The contrast between the two opportunities was too great — except for frothing criticism. Gladly, to help our neighbours out of a difficulty, we divided a big classroom into two parts, added a third teacher to our school, and were thus able to make an intermediate grade.

The great majority of the whole reconstruction and work of the school was made possible by the generous and loving interest of a lady in Chicago. Added to the other anxieties of meeting our annual budget, we did not feel able to bear the additional burden for which this venture called. One cannot work at one's best at any time with an anxious mind. The lady, however, was generous enough to give sufficient endowment to secure two teachers among other things, though she absolutely refused to let even her name be known in connection with the school. Our consolation is that we know that she has vision enough to realize the value of her gift and to accept that as a more than sufficient return.

Seeing that some of our older scholars were able to find really useful and remunerative employment in teaching, and as only for those who held certificates of having passed the local examinations were augmentation grants available, we decided to make special efforts to have our scholars pass by the local standards. We, therefore, thanks to the endowment, engaged teachers trained in the country, and instituted the curriculum of the Colony. These teachers told us that our school was better than almost any outside St. John's. Four scholars have passed this year; and now we have as head mistress a delightful lady who holds the best percentage record for passing children through the requirements of the local examinations of any in the country.

So much more deeply, however, do idle words sink into some natures than even deeds, that one family preferred to keep their children at home to risk sending them to our undenominational school; and there is no law to compel better wisdom with us here in the North.

On the other hand, we had already obtained a scale of our own for grading success. For a number of our most promising boys and girls we had raised the money for them to get outside the country what they could never get in it, namely, the technical training which is so much needed on a coast where we have to do everything for ourselves, and the breadth of view which contact with a more progressive civilization alone can give them. The faculty of Pratt Institute gave us a scholarship, and later two of them; and with no little fear as to their ability to keep up, we sent two young men there. The newness of our school forced us to select at the beginning boys who had only received teaching after their working hours. Both boys and girls have always had to earn something to help them on their way through. But they have stood the test of efficiency so well that we look forward with confidence to the future. A girl who took the Domestic Economy course at the Nasson Institute told me only to-day, "It gave me a new life altogether, Doctor"; and she is making a splendid return in service to her own people here.

The real test of education is its communal effect; and no education is complete which leaves the individual ignorant of the things that concern his larger relationship to his country, any more than he is anything beyond a learned animal if he knows nothing of his opportunities and responsibilities as a son of God. But though example is a more impelling factor than precept, undoubtedly the most permanent contributions conferred on the coast by the many college students, who come as volunteers every summer to help us in the various branches of our work, is just this gift of their own personalities. Strangely enough, quite a number of these helpers who have to spend considerable money coming and returning, just to give us what they can for the sole return of what that means to their own lives, have not been the sons of the wealthy, but those working their way through the colleges. These men are just splendid to hold up as inspirational to our own.

The access to books, as well as to sermons, may not be neglected. Our faculties, like our jaws, atrophy if we do not use them to bite with. The Carnegie libraries have emphasized a fact that is to education and the colleges what social work is to medicine and the hospitals. We were running south some years ago on our long northern trip before a fine leading wind, when suddenly we noticed a small boat with an improvised flag hoisted, standing right out across our bows. Thinking that it was at least some serious surgical case, we at once ordered "Down sail and heave her to," annoying though it was to have the trouble and delay. When at last she was alongside, a solitary, white-haired old man climbed with much difficulty over our rail. "Good-day. What's the trouble? We are in a hurry." The old man most courteously doffed his cap, and stood holding it in his hand. "I wanted to ask you, Doctor," he said slowly, "if you had any books which you could lend me. We can't get anything to read here." An angry reply almost escaped my lips for delaying a steamer for such a purpose. But a strange feeling of humiliation replaced it almost immediately. Which is really charity — skilfully to remove his injured leg, if he had one, or to afford him the pleasure and profit of a good book? Both services were just as far from his reach without our help.

"Haven't you got any books?"

"Yes, Doctor, I've got two, but I've read them through and through long ago."

"What kind are they?"

"One is the 'Works of Josephus,'" he answered, "and the other is 'Plutarch's Lives.'"

I thought that I had discovered the first man who could honestly and truthfully say that he would prefer for his own library the "best hundred books," selected by Mr. Ruskin and Dr. Eliot, without even so much as a sigh for the "ten best sellers."

He was soon bounding away over the seas in his little craft, the happy possessor of one of our moving libraries, containing some fifty books, ranging from Henty's stories to discarded tomes from theological libraries.

Each year the hospital ship moves these library boxes one more stage along the coast. As there are some seventy-five of them, they thus last the natural life of books, since we have only rarely enjoyed the help of a trained librarian enabling us to make the most use of these always welcome assets for our work. Later, some librarian friends from Brooklyn, chief among whom was Miss Marion Cutter, came down to help us; but our inability to have continuity when the ladies cannot afford to give their valuable services, has seriously handicapped the efficiency of this branch of the work. This, however, only spells opportunity, and when this war releases the new appreciation of service, we feel confident that somehow we shall be able to fill the gap, and some one will be found to come and help us again to meet this great need.

The coöperation of teachers and librarians more than

doubles the capacity of each alone, and we believe sincerely that they do that of doctors, as they unquestionably do that of the clergy. All the world's workers have infinitely more to gain by coöperation than they often suspect. And indeed we who are apostles of coöperation, as essential for economy in distribution and efficiency in production, realize that groups of workers pulling together always increase by geometrical progression the result obtained.

None of our methods, however, tackled the smallest settlements, hidden away here and there in these fjords, especially those unreached by the mail steamers and devoid of means of transportation. Mahomet just could not come to the mountain, so it had to go to him. A lady and a Doctor of Philosophy, Miss Ethel Gordon Muir, whose life had been spent in teaching, and who would have been excused for discontinuing that function during her long vacations, came down at her own cost and charges to carry the light to one of these lonely settlements. She has with loyal devotion continued to carry on and enlarge that work ever since, till finally she has built up a work that the clergyman of the main section of coast affected, and also the Superintendent of Education, have declared is the most effective branch of our Mission. Her band of teachers are volunteers. They come down to these little hamlets for the duration of their summer vacations. They live with the fishermen in their cottages and gather their pupils daily wherever seems best. Lack of proper accommodation and pioneer conditions throughout in no way deter them. We expected that their criticism would be, "It is not worth while." That has never been the case. Before the war they came again and again, as a testimony to their belief in the value of the effort. Some have given promising children a chance for a complete education in the States. Indeed, one such lad, taken down some years ago by one of the students, entered Amherst College last year; while several were fighting with the American boys "Over There."

The only real joy of possession is the power which it confers for a larger life of service. Has it been the reader's good fortune ever to save a human life? A cousin of mine, an officer in the submarine service of the Royal Engineers, told me a year or two before the war that he was never quite happy because he had spent all his life acquiring special capacities which he never in the least expected to be able to put to practical use. This war has given to him, at least, what possessions could never have offered.

It almost requires the fabulous Jack to overcome the hoary giants of prejudice and custom, or the irrepressible energy of the Gorgon. It has been helpful to remember away "down North" the stand which Archbishop Ireland took for public schools. When the Episcopal clergyman for Labrador, whom we had been influential in bringing out from England, decided to start an undenominational boarding-school on his section of the coast, we began to hope that we might yet live to see our sporadic effort become a policy. Laymen in St. John's, led by the Rev. Dr. Edgar Jones, a most progressive clergyman, sympathized in dollars, and we were able to back the effort. A splendid volunteer head teacher will arrive in the spring to begin work. The effort still needs much help; but I am persuaded that a chain of undenominational schools can be started that will react on the whole country. Already a scheme for a similar uplift for the west coast is being promulgated.

In a letter written to my wife some years ago I find

that my convictions on the subject of education were no less firm than they are to-day. One came to the conclusion that "ignorance is the worst cause of suffering on our coast, and our 'religion' is fostering it. True, it has denominational schools, but these are to bolster up special ecclesiastical bodies, and are not half so good as Government schools would be. The 'goods delivered' in the schools are not educational in the best sense, and are all too often inefficiently offered. Instead of making the children ambitious to go on learning through life, they make them tired. There is no effort to stimulate the play side; and in our north end of the Colony's territory there are no trades taught, no new ideas, no manual training — it is all so-called 'arts' and Creeds."

CHAPTER XVI

"WHO HATH DESIRED THE SEA?"

WE are somewhat superstitious down here still, and not a few believe that shoals and submerged rocks are like sirens which charm vessels to their doom.

On one occasion, as late in the fall we were creeping up the Straits of Belle Isle in the only motor boat then in use there, our new toy broke down, and with a strong onshore wind we gradually drifted in toward the high cliffs. It was a heavy boat, and though we rowed our best we realized that we must soon be on the rocks, where a strong surf was breaking. So we lashed all our lines together and cast over our anchors, hoping to find bottom. Alas, the water was too deep. Darkness came on and the prospect of a long, weary night struggling for safety made us thrill with excitement. Suddenly a schooner's lights, utterly unexpected, loomed up, coming head on toward us. Like Saul and his asses, we no longer cared about our craft so long as we escaped. At once we lashed the hurricane light on the boat-hook and waved it to and fro on high to make sure of attracting attention. To our dismay the schooner, now almost in hail, incontinently tacked, and, making for the open sea, soon left us far astern. We fired our guns, we shouted in unison, we lit flares. All to no purpose. Surely it must have been a phantom vessel sent to mock us. Suddenly our amateur engineer, who had all the time been working away at the scrap-heap of parts into which he had dismembered the motor, got a faint kick out of one cylinder — a second — a third, then two, three, and then a solitary one again. It was exactly like a case of blocked heart. But it was enough with our oars to make us move slowly ahead. By much stimulating and watchful nursing we limped along on the one cylinder, and about midnight found ourselves alongside the phantom ship, which we had followed into the harbour "afar off." Angry enough at their desertion of us in distress, we went aboard just to tell them what we thought of their behaviour. But their explanation entirely disarmed us. "Them cliffs is haunted," said the skipper. "More'n one light 's been seen there than ever any man lit. When us saw you'se light flashing round right in on the cliffs, us knowed it was no place for Christian men that time o' night. Us guessed it was just fairies or devils trying to toll us in."

We had no lighthouses on Labrador in those days, and though hundreds of vessels, crowded often with women and children, had to pass up and down the coast each spring and fall, still not a single island, harbour, cape, or reef had any light to mark it, and many boats were unnecessarily lost as a result.

Most of the schooners of this large fleet are small. Many are old and poorly "found" in running gear. Their decks are so crowded with boats, barrels, gear, wood, and other impedimenta, that to reef or handle sails on a dark night is almost impossible; while below they were often so crowded with women and children going North with their men for the summer fishing on the Labrador shore, that I have had to crawl on my knees to get at a patient, after climbing down through the main hatch. These craft are quite unfitted for a rough night at sea, especially as there always are icebergs or big pans about, which if touched would each spell another "vessel missing." So the craft all creep North and South in the spring and fall along the land, darting into harbours before dark, and

leaving before dawn if the night proves "civil." Yet
many a time I have seen these little vessels with their
precious cargoes becalmed, or with wind ahead, just
unable to make anchorage, and often on moonless nights
when the barometer has been low and the sky threatening. As there were no lights on the land, it would have
been madness to try and make harbours after sundown.

I have known the cruel, long anxiety of heart which
the dilemma involved. It has been our great pleasure
sometimes to run out and tow vessels in out of their distress. I can still feel the grip of one fine skipper, who
came aboard when the sea eased down. The only harbour
available for us had been very small, and the water too
deep for his poor gear. So when he started to drift, we
had given him a line and let him hold on to us through
the night, with his own stern only a few yards from the
cliffs under his lee, and all his loved ones, as well as his
freighters, a good deal nearer heaven than he wished
them to be.

We had frequently written to the Government of this
neglect of lights for the coast. But Labrador has no
representative in the Newfoundland Parliament, and
legislators who never visited Labrador had unimagina-
tive minds. Year after year went by and nothing was
done. So I spoke to many friends of the dire need for a
light near Battle Harbour Hospital. Practically every
one of the Northern craft ran right by us many times as
they fished first in the Gulf and later on the east coast,
and so had to go past that corner of land. I have seen a
hundred vessels come and anchor near by in a single
evening. When the money was donated, our architect
designed the building, and a friend promised to endow
the effort, so that the salary of the light-keeper might be
permanent. The material was cut and sent North, when

DRYING THE SEINES

FISH ON THE FLAKES

we were politely told that the Government could not permit private ownership of lights — a very proper decision, too. They told us that the year before money had been voted by the House for lights, and the first would be erected near Battle Harbour. This was done, and the Double Island Light has been a veritable Godsend to me as well as to thousands of others many times since that day.

One hundred miles north of Indian Tickle, a place also directly in the run of all the fishing schooners, a light was much needed. On a certain voyage coming South with the fleet in the fall, we had all tried to make the harbour, but it shut down suddenly before nightfall with a blanket of fog which you could almost cut with a knife, and being inside many reefs, and unable to make the open, we were all forced to anchor. Where we were exactly none of us knew, for we had all pushed on for the harbour as much as we dared. There were eleven riding-lights visible around us when a rift came in the fog. We hoped against hope that we had made the harbour. A fierce northeaster gathered strength as night fell, and a mighty sea began to heave in. Soon we strained at our anchors in the big seas, and heavy water swept down our decks from bow to stern. Our patients were dressed and our boats gotten ready, though it all had only a psychological value. Gradually we missed first one and then another of the riding-lights, and it was not difficult to guess what had happened. When daylight broke, only one boat was left — a large vessel called the Yosemite, and she was drifting right down toward us. Suddenly she touched a reef, turned on her side, and we saw the seas carry her over the breakers, the crew hanging on to her bilge. Steaming to our anchors had saved us. All the vessels that went ashore became matchwood. But before we could get our anchors or slip them, our main steam pipe gave out and we had to blow down our boilers. It was now a race between the engineers trying to repair the damage and the shortening hours of daylight. On the result depended quite possibly the lives of us all. I cannot remember one sweeter sound than the raucous voice of the engineer just in the nick of time calling out, "Right for'ard," and then the signal of the engine-room bell in the tell-tale in our little wheel-house. The Government has since put a fine little light in summer on White Point, the point off which we lay.

Farther north, right by our hospital at Indian Harbour, is a narrow tickle known as the "White Cockade." Through this most of the fleet pass, and here also we had planned for a lighthouse. When we were forbidden to put our material at Battle Harbour, we suggested moving to this almost equally important point. But it fell under the same category, and soon after the Government put a good light there also. The fishermen, therefore, suggested that we should offer our peripatetic, would-be lighthouse to the Government for some new place each year.

We have not much now to complain of so far as the needs of our present stage of evolution goes. We have wireless stations, quite a number of lights, not a few landmarks, and a ten times better mail and transport service than the much wealthier and more able Dominion of Canada could and ought to give to her long shore from Quebec to the eastern "Newfoundland" boundary on the Straits Labrador.

He is not a great legislator who only makes provision for certainties. True, the West has shown such riches and capacity that it has paid better to develop it first. But there is no excuse now whatever for neglecting the East. The Dominion would have been well advised, indeed,

had she years ago built a railway to the east coast, shortening the steamer communication with England to only
two nights at sea, and saving twenty-four hours for the
mails between London and Toronto. The war has shown
how easily she could have afforded it. Most ardently I
had hoped that she might have turned some of her German prisoner labour in so invaluable a direction.

Had the reindeer installation been handled by the
Newfoundland Government years ago as it should have
been, Labrador would have yielded to our boys in France
a very material assistance in meat and furs. Canada now
could and should, if only in the interest of her native
population, begin on this problem as soon as peace is
declared.

The fact that a thing possesses vitality is a guarantee
that it will grow if it can. Each new focus will expand,
and caterpillar-like cast off its old clothing for better.
The first necessity for economy and efficiency in our
work has been to get our patients quickly to us or to be
able to get to them. Experience has shown us that while
boats entirely dependent on motors are cheapest, it is
not always safe to do open-sea work in such launches
without a secondary and more reliable means of progression. The stories of a doctor's work in these launches
would fill a volume by themselves. The first Northern
Messenger, a small "hot-head" boat, was replaced and
sold to pay part of the cost of Northern Messenger number two. This in its turn was wrecked on an uncharted
shoal with Dr. West on board, and her insurance used
to help to procure Northern Messenger number three —
which is the beautiful boat which now serves Harrington,
our most westerly hospital. We are largely indebted for
her to Mr. William Bowditch, of Milton, Massachusetts.

Dr. Hare, our first doctor at that station, never wrote

his own experiences, but one of the Yale volunteers who worked under him wrote a story founded on fact, from which the following incident is suggestive.

Once, running home before a wind in the Gulf, the doctor suddenly missed his little son Pat, and looking round saw him struggling in the water, already many yards astern. Dr. Hare, who was at the tiller at the time, instantly jumped over after him. The child was finally disappearing when he reached him at last and held his head above water. Meanwhile the engineer, who had been below, jumped on deck to find the sails flapping in the wind and the boat head to sea. With the intuitive quickness of our people in matters pertaining to the sea, he took in the situation in a second, and though entirely alone manœuvred the boat so cleverly as to pick them both up before they perished in these frigid waters. Pat's young life was saved, only to be given a short few years later in France for the same fight for the kingdom of righteousness which his home life had made his familiar ideal.

The forty-five-foot, "hot-head" yawl Daryl, given us by the Dutch Reformed friends in New York, was sold to the Hudson Bay Company. At first she was naturally called the Flying Dutchman, and was most useful; but here we have learned when a better instrument is available that it is the truest economy to scrap-heap the old. We were to give delivery of the boat in Baffin's Land. There were plenty of volunteers for the task, for the tough jobs are the very ones which appeal to real men. It would be well if the churches realized this fact and that therein lies the real secret of Christianity. The impression that being a Christian is a soft job inevitably brings our religion into contempt. I had been in England that spring, and had been able to arrange that the mail steamer bound for Montreal on which I took passage should stop and drop me off Belle Isle if the crusaders who were to take this launch on her long voyage North would stand out across our pathway. Mr. Marconi personally took an interest in the venture. The launch was to wait at our most easterly Labrador station, and we were to keep telling her our position. The boat was in charge of Mr. John Rowland and Mr. Robert English, both of Yale. It created quite a furor among the passengers on our great ship, when she stopped in mid-ocean, as it appeared to them, and lowered an erratic doctor over the side on to a midget, whose mast-tops one looked down upon from the liner's rail. The sensation was all the more marked as we disappeared over the rail clinging to two large pots of geraniums — an importation which we regarded as very much worth while.

With an old Hudson Bay man, Mr. George Ford, to act as interpreter, and a Harvard colleague, who to his infinite chagrin was recalled by a wireless from his parents almost before starting, the little ship and her crew of three disappeared "over the edge" beyond communication. I should mention that the Company had promised an engineer for the launch, but he had begged off when he understood the nature of the projected expedition; so Yale decided that they were men enough to do without any outside help.

September had nearly gone, and no news had come from the boys. I owe some one an infinite debt for a temperament which does not go halfway to meet troubles; but even I was a little worried when unkind rumours that we had sold a boat that was not safe were capped by a father's letter to say that he "had heard the reports"! Fortunately, two days later, as the Strathcona lay taking on whale meat for winter dog food at the northernmost factory, the Northern mail steamer came in. On board were our returned wanderers, and papa, who had gone down as far as the Labrador steamer runs to look for them, as proud and happy as a man has a right to be over sons who do things. The boys had not only reached Baffin's Land, but had explored over a hundred miles of its uncharted coast-line, crossed to Cape Wolstenholme, navigated Stupart's Bay — northeast of Ungava — and finally returned to Baffin's Land, coming back to Cartwright on the Hudson Bay Company's steamer Pelican. It was a splendid record, especially when we remember the fierce currents and tremendous rise and fall of tides in that distant land. This latter was so great that having anchored one night in three fathoms of water in what appeared to be a good harbour, they had awakened in the morning to the fact that they were in a pond a full mile in the country, left stranded by the retiring tide.

Our last "hot-head," the Pomiuk, in a heavy gale of wind was smashed to atoms on a terrible reef of rocks off Domino Point a mile from land — fortunately with no one aboard. Yet another of our fine yawls, the Andrew McCosh, given us by the students of Princeton, was driven from her anchors on to the dangerous Point Amour, where years ago, H.M.S. Lily was lost, and whose bones still lie bleaching on the rocky foreshore at the foot of the cliffs. Much as I love the sea, it made one rather "sore" that it should serve us such a turn as wrecking the McCosh. I have been on the sea for over thirty years and never lost a vessel while aboard her, but to look on while the waves destroyed so beautiful a handmaid almost reconciled me to the statement that in heaven there shall "be no more sea."

It was near this same spot that in November, 1905, a very old vessel, while trying to cross the Straits in a breeze, suddenly sprung a leak which sent her to the bottom in spite of all the pumping which could be done. The six men aboard were able to keep afloat at that time of year in the open Atlantic out of sight of land for five days and nights. They had nothing to eat but dry bread, and no covering of any kind. The winds were heavy and the seas high all the while. By patiently keeping their little boat's head to the wind with the oars, for they had not any sails, day after day and night after night, and backing her astern when a breaker threatened to overwhelm them, they eventually reached land safe and sound.

The special interest about the launches has always been the pleasant connection which they have enabled us to maintain with the universities. Yale crews, Harvard crews, Princeton crews, Johns Hopkins crews, College of Physicians and Surgeons crews, and combined crews of many others, have in succeeding years thus become interested. Occasionally these men have taken back some of their Labrador shipmates to the United States for a year's education, and in that and other ways, so they say, have they themselves received much real joy and inspiration.

In order to maintain the interest which Canada had taken in our work, it had in some way to be organized. We had volunteer honorary secretaries in a few cities, but no way of keeping them informed of our needs and our progress. In New England a most loyal friend, Miss Emma White, who ever since has been secretary and devoted helper of the Labrador work there, had started a regular association with a board of directors and had taken an office in Beacon Street, Boston. This association now and again published little brochures of our work, or ordered out a few copies of the English magazine called "The Toilers of the Deep." It was suggested that we might with advantage publish a quarterly pamphlet of our own. This was made possible by the generous help of the late Miss Julia Greenshields, of Toronto, who undertook not only to edit, but also personally to finance any loss on a little magazine to be entitled "Among the Deep-Sea Fishers." This has been maintained ever since, and has been responsible for helping to raise many of the funds to enable us to "carry on."

We had also begun to get friends in New York. Dr. Charles Parkhurst, famous especially for his plucky exposure of the former rottenness of the police force of that city, had asked me to give an illustrated lecture at his mission in the Bowery. After my talk a gentleman present, to my blank astonishment, gave me a cheque for five hundred dollars. It was the beginning of a lifelong friendship with one who has, for all the succeeding years, given far more than money, namely, the constant inspiration of his own attitude to life and his wise counsel — to say nothing of the value of the endorsation of his name. His eldest son, one of the ablest of the rising New York architects, became chairman of the Grenfell Association of America, and gave us both of his time and talent — he being responsible, as voluntary architect, for many of our present buildings, including the Institute at St. John's, Newfoundland.

This spread of interest in the United States greatly increased our correspondence, with an odd result. Americans apparently all believed that this Colony was part of Canada, and that the postage was two cents as to the Dominion. This mistake left us six cents to pay on every letter, and sixteen on any which were overweight. On one occasion the postmaster offered me so many taxable letters that I decided to accept only one, and let the others go back. That one contained a cheque for a hundred dollars for the Mission. I naturally took the rest, and found every one of them to be bills, gossip, or from autograph-hunters.

On inquiry, our Postmaster-General informed me that it was not possible to arrange a two-cent postal rate with America. It had been tried and abandoned, because Canada wanted a share for carrying the letters through her territory. He told me, however, that he would agree gladly if the United States offered it. On my visit to Washington I had the honour of dining with Lord Bryce, our Ambassador there and an old friend of my father's, and I mentioned the matter to him. He could not, however, commend my efforts to the Government, as I had no credentials as a special delegate. There was nothing to do but take my place in the queue of importunates waiting to interview the Postmaster-General. When at length I had been moved to the top of the bench, I was called in, and very soon explained my mission. I received a most cordial hearing, but merely the information that a note would be made of my request and filed.

It suddenly flashed upon me that Americans had equal fishing rights with ourselves on the Labrador coast, and that quite a number visited there every year. Possibly the grant of a two-cent postage would be a welcome little "sop" to them. Mr. Meyer, who was the Postmaster-General at the time, said that it made all the difference if the reduced rate would in any way encourage the American mercantile marine. He bade me draw a careful list of reasons in favour of my proposal, and promised to give it careful attention.

It so happened that a few days later I mentioned the matter to Colonel McCook at whose home I was staying in New York. Colonel McCook, known as "Fighting

McCook," from the fact that he was the only one of nine brothers not killed in the Civil War, at once took up the cudgels in my behalf, left for Washington the following day, and wired me on the next morning, "All arranged. Congratulations" — and I had the pleasure of telegraphing the Postmaster-General in St. John's that I had arranged the two-cent postage rate with the United States and Newfoundland. A few days later I received a marked copy of a Newfoundland paper saying how capable a Government they possessed, seeing that now they had so successfully put through the two-cent post for the Colony — and that was all the notice ever taken of my only little political intrigue; except that a year or two later, meeting Mr. Meyer in Cambridge, he whispered in my ear, "We were going out of office in four days, or you would never have got that two-cent post law of yours through so easily."

In the spring of 1907 I was in England, and before I left, my old University was good enough to offer me an honorary degree of Doctor of Medicine of Oxford. As it was the first occasion that that respectable old University had ever given that particular degree to any one, I was naturally not a little gratified. The day of the conferring of it will ever live in my memory. My cousin, the Professor of Paleontology, half of whose life was spent in the desert of Egypt digging for papyri in old dustheaps, was considered the most appropriate person to stand sponsor for me — a would-be pioneer of a new civilization in the sub-arctic.

The words with which the Public Orator introduced me to the Vice-Chancellor, being in Latin, seem to me interesting as a relic rather than as a statement of fact:

"Insignissime Vice-Cancellarie vosque egregii Procuratores: Adest civis Britannicus, hujus academiæ olim alumnus, nunc Novum Orbem incolentibus quam nostratibus notus. Hic ille est qui quindecim abhinc annos in litus Labradorium profectus est, ut solivagis in mari Boreali piscatoribus ope medica succurreret; quo in munere obeundo Oceani pericula, quæ ibi formidosissima sunt, contempsit dum miseris et mærentibus solatium ac lumen afferret. Nunc quantum homini licet, in ipsius Christi vestigiis, si fas est dicere, insistere videtur, vir vere Christianus. Jure igitur eum laudamus cujus laudibus non ipse solum sed etiam Academia nostra ornatur.

"Præsenta ad vos Wilfredum Thomassum Grenfell, ut admittatur ad gradum Doctoris in Medicina Honoris Causa."

As we, the only two Doctors Grenfell extant, marched solemnly back down the aisle side by side, the antithesis of what doctorates called for struck my sense of humour most forcibly. I had hired the gorgeous robes of scarlet box cloth and carmine silk for the occasion, never expecting to wear them again. But some years later, when yet another honorary Doctorate, of Laws, was most generously conferred upon me by a University of our American cousins, I felt it incumbent on me to uphold if possible the British end of the ritual. A cable brought me just in time the box-cloth surtout. Commencement ceremonies in the United States are in June; and the latitude was that of Rome. For years I had spent the hot months always in the sub-arctic. The assembly hall was small and crowded to bursting — not even all the graduating class could get in, much less all their friends. The temperature was in three figures. The scarlet box cloth got hotter and hotter as we paraded in and about the campus. My face outrivalled the gown in colour. I have made many lobster

men out of the boiled limbs of those admirable adjuncts
of a Northern diet, but I had never expected to pose as
one in the flesh. The most lasting impression which the
ceremony left on my mind is of my volunteer summer
secretary, who stood almost on my toes as he delivered
the valedictory address of his class. I still see his gradually wilting, boiled collar, and the tiny rivulet which
trickled down his neck as he warmed to his subject. We
were the best of friends, but I felt that glow of semi-
satisfaction that comes to the man who finds that he is
no longer the only one seasick on board.

About this time King Edward most graciously presented me, as one of his birthday honours, with a Companionship in the Order of St. Michael and St. George —
most useful persons for any man to have as companions,
especially in a work like ours, both being famous for
downing dragons and devils. My American friends immediately knighted me. The papers and magazines
knighted me in both the United States and Canada. But
that got me into trouble, for only kings can make pawns
into knights, and I had to appeal several times to the
Associated Press to save myself being dubbed *poseur*.
I have protested at meetings when the chairman has
knighted me; at banquets, when the master of ceremonies has knighted me. I gave it up lest accusation should
arise against me, when at a semi-religious meeting I uttered a feeble protest against the title to which I have no
right, and my introducer merely repeated it the more
firmly, informing the audience meanwhile that I was
"too modest to use it."

There was attached to the conferring of the Order one
elective latitude — it could either be sent out or wait till
I returned to England and attended a levee with the
other recipients. I had a great desire to see the King, and,

though it meant a year's waiting, I requested to be allowed to do so. This not only was most courteously granted, but also the permission to let my presence in England be known to the Hereditary Grand Chamberlain, and the King would give me a private audience. When the day arrived, I repaired to Buckingham Palace, where I waited for an hour in the reception room in company with a small, stout clergyman who was very affable. I learned later that he was the Archbishop of Canterbury, who was carrying a fat Bible from Boston, England, I believe, to be presented to the United States of America.

At last Sir Frederick Treves, who kindly acted as my introducer, took me up to the King's study — that King whose life his skill had saved. There a most courteous gentleman made me perfectly at home, and talked of Labrador and North Newfoundland and our work as if he had lived there. He asked especially about the American helpers and interest, and laughed heartily when I told him how many freeborn Americans had gladly taken the oath of loyalty to His Majesty, when called up to act as special constables for me in his oldest Colony. He left the impression on my mind that he was a real Englishman in spirit, though he had spoken with what I took to be a slight German accent. The sports and games of the Colony I had noticed interested him very much, and all references to the splendid seafaring genius of the people also found an appreciative echo in his heart. When at last he handed me a long box with a gorgeous medal and ribbon, and bade me good-bye, I vowed I could sing "God save the King" louder than ever if I could do so without harrowing the feelings of my more tuneful neighbours.

When later, as a major in an American surgical unit in France, I was serving the R.A.M.C., the ribbon of the

Order was actually of real service to me. It undoubtedly opened some closed doors, though it proved a puzzle to every A.D.M.S. to whom I had to explain the anomaly of my position when I had to go and worry him for permission to cross the road or some new imaginary line. In England, and even in America, I found that the fact that the King had recognized one's work was a real material asset. It was a credential — only on a larger scale — like that from our Minister to the Colonies, the Marquis of Ripon, who kindly had given me his blessing in writing when first I visited Canada.

How far signs of superiority are permissible is to my mind an open question. Hereditary human superiority does not necessarily exist, because selective precautions are not taken, and the environment of the superior is very apt to enfeeble the physical machine, anyhow. The question of the hereditary superiority of a man's soul, being outside my sphere, I leave to the theologians. History, which is the school of experience, belies the theory, whatever current science may say. As for the giving of hereditary titles, it is significant that they do not as a rule go to scholars or even scientific men, but to physical fighters, being physical rewards for material services. When these are in the possession of offspring no longer capable of rendering such services, it appears ridiculous that they should sail under false colours.

To make a man a hereditary duke for being humble and modest, or hereditary marquis for being unselfish and generous, or an earl for being a man of peace, and a benefactor in the things which make for peace, such as a good husband and father and comrade, has, so far as I know, never been tried. Some of the so-called lesser honours, such as knighthood, are reserved for these. However, an order of knightly citizens, so long as they are real knights,

is, after all, little more than the gold key of the Phi Beta
Kappa, or the red triangle of the Y.M.C.A. worker, or the
Red Cross badge of the nurse. We are human, anyhow,
and such concessions, seeing that they do have an undoubted stimulating value in the present stage of our
development, to an Englishman seem permissible.

CHAPTER XVII

THE REINDEER EXPERIMENT

LABRADOR will never be a "vineland," a land of corn and wine, or a country where fenced cities will be needed to keep out the milk and honey. But though there may be other sections of the Empire that can produce more dollars, Labrador will, like Norway and Sweden, produce Vikings, and it is said that the man behind the gun is still of some moment.

In past years we have made quite extensive experiments in trying to adapt possible food supplies to this climate. I had seventeen bags of the hardiest cereal seeds known sent me. They consisted of barley from Lapland, from Russia, from Abyssinia, Mansbury barley and Finnish oats. All the seeds came from the experimental station at Rampart, Alaska, and were grown in latitude 63° 30', which is two degrees north of Cape Chidley.

I find in the notes of one of my earliest voyages my satisfaction at the fact that a storm with lightning and thunder had just passed over the boat and freshened up some rhubarb which I was growing in a box. It had been presented to me by the Governor to carry down to Battle Harbour, and I was very eager that it, my first agricultural venture, should not fail.

Everywhere along the coast the inability to get a proper diet, owing to the difficulties of successful farming even on ever so small a scale, had aroused my mind to the necessity of doing something along that line. In one small cottage I saw a poor woman zealously guarding an aged rooster.

"Have you got a hen?" I asked her.

"No, Doctor; I had one, but she died last year."

"Then why ever do you keep that rooster?"

"Oh! I hopes some day to get a hen. I've had him five years. The last manager of the mill gave him to me, but you'se sees he can't never go out and walk around because of the dogs, so I just keeps he under that settle."

Pathetic as were her efforts at stock farming, I must admit that my sympathies were all with the incarcerated rooster.

The problem of the dogs seemed an insurmountable one. The Moravians' records abound in stories of their destructiveness. Mr. Hesketh Pritchard writes: "Dr. Grenfell records two children and one man killed by the dogs. This is fortunately a much less terrible record than that shown farther north by the Moravian Missions. The savage dogs did great harm at those stations one winter." Among other accidents, a boy of thirteen, strong and well, was coming home from his father's kayak to his mother. After some time, as he did not arrive, they went to search for him and found that the dogs had already killed and eaten a good part of him. A full-grown man, driving to Battle Harbour Hospital, was killed by his dogs almost at our doors.

The wolves of the country only pack when deer are about. As a contrast to our dogs, wolves have never been known to kill a man in Labrador, so it would be more correct to speak of a doggish wolf than a wolfish dog. It is an odd thing and a fortunate one that in this country, where it is very common to have been bitten by a dog, we never have been able to find any trace of hydrophobia.

A visitor returning to New York after a summer on the coast wrote as follows: "One of my lasting remembrances of Battle Harbour will be the dreadful dogs. The Mission team were on an island far removed, but there were a number of settlers' dogs which delighted in making the nights hideous. Never before have I seen dogs stand up like men and grapple with each other in a fight, and when made to move on, renew the battle round the corner."

Our efforts at agriculture had taught us not to expect too much of the country. A New Zealand cousin, Martyn Spencer, a graduate of Macdonald College of Agriculture, gave us two years' work. His experience showed that while dogs continued to be in common use, cattle-raising was impossible. Of a flock of forty Herdwick sheep given by Dr. Wakefield, the dogs killed twenty-seven at one time. Angora goats, which we had imported, perished in the winter for lack of proper food. Our land cost so much to reclaim for hay, being soaked in humic acid, that we had always to import that commodity at a cost which made more cows than absolutely essential very inadvisable. Weasels, rats, hawks, and vermin needed a man's whole time if our chickens were to be properly guarded and repay keeping at all. An alfalfa sent us from Washington did well, and potatoes also gave a fair return, though our summer frosts often destroyed whole patches of the latter. Our imported plum and crabapple trees were ringed by mice beneath the snow in winter. At a farm which we cleared nine miles up a bay, so as to have it removed from the polar current, our oats never ripened, and our turnips and cabbage did not flourish in every case. We could not plant early enough, owing to the ground being frozen till July some years.

On the other hand, when we looked at the hundreds of thousands of square miles on which caribou could live and increase without any help from man, and indeed in spite of all his machinations, our attention was naturally turned to reindeer farming, and I went to Washington to consult Dr. Sheldon Jackson, the Presbyterian missionary from Alaska. It was he who had pioneered the introduction by the United States Government of domestic reindeer into Alaska. At Washington we received nothing but encouragement. Reindeer could make our wilderness smile. They would cost only the protection necessary. They multiply steadily, breeding every year for eight or ten years after their second season. A selected herd should double itself every three years.

The skins are very valuable — there is no better non-conductor of heat. The centre of the hair is not a hollow cylinder, but a series of air bubbles which do not soak water, and therefore can be used with advantage for life-saving cushions. The skins are splendid also for motor robes, and now invaluable in the air service. The meat is tender and appetizing, and sold as a game delicacy in New York. The deer fatten well on the abundant mosses of a country such as ours.

Sir William MacGregor, the Governor of Newfoundland at the time, had samples of the mosses collected around the coast and sent to Kew Botanical Gardens for positive identification. The Cladonia Rangiferina, or Iceland moss, proved very abundant. It was claimed, however, that the reindeer would eat any of such plants and shrubs as our coast offers in summer.

As long ago as the year 1903 my interest in the domestication of deer had led me to experiment with a young caribou. We had him on the Strathcona nearly all one summer. He was a great pet on board, and demonstrated how easily trained these animals are. He followed me about like a dog, and called after me as I left the ship's side in a boat if we did not take him with us. He was as inquisitive as a monkey or as the black bear which we had had two years before. We twice caught him in the chart-room chewing up white paper, for on his first raid there he had found an apple just magnanimously sent us from the shore as a delicacy.

Friends, inspired by Mr. William Howell Reed, of Boston, collected the money for a consignment of reindeer, and we accordingly sent to Lapland to purchase as many of the animals as we could afford. The expense was not so much in the cost of the deer as in the transport. They could not be shipped till they had themselves hauled down to the beach enough moss to feed them on their passage across the Atlantic. Between two hundred and fifty and three hundred were purchased, and three Lapp families hired to teach some of our local people how to herd them. When at last snow enough fell for the sledges to haul the moss down to the landwash, it was dark all day around the North Cape.

Fifty years hence in all probability the Lapps will be an extinct race, as even within the past twelve or fifteen years, districts in which thousands of domesticated reindeer grazed, now possess but a few hundreds.

The good ship Anita, which conveyed the herd to us, steamed in for southern Newfoundland and then worked her way North as far as the ice would permit. At St. Anthony everything was frozen up, and the men walked out of the harbour mouth on the sea ice to meet the steamer bringing the deer. The whole three hundred were landed on the ice in Crémaillière, some three miles to the southward of St. Anthony Hospital, and though many fell through into the sea, they proved hardy and resourceful enough to reach the land, where they gathered around the tinkling bells of the old deer without a single loss from land to land.

One of our workers at St. Anthony that winter wrote that "the most exciting moment was when the woman was lowered in her own sledge over the steamer's side

on to the ice, drawn to the shore, and transferred to one
of Dr. Grenfell's komatiks, as she had hurt her leg on the
voyage. The sight of all the strange men surrounding her
frightened her, but she was finally reassured, threw aside
her coverings, and clutched her frying-pan, which she
had hidden under a sheepskin. When she had it safely in
her arms she allowed the men to lift her and put her on
the komatik." When the doctor at the hospital advised
that her leg would best be treated by operation, the man
said, "She is a pretty old woman, and does n't need a
very good leg much longer." She was thirty-five!

An Irish friend had volunteered to come out and watch
the experiment in our interest — and this he did most
efficiently. The deer flourished and increased rapidly.
Unfortunately the Lapps did not like our country. They
complained that North Newfoundland was too cold for
them and they wanted to return home. One family left
after the first year. A rise in salary kept three of the men,
but the following season they wanted more than we had
funds to meet, and we were forced to decide, wrongly, I
fear, to let them go. The old herder warned me, "No
Lapps, no deer"; but I thought too much in terms of
Mission finances, the Government having withdrawn
their grant toward the herders' salaries. Trusting to the
confidence in their own ability of the locally trained men,
I therefore let the Lapp herders go home. The love of the
Lapps for their deer is like a fisherman's for his vessel,
and seems a master passion. They appeared even to
grudge our having any deer tethered away from their
care.

To us it seemed strange that these Lapps always con-
tended that the work was too hard, and that the only
reason that they were always gone from camp was that
there were no wolves to keep the herd together. They

claimed that we must have a big fence or the deer would go off into the country. They, of course, both when with us and in Lapland as well, lived and slept where the herd was. They told us that the deer no longer obeyed the warning summons of the old does' bells, having no natural enemy to fear; and one told me, "Money no good, Doctor, if herd no increase." Reindeer seemed to be the complement of their souls.

Meanwhile the Alaskan experiment was realizing all of Dr. Jackson's happiest hopes; but it had a strong Government grant and backing and plenty of skilled superintendence. The lack of those were our weaknesses. Our deer thrived splendidly and multiplied as we had predicted. We went thirty miles in a day with them with ease. We hauled our firewood out, using half a dozen hauling teams every day. Every fortnight during the rush of patients at the hospital in summer we could afford to kill a deer. The milk was excellent in quality and sweet, and preserved perfectly well in rubber-capped bottles. The cheese was nourishing and a welcome addition to the local diet. At the close of the fourth year we had a thousand deer.

A paper of the serious standing of the "Wall Street Journal," writing at about that time, under the title "Reindeer Venison from Alaska," had this to say: "At different times in the past twenty years the Government imported reindeer into Alaska — about twelve hundred in all — in hopes to provide food for the natives in the future. The plan caused some amusement and some criticism at the time. Subsequent developments, however, have justified the attempt. The herds have now increased to about forty thousand animals, and are rapidly becoming still more numerous. The natives own about two thirds of the number. Shipments of meat have been made

to the Pacific Coast cities. Last year the sales of venison
and skins amounted to $25,000. It is claimed that the
vast tundra, or treeless frozen plains of Alaska, will
support at least ten million animals. The federal authorities in charge are so optimistic of the future outlook that
the prediction is made that within twenty-five years the
United States can draw a considerable part of its meat
supply from Alaska." What can be done in Alaska can be
done in Labrador, and with its better facilities for shipping and handling the product, the greater future ought
to be the prize of the latter country.

In the spring of 1912 there were five hundred fawns,
and at one time we had gathered into our corral for tag-
ging no less than twelve hundred and fifty reindeer. Of
these we sold fifty to the Government of Canada for the
Peace River District. There they were lost because they
were placed in a flat country, densely wooded with alders,
and not near the barren lands. We also sold a few to
clubs, in order to try and introduce the deer. These sales
would have done the experiment no injury, but with the
fifty to Canada went my chief herder and two of my other
herders from Labrador. This loss, from which we never
recovered, coincided with an outbreak of hostility toward the deer among the resident population, who live
entirely on the sea edge. Only long afterwards did we find
out that it was partly because they feared that we would
force deer upon them and do away with their dogs. The
local Government official told me only the other day that
the second generation from this would have very little
good to say of the short-sightedness of these men who
let such a valuable industry fail to succeed.

With the increasing cares of the enlarging Mission,
with Lieutenant Lindsay gone back to Ireland, and no
one to superintend the herding, the successful handling of

the deer imperceptibly declined. The tags on the ears were no longer put in; the bells were not replaced in the old localities. The herd was driven, not led as before — was paid for, not loved. These differences at the time were marked by increasing poaching on the herd by the people. Here and there at first they had killed a deer unknown to us; and finally we caught one hidden in a man's woodpile, and several offenders were sent to jail.

We appealed to the Newfoundland Government for protection, as to be policeman and magistrate for the herd which one held in trust was an anomalous position. I was ordered by them to sit on the bench when these cases were up, as I did not own the deer. The section of land on which we had the animals is a peninsula of approximately one hundred and fifty square miles. It is cut off by a narrow, low neck about eight miles long. During all our years of acquaintance with the coast not a dozen caribou had been killed on it, for they do not cross the neck to the northward. But when we applied for a national preserve, that no deer at all might be killed on the peninsula, and so we might run a big fence across the neck with a couple of herders' houses along the line of it, a petition, signed by part of the "voters," went up to St. John's, against such permission being granted us. The petition stated that the deer destroyed the people's "gardens," that they were a danger to the lives of the settlers, whose dogs went wild when they crossed their path, and they claimed that the herd "led men into temptation," because if there were no reindeer to tempt men to kill them, there would be none killed. The deer thus were supposed to be the cause of making cattle-thieves out of honest men! The result was that a law was passed that no domestic reindeer might be shot north of the line of the neck for which we had applied, and which we

A PART OF THE REINDEER HERD

REINDEER TEAMS MEETING A DOG TEAM

intended to fence. This only made matters ten times worse, for if the deer either strayed or else were driven across the line, the killing of them was thus legalized.

The deer had cost us, landed, some fifty-one dollars apiece. Three years of herding under the adverse conditions of lack of support from either Government or people had not lessened the per caput expense very materially. If we had shot some one's fifty-dollar cow, our name would have been anathema — but we lost two hundred and fifty deer one winter. In addition to this, when we moved the deer to a spot near another village on a high bluff, over a hundred died in summer, either — according to the report of the herders — from falling over the cliffs driven by dogs, or of a sickness of which we could not discover the nature, though we thought that it resembled a kind of pneumonia.

The poaching got so bad that we took every means in our power to catch the guilty parties. But it was a very difficult thing to do. A dead deer lies quiet, keeps for weeks where he falls in our winter climate, and can be surreptitiously removed by day or night. The little Lapp dogs occasionally scented them beneath the snow, and many tell-tale "paunches" showed where deer had been killed and carried off.

I had been treating the hunchback boy and only child of a fisherman for whom I had very great respect. His was the home where the Methodist minister always boarded, and he was looked upon as a pillar of piety. After a straightening by frame treatment, the boy's spine had been ankylosed by an operation; and as every one felt sorry for the little fellow, we were often able to send him gifts. One day the father came to me, evidently in great trouble, to have what proved to be a most uncommon private talk. To my utter surprise he began: "Doctor, I can no longer live and keep the secret that I shot two of your reindeer. I have brought you ninety dollars, all the cash that I have, and I want to ask your forgiveness, after all you have done for me." Needless to say, it was freely given, but it made me feel more than ever that the deer must be moved to some other country.

It was about this year that the Government for the first time granted us a resident policeman — previously we had had to be our own police. Fortunately the man sent was quite a smart fellow. A dozen or so deer had been killed along the section of our coast, and so skilfully that even though it was done under the noses of the herders no evidence to convict could be obtained. It so happened, however, that while one of the herders was eating a piece of one of the slaughtered animals which he had discovered, and that the thieves had not been able to carry off, his teeth met on a still well-formed rifle bullet of number 22 calibre. This type of rifle we knew was scarcely ever used on our coast, and the policeman at once made a round to take every one. He returned with three, which was really the whole stock.

A piece of meat was now placed at a reasonable distance, also some bags of snow, flour, etc., and a number of bullets fired into them. These bullets were then all privately marked, and shuffled up. Our own deductions were made, and a man from twenty miles away summoned, arrested, and brought up. He brought witnesses and friends, apparently to impress the court — one especially, who most vehemently protested that he knew the owner of the rifle, and that he was never out of his house at the time that the deer would have been killed. In court was a man, for twenty-seven years agent in Labrador for the Hudson Bay Company — a crack shot and a most expert hunter. He was called up, given the big pile of bullets, and told to try and sort them, by the groove marks, into those fired by the three different rifles. We then handed him the control bullet, and he put it instantly on one of the piles. It was the pile that had been fired from the rifle of the accused. This man, in testifying, in order to clear himself, had let out the fact that his rifle had not been kept in his house, but in the house of the vociferous witness — whom we now arrested, convicted, and condemned to jail for six months or two hundred dollars fine — the latter alternative being given only because we knew that he had not the necessary sum. Protesting as loudly as he had previously witnessed, he went to jail; but the rest let out threats that they were coming back with others to set him free. We had only a frame wooden jail, and a rheumatic jailer of over seventy years, hired to hobble around by day and see that the prisoners were fed and kept orderly. We announced, therefore, that our Hudson Bay friend, with his rifle loaded, would be night jailer.

A few days passed by. The prisoner did not like improving the public thoroughfare for our benefit, while those "who were just as bad as he" went free. Our old jailer took good care that he should hear what good times they were having and laughing at him for being caught. Indeed, he liked it so little that he gave the whole plot away — at least what he called the whole. This landed four more of his friends in the same honest and public-spirited occupation which he was himself pursuing; though all escaped shortly afterwards by paying fines to the Government which aggregated some eight hundred dollars — which sum was largely paid by others for them.

There was no way, however, definitely to stop the steady decrease in the numbers of the herd; and though we moved them to new pastures around the coast, and fenced them in such small mobile corrals as we could afford, they were not safe. On several occasions we found dead deer with buckshot in them, which had "fallen over the cliffs." Twice we discovered that deer had even been killed within our own corral. One had been successfully removed, and the other trussed-up carcass had been hidden until a good opportunity offered for it to follow suit. I do not wish to leave the impression on the minds of my readers that every man on this part of the coast is a poacher. Far from it. But the majority of the best men were against the reindeer experiment from the moment that the first trouble arose. A new obligation of social life was introduced. This implied restraint in such trifling things as their having to fence their tiny gardens, protect small stray hay-pooks, and discriminate into what they discharged their ubiquitous blunderbusses.

Meanwhile the steadily increasing demand for meat, especially since the war began, caused outside interest in the experiment; and both the owners of Anticosti Island, and a firm in the West who were commencing reindeer farming on a commercial basis, opened negotiations with us for the purchase of our herd. In the original outlay, however, the Canadian Dominion Government had taken an interest to the amount of five thousand dollars, so it was necessary to get their opinion on the subject. Their Department of Indian Affairs happened to be looking for some satisfactory way of helping out their Labrador Indian population. They sent down and made inquiries, and came to the conclusion that they would themselves take the matter up, as they had done with buffalo, elk, and other animals in the West.

In 1917 all preparations for transferring the deer were made, but war conditions called their steamer away and transport was delayed until 1918. Again their steamer was called off, so we decided to take the deer across ourselves in our splendid three-masted schooner, the George B. Cluett. She, alas, was delayed in America by the submarine scare, and it was the end of September instead of June when she finally arrived. It was a poor season for our dangerous North coast and a very bad time for moving the deer, whose rutting season was just beginning. My herders, too, were now much reduced in numbers. Most of them had gone to the war, and as one had been sick all summer, practically only two were available. To add to the difficulty, many small herds of reindeer were loose in the country outside the corral.

However, we felt that the venture must be attempted at all hazards, even if it delayed our beautiful ship taking a cargo of food to the Allies — as she was scheduled to do as soon as possible — and though it was a serious risk to remain anchored in the shallow open roadstead off the spot where the deer had to be taken aboard. The work was all new to us. The deer, instead of being tame as they had previously been, were wild at best, and wilder still from their breeding season. The days went by, and we succeeded in getting only a few aboard. We were all greenhorns with the lassoes and lariats which we improvised. A gale of wind came on and nothing could be done but lie up.

Then followed a fine Sunday morning. It was intensely interesting to note the attitude which my crew could take toward my decision to work all day after morning prayers. We talked briefly over the emphasis laid by the four Evangelists on Christ's attitude toward the day of rest, and what it might mean, if we allowed a rare fine day to go by, to that long section of coast which we had not yet this year visited, and which might thus miss the opportunity of seeing a doctor before Christmas. As since this war has begun I have felt that the Christ whom I wanted to follow would be in France, so now I felt that the Christ of my ideal would go ashore and get those deer in spite of the great breach of convention which it would mean for a "Mission" doctor to work in any way, except in the many ways he has to work every Sunday of his life. The whole crew followed me when I went ashore, saying that they shared my view — all except the mate, who spent his Sunday in bed. Idleness is not rest to some natures, either to body or mind, and when at night we all turned in at ten o'clock, wet through — for it had rained in the evening — and tired out, we were able to say our prayers with just as light hearts, feeling that we had put sixty-eight deer aboard, as if we had enjoyed that foretaste of what some still believe to be the rest of heaven. Rest for our souls we certainly had, and to some of us that is the rest which God calls His own and intends shall be ours also. When later I spoke to some young men about this, it seemed to them a Chestertonian paradox, that we should actually hold a Sunday service and then go forth to render it. They thought that Sunday prayers had to do only with the escaping the consequences of one's sins.

I still believe that we were absolutely right in our theory of the introduction of the deer into this North country, and that we shall be justified in it by posterity. That these thousands of miles, now useless to men, will be grazed over one day by countless herds of deer affording milk, meat, clothing, transport, and pleasure to the human race, is certain. They do not by any means destroy the land over which they rove. On the contrary, the deep ruts made by their feet, like the ponies' feet in Iceland, serve to drain the surface water and dry the land. The kicking and pawing of the moss-covered ground with their spade-like feet tear it up, level it, and cut off the dense moss and creeping plants, bring the sub-soil to the top, and over the whole the big herd spreads a good covering of manure.

Reinder-trodden barrens, after a short rest, yield more grass and cattle food than ever before. No domesticated animal can tolerate the cold of this country and find sustenance for itself as can the deer. It can live as far north as the musk-ox. Peary found reindeer in plenty on the shores of the polar sea. The great barren lands of Canada, from Hudson Bay north of Chesterfield Inlet away to the west, carry tens of thousands of wild caribou. Mr. J. B. Tyrrell's photographs show armies of them advancing; the stags with their lordly horns are seen passing close to the camera in serried ranks that seem to have no end.

Our own experiment is far from being a failure. It has been a success, even if only the corpse is left in Newfoundland. We have proved conclusively that the deer can live, thrive, and multiply on the otherwise perfectly valueless areas of this North country, and furnish a rapidly increasing domesticated "raw material" for a food and clothing supply to its people.

CHAPTER XVIII

THE ICE-PAN ADVENTURE

On Easter Sunday, the 21st of April, 1908, it was still winter with us in northern Newfoundland. Everything was covered with snow and ice. I was returning to the hospital after morning service, when a boy came running over with the news that a large team of dogs had come from sixty miles to the southward to get a doctor to come at once on an urgent case. A fortnight before we had operated on a young man for acute bone disease of the thigh, but when he was sent home the people had allowed the wound to close, and poisoned matter had accumulated. As it seemed probable that we should have to remove the leg, there was no time to be lost, and I therefore started immediately, the messengers following me with their team.

My dogs were especially good ones and had pulled me out of many a previous scrape by their sagacity and endurance. Moody, Watch, Spy, Doc, Brin, Jerry, Sue, and Jack were as beautiful beasts as ever hauled a komatik over our Northern barrens. The messengers had been anxious that their team should travel back with mine, for their animals were slow at best, and moreover were now tired from their long journey. My dogs, however, were so powerful that it was impossible to hold them back, and though I twice managed to wait for the following sledge, I had reached a village twenty miles to the south and had already fed my team when the others caught up.

That night the wind came in from sea, bringing with it both fog and rain, softening the snow and making the travelling very difficult. Besides this a heavy sea began

A SPRING SCENE AT ST. ANTHONY

DOG RACE AT ST. ANTHONY

heaving into the bay on the shores of which lay the little hamlet where I spent my first night. Our journey the next day would be over forty miles, the first ten lying on an arm of the sea.

In order not to be separated too long from my friends I sent them ahead of me by two hours, appointing as a rendezvous the log tilt on the other side of the bay. As I started the first rain of the year began to fall, and I was obliged to keep on what we call the "ballicaters," or ice barricades, for a much longer distance up the bay than I had anticipated. The sea, rolling in during the previous night, had smashed the ponderous layer of surface ice right up to the landwash. Between the huge ice-pans were gaping chasms, while half a mile out all was clear water.

Three miles from the shore is a small island situated in the middle of the bay. This had preserved an ice bridge, so that by crossing a few cracks I managed to get to it safely. From that point it was only four miles to the opposite shore, a saving of several miles if one could make it, instead of following the landwash round the bay. Although the ice looked rough, it seemed good, though one could see that it had been smashed up by the incoming sea and packed in tight again by the easterly wind. Therefore, without giving the matter a second thought, I flung myself on the komatik and the dogs started for the rocky promontory some four miles distant.

All went well till we were within about a quarter of a mile of our objective point. Then the wind dropped suddenly, and I noticed simultaneously that we were travelling over "sish" ice. By stabbing down with my whip-handle I could drive it through the thin coating of young ice which had formed on the surface. "Sish" ice is made up of tiny bits formed by the pounding together of the large pans by the heavy seas. So quickly had the wind veered and come offshore, and so rapidly did the packed slob, relieved of the inward pressure of the easterly breeze, "run abroad," that already I could not see any pan larger than ten feet square. The whole field of ice was loosening so rapidly that no retreat was possible.

There was not a moment to lose. I dragged off my oil-skins and threw myself on my hands and knees beside the komatik so as to give a larger base to hold, shouting at the same time to my team to make a dash for the shore. We had not gone twenty yards when the dogs scented danger and hesitated, and the komatik sank instantly into the soft slob. Thus the dogs had to pull much harder, causing them to sink also.

It flashed across my mind that earlier in the year a man had been drowned in this same way by his team tangling their traces around him in the slob. I loosened my sheath-knife, scrambled forward and cut the traces, retaining the leader's trace wound securely round my wrist.

As I was in the water I could not discern anything that would bear us up, but I noticed that my leading dog was wallowing about near a piece of snow, packed and frozen together like a huge snowball, some twenty-five yards away. Upon this he had managed to scramble. He shook the ice and water from his shaggy coat and turned around to look for me. Perched up there out of the frigid water he seemed to think the situation the most natural in the world, and the weird black marking of his face made him appear to be grinning with satisfaction. The rest of us were bogged like flies in treacle.

Gradually I succeeded in hauling myself along by the line which was still attached to my wrist, and was nearly up to the snow-raft, when the leader turned adroitly round, slipped out of his harness, and once more leered at me with his grinning face.

There seemed nothing to be done, and I was beginning to feel drowsy with the cold, when I noticed the trace of another dog near by. He had fallen through close to the pan, and was now unable to force his way out. Along his line I hauled myself, using him as a kind of bow anchor — and I soon lay, with my dogs around me, on the little island of slob ice.

The piece of frozen snow on which we lay was so small that it was evident we must all be drowned if we were forced to remain on it as it was driven seaward into open water. Twenty yards away was a larger and firmer pan floating in the sish, and if we could reach it I felt that we might postpone for a time the death which seemed inescapable. To my great satisfaction I now found that my hunting knife was still tied on to the back of one of the dogs, where I had attached it when we first fell through. Soon the sealskin traces hanging on the dogs' harnesses were cut and spliced together to form one long line. I divided this and fastened the ends to the backs of my two leaders, attaching the two other ends to my own wrists. My long sealskin boots, reaching to my hips, were full of ice and water, and I took them off and tied them separately on the dogs' backs. I had already lost my coat, cap, gloves, and overalls.

Nothing seemed to be able to induce the dogs to move, even though I kept throwing them off the ice into the water. Perhaps it was only natural that they should struggle back, for once in the water they could see no other pan to which to swim. It flashed into my mind that my small black spaniel which was with me was as light as a feather and could get across with no difficulty. I showed him the direction and then flung a bit of ice toward the desired goal. Without a second's hesitation he made a dash and reached the pan safely, as the tough layer of sea ice easily carried his weight. As he lay on the white surface looking like a round black fuss ball, my leaders could plainly see him. They now understood what I wanted and fought their way bravely toward the little retriever, carrying with them the line that gave me yet another chance for my life. The other dogs followed them, and all but one succeeded in getting out on the new haven of refuge.

Taking all the run that the length of my little pan would afford, I made a dive, slithering along the surface as far as possible before I once again fell through. This time I had taken the precaution to tie the harnesses under the dogs' bellies so that they could not slip them off, and after a long fight I was able to drag myself onto the new pan.

Though we had been working all the while toward the shore, the offshore wind had driven us a hundred yards farther seaward. On closer examination I found that the pan on which we were resting was not ice at all, but snow-covered slob, frozen into a mass which would certainly eventually break up in the heavy sea, which was momentarily increasing as the ice drove offshore before the wind. The westerly wind kept on rising — a bitter blast with us in winter, coming as it does over the Gulf ice.

Some yards away I could still see my komatik with my thermos bottle and warm clothing on it, as well as matches and wood. In the memory of the oldest inhabitant no one had ever been adrift on the ice in this bay, and unless the team which had gone ahead should happen to come back to look for me, there was not one chance in a thousand of my being seen.

To protect myself from freezing I now cut down my long boots as far as the feet, and made a kind of jacket, which shielded my back from the rising wind.

By midday I had passed the island to which I had crossed on the ice bridge. The bridge was gone, so that if

I did succeed in reaching that island I should only be
marooned there and die of starvation. Five miles away to
the north side of the bay the immense pans of Arctic ice
were surging to and fro in the ground seas and thundering against the cliffs. No boat could have lived through
such surf, even if I had been seen from that quarter.
Though it was hardly safe to move about on my little
pan, I saw that I must have the skins of some of my dogs,
if I were to live the night out without freezing. With some
difficulty I now succeeded in killing three of my dogs —
and I envied those dead beasts whose troubles were over
so quickly. I questioned if, once I passed into the open
sea, it would not be better to use my trusty knife on myself than to die by inches.

But the necessity for work saved me from undue philos-
ophizing; and night found me ten miles on my seaward voyage, with the three dogs skinned and their fur
wrapped around me as a coat. I also frayed a small piece
of rope into oakum and mixed it with the fat from the
intestines of my dogs. But, alas, I found that the matches
in my box, which was always chained to me, were soaked
to a pulp and quite useless. Had I been able to make a fire
out there at sea, it would have looked so uncanny that
I felt sure that the fishermen friends, whose tiny light
I could just discern twinkling away in the bay, would see
it. The carcasses of my dogs I piled up to make a wind-
break, and at intervals I took off my clothes, wrung them
out, swung them in the wind, and put on first one and
then the other inside, hoping that the heat of my body
would thus dry them. My feet gave me the most trouble,
as the moccasins were so easily soaked through in the
snow. But I remembered the way in which the Lapps who
tended our reindeer carried grass with them, to use in
their boots in place of dry socks. As soon as I could sit

down I began to unravel the ropes from the dogs' harnesses, and although by this time my fingers were more or less frozen, I managed to stuff the oakum into my shoes.

Shortly before I had opened a box containing some old football clothes which I had not seen for twenty years. I was wearing this costume at the time; and though my cap, coat, and gloves were gone, as I stood there in a pair of my old Oxford University running shorts, and red, yellow, and black Richmond football stockings, and a flannel shirt, I remembered involuntarily the little dying girl who asked to be dressed in her Sunday frock so that she might arrive in heaven properly attired.

Forcing my biggest dog to lie down, I cuddled up close to him, drew the improvised dogskin rug over me, and proceeded to go to sleep. One hand being against the dog was warm, but the other was frozen, and about midnight I woke up shivering enough, so I thought, to shatter my frail pan to atoms. The moon was just rising, and the wind was steadily driving me toward the open sea. Suddenly what seemed a miracle happened, for the wind veered, then dropped away entirely leaving it flat calm. I turned over and fell asleep again. I was next awakened by the sudden and persistent thought that I must have a flag, and accordingly set to work to disarticulate the frozen legs of my dead dogs. Cold as it was I determined to sacrifice my shirt to top this rude flagpole as soon as the daylight came. When the legs were at last tied together with bits of old harness rope, they made the crookedest flagstaff that it has ever been my lot to see. Though with the rising of the sun the frost came out of the dogs' legs to some extent, and the friction of waving it made the odd pole almost tie itself in knots, I could raise it three or four feet above my head, which was very important.

Once or twice I thought that I could distinguish men against the distant cliffs — for I had drifted out of the bay into the sea — but the objects turned out to be trees. Once also I thought that I saw a boat appearing and disappearing on the surface of the water, but it proved to be only a small piece of ice bobbing up and down. The rocking of my cradle on the waves had helped me to sleep, and I felt as well as I ever did in my life. I was confident that I could last another twenty-four hours if my boat would only hold out and not rot under the sun's rays. I could not help laughing at my position, standing hour after hour waving my shirt at those barren and lonely cliffs; but I can honestly say that from first to last not a single sensation of fear crossed my mind.

My own faith in the mystery of immortality is so untroubled that it now seemed almost natural to be passing to the portal of death from an ice-pan. Quite unbidden, the words of the old hymn kept running through my head:

"My God, my Father, while I stray
Far from my home on life's rough way,
Oh, help me from my heart to say,
Thy will be done."

I had laid my wooden matches out to dry and was searching about on the pan for a piece of transparent ice which I could use as a burning-glass. I thought that I could make smoke enough to be seen from the land if only I could get some sort of a light. All at once I seemed to see the glitter of an oar, but I gave up the idea because I remembered that it was not water which lay between me and the land, but slob ice, and even if people had seen me, I did not imagine that they could force a boat through. The next time that I went back to my flag-waving, however, the glitter was very distinct, but my snow-glasses having been lost, I was partially snow-blind and distrusted my vision. But at last, besides the glide of an oar I made out the black streak of a boat's hull, and knew that if the pan held out for another hour I should be all right. The boat drew nearer and nearer, and I could make out my rescuers frantically waving. When they got close by they shouted, "Don't get excited. Keep on the pan where you are." They were far more excited than I, and had they only known as I did the sensations of a bath in the icy water, without the chance of drying one's self afterwards, they would not have expected me to wish to follow the example of the Apostle Peter.

As the first man leaped on my pan and grasped my hand, not a word was spoken, but I could see the emotions which he was trying to force back. A swallow of the hot tea which had been thoughtfully sent out in a bottle, the dogs hoisted on board, and we started for home, now forging along in open water, now pushing the pans apart with the oars, and now jumping out on the ice and hauling the boat over the pans.

It seems that the night before four men had been out on the headland cutting up some seals which they had killed in the fall. As they were leaving for home, my ice-raft must have drifted clear of Hare Island, and one of them, with his keen fisherman's eyes, had detected something unusual on the ice. They at once returned to their village, saying that something living was adrift on the floe. The one man on that section of coast who owned a good spy-glass jumped up from his supper on hearing the news and hurried over to the lookout on the cliffs. Dusk though it was, he saw that a man was out on the ice, and noticed him every now and again waving his hands at the shore. He immediately surmised who it must be; so little as I thought it, when night was closing in the men at the village were trying to launch a boat. Miles of ice lay between them and me, and the angry sea was hurling great blocks against the land. While I had considered myself a laughing-stock, bowing with my flag at those unresponsive cliffs, many eyes were watching me.

By daybreak a fine volunteer crew had been organized, and the boat, with such a force behind it, would, I believe, have gone through anything. After seeing the heavy breakers through which we were guided, as at last we ran in at the harbour mouth, I knew well what the wives of that crew had been thinking when they saw their loved ones depart on such an errand.

Every soul in the village was waiting to shake hands as I landed; and even with the grip that one after another gave me, I did not find out that my hands were badly frostburnt — a fact which I have realized since, however. I must have looked a weird object as I stepped ashore, tied up in rags, stuffed out with oakum, and wrapped in the bloody dogskins.

The news had gone over to the hospital that I was lost, so I at once started north for St. Anthony, though I must confess that I did not greatly enjoy the trip, as I had to be hauled like a log, my feet being so frozen that I could not walk. For a few days subsequently I had painful reminders of the adventure in my frozen hands and feet, which forced me to keep to my bed — an unwelcome and unusual interlude in my way of life.

In our hallway stands a bronze tablet:

> "To the Memory of
> Three Noble Dogs
> Moody
> Watch
> Spy
> Whose lives were given
> For mine on the ice
> April 21st, 1908."

The boy whose life I was intent on saving was brought to the hospital a day or so later in a boat, the ice having cleared off the coast temporarily; and he was soon on the highroad to recovery.

We all love life, and I was glad to have a new lease of it before me. As I went to sleep that night there still rang through my ears the same verse of the old hymn which had been my companion on the ice-pan:

"Oh, help me from my heart to say,
Thy will be done."

CHAPTER XIX
THEY THAT DO BUSINESS IN GREAT WATERS

CONTRARY to her ungenerous reputation, even if vessels are lost on the Labrador, her almost unequalled series of harbours — so that from the Straits of Belle Isle to those of Hudson Bay there is not ten miles of coast anywhere without one — enables the crew to escape nearly every time.

In 1883, in the North Sea in October, a hurricane destroyed twenty-five of our stout vessels on the Dogger Bank, cost us two hundred and seventy good lives, and left a hundred widows to mourn on the land. In 1889 a storm hit the north coast of Newfoundland, but too late in the season to injure much of the fishing fleet, which had for the most part gone South. But it caused immense damage to property and the loss of a few lives. As one of the testimonials to its fury, I saw the flooring and seats of the church in the mud of the harbour at St. Anthony at low tide even though that church had been founded entirely on a rock. We now concede that it is good economy on our coast to have wire stays to ringbolts leaded into rocky foundations, to anchor small buildings. Our storms are mostly cyclones with wide vortices, and coming largely from the southwest or northwest, are offshore, and therefore less felt.

We were once running along at full speed in a very thick fog, framing a course to just clear some nasty shoals on our port bow. There was nothing outside us and we had seen no ice of late, so I went below for some lunch, telling the mate to report land as soon as he saw any, and instructing the man at the wheel, if he heard a shout, to port his helm hard. The soup was still on the table when a loud shouting made us leap on the deck to see the ship going full tilt into an enormous iceberg, which seemed right at the end of the bowsprit. This unexpected monster was on our starboard bow, and the order to avoid the shoal was putting us headfirst into it. Our only chance was full speed and a starboard helm, and we actually grazed along the side of the berg. It seemed almost ludicrous later to pick up a large island and run into a harbour with grassy, sloping sides, out of which the fog was shut like a wall, and then to go ashore and bargain over buying a couple of cows, which were being sold, as the settler was moving to the mainland.

Among the records of events of importance to us I find in 1908 that of the second real hurricane which I have ever seen. It began on Saturday, July 28, the height of our summer, with flat calm and sunshine alternating with small, fierce squalls. Though we had a falling barometer, this deceived us, and we anchored that evening in a shallow and unsafe open roadstead about twenty miles from Indian Harbour Hospital. Fortunately our suspicions induced us to keep an anchor watch, and his warning made us get steam at midnight, and we brought up at daylight in the excellent narrow harbour in which the hospital stands. The holding ground there is deep mud in four fathoms of water, the best possible for us. Our only trouble was that the heavy tidal current would swing a ship uneasily broadside against an average wind force.

It was blowing so strongly by this time that the hospital yawl Daryl had already been driven ashore from her anchors, but still we were able to keep ours in the water, and getting a line to her, to heave her astern of our vessel with our powerful winch. The fury of the breeze grew worse as the day went on. All the fishing boats in the harbour filled and sank with the driving water. With the increase of violence of the weather we got up steam and steamed to our anchors to ease if possible the strain on our two chains and shore lines — a web which we had been able to weave before it was too late. By Sunday the gale had blown itself entirely away, and Monday morning broke flat calm, with lovely sunshine, and only an enormous sullen ground sea. This is no uncommon game of Dame Nature's; she seemed to be only mocking at the destruction which she had wrought.

Knowing that there must be many comrades in trouble, we were early away, and dancing like a bubble, we ran north, keeping as close inshore as we could, and watching the coast-line with our glasses. The coast was littered with remains. Forty-one vessels had been lost; in one uninhabited roadstead alone, some forty miles away from Indian Harbour, lay sixteen wrecks. The shore here was lined with rude shelters made from the wreckage of spars and sails, and the women were busy cooking meals and "tidying up" the shacks as if they had lived there always.

We soon set to work hauling off such vessels as would float. One, a large hardwood, well-fastened hull, we determined to save. Her name was Pendragon. The owner was aboard — a young man with no experience who had never previously owned a vessel. He was so appalled at the disaster that he decided to have her sold piecemeal and broken up. We attended the auction on the beach and bought each piece as it came to the hammer. Getting her off was the trouble. We adopted tactics of our own invention. Mousing together the two mastheads with a bight of rope, we put on it a large whoop traveller, and to that fastened our stoutest and longest line. Then first backing down to her on the very top of high water, we went "full speed ahead." Over she fell on her side and bumped along on the mud and shingle for a few yards. By repeated jerks she was eventually ours, but leaking so like a basket that we feared we should yet lose her. Pumps inside fortunately kept her free till we passed her topsail under her, and after dropping in sods and peat, we let the pressure from the outside keep them in place. When night fell I was played out, and told the crew they must let her sink. My two volunteer helpers, Albert Gould, of Bowdoin, and Paul Matheson, of Brown, however, volunteered to pump all night.

While hunting for a crew to take her South we came upon the wreck of a brand-new boat, only launched two months previously. She had been the pride of the skipper's life. He was an old friend of mine, and we felt so sorry for him that we not only got him to take our vessel, but we handed it over for him to work out at the cost which we had paid for the pieces. He made a good living out of her for several years, but later she was lost with all hands on some dangerous shoals near St. Anthony on a journey North.

With fifty-odd people aboard, and a long trail of nineteen fishing boats we eventually got back to Indian Harbour, where every one joined in helping our friends in misfortune till the steamer came and took them South. They waved us farewell, and, quite undismayed, wished for better luck for themselves another season.

The case of one skipper is well worth relating as showing their admirable optimism. He was sixty-seven years old, and had by hard saving earned his own schooner — a fine large vessel. He had arranged to sell her on his return trip and live quietly on the proceeds on his potato patch in southern Newfoundland. His vessel had driven on a submerged reef and turned turtle. The crew had jumped for their lives, not even saving their personal clothing, watches, or instruments. We photographed the remains of the capsized hull floating on the surf. Yet this man, in the four days during which he was my guest, never once uttered a word of complaint. He had done all he could, and he " 'lowed that t' Lord knew better than he what was best."

"But what will you do now, Skipper?" I asked.

"Why, get another," he replied; "I think them'll trust me."

One of our older vessels started a plank in a gale of wind in the Atlantic and went to the bottom without warning. In an open boat for six days with only a little dry bread and no covering of any sort, the crew fought rough seas and heavy breezes. But they handled her with the sea genius of our race; made land safely at last, and never said a word about the incident. On another occasion two men, who had been a fortnight adrift, had rowed one hundred and fifty miles, and had only the smallest modicum of food, came aboard our vessel. When I said, "You are hungry, are n't you?" they merely replied, "Well, not over-much" — and only laughed when I suggested that perhaps a month in the open boat might have given them a real appetite.

One October, south of St. Anthony, we were lying in the arm of a bay with two anchors and two warps out, one to each side of the narrow channel. The wind piled up the waters, much as it did in Pharaoh's day. We were flung astern yard by yard on the top of the seas, and when it was obvious that we must go ashore, we reversed our engines, slipped our line, and drove up high and dry to escape the bumping on the beach which was inevitable. There we lay for days. Meanwhile I had taken our launch into the river-mouth and was marooned there. For the launch blew right up on the bank in among the trees, and strive as we would, for days we could not even move her out again.

Another spring we had a very close squeak of losing the Strathcona. While we were trying one morning to get out of a harbour, a sudden gale of wind came down upon us and pinned us tight, so that we could not move an inch. The pressure of the ice became more severe moment by moment, and meanwhile the ice between us and the shore seemed to be imperceptibly melting away. Naturally we tried every expedient we could think of to keep enough ice between us and the shore rocks to save the vessel being swept over the rocky headland, toward which the irresistible tidal current was steadily forcing us. To make matters worse, we struck our propeller against a pan of ice and broke off one of the flanges close to the shaft. It became breathlessly exciting as the ship drew nearer and nearer to the rocks. We abandoned our boat when we saw that by trying to hold on to it any longer we should be jeopardizing the steamer. Twisting round helplessly as in a giant's arms, we were swept past the dangerous promontory and to our infinite joy carried out into the open Atlantic where there is room for all. Our boat was subsequently rescued from the shore, and we were able to screw on a new blade to the propeller.

Just after the big gale in 1908 His Excellency, Sir William MacGregor, then Governor, was good enough to come and spend a short time surveying on our north coast. He was an expert in this line, as well as being a gold-medallist in medicine. Later he changed over from the Strathcona to the Government steamer Fiona. I acted as pilot among other capacities on that journey, and was unlucky enough to run her full tilt onto one of the only sandbanks on the coast in a narrow passage between some islands and the mainland! The little Strath-

ICEBERGS

cona, following behind, was in time to haul us off again, but the incident made the captain naturally distrust my ability, and as a result he would not approach the shore near enough for us to get the observations which we needed. Although we went round Cape Chidley into Ungava Bay I could not regain his confidence sufficiently to go through the straits which I had myself sounded and surveyed. So we accomplished it in a small boat, getting good observations. Our best work, however, was done when His Excellency was content to be our guest. The hospital on board was used for the necessary instruments — four chronometers, two theodolites, guns, telescopes, camp furniture, and piles of books and printed forms. Mr. Albert Gould of Bowdoin was my secretary on board that year, and was of very great value to us.

Though the work of an amateur, Sir William's surveying was accepted by the Admiralty and the Royal Geographical Society — his survey in Nigeria having proved to have not one single location a mile out of place when an official survey was run later.

Many a time in the middle of a meal, some desired but unlucky star would cross the prime vertical, and all hands had to go up on deck and shiver while rows of figures were accumulated. Sir William told us that he would rather shoot a star any time than all the game ever hunted. One night my secretary, after sitting on a rock at a movable table from 5 P.M. till midnight, came in, his joints almost creaking with cold, and loaded with a pile of figures which he assured us would crush the life out of most men. My mate that year was a stout and very short, plethoric person. When he stated that he preferred surveying to fishing, as it was going to benefit others so much, and that he was familiar with the joys of service, he was taken promptly at his word. It was a hot summer.

The theodolite was a nine-inch one and weighed many pounds. We had climbed the face of a very steep mountain called Cape Mugford, some three thousand feet high — every inch of which distance we had to mount from dead sea-level. When at last Israel arrived on the summit, he looked worried. He said that he had always thought surveying meant letting things drop down over the ship's side, and not carrying ballast up precipices. For his part he could now see that providing food for the world was good enough for him. He distinctly failed to grasp where the joy of this kind of service came in — and noting his condition as he lay on the ground and panted I decided to let it go at that.

The Governor was a real MacGregor and a Presbyterian, and was therefore quite a believer in keeping Sunday as a day of rest. But after morning prayers on the first fine day, after nearly a week of fog, he decided that he had had physical rest enough, and to get good observations would bring him the recreation of spirit which he most needed. So he packed up for work, and happened to light on the unhappy Israel to row him a mile or so to the land. "Iz" was taken "all aback." He believed that you should not strain yourself ever — much less on Sundays. So from religious scruples he asked to be excused, though he offered to row any one ashore if he was only going to idle the hours away. After all, however, our Governor represented our King, and I was personally horrified, intending to correct Israel's position with a round turn, and show him that we are especially enjoined to obey "Governors and Rulers" — as better also than the sacrifice of loafing. But the Governor forbade it, quietly unpacked, put his things away, and stayed aboard. Israel subsequently cultivated the habit of remaining in bed on Sundays — thereby escaping being led into temptation, as even Governors would not be likely to go and tempt him in his bunk.

I have had others refuse to help in really necessary work on Sunday. One skipper would not get the Strathcona under way in answer to a wireless appeal to come to a woman in danger of dying from hemorrhage forty miles distant. When we prepared to start without him, he told me that he would go, but that it would be at the price of his soul and we would have to be responsible for that loss. We went all the same.

Our charts, such as they were, were subsequently accepted by the Royal Geographical Society of England, who generously invited me to lecture before them. They were later good enough to award me the Murchison Prize in 1911. Much of the work was really due to Sir William, and as much of it as I could put on him to the Sabbatarian "Iz."

In connection with the scientific work on the coast I well remember the eclipse of October, 1905. All along the land it was perfectly visible. A break in the clouds occurred at exactly the right moment: one fisherman, to console the astronomers, said that he was very sorry, but that he supposed it did not much matter, as there would be another eclipse next week. The scientific explorer, who was devoting his attention to the effect on the earth's magnetism, spent the time of the eclipse in a dark cellar. Most wonderful magnetic disturbances had been occurring almost every night, and the night before the event a far from ordinary storm had upset his instruments, so that the effect of the eclipse on the magnetic indicators was scarcely distinguishable. He had just time after the thing was over to peep out and see the light returning. He had watched his thermometer and found that it fell three degrees during totality.

The year 1908 at the mill we had built a new large schooner in honour of that devoted friend of Labrador, our secretary in Boston, and had named the vessel for her, the Emma E. White. She fetched Lloyd's full bounty for an A 1 ship. This was a feather in our caps, since she was designed and built by one of our own men, who was no "scholard," having never learned to read or write. Will Hopkins can take an axe and a few tools into the green woods in the fall, and sail down the bay in a new schooner in the spring when the ice goes. To see him steaming the planking in the open in his own improvised boxes on the top of six feet of snow made me stand and take off my hat to him. He is no good at speech-making; he does not own a dress-suit, and he cannot dance a tango; but he is quite as useful a citizen as some who can, and his type of education is one which endears him to all. He gave me the great pleasure of having our friend come sailing into St. Anthony in the middle of a fine day, seated on the bow of her namesake, the beautiful and valuable product of his skill, just when we were all ready on the wharf to "sketch them both off," as our people call taking a photograph.

Our increasing buildings being all of wood, and as the two largest were full of either helpless sick people or an ever-increasing batch of children, we wanted something safer than kerosene lamps to illuminate the rooms. The people here had never seen electric light "tamed," as it were, and to us it seemed almost too big a venture to install a plant of our own. Home outfits were not common in those days even in the States, and we feared in any case that we could not run it regularly enough. No one except the head of the machine shop, a Labrador boy and Pratt graduate, knew the first thing about electricity, and he would not always be available.

However, with the help of friends we were able to purchase a hot-head vertical engine to generate our current; for our near-by streams freeze solid in winter. That engine has now been running for over ten years, and has given us electricity in St. Anthony Hospital for operating and X-ray work as well as all our lighting. Until he died, it was run the greater part of the time by an Eskimo boy whom we had brought down from the North Labrador, and who was convalescing from empyema. The installation was efficiently done by a volunteer student from the Pratt Institute, Mr. Hause.

On my lecture trip the previous winter a gentleman at whose house I was a guest told me that when quite a youth he had fought in the Civil War, been invalided home, and advised to take a sea voyage for his health. He therefore took passage with some Gloucester fishermen and set sail for the Labrador. The crew proved to be Southern sympathizers, and one day, while my friend was ashore taking a walk, the skipper slipped out and left him marooned. He had with him neither money, spare clothing, nor anything else; and as British sympathies were also with the South, he had many doubts as to how the settlers would receive a penniless stranger and Northerner. So seeing his schooner bound in an easterly direction, he started literally to run along the shore, hoping that he might find where she went and catch her again. Mile after mile he went, tearing through the "tuckamore" or dense undergrowth of gnarled trees, climbing over high cliffs, swimming or wading the innumerable rivers, skirting bays, and now and again finding a short beach along which he could hurry. At night, wet, dirty, tired, hungry, penniless, he came to a fisherman's cottage and asked shelter and food. He explained that he was an American gentleman taking a holiday, but had n't a penny of money. It spoke well for the people that they accepted his story. He told me that they both fed and clothed him, and one kind-hearted man actually the next day gave him some oilskin clothing and a sou'wester hat — costly articles "on Labrador" in those days. So on and on and on he went, till at last arriving at Red Bay he found his schooner at anchor calmly fishing. He went aboard at once as if nothing had happened, and stayed there (having enjoyed enough pedestrian exercise for the time being) and no one ever referred to his having been left behind. He was now, however, forty years later, anxious to do something for the people of that section of the shore, and he gave me a thousand dollars toward building a small cottage for a district nurse. Forteau was the village chosen, and Dennison Cottage erected as a nursing station and dispensary. The people at first each gave a week toward its upkeep; and even now every man gives three days annually. The house has a good garden, little wards for in-patients, and is the centre of much useful industrial work, especially the making of artificial flowers. For twelve years now, Miss Florence Bailey, a nurse from the Mildmay Institute in London, has presided over its destinies, endeared herself to the people, and done most unselfish and heroic work in that lonely station, which she has greatly enlarged and improved by her untiring efforts. It forms an admirable halfway house between Battle and Harrington Hospitals, each being about a hundred miles distant. A local trader once wrote me: "Sister Bailey did good work last year. That cottage hospital is a blessing to the people of this part of the shore. Who would think that by a little act of kindness done forty-odd years ago to an old soldier, we would now be reaping the benefit of such an act."

Only one longer journey on foot on the Labrador coast

is on record. The traveller started from Quebec and walked
to Battle Harbour. There he turned north and walked to
Nakvak Bay. The distance as the crow flies is about fourteen hundred miles. But the man had no boat of his own
and only in one or two places accepted a passage. One bay
on the east coast runs in for some hundred and fifty miles.
Over this he got a boat fifty miles from the mouth. Round
Kipokak and Makkovik, and the bays south of Hopedale, he walked most of the way, and these run in for
forty miles. He carried practically nothing with him, and
depended on what boots and clothing the people gave
him, eating berries and whatever else he could find while
he was in the country. Those who housed him told me that
they did not see any signs of madness about him, except
his avoidance of men and refusal to go in boats or mix
with others if he could in any way avoid it. He carried no
gun. No one knew who he was nor why he went on such
a "cruise." Long before he reached the North the theory
that he was a murderer fleeing from justice got started,
and at some places a very careful watch was kept over
him. Arrived at Nakvak, he went to the house of everyone's friend, George Ford. That is one of the most inac-
cessible places in the world. No mail steamer ever goes
there, and no schooner ever anchors nearer than a few
miles. It is at the bottom of a fjord twenty-five miles long,
with very precipitous cliffs two thousand feet high on
each side and bottomless water below. It was then thirty
miles from the nearest house, with ranges of mountains
between, and was the most northerly house on the Labrador. Here this phenomenon celebrated his arrival by
climbing up onto the ridge of the house, when lo! most
prosaic of accidents, he fell off and broke his neck. The
puzzle has always been why he elected to carry an unbroken neck at such cost all that long distance.

Many inexplicable things happen "on Labrador." Thus, one year while visiting at the head of Hamilton Inlet, a Scotch settler came aboard to ask my advice about a large animal that had appeared round his house. Though he had sat up night after night with his gun, he had never seen it. His children had seen it several times disappearing into the trees. The French agent of Révillon Frères, twenty miles away, had come over, and together they had tracked it, measured the footmarks in the mud, and even fenced some of them round. The stride was about eight feet, the marks as of the cloven hoofs of an ox. The children described the creature as looking like a huge hairy man; and several nights the dogs had been driven growling from the house into the water. Twice the whole family had heard the creature prowling around the cottage, and tapping at the doors and windows. The now grown-up children persist in saying that they saw this wild thing. Their house is twenty miles up the large Grand River, and a hundred and fifty miles from the coast.

An old fellow called Harry Howell was one winter night missing from his home. He had been hunting, and only too late, after a blizzard set in, was it discovered that he was absent. In the morning the men gathered to make a search, but at that moment in walked "old Harry"! He told me later that he was coming home in the afternoon when the blizzard began. It was dirty, thick of snow, and cold. Suddenly he heard bells ringing, and knew that it was fairies bidding him follow them — because he had followed them before. So off he went, pushing his way through the driving snow. When at last he reached the foot of a gnarled old tree in the forest, the bells stopped, and he knew that was the place where he must stay for the night. So he laid some of the partridges which he had killed into a hole in the snow close to the trunk, crawled down and used them for a seat, and placed the rest of the frozen birds at his feet. Then he pulled up his dickey, or kossak, over his head, and with his back to the tree, went to sleep while the snow was still driving. There was no persuading that man that the ringing bells were in his own imagination.

Many years ago a Norwegian captain on the Labrador told me the following story. One day the carpenter of his schooner, a man whom he had known for three voyages, and trusted thoroughly, was steering on the course which the mate had given him. All at once the mate came and found the man steering four points out. When he upbraided him, he answered, "He came and told me to." "Nobody did," replied the mate. "Go northwest."

Three times the experience was repeated, and at last the mate reported the matter to the skipper. He immediately suggested, "Well, let us go on running in the direction he insists on taking for a while and see if anything happens." At the end of two hours they came upon a square-rigger with her decks just awash, and six men clinging to her rigging. As they came alongside the sinking vessel the carpenter pointed aghast to one of the rescued crew and cried out, "There's the man who came and told me the skipper said to change the course."

In medicine, too, things happen which we professional men are just as unable to explain. A big-bodied, successful fisherman came aboard my steamer one day, saying that he had toothache. This was probable, for his jaw was swollen, his mouth hard to open, and the offending molar easily visible within. When I produced the forceps he protested most loudly that he would not have it touched for worlds.

"Why, then, did you come to me?" I asked. "You are wasting my time."

"I wanted you to charm her, Doctor," he answered, quite naturally.

"But, my dear friend, I do not know how to charm, and don't think it would do the slightest good. Doctors are not allowed to do such things."

He was evidently very much put out, and turning round to go, said, "I knows why you'se won't charm her. It's because I'm a Roman Catholic."

"Nonsense. If you really think that it would do any good, come along. You'll have to pay twenty-five cents exactly as if you had it pulled out."

"Gladly enough, Doctor. Please go ahead."

He sat on the rail, a burly carcass, the incarnation of materialism, while the doctor, feeling the size of a sandflea, put one finger into his mouth and touched the molar, while he repeated the most mystic nonsense he could think of, "Abracadabra Tiddlywinkum Umslopoga" — and then jumped the finger out lest the patient might close his ponderous jaw. The fisherman took a turn around the deck, pulled out the quarter, and solemnly handed it to me, saying, "All the pain has gone. Many thanks, Doctor." I found myself standing alone in amazement, twiddling a miserable shilling, and wondering how I came to make such a fool of myself.

A month later the patient again came to see me when we happened to be in his harbour. The swelling had gone, the molar was there. "Ne'er an ache out of her since," the patient laughed. I have not reported this end result to the committee of the American College of Surgeons, though much attention is now devoted to the follow-up and end-result department of surgery and medicine.

CHAPTER XX

MARRIAGE

It was now the fall of 1908, and the time had come for me to visit England again and try and arouse fresh interest in our work; and this motive was combined with the desire to see my old mother, who was now nearing her fourscore years. I decided to leave in November and return *via* America in the spring to receive the honorary degree of LL.D. from Williams College and of M.A. from Harvard, which I had been generously offered.

My lecture tour this winter was entrusted to an agency. Propaganda is a recognized necessity in human life, though it has little attraction for most men. To me having to ask personally for money even for other people was always a difficulty. Scores of times I have been blamed for not even stating in a lecture that we needed help. The distaste for beating the big drum, which lecturing for your own work always appears to be, makes me quite unable to see any virtue in not doing it, but just asking the Lord to do it. If I really were convinced that He would meet the expenses whether I worked or not, I should believe that neither would He let people suffer and die untended out here or anywhere else. Indeed, it would seem a work of supererogation to have to remind Him of the necessity that existed.

The fact that we have to show pictures of the work which we are doing is tiresome and takes time, but it encourages us to have pictures worth taking and to do deeds which we are not ashamed to narrate. It also stimulates others to give themselves as well as their money to similar kinds of work at their own doorsteps, to see how much like themselves their almoners are. Only to-day my volunteer secretary told me that he honestly expected to meet "a bearded old fogey in spectacles," not a man who can shoot his own dinner from the wing or who enjoys the justifiable pleasures of life.

The religion of Christ never permitted me to accept the idea that there is "nothing to do, only believe." Every man ought to earn his own bread and the means to support his family. Why, then, should you have only to ask the Lord to give unasked the wherewithal to feed other people's families?

Lecturing for philanthropies, only another word for the means to help along the Kingdom of God on earth, is in England usually carried on through the ordinary missionary meetings; and in my previous experience they were not generally much credit to the splendid objects in view. The lectures were aften patronized by small audiences largely composed of women and children.

That particular winter in England I had the privilege of addressing all sorts of workmen's clubs and city lecture-course audiences, people who would have "the shivers" almost if one had asked them to attend a "missionary" lecture. The collection, or even the final monetary outcome, is far from being the test of the value of the address. To commend Christ's religion by minimizing in any way the prerogative He gave men of carrying on the work of His kingdom in their human efforts is to sap the very appeal that attracts manhood to Him. I never wanted to sing, "Oh! to be nothing, nothing." I always wished to sing, "Oh! make me something, something" — that shall leave some footprints on the sands of time, and have some record of talents gained to offer a Master whom we believe to be righteous.

When spring came and the lectures were over, a new

idea suddenly dawned upon me. If I were going to
America to festive gatherings and to have some honours
conferred, why leave the mother behind? Seventy-eight
years is not old. She was born in India, had lived in England, and suppose anything did happen, why not sleep
in America? — she would be just as near God there. The
splendid Mauretania not only took us safely over, but
gave me also that gift which I firmly believe God designed for me — a real partner to share in my joys and
sorrows, to encourage and support in trouble and failures,
to inspire and advise in a thousand ways, and in addition
to bring into my distant field of work a personal comrade
with the culture, wisdom, and enthusiasm of the American life and the training of one of the very best of its
Universities.

We met on board the second day out. She was travelling with a Scotch banker of Chicago and his wife, Mr.
W. R. Stirling, whose daughter was her best friend. They
were returning from a motor tour through Europe and
Algeria. The Mauretania takes only four and a half days
in crossing, and never before did I realize the drawbacks
of "hustle," and yet the extreme need of it on my part.
The degrees of longitude slipped by so quickly that I
felt personally aggrieved when one day we made over
six hundred miles, and the captain told us in triumph that
it was a new record. The ship seemed to be paying off
some spite against me. My mother kept mostly to her
cabin. Though constantly in to see her, I am afraid I did
not unduly worry her to join me on the deck. When just
on landing I told her that I had asked a fellow passenger
to become my wife, I am sure had the opportunity arisen
she would have tumbled down the Mauretania's staircase. When she had the joy of meeting the girl, her equanimity was so far upset as to let an unaccustomed tear roll

down her cheek. That, at least, is one of the tears which I have cost her which brings no regrets. For she confesses that it often puzzles her to which of our lives the event has meant most.

The constant little activities of my life had so filled every hour of time, and so engrossed my thoughts, that I had never thought to philosophize on the advisability of marriage, nor stopped to compare my life with those of my neighbors. There is no virtue in keeping the Ninth Commandment and not envying your neighbour's condition or goods when it never enters your head or heart to worry about them; and when you are getting what you care about no halo is due you for not falling victim to envy or jealousy of others. I have not been in the habit of praying for special personal providences like fine weather in my section of the earth, or for head wind for the schooners so as to give me a fair wind for my steamer, except so far as one prays for the recognition of God's good hand in everything.

I can honestly protest that nothing in my life ever came more "out of the blue" than my marriage; and beyond that I am increasingly certain each day that it did come out of that blue where God dwells.

I knew neither whence she came nor whither she was going. Indeed, I only found out when the proposition was really put that I did not even know her name — for it was down on the passenger list as one of the daughters of the friends with whom she was travelling. Fortunately it never entered my head that it mattered. For I doubt if I should have had the courage to question the chaperon, whose daughter she presumably was. It certainly was a "poser" to be told, "But you don't even know my name." Had I not been a bit of a seaman, and often compelled on the spur of the moment to act first and think afterwards, what the consequences might have been I cannot say. Fortunately, I remembered that it was not the matter at issue, and explained, without admitting the impeachment, that the only question that interested me in the least was what I hoped that it might become. Incidentally she mentioned that she had only once heard of me. It was the year previous when I had been speaking at Bryn Mawr and she had refused in no measured terms an invitation to attend, as sounding entirely too dull for her predilections. I have wondered whether this was not another "small providence."

A pathological condition of one's internal workings is not unusual even in Britons who "go down to the sea in ships," but such genius as our family has displayed has, so history assures us, shone best on a quarter-deck; and on this occasion it pleased God ultimately to add another naval victory to our credit. It is generally admitted that an abnormal mentality accompanies this not uncommon experience of human life, and I found my lack of appreciation of the rapid voyage paralleled by a wicked satisfaction that my mother preferred the brass four-poster, so thoughtfully provided for her by the Cunard Company, to the risks of the unsteady promenade deck.

When the girl's way and mine parted in that last word in material jostlings, the custom-house shed in Manhattan, after the liner arrived, I realized that it was rather an armistice than a permanent settlement which I had achieved. Though there was no father in the case, I learned that there was a mother and a home in Chicago. These were formidable strongholds for a homeless wanderer to assault, but rendered doubly so by the fact that there was neither brother nor sister to leave behind to mitigate the possible vacancy. The "everlasting yea" not having been forthcoming, under the circumstances it was no easy task for me to keep faith with the many appointments to lecture on Labrador which had been made for me. The inexorable schedule kept me week after week in the East. Fortunately the generous hospitality of many old friends who wanted the pleasure of meeting my mother kept my mind somewhat occupied. But I confess at the back of it the forthcoming venture loomed up more and more momentous as the fateful day drew near for me to start for Chicago.

This visit to my wife's beautiful country home among the trees on the bluff of Lake Michigan in Lake Forest was one long dream. My mother and I were now made acquainted with the family and friends of my fiancée. Her father, Colonel MacClanahan, a man of six feet five inches in height, had been Judge Advocate General on the Staff of Braxton Bragg and had fought under General Robert E. Lee. He was a Southerner of Scotch extraction, having been born and brought up in Tennessee. A lawyer by training, after the war, when everything that belonged to him was destroyed in the "reconstruction period," and being still a very young man, he had gone North to Chicago and begun life again at his profession. There he met and married, in 1884, Miss Rosamond Hill, who was born in Burlington, Vermont, but who, since childhood and the death of her parents, had lived with her married sister, Mrs. Charles Durand, of Chicago. The MacClanahans had two children — the boy, Kinloch, dying at an early age as the result of an accident. Colonel MacClanahan himself died a few months later, leaving a widow and one child, Anna Elizabeth Caldwell MacClanahan. She and her mother had lived the greater part of the time with Mrs. Durand, who died something more than a year before our engagement.

The friends with whom my fiancée had been travelling were almost next-door neighbours in Lake Forest. They made my short stay doubly happy by endless kindnesses; and all through the years, till his death in 1918, Mr. Stirling gave me not only a friendship which meant more to me than I can express, but his loving and invaluable aid and counsel in our work.

In spite of my many years of sailor life, I found that I was expected among other things to ride a horse, my fiancée being devoted to that means of progression. The days when I had ridden to hounds in England as a boy in Cheshire stood me in some little stead, for like swimming, tennis, and other pastimes calling for coördination, riding is never quite forgotten. But remembering Mr. Winkle's experiences, it was not without some misgivings that I found a shellback like myself galloping behind my lady's charger. My last essay at horseback riding had been just eleven years previously in Iceland. Having to wait a few days at Reikkavik, I had hired a whole bevy of ponies with a guide to take myself and the young skipper of our vessel for a three days' ride to see the geysers. He had never been on the back of any animal before, and was nevertheless not surprised or daunted at falling off frequently, though an interlude of being dragged along with one foot in the stirrup over lava beds made no little impression upon him. Fodder of all kinds is very scarce in the volcanic tufa of which all that land consists, and any moment that one stopped was always devoted by our ponies to grubbing for blades of grass in the holes. On our return to the ship the crew could not help noticing that the skipper for many days ceased to patronize the lockers or any other seat, and soon they were rejoicing that for some reason he was unable to sit down at all. He explained it by saying that his ponies ate so much lava that it stuck out under their skins, and I myself recall feeling inclined to agree with him.

The journey from Lake Forest to Labrador would have been a tedious one, but by good fortune a friend from New York had arranged to come and visit the coast in his steam yacht, the Enchantress, and was good enough to pick me up at Bras d'Or. Dr. Alexander Graham Bell, who had previously shown me much kindness, permitted us to rendezvous at his house, and for a second time I enjoyed seeing some of the experiments of his most versatile brain. His aeroplanes, telephones, and other inventions were all intensely interesting, but among his other lines of work the effort to develop a race of sheep, which had litters just as pigs do, interested me most.

Francis Sayre, whom I had heard win the prize at Williams with his valedictory speech, was again to be my summer secretary. On our arrival at St. Anthony we found a great deal going on. The fame as a surgeon of my colleague, Dr. John Mason Little, had spread so widely that St. Anthony Hospital would no longer hold the patients who sought assistance at it. Fifty would arrive on a single mail boat. They were dumped down on the little wharf, having been landed in small punts from the steamer, as in those days we had no proper dock to which the boats could come. The little waiting-room in the hospital at night resembled nothing so much as a newly opened sardine tin; and to cater for the waiting patients was a Sisyphean task without the Hercules. Through the instrumentality of Dr. Little's sister a fund of ten thousand dollars was raised to double the size of the hospital, and the work of building was begun on my return. Although the capacity was greatly increased thereby we have really been unable ever to make our building what it ought to be to meet the problem. The first part, constructed of green lumber hauled from the woods, and other wings added at different periods of growth, the endeavour to blast out suitable heating-plant accommodations — all this has left the hospital building more or less a thing of rags and patches, and most uneconomical to run. We are urgently in need of having it rebuilt entirely of either brick or stone, in order to resist the winter cold, to give more efficiency and comfort to patients and staff and to conserve our fuel, which is the most serious item of expense we have to meet.

But at that time with all its capacity for service the new addition was rising, sounding yet one more note of praise in better ability to meet the demands upon us.

And *pari passu* came the beautiful offer of my friend, Mr. Sayre, to double the size of our orphanage, putting up the new wing in memory of his father. This meant that instead of twenty we might now accommodate forty children at a pinch. Life is so short that it is the depths of pathos to be hampered in doing one's work for the lack of a few dollars. Of great interest to my fiancée and myself was the selection of a piece of ground adjoining the Mission land, and the erection for ourselves of the home which we had planned and designed together before I had left Lake Forest. We chose some land up on the hillside and overlooking the sea and the harbour, where the view should be as comprehensive as possible. But we feared that even though our new house was very literally "founded upon a rock," the winds might some day remove it bodily from its abiding-place, and therefore we riveted the structure with heavy iron bolts to the solid bedrock.

One excitement of that season was Admiral Peary's return from the North Pole. We were cruising near Indian

Harbour when some visitors came aboard to make use of our wireless telegraph, which at that time we had installed on board. It proved to be Mr. Harry Whitney. It was the first intimation that we had had that Peary was returning that year. Whitney had met Cook coming back from the polar sea on the west side of the Gulf, where he had disappeared about eighteen months previously. I had met Dr. Cook several times myself, and indeed I had slept at his house in Brooklyn. He had visited Battle Harbour Hospital in 1893 when he was wrecked in the steamer in which he was conducting a party to visit Greenland. We had again seen him as he went North with Mr. Bradley in the yacht, and he had sent us back some Greenland dogs to mix their blood with our dogs, and so perhaps improve their breed and endurance. These, however, I had later felt it necessary to kill, for the Greenland dogs carry the dangerous tapeworm which is such a menace to man, and of which our Labrador dogs are entirely free so far.

The picture of this meeting on the ice between Cook and Whitney gave us the impression of another Nansen and Jackson at Spitzbergen. Whitney had welcomed Cook warmly, had witnessed his troubles at Etah, and his departure by komatik, and had taken charge of his instruments and records to carry South with him when he came home. But his ship was delayed and delayed, and when Peary in the Roosevelt passed on his way South, fearing to be left another winter Whitney had accepted a passage on her at the cost of leaving Cook's material behind. He had met his own boat farther south and had transferred to her. He left the impression very firmly on all our minds that both he and Dr. Cook really believed that the latter had found the long-sought Pole.

A little later, while cruising in thick weather in the

COMMODORE PEARY ON HIS WAY BACK FROM THE POLE, 1909

Gulf of St. Lawrence, my wireless operator came in and said: "There can be no harm telling you, Doctor, that Peary is at Battle Harbour. He is wiring to Washington that he has found the Pole, and also he is asking his committee if he may present the Mission with his superfluous supplies, or whether he is to sell them to you." Seeing that it is not easy to know whence wireless messages come if the sender does not own up to his whereabouts, I at once ordered him to wireless to Peary at Battle the simple words: "Give it to them, of course," and sign it "Washington." I knew that the Commander would see the joke, and if the decision turned out later to be incorrect, it could easily be rectified by purchasing the goods. A tin of his brown bread now lies among my curios and one of his sledges is in my barn.

On our arrival at Battle Harbour we found the Roosevelt lying at the wharf repainting and refitting. A whole host of newspaper men and other friends had come North to welcome the explorer home. Battle was quite a gay place; but it was living up to its name, for Peary not only claimed that he had found the Pole, but also that Cook had not; and he was realizing what a hard thing it is to prove a negative. We had a very delightful time with the party, and greatly enjoyed meeting all the members of the expedition. Among them was the ill-fated Borup, destined shortly to be drowned on a simple canoe trip, and the indomitable and athletic Macmillan who subsequently led the Crocker Land expedition, our own schooner George B. Cluett carrying them to Etah.

My secretary, Mr. Sayre, was just about to leave for America, and at Peary's request he transferred to the Roosevelt with his typewriter, to help the Commander with a few of his many notes and records. I dare say that he got an inside view of the question then agitating the world from Washington to Copenhagen; but if so, he has remained forever silent about it. For our part we were glad that some one had found the Pole, for it has been a costly quest in both fine men and valuable time, energy, and money. It has caused lots of trouble and sorrow, and so far at least its practical issues have been few.

Our wedding had been scheduled for November, and for the first time I had found a Labrador summer long. In the late fall I left for Chicago on a mission that had no flavour of the North Pole about it. We were married in Grace Episcopal Church, Chicago, on November 18, 1909. Our wedding was followed by a visit to the Hot Springs of Virginia; and then "heigho," and a flight for the North. We sailed from St. John's, Newfoundland, in January. I had assured my wife, who is an excellent sailor, that she would scarcely notice the motion of the ship on the coastal trip of three hundred miles. Instead of five days, it took nine; and we steamed straight out of the Narrows at St. John's into a head gale and a blizzard of snow. The driving spray froze onto everything till the ship was sugared like a vast Christmas cake. It made the home which we had built at St. Anthony appear perfectly delightful. My wife had had her furniture sent North during the summer, so that now the "Lares and Penates" with which she had been familiar from childhood seemed to extend a mute but hearty welcome to us from their new setting.

We have three children, all born at St. Anthony. Our elder son, Wilfred Thomason, was born in the fall of 1910; Kinloch Pascoe in the fall of 1912, two years almost to a day behind his brother; and lastly a daughter, Rosamond Loveday, who followed her brothers in 1917. In the case of the two latter children the honours of the

name were divided between both sides of the family,
Kinloch and Rosamond being old family names on my
wife's side, while, on the other hand, there have been
Pascoe and Loveday Grenfells from time immemorial.

Nearly ten years have now rolled away since our
marriage. The puzzle to me is how I ever got along before; and these last nine years have been so crowded with
the activities and worries of the increasing cares of a
growing work, that without the love and inspiration and
intellectual help of a true comrade, I could never have
stood up under them. Every side of life is developed and
broadened by companionship. I admit of no separation
of life into "secular" and "religious." Religion, if it
means anything, means the life and activities of our
divine spirit on earth in relation to our Father in heaven.
I am convinced from experience of the supreme value to
that of a happy marriage, and that "team work" is
God's plan for us on this earth.

CHAPTER XXI

NEW VENTURES

No human life can be perfect, or even be lived without troubles. Clams have their troubles, I dare say. A queer sort of sinking feeling just like descending in a fast elevator comes over one, as if trouble and the abdominal viscera had a direct connection. Some one has said that it must be because that is where the average mind centres. Thus, when we lost the little steamer Swallow which we were towing, and with it the evidence of a crime and the road to the prevention of its repetition, it absolutely sickened me for two or three days, or, to be more exact, during two or three nights. It was all quite unnecessary, for we can see now that the matter worked out for the best. The fact that troubles hurt most when one is at rest and one's mind unoccupied, and in the night when one's vitality is lowest, is a great comfort, because that shows how it is something physical that is at fault, and no physical troubles are of very great importance.

The summer of 1910 brought me a fine crop of personal worries, and probably deservedly so, for no one should leave his business affairs too much to another, without guarantees, occasionally renewed, that all is well. Few professional men are good at business, and personally I have no liking for it. This, combined with an over-readiness to accept as helpers men whose only qualifications have sometimes been of their own rating, was really spoiling for trouble — and mine came through the series of coöperative stores.

To begin with, none of the stores were incorporated, and

their liabilities were therefore unlimited. Though I had always felt it best not to accept a penny of interest, I had been obliged to loan them money, and their agent in St. John's, who was also mine, allowed them considerable latitude in credits. It was, indeed, a bolt from the blue when I was informed that the merchants in St. John's were owed by the stores the sum of twenty-five thousand dollars, and that I was being held responsible for every cent of it — because on the strength of their faith in me, and their knowledge that I was interested in the stores, having brought them into being, they had been willing to let the credits mount up. Even then I still had all my work to carry on and little time to devote to money affairs. Had I accepted, on first entering the Mission, the salary offered me, which was that of my predecessor, I should have been able to meet these liabilities, and very gladly indeed would I have done so. As it was I had to find some way out. All the merchants interested were told of the facts, and asked to meet me at the office of one of them, go over the accounts with my agent, and try and find a plan to settle. One can have little heart in his work if he feels every one who looks at him really thinks that he is a defaulter. The outcome of the inquiry revealed that if the agent could not show which store owed each debt, neither could the merchants; some had made out their bills to separate stores, some all to one store, and some in a general way to myself, though not one single penny of the debt was a personal one of my own.

The next discovery was that the manager of the St. Anthony store, who had been my summer secretary before, and was an exceedingly pious man — whose great zeal for cottage prayer meetings, and that form of religious work, had led me to think far too highly of him — had neglected his books. He had given credit to every one who came along (though it was a cardinal statute under his rules that no credit was to be allowed except at his own personal risk). The St. John's agent claimed that he had made a loss of twelve thousand dollars in a little over a year, in which he professed to have been able to pay ten per cent to shareholders and put by three hundred dollars to reserve. Besides this, the new local store secretary had mixed up affairs by both ordering supplies direct from Canada and sending produce there, which the St. John's agent claimed were owed to the merchants in that city.

These two men, instead of pulling together, were, I found, bitter enemies; and it looked as if the whole pack of cards were tumbling about my ears. I cashed every available personal asset which I could. The beautiful schooner, Emma E. White, also a personal possession, arrived in St. John's while we were there with a full load of lumber, but it and she sailed straight into the melting-pot. The merchants, with one exception, were all as good about the matter as men can be. They were perfectly satisfied when they realized that I meant facing the debt squarely. One was nasty about it, saying that he would not wait — and oddly enough in ordinary life he was a man whom one would not expect to be ungenerous, for he too was a religious man. Whether he gained by it or not it is hard to say. He was paid first, anyhow. The standard of what is really remunerative in life is differently graded. The stores have dealt with him since, and his prices are fair and honest; but he was the only one among some twenty who even appeared to kick a man when he was down. I have nothing but gratitude to all the rest.

I should add that the incident was not the fault of the people of the coast. Often I had been warned by the merchants that the coöperative stores would fail and that the people would rob me. It is true that there was trouble over the badly kept books, and a number of the fishermen disclaimed their debts charged against them; but with one exception no one came and said that he had had things which were not noted on the bills. I am confident, however, that they did not go back on me willingly, and when my merchant friends said, "I told you so," I honestly was able to state that it was the management, not the people or the system, that was at fault. Indeed, subsequent events have proved this. For five of the stores still run, and run splendidly, and pay handsomer dividends by far than any investment our people could possibly make elsewhere.

With the sale of a few investments and some other available property, the liability was so far reduced that, with what the stores paid, only one merchant was not fully indemnified, and he generously told me not to worry about the balance.

This same year, on the other hand, one of our most forward steps, so far as the Mission was concerned, was taken, through the generosity of the late Mr. George B. Cluett, of Troy, New York. He had built specially for our work a magnificent three-masted schooner, fitted with the best of gear including a motor launch. She was constructed of three-inch oak plank, sheathed with hardwood for work in the ice-fields. She was also fitted with an eighty horse-power Wolverine engine. The bronze tablet in her bore the inscription, "This vessel with full equipment was presented to Wilfred T. Grenfell by George B. Cluett." He had previously asked me if I would like any words from the Bible on the plate, and I had suggested, "The sea is His and He made it." The designer unfortunately put the text after the inscription; so that I have been frequently asked why and how I came to make it, seeing that it is believed by all good Christians that in heaven "there shall be no more sea."

To help out with the expenses of getting her running, our loved friend from Chicago, Mr. W. R. Stirling, agreed to come North on the schooner the first season, bringing his two daughters and three friends. Even though he was renting her for a yachting trip, he offered to bring all the cargo free and make the Mission stations his ports of call.

Mr. Cluett's idea was that, as we had big expenses carrying endless freight so far North, and as it got so broken and often lost in transit, and greatly damaged in the many changes involved from rail to steamer, and from steamer to steamer, if she carried our freight in summer, she could in winter earn enough to make it all free, and possibly provide a sinking fund for herself as well. There was also good accommodation in her for doctors, nurses, students, etc., who every summer come from the South to help in various ways in the work of the Mission.

All our freight that year arrived promptly and in good condition, which had never happened before. Later the vessel was chartered to go to Greenland by the Smithsonian. On this occasion her engine, never satisfactory, gave out entirely, which so delayed her that she got frozen in near Etah and was held up a whole twelve-month. Meanwhile the war had broken out, and when she at last sailed into Boston, we were able to sell her, by the generous permission of Mrs. Cluett, and use the money to purchase the George B. Cluett II.

Illustrating the advantage of getting our freight direct, among the many instances which have occurred, that of the lost searchlight for the Strathcona comes to my mind. As she had often on dark nights to come to anchor among vessels, and to nose her way into unlit harbours, some friends, through the Professor of Geology at Harvard, who had himself cruised all along our coast in a schooner, presented me with a searchlight for the hospital ship and despatched it *via* Sydney — the normal freight route. Month after month went by, and it never appeared. Year followed year, and still we searched for that searchlight. At length, after two and a half years, it suddenly arrived, having been "delayed on the way." Had it been provisions or clothing or drugs, or almost anything else, of course, it would have been useless. It has proved to us one of the almost *de luxe* additions to a Mission steamer.

For a long time I had felt the need of some place in St. John's where work for fishermen could be carried on, and which could be also utilized as a place of safety for girls coming to that city from other parts of the island. My attention was called one day to the fact that liquor was being sent to people in the outports C.O.D., by a barrel of flour which was being lowered over the side of the mail steamer rather too quickly on to the ice. As the hard bump came, the flour in the barrel jingled loudly and leaked rum profusely from the compound fracture. When our sober outport people went to St. John's, as they must every year for supplies, they had only the uncomfortable schooner or the street in which to pass the time. There is no "Foyer des Pêcheurs"; no one wanted fishermen straight from a fishing schooner in the home; and in those days there were no Camp Community Clubs. As one man said, "It is easy for the parson to tell us to be good, but it is hard on a wet cold night to be good in the open street" and nowhere to go, and harder still if you have to seek shelter in a brightly lighted room, where music was being played. The boarding-houses for the fishermen, where thousands of our young men flocked in the spring to try for a berth in the seal fishery, were ridiculous, not to say calamitous. Lastly, unsophisticated girls coming from the outports ran terrible risks in the city, having no friends to direct and assist them; and the Institute which we had in mind was to comprise also a girls' lodging department. No provision was made for the accommodation of crews wrecked by accident, and our Institute has already proved invaluable to many in such plights.

Seeing the hundreds of craft and the thousands of fishermen, and the capital and interest vested against us as prohibitionists, it would have been obviously futile to put up a second-rate affair in a back street. It would only be sneered at as a proselytizing job. I had almost forgotten to mention that there was already an Old Seamen's Home, but it had gradually become a roost for boozers, and when with the trustees we made an inspection of it, it proved to be only worthy of immediate closure. This was promptly done, and the money realized from the sale of it, some ten thousand dollars, was kindly donated to the fund for our new building.

After a few years of my collecting funds spasmodically, a number of our local friends got "cold feet." Reports started, not circulated by well-wishers, that it was all a piece of personal vanity, that no such thing was needed, and if built would prove a white elephant, to support which I would be going round with my hat in my hand worrying the merchants. We had at that time some ninety thousand dollars in hand. I laid the whole story before the Governor, Sir Ralph Williams, a man by no means prejudiced in favour of prohibition. He was, however, one who knew what the city needed, and realized that it was a big lack and required a big remedy.

A letter which I published in all the St. John's papers, describing my passing fifteen drunken men on the streets before morning service on Christmas Day, brought forth angry denials of the actual facts, and my statement of the number of saloons in the city was also contradicted. But a saloon is not necessarily a place licensed by the Government or city to make men drunk — for the majority are unlicensed, and a couple of experiences which my men had in looking for sailors who had shipped, been given advances, and gone off and got drunk in shebeens, proved the number to be very much higher than even I had estimated it.

Sir Ralph thought the matter over and called a public meeting in the ballroom of Government House. He had a remarkable personality and no fear of conventions. After thoroughly endorsing the plan for the Institute, and the need for it, he asked each of the many citizens who had responded to his invitation, "Will you personally stand by the larger scheme of a two hundred thousand dollar building, or will you stand by the sixty thousand dollar building with the thirty thousand dollar endowment fund, or will you do nothing at all?" It was proven that when it came to the point of going on record, practically all who really took the slightest interest in the matter were in favour of the larger plan — if I would undertake to raise the money. My own view, since more than justified, was that only so large a building could ever hope to meet the requirements and only such a comprehensive institution could expect to carry its own expenses. I preferred refunding the ninety thousand dollars to the various donors and dropping the whole business to embarking on the smaller scheme.

That meeting did a world of good. It cleared the atmosphere; and it is only fresh air which most of these things really need — just as does a consumptive patient. The plan was now on the shoulders of the citizens; it was no longer one man's hobby. Enemies, like the Scribes and Pharisees of old, knew better than to tackle a crowd, and with the splendid gift of Messrs. Bowring Brothers of a site on the water-side on the main street, costing thirteen thousand dollars, and those of Job Brothers, Harvey and Company, and Macpherson Brothers of twenty-five hundred dollars each, the fund grew like Jonah's gourd; and in the year of 1911, with approximately one hundred and seventy-five thousand dollars in hand, we actually came to the time for laying the foundation stone. The hostility of enemies was not over. Such an institute is a fighting force, and involves contest and therefore enemies. So we decided to make this occasion as much of an event as we could. Through friends in England we obtained the promise of King George V that if we connected the foundation stone with Buckingham Palace by wire, he would, after the ceremony in Westminster Abbey on his Coronation Day, press a button at three in the afternoon and lay the stone across the Atlantic. The good services of friends in the Anglo-American Telegraph Company did the rest.

On the fateful day His Excellency the Governor came down and made an appropriate and patriotic speech. Owing to the difference in time of about three hours and twenty minutes, it was shortly before twelve o'clock with us. The noonday gun signal from the Narrows was fired during His Excellency's address. Then followed a prayer of invocation by His Lordship the Bishop of Newfoundland and Bermuda — and then, a dead silence and pause. Every one was waiting for our newly crowned King to put that stone into place. Only a moment had passed, the Governor had just said, "We will wait for the King," when "Bing, bang, bang," went the gong signifying that His Majesty was at the other end of the wire. Up went the national flag, and slowly but surely the great stone began to move. A storm of cheering greeted the successful effort; and all that was left for our enemies to say was, "It was a fake." They claimed that we had laid the stone ourselves. Nor might they have been so far off the mark as they supposed, for we had a man with a knife under that platform to make that stone come down if anything happened that the wire device did not work. You cannot go back on your King whatever else you do, and to permit any grounds to exist for supposing that he had not been punctual was unthinkable. But fortunately for all concerned our subterfuge was unnecessary.

I have omitted so far to state one of the main reasons why the Institute to our mind was so desirable. That was because no undenominational work is carried on practically in the whole country. Religion is tied up in bundles and its energies used to divide rather than to unite men. No Y.M.C.A. or Y.W.C.A. could exist in the Colony for that reason. The Boys' Brigade which we had originally started could not continue, any more than the Boy Scouts can now. Catholic Cadets, Church Lads Brigade, Methodist Guards, Presbyterian Highland Brigade — are all names symbolic of the dividing influences of "religion." In no place of which I know would a Y.M.C.A. be more desirable; and a large meeting held in the Institute this present spring decided that in no town anywhere was a Y.W.C.A. more needed.

In another place in this book I have spoken of the problem of alcohol and fishermen. A man does not need alcohol and is far better without it. A man who sees two lights when there is only one is not wanted at the wheel. The people who sell alcohol know that just as well as we do, but for paltry gain they are unpatriotic enough to barter their earthly country as well as their heavenly one, and to be branded with the knowledge that they are cursing men and ruining families. The filibuster deserves the name no less because he does his destructive work secretly and slowly, and wears the emblems of respectability instead of operating in the open with "Long Toms" under the shadow of the "Jolly Roger."

As a magistrate on this coast I have been obliged more than once to act as a policeman, and though one hated the ill-feeling which it stored up, and did not enjoy the evil-speaking to which it gave rise, I considered that it was really only like lancing a concealed infection — the ill-feeling and evil-speaking were better tapped and let out.

On one occasion at one of our Labrador hospitals a beardless youth, one of the Methodist candidates for college who every year are sent down to look after the interests of that denomination on our North coast, came to inform me that the only other magistrate on the coast, the pillar of the Church of England, and shortly to be our stipendiary, who had many political friends of great influence in St. John's, was keeping a "blind tiger," while many even of his own people were being ruined body and soul by this temptation under their noses.

"Well," I replied, "if you will come and give the evidence which will lead to conviction, I will do the rest."

"I certainly will," he answered. And he did. So we got the little Strathcona under way, and after steaming some fifteen miles dropped into a small cove a mile or two from the place where our friend lived. In the King's name we constrained a couple of men to come along as special constables. Our visit was an unusual one. To divert suspicion we dressed our ship in bunting as if we were coming for a marriage license. When we anchored as near his

THE INSTITUTE

stage as possible, we dropped our jolly-boat and made
for the store. The door was, however, locked and our
friend nowhere to be seen. "He is in the store" was the
reply of his wife to our query. We knew then that there
was no time to be lost, and even while we battered at the
door, we could hear a suspicious gurgle and smell a curious
odour. Rum was trickling down through the cracks of the
store floor on to the astonished winkles below. But the
door quickly gave way before our overtures, and we
caught the magistrate *flagrante delicto*. We were threatened with all sorts of big folk in St. John's; but we held
the trial on board straightaway just the same. When
court was called, the defendant demanded the name of
the prosecutor — and to his infinite surprise out popped
the youthful aspirant to the Methodist ministry. When
he learned that half of his fine of seventy dollars had to
be paid to the prosecutor and would be applied toward
the building of a Methodist school, his temper completely
ran away with him; and we had to threaten auction on
the spot of the goods in the store before we could collect
the money. We left him breathing out threatenings and
slaughter.

Only once was I really caught. Two mothers in a little
village had appealed to me because liquor was being sold
to their boys who had no money, while people were com-
plaining simultaneously that fish was being stolen from
their stages. No one would tell who was selling it, so we
had a systematic search made of all the houses, and the
guilty man was convicted on evidence discovered under
the floor of his sitting-room. The fine of fifty dollars he
paid without a murmur and it was promptly divided between the Government and the prosecutor. It so happened, however, that he had obtained from us for a close
relative a new artificial leg, and there was fifty dollars

owing to us on it. Unknown to us at the time, he had collected that fifty dollars from the said relative and with it paid his fine. To this day we never got a cent for our leg, and so really fined ourselves. Nor could we with any propriety distrain on one of a poor woman's legs!

CHAPTER XXII

PROBLEMS ON LAND AND SEA

THE year 1912 was a busy season. The New Year found us in Florida with the donor of the ship George B. Cluett, consulting him concerning its progress and future. Lecturing then as we went west we reached Colorado, visited the Grand Canyon, and lectured all along the Pacific Coast from San Diego to Victoria — finding many old friends and making many new ones.

At Oaklands I was asked to deliver the Earle Lectures at the University of California; and I also spoke to an immense audience in the open Greek theatre — a most novel experience. At Santa Barbara a special meeting had been arranged by our good friend Dr. Joseph Andrews, who every year travels all the way from California to St. Anthony at his own expense to afford the fishermen of our Northern waters the inestimable benefits of his skill as a consulting eye specialist. Many blind he has restored to sight who would otherwise be encumbrances to themselves and others. Only last year I received the following communication from an eager would-be patient: "Dear Dr. Grandfield, when is the eye spider coming to St. Anthony? I needs to see him bad."

While we were at Tacoma a visitor, saying that he was an old acquaintance of mine, sent up his card to our room. He had driven over in a fine motor car, and was a great, broad-shouldered man. The grip which he gave me assured me that he had been brought up hard, but I utterly failed to place him. With a broad grin he relieved the situation by saying: "The last time that we met, Doctor, was on the deck of a fishing vessel in the North Sea. I was

second hand aboard, sailing out from Grimsby." The
tough surroundings of that life were such a contrast to his
present apparently ample means that I could only say,
"How on earth did you get out here?"

"A friend," said he, "gave me a little book entitled
'One Hundred Ways to Rise in the World.' The first
ninety-nine were no good to me, but the hundredth said,
'Go to Western America,' so I just cleared out and came
here." He was exceedingly kind to us, even accompanying
us to Seattle, and his story of pluck and enterprise was a
splendid stimulus.

Six weeks of lecturing nearly every single night in a
new town in Canada gave me a real vision of Canadian
Western life, and a sincere admiration for its people who
are making a nation of which the world is proud.

In April a large meeting was held in New York to reorganize the management of the Mission. The English
Royal National Mission to Deep-Sea Fishermen was no
longer able or willing to finance, much less to direct,
affairs which had gone beyond their control, and was hoping to arrange an organization of an international character to which all the affairs of the enterprise could be
turned over. This organization was formed at the house
of Mr. Eugene Delano, the head of Brown Brothers,
bankers, whose lifelong help has meant for Labrador
more than he will ever know.

The International Grenfell Association was incorporated to comprise the Labrador branches of the Royal
National Mission to Deep-Sea Fishermen as its English
component, the Grenfell Association of America and the
New England Grenfell Association to represent the American interests, the Labrador Medical Mission as the Canadian name for its Society, and the Newfoundland Grenfell Association for the Newfoundland branch. Each one

of these component societies has two members in the
Central Council, and together they make up the Board
of Directors of the International Grenfell Association.
These directors ever since have generously been giving
their time and interest in the wise and efficient adminis-
tration of this work. To these unselfish men Labrador
and northern Newfoundland, as well as I, owe a greater
debt than can ever be repaid.

On the 1st of May I was due to speak at the annual
meeting of the English Mission in London, and the swift
heels of the Mauretania once more stood us in good stead;
for we reached England the evening before May 1, arrived in London at 2 A.M., and I spoke three times that
day. After a day or so at my old home with my mother we
ran about in a Ford car for a fortnight, lecturing every
evening. The little motor saved endless energy otherwise
lost in endeavouring to make connections, and gave us
the opportunity to see numbers of old friends whom we
must otherwise have missed. One day we would be at a
meeting of miners at Redmuth in Cornwall, on another
at Harrow or Rugby Schools. At the latter, an old college
friend, who is now head master there, gave us a royal
welcome. During the last fortnight at home a splendid
chance was afforded me to visit daily the clinics of an old
friend, Sir Robert Jones, England's famous orthopedic
surgeon. He is one of the most wonderful and practical
of men, and he opened our eyes to the possibility of medical mission work in the very heart of England — for if
ever there was an apostle of hope for the deformed and
paralyzed he certainly is the man. His Sunday morning
free clinics crowded even the street opposite his office
door with waiting patients of the poorest class. Equally
beneficent also is the large and wonderful hospital built
specially for derelict children on the heather-covered hills

just above our home in Cheshire. But most unique of all was his Basschurch Hospital, constructed mostly of sheet iron, standing in the middle of a field in the country forty miles away from Liverpool. Every second Sunday, Sir Robert Jones used to motor over there and operate "in the field." No expedition have I ever enjoyed better in my life than when he was good enough to pick us up on his way, and we saw him tackle the motley collection of halt and lame, whom the lady of the hospital, herself a marvellous testimony to his skill, collected from the neighbouring town slums between his visits. The hospital was the nearest thing I know to our little "one-horse shows" scattered along the Labrador coast; and there was a homing feeling in one's heart all the time at these open-air clinics.

As commander-in-chief of the orthopedic work of the British Army in the war, I am certain that Colonel Sir Robert Jones has found the experiences of his improvised clinics among the most valuable assets he could have had. One day he has promised that he will bring his magic wand to Labrador; for he is a sportsman in the best sense of the word as well as a healer of limbs.

The quickest way back to St. John's being *via* Canada, we returned by the Allan Line, and lectured in the Maritime Provinces as we passed North.

It would appear that one must possess an insatiable love of lecturing. As a matter of fact, nothing is farther from the truth. But the brevity of life is an insistent fact in our existence, and the inability to do good work for lack of help that is so gladly given when the reasonableness of the expenditure is presented, makes one feel guilty if an evening is spent doing nothing. The lecturing is by far the most uncongenial task which I have been called upon to do in life, but in a mission like ours, which is not under any special church, the funds must be raised to a very great extent by voluntary donations, and in order to secure these friends must be kept informed of the progress of the work which their gifts are making possible.

For the first seven years of my work I never spent the winters in the country — nor was it my intention ever to do so. Besides the general direction of the whole, my work as superintendent has meant the raising of the necessary funds, and my special charge on the actual coast has been the hospital ship Strathcona. Naturally, owing to our frozen winter sea this is only possible during open water. Since 1902 it has been my custom when possible to spend every other winter as well as every summer in the North. The actual work and life there is a tremendous rest after the nervous and physical tax of a lecture tour. At first I used to wonder at the lack of imagination in those who would greet me, after some long, wearisome hours on the train or in a crowded lecture hall, with "What a lovely holiday you are having!" Now this oft-repeated comment only amuses me.

It was just after the first of June when again we found ourselves heading North for St. Anthony, only once more to be caught in the jaws of winter. For the heavy Arctic ice blockaded the whole of the eastern French shore, and we had to be content to be held up in small ice-bound harbours as we pushed along through the inner edge of the floe, till strong westerly winds cleared the way.

Having reached St. Anthony and looked into matters there, we once again ran south to St. John's to inspect the new venture of the Institute. To help out expenses we towed for the whole four hundred miles a schooner which had been wrecked on the Labrador coast, having run on the rocks, and knocked a hole in her bottom. She had a

number of sacks of "hard bread" on board. These had
been thrown into the breach and planking nailed on over
them. The bread had swelled up between the two casings
and become so hard again that the vessel leaked but little; and though the continual dirge of the pumps was
somewhat dismal as we journeyed, we had no reason to
fear that she would go to the bottom.

Flour resists water in a marvellous way. On one occasion our own vessel in the North Sea was run into by another. The latter's cutwater went through her side and
deck almost to the combing of the hatch, and the water
began to pour in. By immediately putting the vessel on
the other tack, the rent was largely lifted out of water.
A heavy topsail was hastily thrown over her side, and
eventually hauled under the keel — the inrushing water
keeping it there. Then sacks of flour were rammed into
the breach. The ship in this condition, favoured by the
wind which enabled her to continue on that tack, reached
home, two hundred miles distant, with her hand-pumps
keeping her comparatively free, though there was the
greatest difficulty to keep her afloat directly she was
towed into the harbour and lay at the wharf.

On another occasion when a Canadian steamer, loaded
with provisions, ran into a cliff two hundred feet high in
a fog on the northeast end of Belle Isle, and became a
total wreck, her flour floated all up and down the Straits.
I remember picking up a sack that had certainly been in
the water some weeks; and yet only about a quarter of
an inch of outside layer was even wet.

The opening of the Institute was a great day. Dr.
Henry van Dyke had come all the way from New York
to give an address. Sir William Archibald, chairman of
the Royal National Mission to Deep-Sea Fishermen, had
travelled from England to bring a blessing from the old

home country; and the merchants and friends in St. John's did their best to make it a red-letter day. Sir Edward Morris, the Prime Minister, and other politicians, the Mayor and civic functionaries were all good enough to come and add their quota to the launching of the new ship. There were still pessimistic and croaking individuals, however, as well as joyful hearts, when a few days later we again ran North.

We started almost immediately for our Straits trip after reaching St. Anthony. On our way east from Harrington, our most westerly hospital, commenced in 1907, a telegram summoning me immediately to St. John's dropped upon me like a bolt from the blue. Without a moment's delay we headed yet again South, full of anxiety as to what could be the cause of this message.

On arrival there we found that trouble had arisen concerning the funds of the Institute and a prosecution was to follow. It was the worst time of my life. Things were readjusted; the money was refunded, punishment meted out — but such damage is not made right by reconstruction. It left permanent scars and made the end of an otherwise splendid year anxious and sorrowful.

The work on East Labrador was also extended this year. While walking down the street in New York with a young doctor friend who had once wintered with me, we met a colleague of his at the College of Physicians and Surgeons. In the conversation it was suggested that he should spend a summer in Labrador, and we would place him in a virgin field. As a result Dr. Wiltsie, now in China, came North, started in work with a little school, club, and dispensary, at a place called Spotted Islands, in a very barren group of islands about a hundred miles north of the Straits of Belle Isle. His work became permanent as the summer mission of the Y.M.C.A. of the College, which organization now carries all its expenses. It has a dwelling-house, school, dispensary, small operating room, and accommodation for a couple of patients, all under one roof, and owns a fast motor boat called the P. and S., which has made itself known as an angel of mercy, every summer since, over a hundred miles of coast and islands. It is only a summer work, and is mainly among a schooner population; but as a testimonial to the value of pluck and unselfishness I know of no better example.

Among other ways to help Labrador we had always tried to induce tourists and yachtsmen to come and visit us. Mr. Rainey's Surf, Mr. McCready's Enchantress, Dr. Stimson's Fleur de Lys, Mr. Arthur James's Aloha, and a few other yachts had come part of the way, but no one had yet explored north of Hopedale — the latitude at which the fine Northern scenery may be said only to begin. The large power vessels or even the best type of yacht are by no means necessary for a visit to Labrador. For the innumerable fjords and islands make it much more interesting to be in a smaller boat, which allows one to go freely in and out of new by-ways, even when the survey is only that of your own making. The most sporting visits of that kind have been the honeymoon of a Philadelphia friend, who, with his wife, one man, and a canoe, went by river to James's Bay, then *via* Hudson Bay to Richmond Gulf, then by portage and river to Ungava Bay, and thence home by way of the Hudson Bay Company's steamer; the canoe trips of Mr. Kennedy all along the outside eastern coast, and those of Mr. William Cabot on the section of the northeastern coast between Hopedale and Nain. In this year of 1912 a new little yacht appeared, the Sybil, brought down from Boston by her owner, Mr. George Williams. I had promised that if ever he would sail down to see us in his own boat, we would escort him up a salmon river for a fishing expedition — a luxury which we certainly never anticipated would materialize. But on arriving North, there was the beautiful little boat; and in it we sailed up into the fine salmon stream in the bay close to the hospital. Subsequently Mr. Williams came year after year, pushing farther North each time. The Sybil he eventually gave to the Mission, and built a large boat, the Jeanette, in which I had the pleasure later of exploring with him and roughly charting three hitherto unrecorded bays.

One unusual feature of our magisterial work in 1912 was the settlement of a fisherman's strike "down North." It would at first seem difficult to understand how fishermen could engineer a strike, they are so good-natured and so long-suffering. But this time it was over the price of fish, naturally a matter of immense importance to the catcher. The planters, or men who give advances to come and fish around the mouth of Hamilton Inlet, were to ship their fish on a steamer coming direct from England and returning direct— thus saving delay and very great expense. But the price did not please the men, and they knew if they once put the fish on board at $3.50 per quintal, the amount offered, they would never recover the $5, which was the price for which fish was selling in St. John's that year. The more masterful men decided that not only would they not put the fish on board till they had cash orders or Révillon agreements for their price, but they would not allow any of the weaker brethren to do so either. There were but few hard words and no violent deeds, but when one blackleg was seen to go alongside the waiting steamer, which was costing a hundred dollars a day to the fish-carrying merchant, a crowd of boats dashed out from creeks and corners and pounced like a vulture on the big boat, fat with a fine load of fish, and not only towed her away and tied her up, but hauled her out of the water with the cargo and all in her, and dragged her so far up the side of a steep hill that the owner was utterly unable without assistance to get her down again.

Each day we had a conference with one side or the other, the Government having asked us to remain and see things settled. While each side was fencing for an advantage, a good-sized schooner sailed into the harbour, brought up alongside the steamer, and was seen to begin unloading dry fish. A dash was made for her by the boats as before; only this time it was the attack of Lilliputians on Gulliver. We on the shore could not help laughing heartily when shortly we saw a string of over a dozen fishing boats harnessed tandem in one long line towing the interloper — as they had the blackleg — away up the inlet where they moored and guarded her. It appeared that the buyer had sent her to a far-off anchorage, and unknown to the strikers had had fish put into her there. The steamer might have followed and got away with the ruse. But the skipper underestimated the enemy, always a fatal mistake, and lost out.

The agreement made a day or so later was perfectly peaceful, and perfectly satisfactory to both sides, for the fish turned out a good price, and the buyer did not lose anything on the transaction but the demurrage on his steamer and a little kudos, which I must confess he took in very good spirit. Even if he did have a grasping side to his character, he was fortunate in possessing a sense of humour also.

The fall brought yet another call to go South to St. John's, and once more in the little Strathcona we ploughed our way through the long miles to the southward. This time it was for the reorganization of the Institute government, to form a council and to install the new manager from England. This was Mr. Walter Jones, a man whose wide experience among naval "Jackies" had been gained in a large institute of much the same kind. This gave him the credentials which we needed, for he had made it not only a social but an economic success. He has been much sought by the various churches in St. John's as a speaker to men, and his Sunday evening lantern services and lectures at the Institute are a real source of uplift and help to men of every religious denomination.

The fall of the year was very busy. Dr. Seymour Armstrong, formerly surgical registrar at the Charing Cross Hospital in London, an able surgeon, and a man of independent means, joined me for that winter at St. Anthony. He had already wintered twice at our Labrador hospitals, and was fully expecting to give us much further help, but two years later the great war found him at the front, where he gladly laid down his life for his country.

One sick call that winter lives in my memory. It was a case where a nurse was really more needed than a doctor. The way was long, the wind was cold, and the snow happened to be particularly deep. One of the nurses, however, volunteered for the journey, and I arranged to carry her on a second komatik, while my driver broke the path with our impedimenta. Things did not go altogether well. Since I have enjoyed the luxury of a driver, or a "carter" as we call them, my cunning in wriggling a komatik at full speed down steep mountain-sides through trees has somewhat waned. Comparatively early in the day we looped the loop — and we were both heavy weights. It was nearly dark when we reached the last lap — an enormous bay with a direct run of seven miles over sea ice. We should probably have made it all right, but suddenly fog drifted in from the Straits of Belle Isle, and steering with a small compass and no binnacle, while attending to hauling a heavy nurse over hummocky sea ice in the dark, satisfied all my ambition for problems. At length the nature of the ice indicated that we were approaching either land or the sea edge. We stopped the komatiks, and it fell to my lot to go ahead and explore. Finding nothing I called to the driver, and his voice returned out of the fog right ahead of me, and almost in my ear. I had told them not to move or we might miss our way, and I reminded him of that fact. "Have n't budged an inch" came the reply from the darkness. I had been describing a large circle. I can still hear that nurse laughing.

At last we struck the huge blocks of ice, raised on the boulder rocks by the rise and fall of tide in shallow water, and we knew that we should make the land. The perversity of nature made us turn the wrong way for the village toward which we were aiming, and we found ourselves "tangled up" in the Boiling Brooks, a place where some underground springs keep holes open through the ice all winter. Suddenly, while marching ahead with the compass, seeking to avoid these springs, the ground being level enough for the nurse to act as her own helmsman, a tremendous "whurr! whurr!" under my feet restored sufficient leaping power to my weary legs to leave me head down and only my racquets out of the snow — all for a covey of white partridges on which I had nearly trodden. At length we made a tiny winter cottage. The nurse slept on the bench, the doctor on the floor, the driver on a shelf. Our generous host had almost to hang himself on a hook. The dogs went hungry. But as we boiled our kettle, all agreed that we would not have exchanged the experience for ten rides in a Pullman Car.

Largely through the zeal of my colleague, Dr. Arthur Wakefield, of Kendal, England, and that of my cousin,

On the Way Home

Carrying a Sick Dog

DOG TRAVEL

Mr. Martyn Spencer, of New Zealand, a band of the Legion of Frontiersmen had been brought into being all along this section of coast, in spite of the scattered nature of the population. The idea was that having to depend so largely on the use of their guns, and being excellent shots with a bullet, the men would make good snipers and scouts if ever there were war. True, most of our people called it "playing soldiers," and no one took seriously that we were ever likely to be called upon to fight; but all Dr. Wakefield's hopes and fears were realized and our lads made both brave soldiers and excellent marksmen.

Dr. and Mrs. Wakefield have given several years of both medical and industrial work for the people of this coast, both in St. Anthony, Forteau, Mud Lake, and Battle Harbour.

Alas, the functions of superintendent involved executive duties, and I had once again to run to St. John's, during the following summer, for a meeting of the Board of Directors. With true Christian unselfishness these men come all the way from Ottawa, New York, and Boston, to help with their counsel so relatively unimportant a work as ours. Sir Walter Davidson again lent his heartiest co-operation. The people owe him, Sir Herbert Murray, Sir Henry MacCallum, Sir William MacGregor, Sir Ralph Williams, Sir Alexander Harris, and all the long line of their Governors, more than most of them realize. They bring all the inspiration of the best type of educated, widely experienced, and travelled Englishmen to this Colony. They are specially trained and specially selected men, and can give their counsel and leadership absolutely untrammelled by any local prejudices.

One excellent outcome of this particular meeting was the reorganization on a larger scale of the Girls' Committee for the Institute. The success of it has been phenom-

enal. Together with its protective work it has aimed at
that most difficult task of creating in them sufficient ambition to make the girls receiving very small wages want
to pay for a better environment. The committee has always been strictly interdenominational, with Mrs. W. C.
Job and Mrs. W. E. Gosling as its presidents. It has made
a "show place" of the Girls' Department of the Institute,
and that department has become self-supporting — a
most desirable goal for every philanthropy.

The lumber mill and schooner building work were in
slings. Our men, made far better off by the winter work
thus provided, had acquired gear so much better for
fishing than their former equipment that they could not
resist engaging in the more remunerative work of the fishery in the summer months. For two years previous they
had left before the drive was complete and the logs out
of the woods. Now the local manager had also decided to
fish during the three summer months — which is really
the only time available for mill operations also. I was
fortunate enough on my way North to persuade an expert
lumber operator from Canada, and an entirely kindred
spirit, Mr. Harry Crowe, to come down and help me out
with the problem. We spent a few delightful days together, in which he taught me as many things that every
mill man should know as he would have had to learn had
he been dabbling in pills. Like myself, Mr. Crowe is an
ardent believer in Confederation with Canada for this little
country. Before Mr. Crowe's efforts on our behalf had materialized, a new friend, Mr. Walter Booth, of New York,
well known in American football circles as one of the best
of all-American forwards, came North and carried the mill
for a year. The one and only fault of his régime was that
it was too short. The field of work was one for which he was
admirably equipped, but home reasons made him return

after his time expired. He has often told me since, however, that he has fits of wishing that he could have put in a life with us in the North, rather than spending it in the more civilized circles of the New York Bar.

Many invitations to speak, especially at universities in America, and through a lecture agency in England to numerous societies and clubs, led me to devote the winter of 1913–14 to a lecture tour. My wife induced me also to renew my youth by a holiday of a month on the Continent.

A lecture tour includes some of the most delightful experiences of life, bringing one into direct personal contact with so many people whom it is a privilege to know. But it also has its anxieties and worries, and eternal vigilance is the price of avoiding a breakdown at this the most difficult of all my work. One's memory is taxed far beyond its capacity. To forget some things, and some people and some kindnesses, are unforgivable sins. A new host every night, a new home, a new city, a new audience, alone lead one into lamentable lapses. In a car full of people a man asked me one day how I liked Toledo. I replied that I had never been there. "Strange," he murmured, " because you spent the night at my house!" On another occasion at a crowded reception I was talking to a lady on one side and a gentleman on the other. I had been introduced to them, but caught neither name. They did not address each other, but only spoke to me. I felt that I must remedy matters by making them acquainted with each other, and therefore mumbled, "Pray let me present to you Mrs. M-m-m." "Oh! no need, Doctor," he replied. "We've been married for thirty years." Shortly after I noticed at a reception that every one wore his name pinned onto his breast, and I wondered if there were any connection.

It is my invariable custom in the North to carry a water-tight box with matches and a compass chained to my belt. One night, being tired, I had turned into bed in a very large, strange room without noting the bearings of the doors or electric switches. My faithful belt had been abandoned for pyjama strings. It so happened that to catch a train I had to rise before daylight, and all my possessions were in a dressing-room. I soon gave up hunting for the electric light. It was somewhere in the air, I knew, but beating the air in the dark with the windows wide open in winter is no better fun in your nightclothes in New York than in Labrador. A tour of inspection discovered no less than five doors, none of which I felt entitled to enter in the dark in *déshabille*. The humour of the situation is, of course, apparent now, but even one's dog hates to be laughed at.

An independent life has somehow left me with an instinctive dislike for asking casual acquaintances the way to any place that I am seeking. The aversion is more or less justified by the fact that outside the police force very exceptional persons can direct you, especially if they know the way themselves. On my first visit to New York I could see how easy a city it was to navigate, and returned to my host's house near Eighth Street in good time to dress for dinner after a long side trip near Columbia University and thence to the Bellevue Hospital. "How did you find your way?" my friend asked. "Why, there was sufficient sky visible to let me see the North Star," I answered. I felt almost hurt when he laughed. It is natural for a polar bear not to have to inquire the way home.

The aphorism attributed to Dr. John Watson, of "Beside the Bonnie Briar Bush," suggests itself. "My fee is one hundred dollars if I go to a hotel, two hundred if I am entertained, because in the latter event one can only live half so long." I conclude that he made the choice of Achilles, for he died on a lecture tour. So far fate has been kinder to me.

The greatest danger is the reporter, especially the emotional reporter, who has not attended your meeting. I owe such debts to the press that this statement seems the blackest of ingratitude. On the contrary, I must plead that doctors are privileged. My controversy with this class of reporters is their generosity, which puts into one's mouth statements that on final analysis may be cold facts, but which, remembering that one is lecturing on work among people whom one loves and respects, it would never occur to me to slur at a public meeting. No one who tries to alter conditions which exist can expect to escape making enemies. I have seen reports of what I have said at advertised meetings, that were subsequently cancelled. I have followed up rumours, and editors have expressed sorrow that they accepted them from men who had been too busy to be present. But "qui s'excuse, s'accuse"; and my conclusion is that the lecturer is practically defenceless.

Since our marriage my wife has generously acted as my secretary, having specially learned shorthand and typewriting in order to free me from carrying such a burden, and has helped me enormously ever since on this line. But lecture tours used to make me despair of keeping abreast of correspondence. I sometimes was forced to treat letters as Henry Drummond did — who allowed them to answer themselves — if I wished free mornings in which to visit the hospitals, just at the time that all their professional work was in progress. These clinics are invaluable and almost unique experiences. They persuaded me more than ever how much depends in surgery as well as in medicine on "the man behind the gun"; and that mere mileage is not the real handicap on members of our profession whose fields of work lie away from the centres of learning. They also imbued me with the profoundest spirit of respect for the leaders of the healing art.

To no one but myself did it seem odd that a plain Englishman should be invited to perform the function of best man at the wedding of the daughter of the President of the United States of America at the White House. The matter was never even noticed either in the press or in conversation. The only citizen to whom I suggested the anomaly merely said, "Well, why not? "

My long-time fellow worker and one of my best of friends, Francis B. Sayre, was to be married on November 25, 1913, to Miss Jessie Wilson. Her father, who, when first I had had the honour of his acquaintance, happened to be the President of Princeton University, was now the President of the United States. So we had all the fun of a White House wedding. Not less than fifty of our fishermen friends from Labrador and North Newfoundland were invited, and some members of our staff were present.

We started the wedding procession upstairs, and came down to the fanfare of uniformed trumpeters. Our awkwardness in keeping step, though we had rehearsed the whole business several times, only relieved the tension that must exist at so important an event in life.

Trying to dodge the reporters added heaps of fun, which I am sure that they shared, for they generally got the better of us; though the thrill of escape from the White House and Washington, so that the honeymoon rendezvous should not be known, was practically a victory for the wedding party. As it would never be safe to use the tactics again, I am permitted after the lapse of many years to give them away. As soon as dark fell, and while the guests were still revelling, the bride and groom were hustled into a secret elevator in the thickness of the wall, whisked up to the robing chambers, and completely disguised. Meanwhile a suitable camouflage of automobiles had arrived ostentatiously at the main entrance, to carry and escort the illustrious couple in fitting pomp to the great station. From the landing the couple were dropped direct to the basement to a prearranged oubliette. The password was the sound of the wheels of an ordinary cab at the kitchen entrance. The moments of suspense were not long. At the sound of the crush on the gravel a silent door was opened, two completely muffled figures crept out, and the conspirators drove slowly along round a few corners where a swift automobile lay panting to add *liberté* to *égalité* and *fraternité*.

CHAPTER XXIII

A MONTH'S HOLIDAY IN ASIA MINOR

AFTER the fall spent in America in raising the necessary funds, it was the now famous Carmania which carried us to England. In spite of a few days' rest at my old home, and the stimulus of a Grenfell clan gathering in London, my wife and I were both in need of something which could direct our minds from our problems, and Boxing Day found us bound for Paris, Turin, Milan, and Rome.

Just before Christmas I had had a meeting at the famous office of the Hudson Bay Company in London, and attended another of their interesting luncheons where their directors meet. My old friend Lord Strathcona presided. I could not help noting that after all the lapse of years since we first met at Hudson Bay House in Montreal, he still retained his abstemious habits. He was ninety-three, and still at his post as High Commissioner for a great people, as well as leading councillor of a dozen companies. His memory of Labrador and his days there, and his love for it, had not abated one whit. Hearing that the hospital steamer Strathcona needed a new boiler and considerable repairs, he ordered me to have the work undertaken at once and the bill sent to him. He, moreover, insisted that we should spend some days with him at his beautiful country house near London, an invitation which we accepted for our return, but which we were never fated to realize, for before the appointed date that able man had crossed the last bar.

It is said to be better to be lucky than rich. We had expected in Rome to do only what the Romans of our pocket-book do. But we fell in with some old acquaintances whose pleasure it is to give pleasure, and New Year's night was made memorable by a concert given by the choir of the Sistine Chapel, to which we were taken by the editor of the "Churchman" and later of the "Constructive Quarterly," an old friend of ours, Dr. Silas McBee. A glimpse into the British Embassy gave us an insight into the problem of Roman modern politics and the factions of the Black and White.

Rome is always delightful. One is glad to forget the future and live for the time in the past. Sitting in the Coliseum in the moonlight I could see the gladiators fighting to amuse the civilized man of that period, and gentle women and innocent men dying horrible deaths for truths that have made us what we are, but which we now sometimes regard so lightly.

I confess that religious buildings, religious pictures, religious conventions of all kinds very soon pall on my particular temperament. It is possibly a defect in my development, like my inability to appreciate classical music. On the other hand, like Mark Twain, I enjoy an ancient mummy just because he is ancient; and were it not for the irritation of seeing so much religious display associated with such miserable social conditions in so beautiful a country, I should have more sympathy with those who would "see Rome and die." The sanitation of the one-time Mistress of the world suggests that it could not be difficult to accomplish that feat in the hot weather.

Brindisi is a household word in almost every English home, especially one like ours with literally dozens of Anglo-Indian relatives. I was therefore glad to pass *via* Brindisi on the road to Athens. Patras also had its interest to me as a distributing centre for our Labrador fish. We actually saw three forlorn-looking schooners, with cargoes from Newfoundland, lying in the harbour.

One poignant impression left on my mind by Greece, as well as Rome, was its diminutive size. I almost resented the fact that a place civilized thousands of years ago, and which had loomed up on my imagination as the land of Socrates, of Plato, of Homer, of Achilles, of Spartan warriors, and immortal poets, all seemed so small. The sense of imposition on my youth worried me.

In Athens one saw so many interesting relics within a few hundred yards that it left one with the feeling of having eaten a meal too fast. The scene of the battle of Salamis fascinated me. When we sat in Xerxes' seat and conjured up the whole picture again, and saw the meaning to the world of the great deed for which men so gladly gave their lives to defeat a tyrant seeking for world power, it made me love those old Greeks, not merely admire their art.

On Mars Hill we stood on the spot where, to me, perhaps the greatest man in history, save one, pleaded with men to accept love as the only durable source of greatness and power. But every monument, every bas-relief, every tombstone showed that the fighting man was their ideal.

The idea of sailing from the Piræus reconciled us to the very mediocre vessel which carried us to Smyrna. Our visit to Asia Minor we had inadvertently timed to the opening of the International College at Paradise near Smyrna. This college is the gift of Mrs. John Kennedy of New York. Mr. Ralph Harlow, our host and a professor at the college, with Mr. Cass Reid and other friends, made it possible for us to enjoy intelligently our brief visit. It was just a dream of pleasure. Time forbids my describing the marvellous work of that and other colleges. Men of ambition, utterly irrespective of race, colour, creed, or sect, sit side by side as the alumni. The humanity, not the other-worldliness, of the leaders has made even the Turks, steeped in the blood of their innocent Christian subjects, recognize the untold value of these Christian universities, and kept them, their professors, and buildings, safe during the war.

Dr. Bliss, of Beyrout, once told us a humorous story about himself. He had just been addressing a large audience in New York, when immediately after his speech the chairman rose and announced, "We will now sing the one hundred and fiftieth hymn, 'From the best bliss that earth imparts, we turn unfilled to Thee again.'"

The preservation of Ephesus was a surprise to us, though of late the Turks have been carrying off its precious historic marble to burn for lime for their fields. One large marble font in an old Byzantine baptistry was broken up for that purpose while we were there. We stood on the very rostrum in the theatre where St. Paul and the coppersmith had trouble — while at the time of our visit, the only living inhabitant of that once great city was a hungry ass which we saw harboured in a dressing-room beneath the platform.

The anachronism of buzzing along a Roman road, which had not been repaired since the days of the Cæsars, on our way to Pergamos, in the only Ford car in the country, was punctuated by having to get out and shove whenever we came to a cross-drain. These always went over instead of under the road — only on an exaggerated Baltimorian plan. One night at Soma, which is the end of the branch railroad in the direction of Pergamos, we were in the best hotel, which, however, was only half of it for humans. A detachment of Turkish soldiers were billeted below in the quarters for the other animals. Snow was on the ground, and it was bitterly cold. The poor soldiers slept literally on the stone floor. We were cold, and we felt so sorry for them, that after we had enjoyed a hot breakfast, in a fit of generosity we sent them a couple of baskets of Turkish specialties. Later in the day we noticed that wherever we went a Turkish soldier with a rifle followed us. So we turned off into a side street and walked out into the country. Sure enough the soldier came along behind. As guide to speak the many languages for us, we had a Greek graduate of International College, a very delightful young fellow, very proud of a newly acquired American citizenship. At last we stopped and bribed that soldier to tell us what the trouble was. "Our officer thought that you must be spies because you sent gifts to Turkish soldiers."

At Pergamos, a Greek Christian — very well off — invited us to be his guests on Greek Christmas Eve. It was the occasion of a large family gathering. There were fine young men and handsome, dark-eyed girls, and all the accessories of a delightful Christian home. When the outer gates had been locked, and the inner doors bolted and blinds drawn down, and all possible loopholes examined for spies, the usual festivities were observed. These families of the conquered race have lived in bondage some four hundred years, but their patriotism has no more dimmed than that of ancient Israel under her oppressors. Before we left they danced for us the famous Souliet Dance — memorial to the brave Greek girls who, driven to their last stand on a rocky hilltop, jumped one by one over the precipice as the dance came round to each one, rather than submit to shame and slavery. From our friends at Smyrna we learned subsequently that when, a few months later, and just before the war, the German general visited the country, making overtures to the Turks, the blow fell on this family like many others, and they suffered the agony of deportation.

At Constantinople the kindness of Mr. Morgenthau,

the American Ambassador, and the optimism bred by Robert College and the Girls' School, left delightful memories of even the few days in winter that we spent there. The museum alone is worth the long journey to it, and when a teacher from the splendid Girls' School, herself a specialist on the Hittites, was good enough to show it to us, it was like a leap back into the long history of man. It seemed but a step to the Neanderthal skull and our Troglodyte forbears.

Owing to shortage of time we returned to England through Bulgaria, passing through Serbia, and stopping for a day at Budapest and two at Vienna. We would have been glad to linger longer, for every hour was delightful.

The month's holiday did me lots of good and sent me back to England a new man to begin lecturing again in the interests of the distant Labrador; and with the feeling that, after all, our coast was a very good place for one's life-work.

We helped to lessen the tedium of the lectures by doing most of the travelling in an automobile of my brother's, in which we lived, moved, and had our meals by the roadside. The lectures took us everywhere from the drawing-room of a border castle on the line of the old Roman Wall — which Puck of Pook's Hill had made as fascinating for us as he did for the children — to the Embassy in Paris.

Once more the Mauretania carried us to America. April was spent partly in lecturing and partly in attending surgical clinics — a very valuable experience being a week's work with Dr. W. R. MacAusland, of Boston, at his orthopedic clinics in and around that city. He and his brother "Andy" had passed a summer with us in Labrador. May found us in Canada visiting our helpers, and stimulating various branches by lectures. While loading the George B. Cluett in early June in St. John's, Newfoundland, we organized an education committee to work with the Institute Committee, to give regular educational lectures throughout the winter. Dr. Lloyd, our present Prime Minister, and Sir Patrick McGrath, always a stanch friend of the Mission, helped materially in this new activity.

The Institute at the time was housing some of the crew of the Greenland, who had come through the terrible experiences at the seal fishery in the spring of 1914. Caught on the ice in a fearful blizzard, almost all had perished miserably. Some few had survived to lose limbs and functions from frostburns. The occasion gave the Institute one of the many opportunities for a service rather more dramatic than the routine, which did much to win it popularity.

Midsummer's Day and the two following days we were stuck in a heavy ice-jam one hundred miles south of St. Anthony. My wife and boys had arrived in St. Anthony before me, and to find them in our own house, and the hospital full of opportunity for the line of help which I especially enjoy, afforded all that heart could wish.

Early in July the Duke of Connaught, the Governor-General of Canada, paid us a long-promised visit. It was highly appreciated by all our people, who would possibly have paid him more undivided attention had he not been kind enough to send his band ashore — the first St. Anthony had ever heard. The resplendent uniforms of the members totally eclipsed that of the Duke, who was in "mufti"; but he readily understood that the division of attention was really not attributable to us. He proved to be a thorough good sport and a most democratic prince.

The war having broken out in August, we had only one

idea — economy on every side, that we might all be able
to do what we could. We had not then begun to realize
the seriousness of it sufficiently to dream that we should
be welcome ourselves. We closed up all activities not entirely necessary, and even the hospital ship went into
winter quarters so early that my fall trip was made from
harbour to harbour in the people's own boats or by mail
steamer or schooner, as opportunity offered.

CHAPTER XXIV

THE WAR

In the fall of 1915, I was urged by the Harvard Surgical Unit to make one of their number for their proposed term of service that winter at a base hospital in France. Having discussed the matter with my directors, we decided that it was justifiable to postpone the lecture tour which had been arranged for me, in view of this new need.

We sailed for England on the Dutch liner New Amsterdam and landed at Falmouth, passing through a cordon of mine-sweepers and small patrols as we neared the English shores. My wife's offer to work in France not being accepted, since I held the rank of Major, we ran down to my old home, where she decided to spend most of her time. My uniform and kit were ready in a few days; and in spite of the multitudinous calls on the War Office officials, I can say in defence of red tape that my papers were made out very quickly. I was thus able to leave promptly for Boulogne, near which I joined the other members of my Unit, who had preceded me by a fortnight.

It was Christmas and the snow was on the ground when I arrived in France. There was much talk of trench feet and the cold. Our life in the North had afforded experiences more like those at the front than most people's. We are forced to try and obtain warmth and mobility combined with economy, especially in food and clothing. At the request of the editor, I therefore sent to the "British Medical Journal" a summary of deductions from our Northern experiences. Clothes only keep heat in and damp out. Thickness, not even fur, will warm a statue, and our ideal has been to obtain light, wind- and waterproof material, and a pattern that prevents leakage of the body's heat from the neck, wrists, waist, knees, and ankles. Our skin boots, by being soft, water-tight, and roomy, remove the causes of trench feet. Later when I returned to England I was invited to the War Office to talk over the matter. The defects, either in wet and cold or in hot weather, of woolen khaki cloth are obvious, and when subsequently I visited the naval authorities in Washington about the same subject, I was delighted to be assured that on all small naval craft our patterns were being exclusively used. Who introduced them did not matter.

I had also advocated a removable insert of sheet steel in a pocket on the breast of the tunic, this plate to be kept in the trenches and inserted on advancing; and a lobster-tail steel knee-piece in the knickers. Of this latter Sir Robert Jones, the British orthopedic chief, appreciated the value, knowing how many splendid men are put *hors de combat* by tiny pieces of shell splinters infecting that joint. But the "Journal" censored all these references to armour. A wounded Frenchman at Berck presented me with a helmet heavily dented by shrapnel, and told me that he owed his life to it. Later at General Headquarters, General Sir Arthur Sloggett showed me a collection of a dozen experimental helmets, each of which stood for a saved life.

One of the soldiers who came under my care had a bullet wound through the palm of his hand. I happened to ask him where his hand had been when hit. He said, "On my hip. We were mending a break in our barbed wire at night, and a fixed rifle got me, exactly where it got my chum just afterwards, but it went through him."

"Where did your bullet go?"

"I don't know," he answered.

An examination of his trousers showed the bullet in his

pocket. It was embedded in three pennies and two francs which he happened to be carrying there, and which his wounded hand had prevented his feeling for afterwards.

Pathos and humour, like genius and madness, are close akin. One of the boys told me of a chum who was very "churchy," and always carried an Episcopal Prayer Book in his pocket — for which he was not a little chaffed. For a joke one day he was presented with a second that a messmate had received, but for which he had no use. His scruples about "wasting it" made him put it in his pocket with the other. Soon after this, in an advance, he was shot in the chest. The bullet passed right through the first Prayer Book and lodged in the second, where it was found on his arrival at hospital for another slight wound. He at least will long continue to swear by the Book of Common Prayer.

One day, walking with other officers in the country, we stumbled across a tiny isolated farm. As usual the voice of the inevitable Tommy could be heard from within. They were tending cavalry horses, which filled every available nook and corner behind the lines at a period when cavalry was considered useless in action. Having learned that one of these men had been body servant to a cousin of mine, who was a V.C. at the time that he was killed, I asked him for the details of his death. The Germans had broken through on the left of his command, and it was instantly imperative to hold the morale while help from the right was summoned. Jumping on the parapet, my cousin had stood there encouraging the line amid volleys of bullets. At the same time he ordered his servant to carry word to the right at once. Suddenly a bullet passed through his body and he fell into the trench. Protesting that he was all right, he declared that he could hold out till the man should come back. On his return he found that my cousin was dead. But help came, the line held, and the German attack was a costly failure. His servant had collected and turned in all the little personal possessions of any value which he had found on the body.

"I think that you should have got a Military Cross," I said.

"I did get an M.C.," he answered.

"I congratulate you," I replied.

"It was a confinement to barracks. A bullet had smashed to pieces a little wrist watch which the captain always carried. It was quite valueless, and I had kept the remnants as a memento of a man whom every one loved. But a comrade got back at me by reporting it to headquarters, and they had to punish me, they said."

It is true, "strafing" was at a low ebb at the time that I arrived in France; but even I was not a bit prepared for the amount of leisure time that our duties allowed us. There were in France hundreds of sick and wounded for every one in the lonely North; but in Labrador you are always on the go, being often the only available doctor. Our Unit had at the time only some five hundred beds and a very strong staff, both of doctors and nurses. In spite of lending one of our colonels and several of our staff to other hospitals, we still had not enough beds to keep us fully occupied. It gave me ample time to help out occasionally in Y.M.C.A. activities, and to do some visiting among the poor French families and refugees in Boulogne, close to which city our hospital was located. I could also visit other Units, and give lantern shows, which had, I thought, special value when psychic treatment was badly needed. Shell-shock was but very imperfectly understood at the beginning of the war. The football matches and athletic sports did not need the asset of being an antidote to shell-shock to attract my patronage. Never in my life had I realized quite so keenly what a saving trait the sporting instinct is in the Anglo-Saxon — a strain of it in the Teuton might have even averted this war.

My stay in France enabled me to enjoy that which life on the Labrador largely denies one — the contact with many educated minds. It was the custom, if an officer needed a lift along the road, to hail any passing motor. While walking one day, I took advantage of this privilege, and found myself driving with Sir Bertrand Dawson, the King's physician, with whom I thus renewed a most valued acquaintanceship. On another occasion our host or guest might be Sir Almroth Wright, the famous pathologist, or Sir Robert Jones would pay us a visit, or Sir Frederick Treves. In fact, we had chances to meet many of the great leaders of our profession. Sir Arthur Lawley, the head of our Red Cross in France, gave me some delightful evenings. Unquestionably there is an intense pleasure in hearing and seeing personally the men who are doing things.

Food grew perceptibly scarcer in Boulogne even during my stay. The *petits gâteaux* got smaller, the hours during which officers might enter restaurants for afternoon tea became painfully shorter. But they were not a whit less enjoyable, reminding one as they did of the dear old days, long before the war was thought of, and before the war of life had taken me to Labrador. If one had hoped that a life in the wilds had succeeded in eradicating natural desires, those relapses in the midst of war-time completely destroyed any such delusion. Every day was full of excitement. Bombs fell on the city only twice while I was there, and, moreover, we were bitterly disappointed that we did not know it till we read the news in the morning paper. But every day flying machines of all sorts sailed overhead. My interest never failed to respond to the buzzing of some hurrying airship, or the sight of a seaplane dropping out of heaven into the water and swimming calmly ashore, waddling up the beach into its pen exactly like a great duck.

One day it was the excitement of watching trawlers from the cliffs firing-up mines; another, hunting along the beach among the silent evidences of some tragedy at sea, or riding convalescent horses that needed exercise, flying along the sands to see some special sight, such as the carcass of a leviathan wrecked by butting into minefields.

Close to us was a large Canadian Unit. They were changing their location, and for three months had been in the sorry company of those who have no work to do. The matron, however, told me that she found plenty to occupy her time — in such a beehive of officers, with seventy-five nurses to look after.

When at the close of the period for which I had volunteered I had to decide whether to sign on again, my whole inclination was to stay just another term; but as my commandant, Colonel David Cheever, informed me that he and a number of the busier men felt that duty called them home, and that there were plenty of volunteers to take our places, my judgment convinced me that I was more needed in Labrador.

I shall not say much of the Y.M.C.A. They need no encomium of mine, but I am prepared to stand by them to the last ditch. They were doing, not talking, and were wise enough to use even those agents whom they knew to be imperfect, as God Himself does when He uses us. The folly of judging for all cases by one standard is common and human, but it is not God's way. This conviction was brought home to me in a very odd manner. I had gone to lecture at an English Y.M.C.A. hut at the invitation of the efficient director, who knew me only for a "medical missionary." On my arrival he most hospitably took me to the cupboard which he called "his rooms." It was a raw, cold night, and among other efforts to show his gratitude for my help, to my amazement he offered me "a drop of Scotch." Astonishment so outran good-breeding that I unwittingly let him perceive it. "I am not a regular 'Y' man, Major," he explained. "I'm an Australian, and was living on my little pile when the war began. They turned me down each place I volunteered on account of my age. But I was crazy to do my bit, and I offered to work with the Y.M.C.A. as a stopgap. The War Office has commandeered so many of their men that they had to take me to 'carry on.' I'm afraid I'm a poor apology, but I'm doing my best."

The freedom from convention lent another peculiar charm to the life in France. The mess sergeant of a headquarters where I was dining one night, close behind the lines, presented the colonel with a beautifully illustrated monograph on a certain unmentionable and unwelcome member of war camps and trench life. The beautiful work and the evidences of scientific training led me to ask who the mess sergeant might have been in civil life. "Professor of Biology at the University of ———," was the reply.

The most inspiring fact about the Channel ports at that time was the regularity with which steamers arrived, crowded with soldiers, and returned with wounded. We could see England on clear days from our quarters, and could follow the boats almost across. The number of trawlers at work all the year round, even in heavy gales that almost blew us off the cliffs, was enough to tell how vigilant a watch was being kept all the while. One morning only we woke to find a large stray steamer, that had entered the roads overnight, sunk across the harbour mouth, her decks awash at low water — torpedoed, we supposed. Another day a small patrol, literally cut in half by a mine, was towed in. But though both in the air and under the sea all the ingenuity of the enemy from as near by as Ostend was unceasingly directed against that living stream, not one single disaster happened the whole winter that I was out. Our mine-fields were constantly being changed. The different courses the traffic took from day to day suggested that. But who did it, and when, no one ever knew. The noise of occasional bomb-firing, once a mine rolling up on the shore, exploding and throwing some incredibly big fragments onto the golf links, the incessant tramp of endless soldiers in the street, the ever-present but silent motors hurrying to and fro, and the nightly arrival of convoys of wounded, were all that reminded us that any war was in progress. Had it been permitted, the beach would have been crowded as usual with invalids, nursemaids, and perambulators.

The second marvel was that in spite of the enormous numbers of people coming and going, no secrets leaked out. We gave up looking for news almost as completely as in winter in Labrador. We seemed to be shut off entirely in an eddy of the stream, as we are in our Northern wastes.

The spirit of humour in the wounded Briton was as invaluable as the love of sport when he is well. On one occasion a small party were going to relieve a section of the line. The Boches had the range of a piece of the road over which they had to pass, and the men made dashes singly or in small numbers across it. A lad, a well-known athlete, was caught by a shell and blown over a hedge into a field. When they reached him, his leg was gone and one arm badly smashed. He was sitting up smoking a cigarette, and all he said was, "Well, I fancy that's the end of my football days." One very undeveloped man, who had somehow leaked into Kitchener's Army, told me, "Well, you see, Major, I was a bit too weak for a labouring man, so I joined the army. I thought it might do my 'ealth good!" One of the English papers reported that when a small Gospel was sent by post to a prisoner in Germany the Teuton official stamped every page, "Passed by the Censor."

The practice of listening to the yarns of the wounded was much discouraged, chiefly for one's own sake, for their knowledge was less accurate than our own, while shell-shock led them to imagine more. The censor had always good yarns to tell. The men showed generally much good-humour and a universal light-heartedness. Our wounded hardly ever "groused." They hid their troubles and cheered their families, seldom or never by pious sentiments. One man writing from a regimental camp close to Boulogne, after a painfully uneventful Channel crossing, announced, "Here we are in the enemies' country right under the muzzles of the guns. We got over quite safely, though three submarines chased us and shelled us all the way. Food here is very short. I have n't looked at a bun for weeks. A bit more of that cake of yours would do nicely, not to talk o' smokes. Your loving husband." Another letter was quoted in the "Daily Mail." It ran: "Dear Mother — This comes hoping that it may find you as it leaves me at present. I have a broken leg, and a bullet in my left lung. Your affectionate son."

Yet the men were far from fatalists, and the psychic stimulus of being able to tell your patient that he was ordered to "Blighty" was demonstrable on his history chart. One poor fellow whose right arm was infected with gas bacillus was so anxious to save it that we left it on too long and general blood poisoning set in. He was on the dying list. The Government under these circumstances would pay the expenses of a wife or mother to come over and say the last good-bye. After the message went, it seemed that our friend could not last till their arrival, and the colonel decided as a last chance to try intra-venous injections of Eusol, the powerful antiseptic in use at that time in all the hospitals. On entering the ward the next morning the nurse told me with a smiling face, "B. is ever so much better. I think that he will pull through all right." "Then the Eusol injection has done good, I suppose?" "His wife and mother came last night and sat up with him" — and I saw a twinkle in the corner of her eye. Eusol injections are now considered inert.

With so many patients who only remained so short a time, there was an inevitable tendency to relapse into treating men as "cases," not as brothers. To get through their exterior needed tact and experience. But if love is a force stronger than bayonets and guns, it certainly has its place in modern — and all time — surgery. I have a shrewd suspicion that it is better worth exhibiting than quite a number of the drugs still on the world's pharma-copœias. Many of the nurses kept visitors' books, and in these their patients were asked to write their names or anything they liked. The little fact made them feel more at home, as if some person really cared for them. One could not help noticing how many of them broke out into verse, though most of them were labouring men at home. Although some was not original, it showed that they liked poetry. Some was extempore, as the following:

"Good-bye, dear mother, sister, brother,
Drive away those bitter tears.
For England's in no danger
While there are bomb throwers in the Tenth Royal Fusiliers."

The following effusion I think was doubtless evolved gradually. It runs:

> "There's a little dug-out in a trench,
> Which the rainstorms continually drench.
> With the sky overhead, and a stone for a bed,
> And another that acts for a bench.

> "It's hard bread and cold bully we chew;
> It is months since we've tasted a stew;
> And the Jack Johnsons flare through the cold wintry air,
> O'er my little wet home in the trench.

> "So hurrah for the mud and the clay,
> Which leads to 'der Tag,' that's the day
> When we enter Berlin, that city of sin,
> And make the fat Berliners pay."

I have never been in any sense what is generally understood by the term "faith healer," but I am certain that you can make a new man out of an old one, can save a man who is losing ground, and turn the balance and help him to win out through psychic agencies when all our chemical stimulants are only doing harm. That seemed especially true in those put *hors de combat* by the almost superhuman horrors of this war. It seemed to me to pay especially to get the confidence of one's patients. Thus one man would be drawn out by the gift of a few flowers, a little fruit, cigarettes, as so many of the kindly visitors discovered. One man with shrapnel splinters in his abdomen expressed a craving for Worcester sauce. It appeared to him so unobtainable in a hospital in France. From the point of view of his recovery I am convinced that the bottle which we procured in Boulogne was a good investment.

We eagerly awaited the illustrated papers each week for the same reason. But personal interest shown in themselves, by the time spared for chatting, was far the most appreciated. We had been very rightly warned against listening to the wounded men. It was with them in the base hospitals that the story of the angels of Mons originated. I never met any one personally who saw anything nearer the supernatural than that marvellous fight itself — the pluck and endurance of our "contemptible little army." But some claimed to have seen a spirit but visible army, such as Elijah at Dothan showed to his servant, or Castor and Pollux at Lake Regillus, fighting in front of our lines. A Canadian in command of the C.A.M.C. contingent, who treated thousands of the wounded as they came back from the front, told me that early in the day he heard the rumour, and ordered his men to ask as many as possible if they had seen any such phenomenon. Not one claimed to have done so. Yet a few days later from the base he heard a great many of these same men had declared that they had seen the "angels." He considered that the whole matter arose originally through some hysterical woman, and then was augmented by the suggestion of the question which he himself had put to them, made to men shell-shocked and in abnormal mental conditions.

Among other deductions from voluminous notes I judged that the Saxons really did not want to fight, the impression coming from so many different sources. Some said that they let us know, shouting across "No Man's Land," that they did not wish to fight, that they were Christians, had wives and children of their own, that they did not want to kill any one, and would fire in the air when forced to fire, were keen to renew the Christmas "pour-parlers." Our men claimed that it was comparative peace when the Saxons were in the trenches opposite, and they made friendly overtures as often as they dared.

They were capable of attributing honour to others, and those who came over into our lines asserted that hundreds were anxious to do so, only they were so watched from behind. Moreover, the outrages committed by the Prussians under flags of truce had made it impossible for our men to allow any one to approach. To sit opposite a Saxon regiment for a month and not exchange shots appeared to be not uncommon. One man told me that they poked up a notice on their bayonets saying, "We are not going to fight"; and another said that once when "strafing" somehow commenced, they shouted from the opposite trenches: "Save your bullets. You'll need them tonight when the Prussian Guard relieves us" — which proved perfectly true. One day an elderly man crawled out of their trench, came to our barbed wire, and called out for bread. We threw him a loaf. He wrapped up something in his cap and threw it over. We tossed it back with more bread, but when he went back he left the watch behind.

After an especially brutal piece of treachery, our men were too maddened to give quarter, and one said, "A Saxon might have had a chance with us even then, but a Prussian would have had about as little as a beetle at a woodpecker's prayer meeting!" The Saxons, on the other hand, displayed the individual courage of the Anglo-Saxon that helped to lessen our losses by enabling us to attack in open formation. Every animal will fight when forced to do so. The cowardly wolf will attack only in packs; and one of the main reasons for the wholesale holocausts of mass attacks seems to have been that same lack of real courage in the boastful and militarist element. He dare not advance alone.

A colonel in command at the first battle of the Aisne described to me an incident that I at least did not hear elsewhere. He said that the Germans opposite him came on sixteen abreast, arm in arm, rifles at the trail or held anyhow. They were singing wildly, and literally jumping up and down, as if dancing. Fire was reserved till they came within a few hundred yards, when machine guns started to mow them down. Hay-pooks, or rather man-pooks, were immediately formed, and the advancing column, instead of coming straight on, went round and round the ever-increasing stacks. He believed that they had been filled with too much dope or too much doctored grog of some kind.

It was my great desire before returning from France to see the conditions at the front. I was told that members of American Units were discouraged from visiting the trenches. Dr. Carrel had twice most kindly invited me to Compiègne to see his new work on wounds, but permission to accept had been denied me. Being a British subject and wearing a British decoration on an American uniform only seemed to worry the authorities. I had almost abandoned hope, when one day an automobile stopped at our headquarters, just at the close of my term of service, and a colonel, a distinguished scientist, jumped out. He told me if I could get to Medical Headquarters, then at St. Omer, he could arrange for me to visit each of the four armies I wished to see. I had no permission to leave the base, though my term of service expired the next day. I had no passes, and our British commandant would not on his own responsibility either give me leave or lend me the necessary outfit. He would only agree to look the other way if I went.

Passing the sentries was not difficult, but once arrived in St. Omer, it was essential to have permission from Headquarters before one could enter any house or hotel. I was accordingly dumped in the dark streets of a strange town and told to be at that exact spot again in two hours, waiting my sponsor's return. Nor did he say where he was going, in case we failed to meet, for no one was allowed to mention the whereabouts of the G.H.Q. After two hours were over, I was at the appointed spot with that pleasurable sense of excitement that seldom comes after one has settled down in life. I could then understand better how a spy must feel. The town naturally was unlit for fear of aircraft, and yet there was a queer feeling that every one was looking at you as you walked up and down in the dark. My colonel friend was at the rendezvous with all the precision of a soldier, not only with the necessary papers and arrangements for the tour of inspection, but also a genial invitation to dine at Headquarters. General Sir Arthur Sloggett and his exceedingly able staff opened my eyes very considerably before the evening was out as to the methods of the R.A.M.C. in war-time. It was such a revelation to me that I felt it would be an infinite comfort to those with loved ones in the trenches to realize how marvellously efficient the provision for the care of the soldier's health had become. The main impression on my mind was the extraordinary developments since the days of the Lady of the Lamp. Formerly, so long as he was fit to fight, the soldier was always looked after. Now the soldier unfit to fight had exactly the same rights, just as after the war let us trust that the broken soldier will be "seen through" back into civil life. I was honestly surprised that he no longer depended on voluntary gifts to a charitable society for a bandage when he lay wounded or for a nurse if sickness overtook him. The marvellous system of the medical intelligence department, even the separate medical secret service, worked so efficiently that in spite of the awful conditions the health of the men in the line was twice as good as that when at home in civil life. Even disease approaching from the enemy's side was "spied," and as far as possible forestalled. All sanitary arrangements, all water supplies, and all public health matters from the North Sea to the Swiss border were handled by regular army officers. For the first time in history the medicals were considered so intimate a part of the fighting force that doctors held the same rank as executive officers. I was a major — no longer a surgeon major or just a sanitary official. Those in command were even trusted in advance with information as to what would likely be required of them on any part of the front by some manœuvre or attack, though I do not think that even the general of the R.A.M.C. was admitted to the council of war.

The chart-room of the G.H.Q. was another revelation. The walls from ceiling to floor were occupied with the usual large-scale maps, with flags on pins; while long, weird, crooked lines of all colours made elaborate tracings over the charts, like those used in hospitals. These flags and lines indicated the surgical and medical front, where battles with typhoid, trench feet, and wounds were being waged by the immense army of workers under General Sloggett's direction. Laboratories in motor cars, special surgeons and ambulances were racing here and there, new hospitals for emergencies were being pushed in different directions, so that though within range of the enemies' guns, men wounded in the chest or abdomen could be treated in time to give them a chance for their lives. Typhoid recurring in any section of the line might mean the reprimand of the medical officer there; trench feet became a misdemeanour, so excellent were the precautions devised and carried out by the N.C.O.'s.

I ventured at table to say quite truthfully that I, a surgeon from a base hospital, where we saw endless Red

Cross motor ambulances, and received so many kindnesses in supplies, and especially luxuries for our wounded from the Red Cross officials, had been under the impression that the R.A.M.C. was a sort of small tail to a very large Red Cross kite, owing to our little army and general unpreparedness when the war broke out. I could see that to my surprised hosts I appeared to be mentally deficient, but I was able to assure them that there were tens of thousands who knew even less than that, and thought that the chances still were that if their loved ones were hurt, they might be left to die because some one had not given their annual contribution to a society. It seemed a very serious omission that the public had not the information that would carry so much consolation with it. The British Red Cross has every one's love and support, but its function in war, as one officer said, must increasingly become, in relation to the R.A.M.C., that of a Sunday-school treat to the staff of the school.

The officialdom of Germany and even of France had always contrasted very unfavourably in my mind with our English methods. I was surprised in America that so many hospitals were Government institutions, and yet worked so well.

At Melville we turned aside to inspect what was apparently a second Valley of Hinnom. It was a series of furnaces, built out of clay and old cans, efficiently disposing of the garbage of a town and a large section of the line. At West Outre an officer found time to show us his ingenious improvised laundry. His share was to fight the enemy by keeping our boys decently clean; and for this purpose he collected their dirty linen into huge piles. He had diverted the only available brook so as to put a portable building over it. His battalion consisted of the whole female strength of the country-side, and had to be prepared to advance or retire *pari passu* with the other fighters. The chattering, shouting crowd, almost invisible in the fog of steam as we walked through, made me realize how difficult a command this regiment of washerwomen constituted. The triumph was that they all appeared to be contented and fraternal.

As every one knows one of the worst problems of the trenches was vermin. We entered a huge building used in peace-time for the purposes of dyeing. A Jack Johnson had only just exploded in the moat that brought the water to the tanks, but provision was made for trifles of this kind. When we peered over the edge of a steaming vat, it was to discover a platoon of Tommies enjoying the "time of their lives," before they joined the line of naked beings, each scrubbing the now happy man ahead. An endless stream of garments advanced through electric superheaters in parallel columns. There seemed as much excitement about the chance of every man getting his own clothing back as there is in the bran pie at a children's Christmas party.

While visiting the mud and squalor of a front trench in Flanders, only a few yards from the enemy's lines, the cheery occupants offered to brew some tea, exactly as we "boil our kettle" and have a good time in the safety of our Northern backwoods. One day I picked up some bright blue crystals. They proved to be "bluestone," or sulphate of copper. When my pilot noticed that its presence puzzled me, he remarked casually, "There was a regimental dressing-station there a day or so ago. Probably that is the remains of it."

On a siding at Calais station a veritable pyramid of filth met my eyes. On inspection it proved to be odd old boots dug from the mud of the battle-fields, and, sorted out from the other endless piles of débris, brought back as salvage. To attack one pair of such boots is depressing. Melancholia alone befitted the pile. Yet I saw close at hand, through a series of sheds, this polluted current entering and coming out at the other end new boots, at the rate of a thousand pairs a day—the talisman not being a Henry Ford of boot-making, but just a smiling English colonel in the sporting trousers of a mounted officer.

The ground was still under snow, and we drove over much ice and through much slush as we returned to our base at Boulogne. My colleagues had gone back to America and it was a terribly lonely journey to London, though both steamer and train were crowded. The war was not yet won, and I could not help feeling an intense desire to remain and see it through with the brave, generous-hearted men who were giving their lives for our sakes. Loneliness scarcely describes my sensations; it felt more like desertion. One road to despair would be the awful realization that one is not wanted. The work looming ahead was the only comforting element, with the knowledge that the best of wives and partners was waiting in London to help me out.

CHAPTER XXV
FORWARD STEPS

My return to the work after serving in France was embittered by a violent attack made upon me in a St. John's paper. It was called forth by a report of a lecture in Montreal where I had addressed the Canadian Club. The meeting was organized by Newfoundlanders at the Ritz Carlton Hotel, and the fact that a large number from the Colony were present and moved the vote of thanks at the end should have been sufficient guarantee of the *bona fides* of my statements. But the over-enthusiastic account of a reporter who unfortunately was not present gave my critics the chance for which they were looking. It was at a time when any criticism whatever of a country that was responding so generously to the homeland's call for help would have been impolitic, even if true. It subsequently proved one factor, however, in obtaining the commission of inquiry from the Government, and so far was really a blessing to our work. In retrospect it is easy to see that all things work together for good, but at the time, oddly enough, even if such reports are absolutely false, they hurt more than the point of a good steel knife. Anonymous letters, on the contrary, with which form of correspondence I have a bowing acquaintance, only disturb the waste-paper basket.

The Governor, the representatives of our Council, the Honourable Robert Watson and the Honourable W. C. Job, and my many other fast friends, however, soon made it possible for me to forget the matter. If protest breeds opposition, it in turn begets apposition, and a good line of demarcation — a "no man's land" between friend and foe — and gives a healthy atmosphere in so-called times of peace.

In the year 1915 a large coöperative store was established at Cape Charles near Battle Harbour, which bred such opposition amongst certain merchants that it proved instrumental also in obtaining for us the Government commission of inquiry sent down a few months later. After a thorough investigation of St. Anthony, Battle Harbour, Cape Charles, Forteau, Red Bay, and Flowers Cove, summoning every possible witness and tracing all rumours to their source, the commissioners' findings were so favourable to the Mission that on their return to St. John's our still undaunted detractors could only attribute it to supernatural agencies.

My colleague at Battle Harbour, Dr. John Grieve, who with his wife had already given us so many years' work there, and whose interest in the coöperative effort at Cape Charles was responsible for its initial success, had worked out a plan for a winter hospital station in Lewis Bay, and had surveyed the necessary land grant. Through the resignation of our business manager, Mr. Sheard, and the selection of Dr. Grieve by the directors as his successor, only that part of the Lewis Bay scheme which enables us to give work in winter providing wood supplies has so far materialized.

In 1915 also, at a place called Northwest River, one hundred and thirty miles up Hamilton Inlet from Indian Harbour, a little cottage hospital and doctor's house combined was built, called the "Emily Beaver Chamberlain Memorial Hospital." Thus the work of Dr. and Mrs. Paddon has been converted into a continuous service, for formerly when Indian Harbour Hospital was closed in the fall, they had no place in which they could efficiently carry on their work during the winter months. Before Dr. Paddon came to the coast, Dr. and Mrs. Norman Stewart gave us several years of valuable service, spending their summers at Indian Harbour and returning for the winter to St. Anthony, according to my original plan when I first built St. Anthony Hospital.

An old friend and worker at St. Anthony, Mr. John Evans of Philadelphia, who had helped us with our deer and other problems, having married our head nurse, the first whom we had ever had from Newfoundland, found it essential to return and take up remunerative work at home.

The increasing number of patients seeking help at St. Anthony made it necessary to provide proportionately increasing facilities. As I have stated elsewhere, the sister of my splendid colleague, Dr. Little, in 1909 had raised the money for the new wing of the hospital for the accommodation of the summer accession of patients. The clinic which had now grown so tremendously, due to Dr. Little's magnificent work, was maintaining a permanent house surgeon, Dr. Louis Fallon, who had faithfully served the Mission at different times at other stations. We had also regular dental and eye departments.

The summer of 1917 was saddened for us all by the loss to the work of my beloved and able colleague, Dr. John Mason Little, Jr., who had given ten years of most valuable labour to the people of this coast. He had married, some years before, our delightful and unselfish helper, Miss Ruth Keese, and they now had four little children growing up in St. Anthony. The education of his family and the call of other home ties made him feel that it had become essential for him to terminate his more intimate connection with the North, and he left us to take up medical work in Boston. The loss of them both was a very heavy one to the work and to us personally, and we are only thankful that we have been able to secure Dr. Little's invaluable assistance and advice on our Board of Directors in Boston. This coast and this hospital owe him a tremendous debt which can never be repaid, for it was he who put this clinic in a position to hold up its head among the best of medical work, and offer to this far-off people the grade of skilled assistance which we should wish for our loved ones if they were ill or in trouble. For Dr. Little offered not only his very exceptional skill as a surgeon, but also the gift of his inspiring and devoted personality.

The winter of 1917–18 was extremely severe, not only in our North country, but in the United States and Canada also. I was lecturing during this winter in both these latter countries, though during the months of December and January travelling became very difficult owing to the continuous blizzards. I was held up for three days in Racine, Wisconsin, as neither trains, electric cars, or automobiles could make their way through the heavy drifts. Had I had my trusty dog team, however, I should not have missed three important lecture engagements. Life in the North has its compensations.

At Toronto I was unfortunate enough to contract bronchitis and pleurisy, and I understand from competent observers that I was an "impossible patient." Be that as it may, so much pressure was brought to bear on me that at last I was forced to obey the doctors and leave for a month's rest in a warmer climate.

Owing to ice and war conditions we did not arrive in St. Anthony until the first of July. In arriving late we were all spared a terrible shock. The previous day some of the boys from the Orphanage had gone fishing in the Devil's Pond, about a mile away, and a favourite resort

THE LABRADOR DOCTOR IN WINTER

with them. Unfortunately that afternoon they were
seized with the brilliant idea of kindling a fire with which
to cook their trout. Greatly to the astonishment of the
would-be cooks, the fire quickly got beyond the one
desired for culinary purposes, and, panic-stricken, they
rushed home to give the alarm. Every man ashore and
afloat came and worked, and the obliteration of the place
was saved by a providential change in the wind and
wide fire-breaks cut through few and ill-to-be-spared
trees. Everything had been taken from our house —
even furniture and linen — and dragged to the wharf
head, where terrified children, fleeing patients, and
heaps of furnishings from the orphanage and elsewhere
were all piled up. Schooners had been hauled in to carry
off what was possible, and the patients in the hospital
were got ready to be carried away at a moment's notice.
Only the most strenuous efforts saved the entire station.
Now all our beautiful sky-line is blackened and charred.
All day long the gravity of the debt was in our hearts,
for if the wooden buildings had once had the clouds of
fiery sparks settle upon them, the whole of those dependent upon us would have been homeless. Surely in a
country like this, the incident of this fire puts an added
emphasis upon our need of brick buildings. Gratitude
for our safe return, for all God's mercies to us, and joy
over the outcome of the at one time apparently inevitable
disaster, made our first day of the season a never-to-be-
forgotten event.

Mr. W. R. Stirling, our Chicago director, who had personally visited the hospitals, insisted that a water supply
must at all costs be secured both for hospital and orphanage. This was not only to avert the reproach of typhoid
epidemics, two of which had previously occurred, but
also to better our protection for so many helpless lives in

old dry wooden buildings, and to economize the great expense of hauling water by dogs every winter, when our little surface reservoir was frozen to the bottom. This water supply has only just been finished; and now we cannot understand how we ever existed without it. But it is an unromantic object to which to give money, and the total cost, even doing the work ourselves, amounted to just upon ten thousand dollars. According to the Government engineer's advice we had a stream to dam and a mile and a quarter of piping to lay six feet underground to prevent the water freezing. It is only in very few places that we boast six feet of soil at all on the rock that forms the frame of Mother Earth here. Hence there was much blasting to do. But the task was accomplished, and by our own boys, and has successfully weathered our bitter winter. The last lap was run by an intensely interesting experiment. The assistant at Emmanuel Church in Boston brought down a number of volunteer Boy Scouts to give their services on the commonplace task of digging the remainder of the trench necessary to complete the water supply. When they first arrived, our Northern outside man, after looking at their clothes of the Boston cut, remarked, "Hm. You'd better give that crowd some softer job than digging." But they did the work, and a whole lot more besides. For their grit and jollity, and above all their readiness to tackle and see through such side tasks as unloading and stowing away some three hundred tons of coal were real "missionary" lessons.

The ever-growing demand for doctors as the war dragged on made it harder and harder to man our far-off stations. The draft in America was the last straw, doctors having already been forbidden to leave England or Canada. Dr. Charles Curtis had taken over Dr. Little's work at St. Anthony, and stood nobly by, getting special permission to do so. Dr. West, who had succeeded our colleague, Dr. Mather Hare, at Harrington, when his wife's breakdown had obliged him to leave us, had already given us a year over his scheduled time, for he had accepted work in India at the hands of those who had specially trained him for that purpose.

We had been having considerable trouble in the accommodation of the heavy batches of patients that came by the mail boat. They were left on the wharf when she steamed away, and only the floors of our treatment and waiting-rooms were available for their reception. For all could not possibly go into the wards, where children, and often very sick patients, were being cared for. The people around always stretched their hospitality to the limit, but this was a very undesirable method of housing sick persons temporarily. Owing to the generosity of a lady in New Bedford and other friends, we were enabled to meet the problem by the erection of a rest house, with first and second class accommodation. This was built in the spring of 1917, and has been a Godsend to many besides patients. It makes people free to come to St. Anthony and stay and benefit by whatever it has to offer, without the feeling that they have no place to which they can go. Moreover, this hostel has been entirely self-supporting from the day that it opened, and every one who goes and comes has a good word for the rest house. It is run by one of our Labrador orphan boys, whose education was finished in America, and "Johnnie," as every one calls him, is already a feature in the life of the place.

Among the advances of the year 1918 must also be noted that more subscribers and subscriptions from local friends have been received than ever before. Our X-ray department has been added to. We have been able also to improve the roads, a thing greatly to be desired.

Look where we will, we have nothing but gratitude that in the last year of a long and exhausting war, here in this far-away section of the world, the keynote has been one of progress.

CHAPTER XXVI
THE FUTURE OF THE MISSION

WHAT is the future of this Mission? I have once or twice been an unwilling listener to a discussion on this point. It has usually been in the smoking-room of a local mail steamer. The subtle humour of W. W. Jacobs has shown us that pessimism is an attribute of the village "pub" also. The alcoholic is always a prophet of doom; and the wish is often father to the thought.

In our medical work in the wilds we have become a repository of some old instruments discarded on the death of their owners or cast aside by the advancing tide of knowledge. Seeing the ingenuity, time, and expense lavished on many of them, they would make a truly pathetic museum. Personally I prefer the habits of India to those of Egypt concerning the departed. If the Pharaoh of the Persecution could see his mummy being shown to tourists as a cheap side show, I am sure that he would vote for cremation if he had the choice over again.

It sounds flippant in one who has devoted his life to this work to say, "Really I don't care what its future may be." I am content to leave the future with God. No true sportsman wants to linger on, a wretched handicap to the cause for which he once stood, like a fake hero with his peg leg and a black patch over one eye. The Christian choice is that of Achilles. Nature also teaches us that the paths of progress are marked by the discarded relics of what once were her corner-stones. The original Moses had the spirit of Christ when he said, "If Thou wilt, forgive their sin — and if not, I pray Thee, blot me out of Thy book." The heroic Paul was willing to be eliminated

for the Kingdom of God. It seems to me that that attitude is the only credential which any Christian mission
can give for its existence. If I felt that my work had
accomplished all it could, I would "lay it down with a
will."

As in India and China the missionaries of the various
societies are uniting to build up a native, national Church
which would wish to assume the responsibility of caring
for its own problems, so when the Government of this
country is willing and able to take over the maintenance
of the medical work, this Mission would have justified its
existence by its elimination. All lines along which the
Mission works should one day become self-eliminating.
Until that time arrives I am satisfied that the Mission
has great opportunities before it. I am an optimist, and
feel certain that God will provide the means to continue
as long as the need exists.

Some believe that the future of this population depends
solely on the attention paid to the development of the
resources of the coast. Not only are its raw products more
needed than ever, but even supposing that unscientific
handling of them has depleted the supply, still there is
ample to maintain a larger population than at present.
This can only be when science and capital are introduced
here, combined with an educated manhood fired by the
spirit of coöperation.

In large parts of China a famine to wipe out surplus
population is apparently a periodical necessity. An orphanage in India for similar reasons does not seem to be
as rationally economic as one for the Labrador children.
I never see a cliff face from which an avalanche has removed the supersoil and herbage without thinking in
pity of the crowded sections of China, where tearing up
even the roots of trees for fuel has permitted so much

arable land to be denuded by rains that the food supply gets smaller while the population grows larger.

The future of all medical work depends on whether people want it and can arrange to get it paid for. If all the world become Christian Scientists, scientific — which we believe to be also Christian — healing will everywhere die a natural death — and possibly the people also. But history suggests that the healing art is one of considerable vitality. My own belief is that in the apparently approaching socialistic age, medicine will be communized and provided by the State free to all. If education for the mind is, why not education for the body?

Certain subtle and very vital psychic influences are probably the best stock in trade of the "Doctor of the old school." These qualities appear at present less likely to be "had for hire" in a Government official. The Chinese may yet return the missionary compliment by teaching us to adopt their method of paying the doctor only when and as long as the patient is cured.

Out of the taxes, the major part of which is paid by the people of the outport districts in this Colony, the Government provides free medical aid in the Capital, presumably because those who have the spending of the money mostly reside there. The Mission provides it in the farthest off and poorest part of the country, Labrador and North Newfoundland, because there is no chance whatever at present for the poor people to obtain it otherwise. Our *pro rata* share of the taxes, if judged by the paltry Government grant toward the work, would not provide anything worth having. The people here pay far better in proportion to their ability for hospital privileges than they do in Boston or London; the Government pays a little, and the rest comes from the loving gifts of those who desire nothing better, when they know of real need, than to make sacrifices to meet it.

One feels that the Chinese and Japanese and all nations will be able some day to pay for their own doctors, whether they do it on individualistic or communistic principles. In the present state of the world I believe the missionary enterprise to be entirely desirable, or I would not be where I am. But being a Christian with a little faith, I hope that it may not be so forever. If anything will stimulate to better methods, it is example, not precept, and perhaps the best work of this and all missions will be their reflex influences on Governments through the governed.

To carry on the bare essentials of this work an endowment of at least a million dollars is necessary. Toward this a hundred and sixty thousand dollars is all that has been contributed, and in addition we can count annually upon a small Government grant. Even if this million dollars were given, it would still leave several thousand dollars to be raised by voluntary subscription each year, a healthy thing for the life of any charitable work. On the other hand, the certainty of being able to meet the main bills is an economy in nerve energy, in time and in money.

Among our patients brought in one season to St. Anthony Hospital was the mother of ten children on whom an emergency operation for appendicitis had to be done — the first time in her life that a doctor had ever tended her. She came from a very poor home, for besides her large family her husband had been all his life handicapped by a serious deformity of one leg caused by a fall. She reminded me of how some years before a traveller had left her the rug from his dog sledge, as, without any bedclothes, she was again about to give birth to a child; how she had actually been unable at times to turn over in bed, because her personal clothing had frozen solid to the wall of the one-roomed hut in which she lived.

In April, 1906, in northern Newfoundland I found a young mother near St. Anthony. She was twenty-six years old, suffering from acute rheumatic fever, lying in a fireless loft, on a rickety bedstead with no bedclothes. She had only one shoddy black dress to her name, and no underwear to keep her warm in bed in a house like that. The floor was littered with débris, including a number of hard buns which she could not now eat, but which some charitable neighbour had sent her. She had a wizened baby of seven months, which every now and then she was trying to feed by raising herself on one elbow and forcing bread and water pap, moistened with the merest suspicion of condensed milk, down its throat. None of her four previous children had lived so long. She had been under my care three years before for sailor's scurvy. Her present illness lasted only a week, and in spite of all that we could do, she died.

The desire of the people to be mutually helpful is undoubted, whether it is to each other or to some "outsider" like ourselves. I question if in the so-called centres of civilization the following incident can be surpassed as evidencing this aspect of their character.

In a little Labrador village called Deep Water Creek I was called in one day to see a patient: an old Englishman, who was reported to have had "a bad place this twelve-month." As I was taken into the tiny cottage, a bright-faced, black-bearded man greeted me. Three children were playing on the hearth with a younger man, evidently their father. "No, Doctor, they are n't ours," replied my host, in answer to my question. "But us took Sam as our own when he was born, and his mother lay dead. These be his little ones. You remember Kate, his wife, what died in hospital."

After the cup of hot tea so thoughtfully provided, I

said, "Skipper John, let's get out and see the old English-man."

"No need, Doctor. He's upstairs in bed."

Upstairs was the triangular space between the roof and the ceiling of the ground floor. At each end was a tiny window, and the whole area, windows included, had been divided longitudinally by a single thickness of hand-sawn lumber. Both windows were open, a cool breeze was blowing through, and a bright paper pasted on the wall gave a cheerful impression. One corner was shut off by a screen of cheap cheesecloth. Sitting bolt upright on a low bench, and leaning against the partition, was a very aged woman, staring fixedly ahead out of blind eyes, and ceaselessly monotoning what was meant for a hymn. No head was visible among the rude collection of bed-clothes.

"Uncle Solomon, it's the Doctor," I called. The mass of clothes moved, and a trembling old hand came out to meet mine.

"No pain, Uncle Solomon, I hope?"

"No pain, Doctor, thank the good Lord, and Skip-per John. He took us in when the old lady and I were starving."

The terrible cancer had so extended its ravages that the reason for the veiled corner was obvious, and also for the effective ventilation.

"He suffers a lot, Doctor, though he won't own it," now chimed in the old woman.

When the interview was over, I was left standing in a brown study till I heard Skipper John's voice calling me. As I descended the ladder he said: "We're so grateful you comed, Doctor. The poor old creatures won't last long. But thanks are n't dollars. I have n't a cent in the world now. The old people have taken what little we had put by. But if I gets a skin t' winter, I'll try and pay you for your visit anyhow."

"Skipper John, what relation are those people to you?"

"Well, no relation 'zactly."

"Do they pay nothing at all?"

"Them has nothing," he replied.

"What made you take them in?"

"They was homeless, and the old lady was already blind."

"How long have they been with you?"

"Just twelve months come Saturday."

I found myself standing in speechless admiration in the presence of this man. I thought then, and I still think, that I had received one of my largest fees.

Ours is primarily a medical mission, and nothing that may have been stated in this book with reference to other branches of the work is meant in any way to detract from what to us as doctors is the basic reason for our being here, though we mean ours to be prophylactic as well as remedial medicine.

St. Anthony having so indisputably become the head-quarters of the hospital stations, there can be but one answer to the question of the advisability of its closing its doors summer or winter in the days to come. For not only is our largest hospital located there — its scope due in great measure to the reputation gained for it by Dr. Little's splendid services, and continued by Dr. Curtis — but also the Children's Home, our school, machine shop, the headquarters of various industrial enterprises, and lastly a large storehouse to be used in future as a distributing centre for the supplies of the general Mission. Moreover, the population of the environs of St. Anthony, owing to their numbers and the fact that they can profit by the employment given by the Mission, should be able increasingly to assist in the maintenance of this hospital, though a large number of its clinic is drawn from distant parts. These patients come not only from Labrador, the Straits of Belle Isle, and southern Newfoundland, but we have had under our care Syrians, Russians, Scandinavians, Frenchmen, and naturally Americans and Canadians, seamen from schooners engaged in the Labrador fishery.

Harrington Hospital, located on the Canadian Labrador, must for many years to come depend on outside support. I am Lloyd Georgian enough to feel that taxation should presuppose the obligation to look after the bodies of the taxed. The Quebec Government gives neither vote, representation, adequate mail service, nor any public health grant for the long section of the coast which it claims to govern, that lies west of the Point des Eskimo. It is to my mind a severe stricture on their qualifications as legislators. That hospital should, we believe, be adequately subsidized and kept open summer and winter. At present we have to thank the Labrador Medical Mission, which is the Canadian branch of the International Grenfell Association, for their generous and continued support of this station.

Battle Harbour and Indian Harbour Hospitals can never be anything but summer stations, owing to their geographical positions on islands in frozen seas, on which islands there is practically no population during the winter months. But gifts and grants sufficient to maintain a doctor at Northwest River Cottage Hospital, and one if possible in Lewis Bay, winter supplements to these summer hospitals, are to my thinking more than justifiable.

As to the future of our hospital stations at Pilley's Islands, Spotted Islands, and Forteau, that will depend upon the changing demands of local conditions. That the

ENTRANCE TO ST. ANTHONY HARBOUR

need of medical assistance exists is unquestionable, as is evidenced from the many appeals which I receive to start hospitals or supply doctors in districts at present utterly incapable of obtaining such help.

One still indispensable requisite in our scattered field of work is a hospital steamer. In fact, not a few of us think that the Strathcona is the keystone of the Mission. She reaches those who need our help most and at times when they cannot afford to leave home and seek it. Her functions are innumerable. She is our eyepiece to keep us cognizant of our opportunities. She both treats and carries the sick and feeds the hospitals. She enables us to distribute our charity efficiently. The invaluable gifts of clothing which the Labrador Needlework Guild and other friends send us could never be used at all as love would wish, unless the Strathcona were available to enlarge the area reached. In spite of all this, those who would quibble over trifles claim that she is the only craft on record that rolls at dry-dock! Her functions are certainly varied, but perhaps the oddest which I have ever been asked to perform was an incident which I have often told. One day, after a long stream of patients had been treated, a young man with a great air of secrecy said that he wanted to see me very privately.

"I wants to get married, Doctor," he confided when we were alone.

"Well, that's something in which I can't help you. Won't any of the girls round here have you?"

"Oh! it is n't that. There's a girl down North I fancies, but I'm shipped to a man here for the summer, and can't get away. Would n't you just propose to her for me, and bring her along as you comes South?"

The library would touch a very limited field if it were not for the hospital ship. She carries half a hundred travelling libraries each year. She finds out the derelict children and brings them home. She is often a court of law, trying to dispense justice and help right against might. She has enabled us to serve not only men, but their ships as well; and many a helping hand she has been able to lend to men in distress when hearts were anxious and hopes growing faint. In a thousand little ways she is just as important a factor in preaching the message of love. To-day she is actually loaned for her final trip, before going into winter quarters, to a number of heads of families, who are thus enabled to bring out fuel for their winter fires from the long bay just south of the hospital.

Her plates are getting thin. They were never anything but three-eighths-inch steel, and we took a thousand pounds of rust out of her after cabin alone this spring. She leaks a little — and no iron ship should. It will cost two thousand dollars to put her into repair again for future use. Money is short now, but when asked about the future of the Mission I feel that whatever else will be needed for many years to come, the hospital ship at least cannot possibly be dispensed with.

The child is potential energy, the father of the future man, and the future state; and the children of this country are integral, determining factors in the future of this Mission. The children who are turned out to order by institutions seem sadly deficient, both in ability to cope with life and in the humanities. The "home" system, as at Quarrier's in Scotland, is a striking contrast, and personally I shall vote for the management of orphanages on home lines every time. This is not a concession to Dickens, whose pictures of Bumble I hope and believe apply only to the dark ages in which Dickens lived; but historically they are not yet far enough removed for me to advocate Government orphanages, though our

Government schools are an advance on Dotheboys Hall.

The human body is the result of physical causes; breeding tells as surely as it does in dogs or cows, and the probability of defects in the offspring of poverty and of lust is necessarily greater than in well-bred, well-fed, well-environed children. The proportion of mentally and morally deficient children that come to us absolutely demonstrates this fact; and the love needed to see such children through to the end is more comprehensive than the mere sentiment of having a child in the home, and infinitely more than the desire to have the help which he can bring.

The Government allows us fifty-two dollars a year toward the expense of a child whose father is dead; nothing if the mother is dead, or if the father is alive but had better be dead. It would be wiser if each case could be judged on its merits by competent officials. But we believe it is a blessing to a community to have the opportunity of finding the balance.

Tested by its output and the returns to the country, our orphanage has amply justified itself. One new life resultant from the outlay of a few dollars would class the investment as gilt-edged if graded merely in cash. The community which sows a neglected childhood reaps a whirlwind in defective manhood.

In view of these facts — to leave out of consideration my earnest personal desire — there can never be any question in my mind as to the imperative necessity of the Mission's continuance of the work for derelict children. This conclusion seems to me safeguarded by the fact that all nations are placing increasing emphasis on "the child in the midst of them."

When Solomon chose wisdom as the gift which he most desired, the Bible tells us that it was pleasing to God.

St. Paul holds out the hope that one day we shall know as we are known. But there is a vast difference between knowledge and being wise. In fact, from the New Testament itself we are led to believe that the devils knew far more than even the Disciples.

The school is an essential part of the orphanage. Seeing that the village children needed education just as much as those for whom we were more directly responsible, and realizing the value to both of the coöperation, and that the denominational system which still persists in the country is a factor for division and not for unity, it became obviously desirable for us to provide such a bond. Friends made the building possible. The generosity of a lady in Chicago in practically endowing it has, we feel, secured its future. We have now a proper building, three teachers, a graded school, modern appliances for teaching, and vastly superior results. In these days when the expenditure of every penny seems a widow's mite, one welcomes the encouragement of facts such as these to enable one to "carry on."

Modern pedagogy has brought to the attention of even the man in the street the realization that education consists not merely in its accepted scholastic aspect, but also that training of the eye and hand which in turn fosters the larger development of the mind. In the latter sense our people are far from uneducated. Taking this aptitude of theirs as a starting-point, some twelve years ago we began our industrial department, first by giving out skin work in the North, and later started other branches under Miss Jessie Luther, who subsequently gave many years of service to the coast.

The coöperative movement is the same question seen from another angle, and is almost contemporaneous with our earliest hospitals.

It is not unnatural that man, realizing that he is himself like "the grass that to-morrow is cast into the oven," should worry over the permanency of the things on which he has spent himself. Though Christ especially warns us against this anxiety, religious people have been the greatest sinners in laying more emphasis upon to-morrow than to-day. The element which makes most for longevity is always interesting, even if longevity is often a mistake. Almost every old parish church in England maintains some skeleton of bygone efforts which once met real needs and were tokens of real love.

The future is a long way off — that future when Christ's Kingdom comes on earth in the consecrated hearts and wills of all mankind, when all the superimposed efforts will be unnecessary. But love builds for a future, however remote; and at present we see no other way than to work for it, and know of no better means than to insure the permanency of the hospitals, orphanage, school, and the industrial and coöperative enterprises, thus to hasten, however little, the coming of Christ in Labrador.

CHAPTER XXVII
MY RELIGIOUS LIFE

No one can write his real religious life with pen or pencil. It is written only in actions, and its seal is our character, not our orthodoxy. Whether we, our neighbour, or God is the judge, absolutely the only value of our "religious" life to ourselves or to any one is what it fits us for and enables us to do. Creeds, when expressed only in words, clothes, or abnormal lives, are daily growing less acceptable as passports to Paradise. What my particular intellect can accept cannot commend me to God. His "well done" is only spoken to the man who "wills to do His will."

We map the world out into black and white patches for "heathen" and "Christian" — as if those who made the charts believed that one section possessed a monopoly of God's sonship. Europe was marked white, which is to-day comment enough on this division. A black friend of mine used often to remind me that in his country the Devil was white.

My own religious experiences divide my life into three periods. As a boy at school, and as a young man at hospital, the truth or untruth of Christianity as taught by the churches did not interest me enough to devote a thought to it. It was neither a disturbing nor a vital influence in my life. My mother was my ideal of goodness. I have never known her speak an angry or unkind word. Sitting here looking back on over fifty years of life, I cannot pick out one thing to criticize in my mother.

What did interest me was athletics. Like most English boys I almost worshipped physical accomplishments.

I had the supremest contempt for clothes except those designed for action or comfort. Since no saint apparently ever wore trousers, or appeared to care about football knickers, I never supposed that they could be the same flesh as myself. It was always a barrier between me and the parsons and religious persons generally that they affected clothing which dubbed my ideals "worldly." It was even a barrier between myself and the Christ that I could not think of Him in flannels or a gymnasium suit. At that time I should have considered such an idea blasphemous — whatever that meant. As soon as religious services ceased to be compulsory for me, I only attended them as a concession to others. The prime object of the prayers and lessons did not appear to be that they might be understood. So far as I could see, common sense and plain natural feelings were at a discount. A long heritage of an eager, restless spirit left me uninterested in "homilies," and aided by the "dim religious light," I was enabled to sleep through both long prayers and sermons. Justice forces me to add that the two endless hours of "prep" lessons after tea had very much the same effect upon me.

At the request of my mother I once went to take a class at the Sunday School. These were for the "poor only" in England in those days. Little effort was expended on making them attractive. I recall nothing but disgust at the dirty urchins with whom I had to associate for half an hour. An incident which happened on the death of one of the boys at my father's school interested me temporarily in religion. The boy's father happened to be a dissenter, and our vicar refused to allow the gates of the parish churchyard to be opened to enable the funeral cortège to enter. My chum had only a legal right to be buried in the yard. The coffin had therefore to be lifted over the wall and as the church was locked, father conducted the service in the open air. His words at the grave-side gave a touch of reality to religion, and still more so did his walking down the aisle out of church the following Sunday when the vicar referred to the destructive influence of anything that lent colour to dissent. Later when father threw up the school for the far more onerous and less remunerative task of chaplain at the London Hospital, even I realized that religion meant something. Indeed, it was that tax on his sensitive, nervous brain that brought his life to its early close. No man ever had a more generous and soft-hearted father. He never refused us any reasonable request, and very few unreasonable ones, and allowed us an amount of self-determination enjoyed by few. How deeply and how often have I regretted that I did not understand him better. His brilliant scholarship, and the friends that it brought around him, his ability literally to speak Greek and Latin as he could German and French, his exceptionally developed mental as compared with his physical gifts, were undoubtedly the reasons that a very ordinary English boy could not appreciate him.

At fourteen years of age, at Marlborough School, I was asked if I wished to be confirmed. Every boy of that age was. It permitted one to remain when "the kids went out after first service." It added dignity, like a football cap or a mustache. All I remember about it was bitterly resenting having to "swat up" the Catechism out of school hours. I counted, however, on the examiner being easy, and he was. I am an absolute believer in boys making a definite decision to follow the Christ; and that in the hands of a really keen Christian man the rite of confirmation is very valuable. The call which gets home to a boy's heart is the call to do things. If only a boy can be led to see that the following of Christ demands a real knighthood, and that true chivalry is Christ's service, he will want all the rites and ceremonies that either proclaim his allegiance or promise him help and strength to live up to it.

What I now believe that D. L. Moody did for me was just to show that under all the shams and externals of religion was a vital call in the world for things that I could do. This marks the beginning of the second period of my religious development. He helped me to see myself as God sees the "unprofitable servant," and to be ashamed. He started me working for all I was worth, and made religion real fun — a new field brimming with opportunities. With me the pendulum swung very far. The evangelical to my mind had a monopoly of infallible truth. A Roman Catholic I regarded as a relic of mediævalism; while almost a rigour went down my spine when a man told me that he was a "Unitarian Christian." Hyphenation was loyalty compared to that. I mention this only because it shows how I can now understand intolerance and dogmatism in others. Yes, I must have been "very impossible," for then I honestly thought that I knew it all.

About this time I began to be interested in reading my Bible, and I learned to appreciate my father's expositions of it. At prayers he always translated into the vernacular from the original of either the Old or the New Testament. To me he seemed to know every sense of every Greek word in any setting. Ever since I have been satisfied to use an English version, knowing that I cannot improve on the words chosen by the various learned translators.

Because I owed so much to evangelical teachers, it worried me for a long while that I could not bring myself to argue with my boys about their intellectual attitude to Christ. My Sunday class contained several Jews whom I loved. I respected them more because they made no verbal professions. I have seen Turkish religionists dancing and whirling in Asia Minor at their prayers. I have seen much emotional Christianity, and I fully realize the value of approaching men on their emotional side. A demonstrative preacher impresses large crowds of people at once. But all the same, I have learned from many disillusionments to be afraid of overdoing emotionalism in religion. Summing up the evidence of men's Christlikeness by their characters, as I look back down my long list of loved and honoured helpers and friends, I am certainly safe in saying that I at least should judge that no section of Christ's Church has any monopoly of Christ's spirit; and that I should like infinitely less to be examined on my own dogmatic theology than I should thirty-five years ago. Combined with this goes the fact that though I know the days of my stay on earth are greatly reduced, I seem to be less rather than more anxious about "the morrow." For though time has rounded off the corners of my conceit, experience of God's dealing with such an unworthy midget as myself has so strengthened the foundations on which faith stood, that Christ now means more to me as a living Presence than when I laid more emphasis on the dogmas concerning Him.

This chapter would not be complete without an endeavour to face the task of trying to answer the questions so often asked: "What is your position now? Do you still believe as you did when you first decided to serve Christ?" I am still a communicant member "in good standing" of the Episcopal Church. One hopes that one's religious ideas grow like the rest of one's life. It is fools who are said to rush in where angels fear to tread. The most powerful Christian churches in the world, the Greek and the Roman, recognizing the great dangers threatening, have countered by stereotyping the answer for all time, assuming all responsibility, and permitting no individual freedom in the matter. The numbers of their adherents testify to how vast a proportion of mankind the course appeals. And yet we are sons of God — and at our best value freedom in every department of our being — spirit as well as mind and body. George Adam Smith says: "The great causes of God and humanity are not defeated by the hot assaults of the Devil, but by the slow, crushing, glacier-like mass of thousands and thousands of indifferent nobodies. God's causes are never destroyed by being blown up, but by being sat upon. It is not the violent and anarchical whom we have to fear in the war for human progress, but the slow, the staid, the respectable; and the danger of these lies in their real skepticism. Though it would abhor articulately confessing that God does nothing, it virtually means so by refusing to share manifest opportunities for serving Him."

Feeble and devious as my own footsteps have been since my decision to follow Jesus Christ, I believe more than ever that this is the only real adventure of life. No step in life do I even compare with that one in permanent satisfaction. I deeply regret that I did not take it sooner. I do not feel that it mattered much whether I chose medicine for an occupation, or law, or education, or commerce, or any other way to justify my existence by working for a living as every honest man should. But if there is one thing about which I never have any question, it is that the decision and endeavour to follow the Christ does for men what nothing else on earth can. Without stultifying our reason, it develops all that makes men godlike. Christ claimed that it was the only way to find out truth.

To me, enforced asceticism, vows of celibacy, denunciation of pleasures innocent in themselves, intellectual monopoly of interpretation of things past or present, written or unwritten, are travesties of common sense, which is to me the Voice within. Not being a philosopher, I do not classify it, but I listen to it, because I believe it to be the Voice of God. That is the first point which I have no fear in putting on record.

The extraordinary revelations of some Power outside ourselves leading and guiding and helping and chastening are, I am certain, really the ordinary experiences of every man who is willing to accept the fact that we are sons of God. Only a child, however, who submits to his father can expect to enjoy or understand his dealings. If we look into our everyday life we cannot fail to see that God not only allows but seeks our coöperation in the establishment of His Kingdom. So the second fundamental by which I stand is the certainty of a possible real and close relationship between man and God. Not one qualm assails my intellect or my intuition when I say that I know absolutely that God is my Father. To live "as seeing Him who is invisible" is my one ideal which embraces all the lesser ideals of my life.

It has been my lot in life to have to stand by many death-beds, and to be called in to dying men and women almost as a routine in my profession. Yet I am increasingly convinced that their spirits never die at all. I am sure that there is no real death. Death is no argument against, but rather for, life. Eternal life is the complement of all my unsatisfied ideals; and experience teaches me that the belief in it is a greater incentive to be useful and good than any other I know.

I have read "Raymond" with great interest. I am neither capable nor willing to criticize those who, with the deductive ability of such men as Sir Oliver Lodge, are brave enough and unselfish enough to devote their talents to pioneering in a field that certainly needs and merits more scientific investigation, seeing that it has possibilities of such great moment to mankind.

The experiences on which rest one's own convictions of continuing life are of an entirely different nature. Even though the first and personal reason may seem foolish, it is because I desire it so much. This is a natural passion, common to all human beings. Experience convinces me that such longings are purposeful and do not go unsatisfied.

No, we do not know everything yet; and perhaps the critic is a shallower fool than he judges to be the patient delvers into the unknown beyond. The evidence on which our deductions have been based through the ages may suddenly be proven fallible after all. It may be that there is no such thing as matter. Chemists and physicists now admit that is possible. The spiritual may be far more real than the material, in spite of the cocksure conceit of the current science of 1918. Immortality may be the complement of mortality, as water becomes steam, and steam becomes power, and power becomes heat, and heat becomes light. The conclusion that life beyond is the conservation of energy of life here may be as scientific as that great natural law for material things. I see knowledge become service, service become joy. I see fear prohibit glands from secreting, hope bring back colour to the face and tone to the blood. I see something not material make Jekyl into Hyde; and thank God, make Hyde over into Jekyl again, when birch rods and iron bars have no effect whatever. I have seen love do physical things which the mere intellectual convictions cannot — make hearts beat and eyes sparkle, that would not respond even to digitalis and strychnine. I claim that the boy is justified in saying that his kite exists in the heaven, even though it is out of sight and the string leads round the corner, on no other presumption than that he feels it tugging. I prefer to stand with Moses in his belief in the Promised Land, and that we can reach it, than to believe that the Celestial City is a mirage.

This attempted analysis of my religious life has revealed to me two great changes in my position toward its intellectual or dogmatic demands, and both of them are reflections of the ever rightly changing attitude of the defenders of our Christian faith. "Tempora mutantur et nos mutamus in illis." Christians should not fret because they cannot escape adapting themselves to the environment of 1918 — which is no longer that of 918, or 18. The one and only hope for any force, Christianity no less than others, is its ability to adapt itself to all time.

I still study my Bible in the morning and scribble on the margin the lessons which I get out of the portion. I can only do it by using a new copy each time I finish, because it brings new thoughts according to the peculiar experiences, tasks, needs, and environments of the day. I change I know. It does not — and yet it does — for we see the old truths in new lights. That to me is the glory of the Scriptures. Somehow it suits itself always to my developing needs. Christ did not teach as did other teachers. He taught for all time. We find out that our attitude to everything changes, to the things that give us pleasure and to those that give us pain. It is but a sign of healthy evolution (in this chapter, I suppose I should call it "grace") that the great churches have ceased to condemn their leaders who are unsound on points which once spelt fagot and stake. To-day predestination no longer involves the same reaction, even if dropped into a conference of selected "Wee Frees." The American section of the Episcopal Church has omitted to insist on our publicly and periodically declaring that we must have a correct view of three Incomprehensibles, or be damned, as is still the case in our Church of England.

I am writing of my religion. The churches are now teaching that religion is action, not diction. There was a time when I could work with only one section of the Church of God. Thank God, it was a very brief period, but I weep for it just the same. Now I can not only work with any section, but worship with them also. If there is error in their intellectual attitudes, it is to God they stand, not to me. Doubtless there is just as much error in mine. To me, he is the best Christian who "judges not." To claim a monopoly of Christian religion for any church, looked at from the point of view of following Jesus Christ, is ridiculous. So I find that I have changed, changed in the importance which I place on what others think and upon what I myself think.

Unless a Christian is a witness in his life, his opinions do not matter two pins to God or man. Of course, to-day *we* should not burn Savonarola, any more than we should actually crucify that brave old fisherman, Peter, or ridicule a Gordon or a Livingstone, or assassinate a Lincoln or a Phillips Brooks, even with our tongues, though they differed from us in their view of what the Christian religion really needs. Oh, of course we should n't!

Perhaps my change spells more and not less faith in the Saviour of the world. As I love the facts of life more, I care less for fusty commentators. As I see more of Christ's living with us all the days, I care less for arguments about His death. I have no more doubt that He lives in His world to-day than that I do. Why should I blame myself because more and more my mind emphasizes the fact that it is because He lives, and only so far as He lives in me, that I shall live also?

THE END

INDEX

INDEX

Agriculture, in Labrador, unsuccessful, 217, 290.
Alaska, reindeer experiment in, 291; 294–295.
Albert, the, hospital ship of Dr. Grenfell, 125, 188, 189.
Among the Deep-Sea Fishers, magazine, 280.
Andrews, Dr. Joseph, eye-specialist, 357.
Archibald, Sir William, chairman of the Royal National Mission to Deep-Sea Fishermen, 362.
Armstrong, Dr. Seymour, his work at St. Anthony, 367.
Arnold, Thomas, of Rugby, 14.
Athletics, Grenfell's fondness of, 21, 32, 44, 50, 51, 53, 81, 424.

Bailey, Florence, nurse, 326.
Barnett, Samuel, of Mile End, head of Toynbee House, 83.
Barter system, the evils of, 131, 132, 133–138, 215–217.
Bartlett, Captain, father of "Captain Bob," 136.
Battle Harbour, Newfoundland, site of hospital, 126, 162, 165, 169, 193.
Beattie, Arthur, 192.
Beetz, Mr., 239.
Begbie, Harold, *Twice-Born Men*, 101.
Bell, Dr. Alexander Graham, 338.
Belle Isle, the Straits of, Labrador, 126, 127, 140, 250.
Besant, Mrs. Annie, associated with Charles Bradlaugh, 81, 82.
Blandford, Captain Samuel, 159, 172.
Bobardt, Dr. Arthur, 126, 159–162.
Booth, Walter, of New York, 370, 371.
Bowditch, William, 275.
Boys' Brigade, the, 101, 353.
Bradlaugh, Charles, religious radical, 81–82.

Cabot, John, 120.
Carpenter, Rev. C. C., 241, 242.
Carrel, Dr. Alexis, in France, 397.

Cartier, Jacques, 158.
Cartwright, George, 158.
Catholic Cadet Corps, the, 159, 353.
Cattle-raising in Labrador unsuccessful, 290.
Cawardine, Miss, nurse, 126.
Charity, prophylactic, more important than remedial, 235.
Cheever, Colonel David, 389.
Chester, England, birthplace of Grenfell, 1, 2.
Chidley, Cape, Labrador, 164, 207, 208.
Children's Home, the, 244–253.
Church Lads Brigade, the, 159, 353.
Clark, Sir Andrew, doctor, 65.
Cluett, George B., of Troy, N.Y., 347, 348.
Cook, Captain, 128, 340, 341.
Coöperative system, the, 215–225.
Corner, the, magazine, 242.
Crookhaven, seat of a dispensary and social centre, 107.
Crowe, Harry, lumber operator, 370.
Curtis, Dr. Charles, 408.
Curtis, Lieutenant Roger, quoted, 158.
Curwen, Dr. Elliott, 126.
Curzon-Howe, Lady, 191.
Curzon-Howe, Lord, 191.
Cutter, Marion, librarian, 266.

Daly, Professor Reginald, head of Department of Geology at Harvard University, quoted, 157, 158.
Dampier, William, 191.
Davis Inlet, Labrador, 154, 155.
Dawson, Sir Betrand, 388.
Dee, the River, 2, 4.
Delano, Eugene, head of Brown Brothers, bankers, 358.
Denominationalism, evils of, 264, 269, 353.
Dogs, Labrador, ferocity of, 198, 289, 290.
Domino Run, Labrador, natural harbour, 120.
Drake, Sir Francis, 191.

The Riverside Press
CAMBRIDGE . MASSACHUSETTS
U . S . A